Adobe Photoshop 2024

Zero to Hero Mastery Guide to the Latest Tools, Techniques, Tricks and Hacks of Adobe Photoshop 2024

Copyright © 2024 **Ronnie Kormah**

All Rights Reserved

This book or parts thereof may not be reproduced in any form, stored in any retrieval system, or transmitted in any form by any means—electronic, mechanical, photocopy, recording, or otherwise—without prior written permission of the publisher, except as provided by United States of America copyright law and fair use.

Disclaimer and Terms of Use

The author and publisher of this book and the accompanying materials have used their best efforts in preparing this book. The author and publisher make no representation or warranties with respect to the accuracy, applicability, fitness, or completeness of the contents of this book. The information contained in this book is strictly for informational purposes. Therefore, if you wish to apply ideas contained in this book, you are taking full responsibility for your actions.

Printed in the United States of America

TABLE OF CONTENTS

TABLE OF CONTENTS III
INTRODUCTION 1
CHAPTER ONE 3
SYSTEM REQUIREMENTS, DOWNLOADING AND INSTALLING PHOTOSHOP 2024 3
    MINIMUM AND RECOMMENDED SYSTEM REQUIREMENTS FOR PHOTOSHOP (WINDOWS) 3
MINIMUM AND RECOMMENDED SYSTEM REQUIREMENTS FOR PHOTOSHOP (MACOS) 3
    PHOTOSHOP SYSTEM REQUIREMENTS BY COMPONENT 3
        Operating system 4
        Processor (CPU) 4
        Memory (RAM) 4
        Graphics card (GPU) 5
        Storage (SSD or HDD) 5
    INSTALLING ADOBE PHOTOSHOP 2024 (VERSION 25.0) 6
CHAPTER TWO 9
PHOTOSHOP 2024 STRIKING FEATURES 9
    GENERATIVE FILL AND GENERATIVE EXPAND ACCESSIBLE IN PHOTOSHOP FOR COMMERCIAL USE 9
    EMBARK ON AN EXCITING LEARNING JOURNEY WITH GENERATIVE FILL 10
    GENERATIVE CREDITS IN PHOTOSHOP 11
    SETTING STANDARDS FOR RESPONSIBILITY AND TRANSPARENCY... 12
    NEW INTERACTIONS IN REMOVE TOOL 13
    ADDED FEATURES TO CONTEXTUAL TASKBAR TO AID WITH MASKING AND CROPPING PROCESSES 14
    PRESET SYNC DISCONTINUED WITH THE RELEASE OF PHOTOSHOP 25.0 15
    USING GENERATIVE FILL 15
        Adding an object 15
    EXPANDING A PHOTO 16
    REMOVING AN OBJECT 17
CHAPTER THREE 18
GETTING STARTED WITH ADOBE PHOTOSHOP SYSTEM 18
    LAUNCHING PHOTOSHOP 18
    ON WINDOWS: 18
    ON MACOS: 18
    GET ACQUAINTED WITH THE HOME SCREEN 19
    HOW TO TURN OFF THE PHOTOSHOP HOME SCREEN. 20
    FAMILIARIZING WITH THE PHOTOSHOP WORKSPACE 21
    OPENING FILES 23
    EXPLORING THE TOOLBAR 24

SELECTION TOOLS GROUP	26
CROP AND SLICE TOOLS GROUP	28
MEASURING TOOLS GROUP	29
DRAWING & TYPE TOOLS GROUP	31
NAVIGATION TOOLS GROUP	33
RETOUCHING & PAINTING TOOLS GROUP	34
SELECTING A TOOL FROM THE TOOLBAR	36
WORKING WITH THE TOOL PROPERTIES	36
KEY POINTS ABOUT THE PROPERTIES PANEL	37
HOW TO UNDERSTAND THE TOOL PROPERTIES IN THE OPTIONS BAR	38
USING THE STATUS BAR	39
ZOOM FACTOR	39
Figure out an image's width and height.	*39*
Some other information	*39*
Adobe Drive	*40*
Document Size	*40*
Document Profile	*40*
Document Dimensions	*40*
Measurement Scales	*40*
Scratch Sizes	*40*
Efficiency	*41*
Timing	*41*
Current Tool	*41*
32-bit Exposure	*41*
Save Progress	*41*
EXPLORING CONTEXT MENUS	41
GETTING USED TO PHOTOSHOP PANELS	43
THE DEFAULT "ESSENTIALS" WORKSPACE	43
Choosing the Essentials Workspace	*44*
Resetting the Essentials Workspace	*44*
WORKING WITH PHOTOSHOP'S PANELS	45
The Panel Area	*45*
The Main Panel Column	*46*
Panel Groups	*47*
Switching Between Panels in a Group	*47*
Changing the Order of Panels in a Group	*48*
Moving Panels between Groups	*49*
Creating New Panel Groups	*50*
Collapsing and Expanding Panel Groups	*52*
Closing a Single Panel	*53*
Closing A Panel or Group from the Tab	*54*
Opening Panels from the Window Menu	*55*
PHOTOSHOP'S STICKY PANELS	56

TABLE OF CONTENTS

TABLE OF CONTENTS III
INTRODUCTION 1
CHAPTER ONE 3
SYSTEM REQUIREMENTS, DOWNLOADING AND INSTALLING PHOTOSHOP 2024 3
    MINIMUM AND RECOMMENDED SYSTEM REQUIREMENTS FOR PHOTOSHOP (WINDOWS) 3
MINIMUM AND RECOMMENDED SYSTEM REQUIREMENTS FOR PHOTOSHOP (MACOS) 3
    PHOTOSHOP SYSTEM REQUIREMENTS BY COMPONENT 3
        Operating system 4
        Processor (CPU) 4
        Memory (RAM) 4
        Graphics card (GPU) 5
        Storage (SSD or HDD) 5
    INSTALLING ADOBE PHOTOSHOP 2024 (VERSION 25.0) 6
CHAPTER TWO 9
PHOTOSHOP 2024 STRIKING FEATURES 9
    GENERATIVE FILL AND GENERATIVE EXPAND ACCESSIBLE IN PHOTOSHOP FOR COMMERCIAL USE 9
    EMBARK ON AN EXCITING LEARNING JOURNEY WITH GENERATIVE FILL 10
    GENERATIVE CREDITS IN PHOTOSHOP 11
    SETTING STANDARDS FOR RESPONSIBILITY AND TRANSPARENCY 12
    NEW INTERACTIONS IN REMOVE TOOL 13
    ADDED FEATURES TO CONTEXTUAL TASKBAR TO AID WITH MASKING AND CROPPING PROCESSES 14
    PRESET SYNC DISCONTINUED WITH THE RELEASE OF PHOTOSHOP 25.0 15
    USING GENERATIVE FILL 15
        Adding an object 15
    EXPANDING A PHOTO 16
    REMOVING AN OBJECT 17
CHAPTER THREE 18
GETTING STARTED WITH ADOBE PHOTOSHOP SYSTEM 18
    LAUNCHING PHOTOSHOP 18
    ON WINDOWS: 18
    ON MACOS: 18
    GET ACQUAINTED WITH THE HOME SCREEN 19
    HOW TO TURN OFF THE PHOTOSHOP HOME SCREEN 20
    FAMILIARIZING WITH THE PHOTOSHOP WORKSPACE 21
    OPENING FILES 23
    EXPLORING THE TOOLBAR 24

SELECTION TOOLS GROUP	26
CROP AND SLICE TOOLS GROUP	28
MEASURING TOOLS GROUP	29
DRAWING & TYPE TOOLS GROUP	31
NAVIGATION TOOLS GROUP	33
RETOUCHING & PAINTING TOOLS GROUP	34
SELECTING A TOOL FROM THE TOOLBAR	36
WORKING WITH THE TOOL PROPERTIES	36
KEY POINTS ABOUT THE PROPERTIES PANEL	37
HOW TO UNDERSTAND THE TOOL PROPERTIES IN THE OPTIONS BAR	38
USING THE STATUS BAR	39
ZOOM FACTOR	39
Figure out an image's width and height.	*39*
Some other information	*39*
Adobe Drive	*40*
Document Size	*40*
Document Profile	*40*
Document Dimensions	*40*
Measurement Scales	*40*
Scratch Sizes	*40*
Efficiency	*41*
Timing	*41*
Current Tool	*41*
32-bit Exposure	*41*
Save Progress	*41*
EXPLORING CONTEXT MENUS	41
GETTING USED TO PHOTOSHOP PANELS	43
THE DEFAULT "ESSENTIALS" WORKSPACE	43
Choosing the Essentials Workspace	*44*
Resetting the Essentials Workspace	*44*
WORKING WITH PHOTOSHOP'S PANELS	45
The Panel Area	*45*
The Main Panel Column	*46*
Panel Groups	*47*
Switching Between Panels in a Group	*47*
Changing the Order of Panels in a Group	*48*
Moving Panels between Groups	*49*
Creating New Panel Groups	*50*
Collapsing and Expanding Panel Groups	*52*
Closing a Single Panel	*53*
Closing A Panel or Group from the Tab	*54*
Opening Panels from the Window Menu	*55*
PHOTOSHOP'S STICKY PANELS	56

OPEN VS. ACTIVE PANELS	56
The Secondary Panel Column	*58*
EXPANDING AND COLLAPSING SECONDARY PANELS	59
MOVING PANEL GROUPS BETWEEN COLUMNS	60
MAKING IT RIGHT WITH UNDO AND REDO COMMANDS	62
EDIT-UNDO (CONTROL/COMMAND + Z)	62
LEGACY UNDO SHORTCUTS	63
ERASING EDITING STEPS WITH THE HISTORY BOX	65
HISTORY BRUSH	67
SETTING PHOTOSHOP PREFERENCES	69
How to Access the Photoshop Preferences	*69*
The Preferences Dialog Box	*69*
THE GENERAL PREFERENCES	70
Export Clipboard	*70*
Interface Preferences	*71*
COLOR THEME	71
HOW TO RESET PHOTOSHOP PREFERENCES	73
WORKING WITH CLOUD DOCUMENTS	73
WHAT IS THE DIFFERENCE BETWEEN CLOUD DOCUMENTS AND ADOBE CREATIVE CLOUD FILES?	74
Am I going to be forced to save my documents to the cloud in Photoshop?	*74*
Do cloud documents in Photoshop have anything to do with Lightroom photos?	*75*
CHAPTER FOUR	**76**
ESSENTIAL REQUIREMENTS FOR IMAGE EDITING	**76**
THE WORD PIXEL	76
The Pixel Grid	*76*
ZOOMING BACK OUT TO VIEW THE IMAGE	77
What is image size?	*77*
The Image Size dialog box	*77*
The pixel dimensions	*77*
Finding the total number of pixels	*78*
WORKING WITH IMAGE RESOLUTION AND DIMENSION	78
THE WIDTH, HEIGHT, AND RESOLUTION CONNECTION	78
THE RESAMPLE OPTION	79
Changing the print size, not the image size	*79*
How does image resolution work?	*80*
CHANGING THE RESOLUTION CHANGES THE PRINT SIZE	81
Changing the print size changes the resolution	*81*
Does image resolution affect file size?	*82*
LOWER RESOLUTION VS. FILE SIZE	83
HIGHER RESOLUTION VS. FILE SIZE	83
DIFFERENCE BETWEEN RESIZING AND RESAMPLING	84
ADJUSTING CANVA SIZE	84

How to Change an Existing Canvas Size in Photoshop 86
How to Change the Canvas Size on Export from Photoshop 87
FILE COMPRESSION 90
CHOOSING FILE FORMATS 91
JPEG (JOINT PHOTOGRAPHER EXPERTS GROUP) 91
    JPEG Basics *91*
    Best Applications *92*
    JPEG Compression Settings *92*
    Image Artifacts *93*
    JPEG Optimization in Photoshop *93*
PNG (PORTABLE NETWORK GRAPHICS) 93
    Key Features of PNG *93*
    Benefits of PNG *94*
    Working with PNG in Photoshop *94*
TIFF (TAGGED IMAGE FILE FORMAT) 95
PDF (PORTABLE DOCUMENT FORMAT) 96
PHOTOSHOP (PSD) 97
    Common Use Cases *98*
DIFFERENT MOTIVES FOR SAVING FILES DIFFERENTLY 99
    SAVING THE IMAGE AS THE ORIGINAL 99
    SAVING IMAGE TO DUPLICATE THE IMAGE FILE 99
SAVE A COPY 99
WORKING WITH THE RULERS AND GUIDES 100
    How to Display Rulers in Photoshop *100*
HOW TO CHANGE UNIT / INCREMENT OF YOUR RULERS 101
    How to Add a Guide Lines in Photoshop *101*
REPOSITION A GUIDE BY CLICKING AND DRAGGING 102
HOW TO LOCK YOUR GUIDES IN PHOTOSHOP 102
    How to Delete a Guide in Photoshop *102*
SNAP OBJECTS ONTO GUIDES OR GRIDS 103
    How to Create a Grid in Photoshop *103*
    How to Change Your Grid Layout *104*
CHANGE PHOTOSHOP RULER TO INCHES 104
COMMON FAQS ABOUT CHANGING PHOTOSHOP RULER TO INCHES 105
    Q: How do I change my Photoshop ruler from pixels to inches? *106*
    Q: Why would I need to change my ruler unit from pixels to inches? *106*
    Q: What is DPI and how does it relate to changing rulers into inches? *106*
    Q: What am I doing wrong? I've tried switching the unit of measurement on my ruler to inches, but it hasn't worked out so far. *107*
PROS AND CONS OF USING THE INCH MEASUREMENT SYSTEM IN PHOTOSHOP 107
    Pros *107*
    Cons *107*
HOW DOES CHANGING THE RULER UNIT AFFECT YOUR FINAL DESIGN OUTPUT? 109

- OPEN VS. ACTIVE PANELS 56
  - *The Secondary Panel Column* 58
- EXPANDING AND COLLAPSING SECONDARY PANELS 59
- MOVING PANEL GROUPS BETWEEN COLUMNS 60
- MAKING IT RIGHT WITH UNDO AND REDO COMMANDS 62
- EDIT-UNDO (CONTROL/COMMAND + Z) 62
- LEGACY UNDO SHORTCUTS 63
- ERASING EDITING STEPS WITH THE HISTORY BOX 65
- HISTORY BRUSH 67
- SETTING PHOTOSHOP PREFERENCES 69
  - *How to Access the Photoshop Preferences* 69
  - *The Preferences Dialog Box* 69
- THE GENERAL PREFERENCES 70
  - *Export Clipboard* 70
  - *Interface Preferences* 71
- COLOR THEME 71
- HOW TO RESET PHOTOSHOP PREFERENCES 73
- WORKING WITH CLOUD DOCUMENTS 73
- WHAT IS THE DIFFERENCE BETWEEN CLOUD DOCUMENTS AND ADOBE CREATIVE CLOUD FILES? 74
  - *Am I going to be forced to save my documents to the cloud in Photoshop?* 74
  - *Do cloud documents in Photoshop have anything to do with Lightroom photos?* 75

CHAPTER FOUR 76

ESSENTIAL REQUIREMENTS FOR IMAGE EDITING 76

- THE WORD PIXEL 76
  - *The Pixel Grid* 76
- ZOOMING BACK OUT TO VIEW THE IMAGE 77
  - *What is image size?* 77
  - *The Image Size dialog box* 77
  - *The pixel dimensions* 77
  - *Finding the total number of pixels* 78
- WORKING WITH IMAGE RESOLUTION AND DIMENSION 78
- THE WIDTH, HEIGHT, AND RESOLUTION CONNECTION 78
- THE RESAMPLE OPTION 79
  - *Changing the print size, not the image size* 79
  - *How does image resolution work?* 80
- CHANGING THE RESOLUTION CHANGES THE PRINT SIZE 81
  - *Changing the print size changes the resolution* 81
  - *Does image resolution affect file size?* 82
- LOWER RESOLUTION VS. FILE SIZE 83
- HIGHER RESOLUTION VS. FILE SIZE 83
- DIFFERENCE BETWEEN RESIZING AND RESAMPLING 84
- ADJUSTING CANVA SIZE 84

How to Change an Existing Canvas Size in Photoshop 86
How to Change the Canvas Size on Export from Photoshop 87
FILE COMPRESSION 90
CHOOSING FILE FORMATS 91
JPEG (JOINT PHOTOGRAPHER EXPERTS GROUP) 91
   JPEG Basics *91*
   Best Applications *92*
   JPEG Compression Settings *92*
   Image Artifacts *93*
   JPEG Optimization in Photoshop *93*
PNG (PORTABLE NETWORK GRAPHICS) 93
   Key Features of PNG *93*
   Benefits of PNG *94*
   Working with PNG in Photoshop *94*
TIFF (TAGGED IMAGE FILE FORMAT) 95
PDF (PORTABLE DOCUMENT FORMAT) 96
PHOTOSHOP (PSD) 97
   Common Use Cases *98*
DIFFERENT MOTIVES FOR SAVING FILES DIFFERENTLY 99
   SAVING THE IMAGE AS THE ORIGINAL *99*
   SAVING IMAGE TO DUPLICATE THE IMAGE FILE *99*
SAVE A COPY 99
WORKING WITH THE RULERS AND GUIDES 100
   How to Display Rulers in Photoshop *100*
How to Change Unit / Increment of Your Rulers 101
   How to Add a Guide Lines in Photoshop *101*
Reposition a Guide by Clicking and Dragging 102
How to Lock Your Guides in Photoshop 102
   How to Delete a Guide in Photoshop *102*
Snap Objects onto Guides or Grids 103
   How to Create a Grid in Photoshop *103*
   How to Change Your Grid Layout *104*
Change Photoshop Ruler to Inches 104
Common FAQs about Changing Photoshop Ruler to Inches 105
   Q: How do I change my Photoshop ruler from pixels to inches? *106*
   Q: Why would I need to change my ruler unit from pixels to inches? *106*
   Q: What is DPI and how does it relate to changing rulers into inches? *106*
   Q: What am I doing wrong? I've tried switching the unit of measurement on my ruler to inches, but it hasn't worked out so far. *107*
Pros and Cons of Using the Inch Measurement System in Photoshop 107
   Pros *107*
   Cons *107*
How Does Changing the Ruler Unit Affect Your Final Design Output? 109

CHAPTER FIVE 112

GETTING STARTED WITH DRAWING ON PHOTOSHOP 112

   BITMAP IMAGES 112
      Bitmap Image Exercise 113
   VECTOR GRAPHICS 117
      When to use vector images. 117
      When to use raster images. 117
      The path to vectors. 117
      Why go from raster to vector? 118
      How to turn a raster image into a vector image in Photoshop. 118
   BITMAP AND VECTOR GRAPHICS STRENGTHS AND WEAKNESSES 119
   WHAT KNOWLEDGE DO YOU HAVE OF PATHS? 120
      How does path work? 120
      How is Paths Utilized? 121
      An example path 121
      Types of line segments 122
      Types of anchor points 122
      About path components 122
   CREATING A SHAPE USING THE PEN TOOL 123
   DRAWING STRAIGHT LINES 124
      Deleting your path 125
      DRAWING CURVED LINES 125
   SWITCHING BETWEEN CURVES AND LINES 127
   CONTINUING PATHS 128
   THE FREEFORM PEN TOOL 129
   SKETCHING A PATH FROM A PHOTO 129
      Step 1: Select the Picture You Want to Use 129
      Step 2: Choose Your Starting Point and Create Path 130
      Step 3: Customizing Clipping Path 131
      Step 4: Save Your Path 132
      Step 5: Turn the Clipping Path into Dotted Lines 132
      Step 6: Erase Unsuitable Background 133
   EDITING PATHS IN PHOTOSHOP 133
      Selecting paths 133
      The Path Component Selection tool 134
      The Direct Selection tool 134
   SOME HANDY SHORTCUTS 135
   MODIFYING PATH SEGMENTS 136
      Moving straight segments 136
      Moving curved segments 136
   RESHAPING CURVED SEGMENTS 137
      Technique 1. Shrinking and stretching 137

Technique 2. Altering the direction lines 138
PERFORMING EDITS ON THE ANCHOR POINTS 138
   Converting from a corner point to a smooth point 138
   Converting from a smooth point to a corner point 139
   Making a corner point without direction lines 139
   Making a corner point with direction lines 139
   Making a corner point with only one direction line 139
   Dragging anchor points 140
   Reopening and joining path components 140

CHAPTER SIX 141

GETTING STARTED WITH TYPE 141

MAJOR GROUPING OF PHOTOSHOP TEXT 141
CREATING A POINT TYPE 142
PARAGRAPH TEXT 143
CREATING A CLIPPING MASK AND APPLYING A SHADOW 143
CREATING TYPE ON A PATH 145
WARPING TEXT 146
   Text Warp Defined 146
   Warp and Distort Text in Photoshop? 146

CHAPTER SEVEN 151

UPDATED SHORTCUTS COMMAND 151

LIST OF MODIFIER KEYS 151
CREATING YOUR KEYBOARD SHORTCUTS 152
EDIT SHORTCUTS 156
IMAGE SHORTCUTS 158
FILE SHORTCUTS 159
LAYER SHORTCUTS 161
   Creating and Selecting Layers 162
   Layer Blending Modes 162
   Layer Opacity 162
   Layer Visibility 162
   Layer Locks 162
   Layer Groups 162
   Layer Masking 163
   Layer Styles 163
   Layer Alignment 163
   Layer Linking 163
   Layer Opacity and Fill 163
SELECT SHORTCUTS 164
   Basic Selection Tools 164
   Advanced Selection Tools 164

Selection Modification *164*
Select All and Deselect *165*
Select Menu Commands *165*
VIEW SHORTCUTS 165
Zooming In and Out *165*
Navigation and Panning *166*
Screen Mode *166*
Rulers, Grids, and Guides *166*
Extras *166*
Snap To *166*
Timeline (for Animation) *166*
Screen Mode for Multiple Monitors *167*
TOOL SHORTCUTS 167
COLOR AND SWATCH SHORTCUTS 168
CLEAR SHORTCUTS FROM A COMMAND OR TOOL 170
Delete a set of shortcuts *170*
View a list of current shortcuts *170*
IMPORTING/EXPORTING KEYBOARD SHORTCUTS 170
EXPORTING KEYBOARD SHORTCUTS IN ADOBE PHOTOSHOP 170
HOW TO RESET TO THE DEFAULT SHORTCUT IN ADOBE PHOTOSHOP 171

CHAPTER EIGHT **172**

EDITING WITH CAMERA RAW EDITOR **172**
UNDERSTANDING VARIOUS RAW FILE FORMATS 172
DO I NEED CAMERA RAW IMAGES INSTEAD OF JPEG IMAGES? 173
Recognizing JPEG and RAW from Camera *173*
When to Choose Camera RAW Images *173*
When to Choose JPEG Images *174*
OPENING IMAGES IN THE CAMERA RAW EDITOR 175
Alternatively *175*
Open images in Photoshop Camera Raw from Photoshop or Bridge *175*
HOW TO MAKE JPEGS AND TIFFS ALWAYS OPEN IN CAMERA RAW 176
GETTING ACQUAINTED WITH CAMERA RAW EDITOR WINDOW 177
GETTING FAMILIAR WITH THE BASIC PANEL 179
SELECTING AN ADOBE RAW PROFILE 181
ADJUSTING IMAGE TONAL USING THE BASIC PANEL 182
FINE-TUNE CURVES 184
SHARPENING IMAGE WITH THE DETAIL PANEL 185
NOTE 187
TIP 188
SAVING CAMERA RAW EDITS AS NEW FILES 188
Save Your Edits as a DNG (Digital Negative) File *188*
Save Your Edits as a TIFF or PSD File *188*

- *Save Your Edits as a JPEG for Sharing* *189*
- *Organize Your Edited Files* *189*
- CORRECTING THE WHITE BALANCE IN THE CAMERA RAW 189
- USING THE PRESETS 190
- USING THE TEMPERATURE & TINT SLIDERS 190
- USING THE WHITE BALANCE TOOL 191
- FROM START TO FINISH 192
- CORRECTING SATURATION IN CAMERA RAW 192

CHAPTER NINE 194

GETTING ACQUAINTED WITH COLOR MODE 194

- WHICH COLOR MODE SHOULD I CHOOSE? 194
  - *Different color modes* *194*
  - *RGB Color mode* *194*
  - *CMYK Color mode* *195*
  - *Lab Color mode* *196*
  - *Grayscale mode* *196*
  - *Bitmap mode* *196*
  - *Duotone mode* *196*
  - *Indexed Color mode* *197*
  - *Multichannel mode* *197*
- UNDERSTANDING CALIBRATION AND PROFILING 197
- CONVERTING RGB IMAGE TO CMYK MODE 199
  - *Step 1: Save a Backup of Your Work* *199*
  - *Step 2: Flatten All Layers* *199*
  - *Step 3: Change the Document Color Profile* *200*
  - *Precautions* *201*
- SAVING YOUR IMAGE AS PHOTOSHOP PDF 201

CHAPTER TEN 202

FINE ART PAINTING WITH THE MIXER BRUSH 202

- CHOOSING A WORKSPACE AND SELECTING BRUSH SETTINGS 202
  - *Choosing a Workspace* *202*
  - *Choosing the Brush Settings* *202*
- WORKING WITH BRUSHES AND WETNESS OPTIONS 203
- THE BASICS 203
  - *Brush Tip* *203*
  - *Foreground Color* *204*
- BRUSH PRESET PICKER CONTEXTUAL MENU 205
  - *Brush Modes* *205*
  - *Modes: Behind, Clear, Normal, and Dissolve* *205*
  - *More Blending Modes* *205*
  - *Opacity* *206*

- *Flow* 206
- WHAT IS THE BRUSH SETTINGS PANEL? 207
  - *MAKE A WET BRUSH* 207
  - *How Do You Make a Wet Brush in Photoshop?* 208
- MIXING COLORS WITH THE MIXER BRUSH 208
  - *Step 1: Select a Color* 208
  - *Step 2: Choose Your Brush Settings* 210
  - *Wet* 210
  - *Load* 211
  - *Mix* 212
  - *Flow* 212
- CREATE AND SAVE A CUSTOM BRUSH PRESET 212
  - *Create a Brush Preset* 212
  - *Brush Tip Shape* 213
  - *Shape Dynamics* 214
  - *Control* 214
  - *Scattering* 214
- COLOR DYNAMICS 215
- DUAL BRUSH 215
  - *Texture* 215
  - *More Dynamics* 216
- HOW TO CREATE A NEW PRESET BRUSH 216
  - *Save and Load Brushes in Photoshop* 217

CHAPTER ELEVEN 218

CREATING MASKS AND CHANNELS IN PHOTOSHOP 218
- UNDERSTANDING MASKS AND ALPHA CHANNELS 218
- ALPHA CHANNELS IN PHOTOSHOP 219
- KEY DIFFERENCES BETWEEN MASKS AND ALPHA CHANNELS 220
- PRACTICAL USES 220
- CREATING A MASK 220
- REFINING A MASK 222
- REFINING MASK EDGE WITH THE GLOBAL REFINEMENTS 222
- GENERATING THE MASK OUTPUT 227
  - *Clipping Masks* 227
  - *Vector Masks* 228
- CREATING A QUICK MASK 228
- CHANGE QUICK MASK OPTIONS 229
- MOULDING AN IMAGE USING THE PUPPET WARP 230
  - *Tips for Using Puppet Warp Effectively* 231
- CREATING A SHADOW WITH AN ALPHA CHANNEL 231
- PUTTING A NEW BACKGROUND FOR THE LAYER MASK 233
  - *Tips for a Professional Finish* 234

CHAPTER TWELVE 234
WORKING WITH SELECTION 234
- MARQUEE TOOLS SELECTION 235
  - *What Does the Marquee Tool Do?* 235
  - *Common Uses for the Tool* 236
  - *Fixed Ratio Selection* 236
  - *Rectangular Marquee tool* 237
  - *Elliptical Marquee tool* 238
  - *Single Row Marquee tool* 240
  - *Single Column Marquee tool* 241
  - *Repositioning a selection marquee while creating it* 243
- MOVING A SELECTION WITH SHORTCUT KEYS 245
- LASSO TOOLS SELECTION 246
  - *The Standard Lasso Tool* 246
  - *Polygonal Lasso Tool* 248
  - *Magnetic Lasso Tool.* 249
- SWITCHING BETWEEN LASSO AND POLYGONAL LASSO TOOLS 251
- ROTATING AND SCALING A SELECTION 252
  - *Selecting from a center point* 253
  - *Resizing and copying a selection* 254
  - *Moving and duplicating a selection simultaneously* 255
- COPYING SELECTIONS 256
- COLOR, EDGE, AND CONTENT-BASED SELECTIONS 257
- MAKING SELECTIONS WITH MAGIC WAND TOOL 257
- MAKING SELECTIONS WITH THE QUICK SELECTION TOOL 260
  - *Moving a selected area* 261
- EXPLORING THE OBJECT SELECTION TOOL 262

CHAPTER THIRTEEN 266
IMAGE RETOUCHING IN PHOTOSHOP 266
- APPROACH FOR RETOUCHING 266
- STRAIGHTENING AND CROPPING AN IMAGE 268
  - *Cropping an image in Photoshop* 268
- STRAIGHTENING AN IMAGE IN PHOTOSHOP 270
- USING A CONTENT-AWARE PATCH 272
- FIXING IMAGE AREAS WITH THE CLONE STAMP TOOL 274
- A FEW HELPFUL HINTS WHILE UTILIZING THE CLONE STAMP TOOL: 276
- REMOVING BLEMISHES AND WRINKLES WITH HEALING BRUSH TOOLS 276
  - *Tips for Effective Use* 277
- ADVANCED TECHNIQUES 278
- SPONGE AND DODGE TOOLS 279
- WORKING WITH THE DODGE, BURN, AND SPONGE TOOLS 279

USING ADOBE PHOTOSHOP'S DODGE AND BURN TOOLS	280
Applying the Sponge Tool in Adobe Photoshop	281
ADJUSTING LEVELS	282
THE PHOTOSHOP LEVELS DIALOG	283
READING THE PHOTOSHOP LEVELS	284
HOW TO ADJUST THE LEVELS IN PHOTOSHOP	284
Step 1 – Add a New Levels Adjustment Layer	284
Step 2 – Adjust the Black Input Level	285
Step 3 – Adjust the White Input Level	285
READING THE INPUT LEVEL NUMBERS	286
ADJUSTING THE PHOTOSHOP OUTPUT LEVELS	286
WHAT'S HAPPENING IN THE PHOTOSHOP LEVELS ADJUSTMENT	288
The Photoshop Midtone Level	288
CORRECTING SKIN TONES	288
Step 1 – Open the Image to Select Skin Tones	288
Step 2 – Select the Target Area	289
Step 3 – Create a Curves Adjustment Layer	290

CHAPTER FOURTEEN 291

WORKING WITH LAYERS 291

ADOBE PHOTOSHOP LAYERS	291
NAVIGATING AROUND THE LAYERS PANEL	292
THE LAYER ROW	294
The Layer Name	294
THE PREVIEW THUMBNAIL	295
ADDING A NEW LAYER	295
Moving Layers	296
The Active Layer	297
Deleting a Layer	297
Copying a Layer	297
Renaming a Layer	297
RENAME A LAYER IN PHOTOSHOP BY MAKING USE OF THE LAYERS PANEL	297
Rename a layer in Photoshop by using "Layer" in the main menu	298
The Layer Search Bar	298
SHOW/HIDE LAYER	300
Locking Layers	301
ADDING LAYER STYLE TO A LAYER	302
LAYERS STACKING ORDER	303
Change the order of layers and layer groups	303
ADJUSTING THE OPACITY OF A LAYER	303
ROTATING AND RESIZING LAYERS	305
BLEND MODES	306
Blending mode descriptions	306

Normal mode 307
Dissolve 307
Behind 307
Clear 307
Darken 307
Multiply 308
Color Burn 308
Linear Burn 308
Lighten 308
Screen 308
Color Dodge 309
Linear Dodge (Add) 309
Overlay 309
Soft Light 309
Hard Light 309
Vivid Light 310
Linear Light 310
Pin Light 310
Hard Mix 310
Difference 311
Exclusion 311
Subtract 311
Divide 311
Hue 311
Saturation 311
Color 312
Luminosity 312
Lighter Color 312
Darker Color 312
APPLYING A FILTER TO CREATE A DESIGN 312
   Step 1: Open Your Image or Start with a New Canvas 312
   Step 2: Create or Import Your Design Elements 313
   Step 3: Select the Layer to Apply the Filter 313
   Step 4: Apply the Filter 313
   Step 5: Review and Modify 313
   Step 6: Combine Filters and Effects (Optional) 313
CREATING TEXT AND ADDING SPECIAL EFFECT 314
APPLYING A GRADIENT TO A LAYER 314
   Step 1: Create a new layer 314
   Step 2: Select the Gradient tool 315
   Step 3: Choose a gradient type 315
   Step 4: Select the colors for your gradient 315
   Step 5: Apply the gradient 315

- Step 6: Adjust the gradient using layer styles 315
- Step 7: Save your work 315
- PHOTOSHOP GRADIENT APPLICATION TIPS 315
- ABOUT ADJUSTMENT LAYERS 316
  - Accessing Photoshop Adjustment Layers 316
  - Adjustment Layer Types 317
- ADDING A BORDER TO THE IMAGE 320
  - Creating a solid border 320
  - Creating a Grunge Border 322
- MERGING LAYERS 323
  - Merge layers into another layer 324
- CONVERT THE BACKGROUND LAYER INTO A REGULAR LAYER 324
- FLATTENING AND SAVING FILES 325
- CREATING A PATTERN TO MAKE A BORDER 327

CHAPTER FIFTEEN 329

IMAGE TRANSFORMATION 329

- RED EYE REMOVAL 329
- THE DETAILED GUIDE TO PHOTOSHOP RED EYE REMOVAL 330
- REMOVING OBJECTS WITH CONTENT-AWARE FILL 333
- RELOCATION WITH THE CONTENT-AWARE TOOL 334
  - Draw a selection 335
  - Reposition, Resize, or Rotate 335
- CORRECTING LENS/CAMERA DISTORTION 335
  - Correct lens distortion and adjust perspective 336
- AUTOMATICALLY CORRECT IMAGE PERSPECTIVE AND LENS FLAWS 336
  - Correction 336
  - Search Criteria 336
  - Lens Profiles 336
- MANUALLY CORRECT IMAGE PERSPECTIVE AND LENS FLAWS 337
- ADJUST THE LENS CORRECTION PREVIEW AND GRID 338
- SAVE SETTINGS AND SET CAMERA AND LENS DEFAULTS 338
- REDUCE IMAGE NOISE AND JPEG ARTIFACTS 339
- CREATING PANORAMA WITH PHOTO MERGE 340
- BRIGHTENING A PHOTOGRAPH 341
  - Method 1: Adjusting Overall Brightness and Contrast 341
  - Method 2: Brightening Selective Areas 341
- ADJUSTING IMAGE WITH LIQUIFY 342
- FORWARD WARP TOOL 343
  - Reconstruct Tool 343
  - Smooth Tool 343
  - Twirl Clockwise Tool 343
  - Pucker Tool 343

- Bloat Tool 344
- Push Left Tool 344
- Freeze Mask Tool 344
- Thaw Mask Tool 344
- Face Tool 344
- Hand Tool 344
- Zoom Tool 345
- Liquify Tool Properties 345
- APPLYING LIQUIFY FILTER AS A SMART FILTER 346

CHAPTER SIXTEEN 347

GROUPS IN PHOTOSHOP 347

- What is a Photoshop Group 347
  - HOW TO CREATE A GROUP IN PHOTOSHOP 348
  - ADDING EFFECTS TO THE GROUP IN PHOTOSHOP 349
  - HIDING A GROUP IN PHOTOSHOP 349
  - DELETING A GROUP IN PHOTOSHOP 350
  - DUPLICATING THE GROUP IN PHOTOSHOP 350
  - UNGROUPING LAYERS IN PHOTOSHOP 350
  - GROUP TEXTS IN PHOTOSHOP 350
- FREQUENTLY ASKED QUESTIONS ON PHOTOSHOP 2024 351
  - What are the system requirements for Photoshop 2024? 351
  - Does Adobe Photoshop 2024 support plugins created by third-party developers? 351
  - How will I be able to become familiar with the new features that have been added to Photoshop 2024? 351
  - Is it possible to install Photoshop 2024 on more than one computer? 351
  - Is Generative Fill a paid add-on? 352
  - What happens if you run out of credits? 352
  - Is the resolution still limited to 1024 x 1024? 352
  - Where is High Resolution? 352
  - Are there going to be any adjustments made to the prices? 352
  - What is the difference between Photoshop 2024 and previous versions? 352
  - What is the Generative Fill feature in Photoshop 2024? 353
  - How can I update to Photoshop 2024? 353
  - What should I do if I am having problems with Adobe Photoshop 2024? 353
  - Does Photoshop 2024 offer any new brushes or filters? 353
  - Can I use Photoshop 2024 on a tablet? 353
  - What are the new features in Photoshop 2024? 354
  - Is there a free trial for Photoshop 2024? 354
  - Can I use my existing Adobe ID to use Photoshop 2024? 354
  - What are the benefits of subscribing to Adobe Creative Cloud? 354
  - How can I learn more about using Photoshop 2024? 355
- CONCLUSION 355

INDEX 356

INTRODUCTION

Welcome to Adobe Photoshop 2024, a place where your creativity is only limited by your imagination. Photoshop is an ageless cornerstone of innovation and creative expression in the ever-changing world of digital design and image modification. It is also one of the most widely used programs in these fields. As we enter the fascinating world of Photoshop in 2024, we would like to take you on a voyage of exploration and mastery, to reveal the full potential of this venerable piece of software. Adobe Photoshop 2024 is more than simply a tool; it is a portal through which your creative ideas can be brought to life. Adobe continues to push the limits of what is possible with each new version of its software, providing users with a wide variety of innovative features and improvements with each new release. This book is your passport to releasing the full potential of Photoshop 2024. Whether you're a seasoned expert trying to keep ahead of the curve or a newbie ready to start on your creative adventure, this guide is the key to unlocking Photoshop's full potential.

Photoshop 2024 draws on its illustrious history while simultaneously embracing the most cutting-edge technology and fashions in the field of digital art and design. You will be able to improve your images, make attractive graphics, and develop compelling visual tales with the help of this program. Photoshop is still the go-to platform for converting your ideas into pixel-perfect reality, and its capabilities range from the most fundamental picture edits to the most complex compositing, retouching, and 3D rendering. You will begin an in-depth investigation of Photoshop's possibilities inside the pages of this guide, beginning with a mastery of the basics and progressing up to an immersion in advanced methods. Your imagination will be stimulated by our novel methods of picture editing, graphic design, and digital arts as we demystify the user interface, give hands-on instruction for crucial tasks, and answer any questions you may have along the way.

In Photoshop 2024, you won't merely be able to repair photographs or manipulate images; rather, the program will serve as a canvas for your creative endeavors. Creating amazing visual storytelling, producing appealing visuals, and bringing your ideas to existence with unmatched accuracy are all part of the process. This book has something to offer everyone interested in visual communication, whether you are a photographer, graphic designer, digital artist, or you just have a general interest in the subject. So, join us as we embark on this exciting journey into Photoshop 2024. Together, we'll navigate the interface, embrace the new features, and uncover the limitless possibilities that await. As the creative landscape continues to evolve, Photoshop remains your trusted companion, and this guide is your trusted roadmap. Let's dive in and harness the boundless creative power of Adobe Photoshop in 2024!

CHAPTER ONE
SYSTEM REQUIREMENTS, DOWNLOADING AND INSTALLING PHOTOSHOP 2024

This chapter discusses the minimum and recommended system requirements for both Windows and macOS platforms. It guides how to install Adobe Photoshop 2024, version 25.0. In general, the purpose of this chapter is to act as an introduction to the process of installing Photoshop 2024 on various operating systems and gaining a concept of the necessary hardware requirements.

MINIMUM AND RECOMMENDED SYSTEM REQUIREMENTS FOR PHOTOSHOP (WINDOWS)

- **CPU**: Intel or AMD processor with 64-bit support, 2 GHz or faster processor
- **RAM**: 8 GB
- **HDD**: 4 GB of storage space
- **GPU**: DirectX 12 support and 2 GB of memory
- **Operating System**: Windows 10 (64-bit) version 1809 or later
- **Screen Resolution**: 1280 x 800
- An Internet connection is needed to activate the software

MINIMUM AND RECOMMENDED SYSTEM REQUIREMENTS FOR PHOTOSHOP (MACOS)

- **CPU**: Intel or AMD processor with 64-bit support, 2 GHz or faster processor
- **RAM**: 8 GB
- **HDD**: 4 GB of storage space
- **GPU**: DirectX 12 support and 2 GB of memory
- **Operating System**: macOS Mojave (version 10.14) or later
- **Screen Resolution**: 1280 x 800
- An Internet connection is needed to activate the software

Photoshop system requirements by component

Now, let's dive a little deeper into the specific components of your computer system and how important each one is to running Adobe Photoshop smoothly.

Operating system

When it comes to how well Photoshop runs on your computer, the operating system (OS) that you use isn't a very important aspect. It doesn't matter whether you're operating on Windows or macOS; as long as the version you're using is relatively current, Photoshop will work just fine on your computer.

To install the most recent version of Photoshop on a computer running Windows, you will need to upgrade to Windows 10. Windows 7 is no longer receiving updates or support. Photoshop can be operated on a Mac running the Mojave operating system, however, the most recent version, Big Sur, is strongly recommended.

Processor (CPU)

Your computer's central processing unit (CPU) is one of the most important system components that determine how well Photoshop runs, but selecting a CPU can also be a contentious issue among Photoshop's legion of devoted users. The following are the facts: in the past, Intel central processing units were by far the finest option; however, as of the year 2021, the distinctions between AMD and Intel processors for the operation of Adobe Photoshop have become insignificant. These days, you can choose whatever brand you want and get results that are quite comparable in terms of performance. You should be aware that Photoshop is unable to take advantage of numerous processor cores; hence, selecting a more powerful central processing unit will not result in a noticeable improvement in terms of speed. When operating Adobe Photoshop, you do not need to prioritize purchasing a computer with a Threadripper or Xeon processor, for example, since they will not provide any further performance benefits.

Memory (RAM)

When it comes to the memory storage components known as RAM, you should always put quantity ahead of quality since this is the component that is the most significant while using Adobe Photoshop or any other creative software for that matter. Try not to let things like greater frequencies, lower latencies, RGB, or any other unique characteristics divert your attention. Aim for 8 gigabytes (GB) as the basic minimum number for your RAM storage, but if your budget allows it, go up to 16 GB since it will offer you a big jump in performance. The more RAM you have, the faster your computer will be. Regardless of the option you choose, remember that there are probably only four memory slots available on your motherboard. As a result, you absolutely must make preparations in advance for the RAM system needs. Let us say that you presently need 16 gigabytes of random access memory (RAM), but shortly, you can decide to increase that to 32 gigabytes. In this scenario, it is recommended that you use two memory sticks, each with an 8 GB capacity, for a total of 16 GB. When compared to having four sticks of memory that are each 4 gigabytes in size, this option is seen as having more adaptability. The total remains the same, which is 16 gigabytes, but spreading it over just two sticks of RAM leaves you with two vacant slots on your motherboard, which means you have space to increase. It is important to keep in mind that if your computer does not have enough RAM, Photoshop will start using up space on your disk to continue working. Because of this, there will be a significant decrease in performance; hence, if you want the greatest results while using Adobe Photoshop, it is recommended that you stock up on RAM as soon as your budget allows for it.

Graphics card (GPU)

Adobe Photoshop does not place a significant demand on the graphics hardware in your computer. It is prudent to allocate a larger portion of your cash toward purchasing a capable central processing unit (CPU), enough random access memory (RAM), and a graphics card that meets your needs. If money is limited, you may want to look into purchasing a central processing unit that also has a graphics card built in. Although this is not the optimal solution, it is the greatest option for those who are open to making upgrades in the near or distant future. This is particularly true considering that the price of graphics processing units (GPU) has soared while there is a shortage of inventories. Instead of purchasing a graphics card at a premium price, you should concentrate on acquiring the most powerful processor you can. When it comes to Adobe Photoshop, this is the part that is considered to be the most crucial. You should consider purchasing a top-selling graphics card in the future if your finances will let it. There is almost no discernible difference in performance between a high-end graphics card and a poor one when it comes to Adobe Photoshop. A 1080p monitor is compatible with any graphics processing unit (GPU) that has at least 2 GB of memory.

Storage (SSD or HDD)

Switching from a traditional hard disk (HDD) to a solid-state drive (SSD) is one of the best ways to significantly boost the speed of Adobe Photoshop. The price of solid-state drives (SSDs) is higher, but the noticeable increase in performance makes the change well worth the additional cost. The vast majority of users are aware that solid-state drives (SSDs) are noticeably quicker than standard hard disk drives (HDDs), but here's the catch: if you want Photoshop to reap the full benefits of your lightning-fast SSD, you must utilize it as a scratch disk. This option can be found just under the heading "**Performance**" in the **Preferences** menu of your app. When you run out of RAM, Photoshop will automatically switch to using scratch drives. The ideal scenario is one in which you have a substantial amount of space on your solid-state drive (SSD), which, given the relatively high cost per gigabyte of SSDs, might be a challenge to obtain.

Because of this, it is recommended that you install Photoshop and other applications on your hard drive rather than your solid-state drive (SSD) so that your SSD remains relatively empty for use as a scratch disk. Even though it may seem paradoxical, installing Photoshop on your solid-state drive will not result in a visible improvement in speed. In general, except for **Photoshop**, the performance of most solid-state drives (SSDs) decreases as more data is written to them. Some people believe that if you fill an SSD to more than 50 percent capacity, you are significantly slowing down its performance. Naturally, this differs from one manufacturer to another and from model to model. If you have at least 20 gigabytes of free space on your solid-state drive (SSD), everything should be OK.

INSTALLING ADOBE PHOTOSHOP 2024 (VERSION 25.0)

The installation of Adobe Photoshop 2024 is a simple procedure; nonetheless, it is essential to follow each step in the installation guide very carefully to guarantee a flawless installation.

Detailed instructions on how to install Adobe Photoshop 2024 can be found here:

1. Prepare Your Computer:
   - Before you start, it is highly recommended that you disable your antivirus software for the time being. Additionally, if you are using Windows, you should temporarily deactivate **Windows Defender**. This is because anti-virus software has the potential to cause complications throughout the installation process.
2. Download the Software:
   - To get started, you will need to download the most recent version of Adobe Photoshop 2024. This program is readily available, in most cases, on the official Adobe website or from another reliable source. Downloading it from a reliable source is necessary if you want to prevent any possible security issues.

3. Extract the Software:

- Once the download is finished, the program will be sent to you in a compressed format (such as a ZIP file), depending on your preferences. It will need to be extracted using software such as **WinRAR or 7-Zip** on your computer. To extract the contents of the downloaded file, right-click on the file and choose "**Extract Here**" or another option of a similar kind.

4. Start the Setup File:
    - Once the program has been extracted, you will be able to locate a setup or installation file. In most cases, it will have an "**.exe**" extension. To start the installation process, double-click on this file.

5. Select the Language:
    - The installation process will begin, and you will be invited to choose the language that you want to use. From the list of available choices, choose "**English**" or the language that best suits your needs.

6. Uncheck Advertising:
    - While you are going through the process of installing Adobe software, you will come across optional components or advertisements that Adobe may recommend you install. It is suggested that you deselect all checkboxes that are connected to supplementary software or advertising unless you particularly desire to install that product or advertisement. Maintaining a discriminating mindset helps keep your system clean and clear of apps that aren't essential.

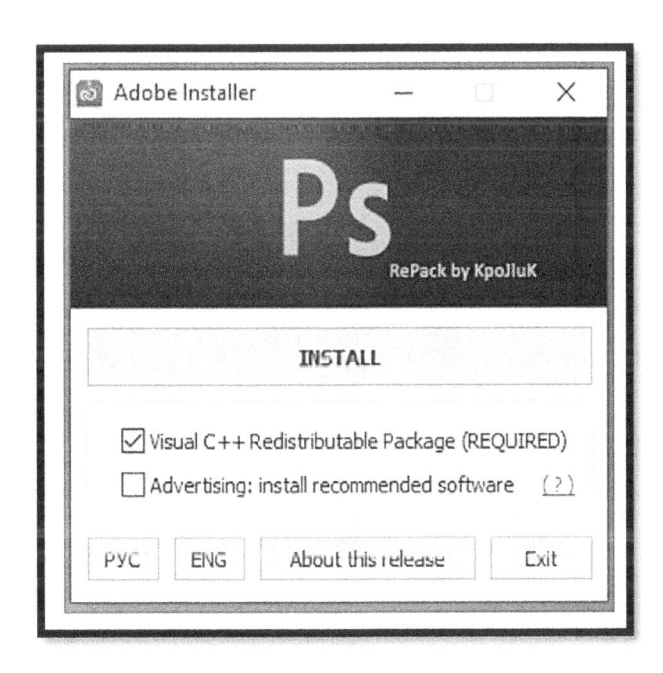

7. Check Microsoft Visual C++ Installation:

- The installer could also check to see whether Microsoft Visual C++ redistributable packages are already present on the system. Both of these checks can be left unchecked if you already have the necessary programs installed on your computer (typically, Visual C++ Redistributable 2019 or a later version). However, if you don't already have them loaded, it's a good idea to activate these checkboxes so that Photoshop will have the appropriate runtime libraries. This will guarantee that Photoshop works properly.

8. Start Installation:
   - After you have made your selections, click the "**Install**" button. The installation of Adobe Photoshop 2024 will begin shortly on your PC.

9. Wait for Installation to Complete:
   - Depending on the capabilities of your computer system, the process of installing the software can take a few minutes to finish. You will notice a progress bar that indicates the current state of the installation.

10. Open Adobe Photoshop:
    - Once the setup process is complete, you will most likely be presented with a confirmation message. Now that Adobe Photoshop 2024 has been updated, you can access it by navigating to the application on your **Start Menu** (on Windows) or the **Applications folder** (on macOS).

Congratulations to you! You should now be able to use Adobe Photoshop 2024 after successfully installing it on your PC. You are now free to explore its features and get started integrating it into your artistic endeavors. If you had to turn off your antivirus software or Windows Defender earlier so that the installation could take place, make sure you remember to turn them back on again.

CHAPTER TWO
PHOTOSHOP 2024 STRIKING FEATURES

This chapter provides an overview of some of the most important new features and adjustments that were made in Photoshop 2024. These include the availability of Generative Fill and Generative Expand for commercial use, enhancements to the Remove Tool, enhancements to the contextual taskbar to assist with masking and cropping, the discontinuation of Preset Sync in Photoshop 25.0, and an improvement in startup performance achieved through on-demand view initialization. All of these changes were made. The purpose of this chapter is to offer an overview of the most significant modifications and additions that were made to Photoshop in this edition.

GENERATIVE FILL AND GENERATIVE EXPAND ACCESSIBLE IN PHOTOSHOP FOR COMMERCIAL USE

Generative Fill and Generative Expand are two game-changing features that have just been added to Photoshop as a result of Adobe's most recent innovation, which is powered by Firefly. These ground-breaking tools make use of the incredible capabilities of generative AI technologies to improve, alter, or even generate information inside your photographs without causing any damage to the originals. What separates these tools from others is how simple it is to use them; all you have to do is follow the on-screen text instructions and watch as your photographs morph in front of your own eyes. You'll have no trouble conveying your imaginative concepts thanks to the support of more than one hundred languages.

Both **Generative Fill and Generative Expand** are intended to surprise you with the outcomes they produce, and they succeed in doing so. These AI-driven tools go above and beyond your expectations by automatically adjusting themselves to the viewpoint, lighting, and style of your photograph. The result will blow your mind since the material will be merged into your picture in such a manner that it seems as if it was always intended to be there. The fact that the created content is stored in a separate layer

Designated as the Generative layer is very astounding. Because of this, a whole new universe of possibilities becomes available to you, as you are now able to make use of the whole power and accuracy of Photoshop to further polish and improve your picture. Because of this synergy, you will realize that you are capable of exceeding even your own creative goals and expectations.

The fact that Generative Fill and Generative Expand are both suitable for use in business settings is one of their primary advantages. Firefly, the artificial intelligence that powers these products, has been carefully trained on Adobe Stock's large collection of professional-grade, high-resolution photographs. This is an acknowledgment of the quality and dependability of Adobe Stock's images. Because of this, you can use these tools with complete assurance for commercial initiatives, secure in the knowledge that the outcomes will live up to the highest expectations prevalent in the sector. Your most powerful tools are Generative Fill and Generative Expand, especially in a world where visual narrative is of the utmost importance. They provide a degree of inventiveness, convenience, and realism that has never been seen before, which will cause you to rethink your approach to picture editing. Accept these tools that are driven by AI, and be ready to be amazed by the limitless possibilities they offer to your creative pursuits.

Embark on an exciting learning journey with Generative Fill

The action starts as soon as you activate the app when you'll be met with the chance to see the wonder of Generative Fill in action. This is where the journey officially begins. Watch how it modifies a scene using a preloaded asset to give you a preview of the creative possibilities that are yet to come. However, this is just the beginning of things. The game Generative Fill is intended to be a learning experience that is both immersive and participatory. You will discover an excess of resources as you explore further its possibilities, which are all easily accessible to you. A contextual approach is provided by Generative Fill to provide even more fluidity in your learning experience. You will get access to example prompts that will get your creative juices flowing and offer a basis for the projects you are working on. Tooltips will appear on-screen at precisely the correct times to provide you with helpful information and hints that will allow you to improve your abilities. In addition to this, you will get an early glance at the Properties panel, which is where you can make precise adjustments and modify your work.

This learning journey is not only about obtaining new skills; rather, it is about releasing your creative potential and experiencing the many possibilities that Generative Fill has to offer. Generative Fill welcomes you to a universe where there are no limitations placed on your ideas, regardless of whether you are an experienced expert or a curious novice. So, embark on this captivating journey, and let Generative Fill be your trusted companion as you discover, create, and redefine what's possible in the realm of digital image editing. Get ready to be inspired, empowered, and amazed by the transformative capabilities of Generative Fill. Your creative adventure awaits!

Generative credits in Photoshop

Exciting news for those who pay for a membership in Creative Cloud or who subscribe to Adobe Express Premium! Your experience with an Adobe membership has just become much more creative and powerful. Generative Credits are a game-changing addition to your plan that opens up a world of possibilities for the development of content. These possibilities are all made possible by the wonderful Firefly technology. Because your membership now includes Generative Credits, you will get monthly credits that provide you access to a variety of content production options that make the most of the enormous potential that Firefly has. This implies that you can take your creative ideas to new heights, discover breakthrough tools, and produce amazing outcomes like never before in your life.

These generative credits are intended to make your creative journey more enjoyable, regardless of whether you are an experienced designer, an aspiring artist, or a professional photographer. You are now in possession of the tools that will allow you to test the limits of what is possible, try out innovative concepts, and bring your dreams to life. These crucial generative credits are now included as a standard component of your Adobe membership plan, regardless of whether that plan is Creative Cloud, Adobe Express, Adobe Firefly, or Adobe Stock. This is a demonstration of Adobe's dedication to giving you access to the greatest and most cutting-edge tools possible so that you can fuel your creativity. Therefore, go ahead and use your generative credits to their full potential.

Dive into the realm of content creation brought to you by Firefly, and let your creativity run wild as you create new things. Discover, try out, and amaze yourself with the incredible powers that can be unlocked with these credits. With the introduction of Generative Credits in Photoshop, your journey into the creative world just became more exciting, brighter, and more unlimited. As you begin this exciting new phase of your creative journey, you can expect to feel inspired, surprised, and empowered in equal measure.

Setting standards for responsibility and transparency

An innovative new feature has been added to the most recent version of Photoshop by Adobe. This feature highlights the company's commitment to ethical sourcing and transparency in the field of generative artificial intelligence. Users of Photoshop will now have access to a Generative AI model that functions ethically by exploiting material that is supplied by Adobe Stock as a result of this upgrade. The fact that Photoshop will now automatically attach **Content Credentials** to photos that have been created using Generative Fill and Generative Expand, as well as those that have been exported as **PNG, JPG,** or via the "**Save as**" tool, is what makes this new enhancement noteworthy. These credentials serve as a visible signal for users, telling them whether or not an image was made or changed in Photoshop utilizing the Generative AI technology provided by Firefly. Users can recognize and distinguish between photos that have undergone generative AI modifications and those that have not with the use of Content Credentials, which offer users vital insights and confidence. This inclusion not only helps promote clear communication and acknowledgment of the creative processes that are involved in the development or alteration of an image, but it also helps guarantee that material is used ethically.

Not only does Adobe's dedication to ethical sourcing and transparency increase consumer confidence, but it also brings the company in line with the norms and best practices of the industry. Adobe is helping to cultivate a culture of accountability and integrity in the creative community by equipping users with the ability to make educated choices about the usage and attribution of pictures via the implementation of this feature. In a world where creative expression and technological innovation collide, Adobe's commitment to the moral and responsible use of AI is a laudable example to follow. This upgrade not only raises the ethical standards that are now in place within the creative software industry, but it also strengthens Adobe's position as a leader in fostering the development of content that is responsible and transparent when powered by artificial intelligence.

NEW INTERACTIONS IN REMOVE TOOL

New and exciting enhancements have been added to the Remove tool in Photoshop, which will improve the editing experience overall and make the program even more effective. These newly added interactions are intended to make the process of deleting undesired objects from your photographs more straightforward while maintaining a high level of accuracy.

Here's what you can look forward to:

1. **Draw Loops for Removal:**
   - Using the Remove tool, you can now create a loop around the precise region you wish to make vanish rather than just brushing over the whole area. This replaces the previous method of simply painting over the entire area. A more precise selection of items or distractions from inside an image is now possible thanks to this innovative technology.

2. **Auto-Connect Loops:**
   - There is no need for you to even be concerned about completely closing the loop. The removal procedure will be made much easier by the intelligence algorithms that are used in Photoshop, which will calculate the distance and automatically link the loop. This function helps to reduce the number of brushing mistakes that occur and can save you a substantial amount of time while editing.

3. **Easy Corrections:**
   - If you make any inadvertent choices when you are surrounding a region, it is quite easy to make any necessary modifications. In the settings box, you can change the mode of the brush stroke from "**addition**" to "**subtraction**." This adjustment enables you to improve your selection by removing undesired regions from your loop, resulting in results that are accurate and error-free.

Because of these interactions inside the Remove tool, you will have a better degree of control over the process of modifying your image. These new tools make the work of eliminating distractions, clearing up backgrounds, or fine tuning your compositions more straightforward and time-efficient than it has ever been before. As Photoshop continues to develop, the program's developers have reaffirmed their dedication to increasing the user experience and developing tools that make difficult editing tasks easier. This devotion has been shown by the new interactions added to the Remove tool in Photoshop, which makes the process of modifying images in Photoshop much more streamlined and fun.

ADDED FEATURES TO CONTEXTUAL TASKBAR TO AID WITH MASKING AND CROPPING PROCESSES

With the recent addition of additional tools and actions to the **Contextual Task Bar**, Photoshop is making it even simpler for users to maintain their creative flow and produce the results they want. This dynamic feature, which is positioned at an accessible location on the canvas, gives you prompt access to frequently used tools and activities that are contextually relevant to your current workflow.

Here's what you can expect:

1. **Streamlined Masking Workflows:**
   - The Contextual Task Bar now provides users who are working on masking tasks with a variety of tools and actions that are conveniently located right at their fingertips. Whether you're working on refining selections, fine-tuning masks, or building complicated composite pictures, you'll have access to the appropriate tools with just a click of the mouse, which will make it easier for you to move fluidly through the many stages of the masking process.

2. **Enhanced Generative AI Workflows:**
   - Users who are engaged in generative AI processes, such as Generative Fill and Generative Expand, will discover that the Contextual Task Bar now enables straightforward access to critical activities. This implies that you can swiftly and effectively direct the modifications made by your generative AI with relative ease.

3. **Learning on the Go:**
   - Users are given the ability to learn as they go thanks to the Contextual Task Bar. It acts as a dynamic, on-the-spot guidance that provides you with applicable tools and activities depending on the unique tasks and projects you have at hand. Users can become more skilled with Photoshop while actively working on artistic efforts thanks to this immersive learning experience that takes place in real time.

4. **Seamless Integration:**
   - Adobe's dedication to user-centric design is reflected in the Contextual Task Bar with the inclusion of these new tools and actions that have been included in it. It is of the utmost importance to make certain that your workflow is uninterrupted, productive, and easy to understand at all times.

The Contextual Task Bar is intended to keep you in the creative zone by freeing your attention from menu navigation so that you can concentrate on your artistic expression rather than looking for options. You can continue to use Photoshop with comfort and confidence, as well as the certainty that the appropriate tools and actions are located just where you need them, regardless of whether you are on the road or have settled into your creative area. Photoshop is still a strong and versatile creative partner, and new updates make it even better at helping you bring your artistic vision to life whenever and wherever inspiration strikes.

PRESET SYNC DISCONTINUED WITH THE RELEASE OF PHOTOSHOP 25.0

It's important to note that **Preset Sync** has been officially phased out as of Photoshop version 25.0; therefore this change has taken effect as of that point. This indicates that the functionality is inoperable and will no longer be accessible for usage inside Photoshop. The **Preset Sync** feature of Adobe Photoshop gave users the ability to synchronize their presets and settings across numerous installations of the software as well as multiple devices. However, as a result of it being discontinued, the option to automatically synchronize settings across several instances of Photoshop will no longer be available to you. Users who depend on **Preset Sync** for the management of their presets should think about using alternate ways of arranging their presets and moving them across their devices and installations. To maintain presets on several devices, these ways may involve manually exporting and importing presets or leveraging various services and tools offered by Adobe Creative Cloud. Certain features and functions may alter over time or be removed altogether as software and technology continues to grow. This is done to better accommodate user requirements and new technological developments. When working with Adobe Photoshop or any other kind of software, it is critical to be current on all available patches and updates to maintain a fluid and productive workflow.

Using Generative Fill

Adding an object

1. Launch your Photoshop app.
2. Import your preferred image.
3. Select the area of the image where you want to add your new element by using any of the selection tools in the left side panel. Use the contextual taskbar's "**Select subject**" button to choose the main subject of your picture if

you want to alter the background of the entire image. After that, choose the background by clicking the inverse icon.
4. Press the **Generate Fill** button. As an alternative, use the menu bar at the top to select **Edit > Generative Fill**.
5. If a legal dialog window shows up, select **Agree**.
6. Type the content you wish to include in the photo in the prompt box. Try to be as detailed as precise as you can. You don't have to begin your prompt with a command like "**make a small campfire here**" or "**add a balloon.**" All you have to do is enter the elements that you want Photoshop to create.

Here are a couple of examples to get you started:

For objects:

- Sitting brown and white corgi with its tongue out
- Opened red wine bottle next to an empty wine glass
- Pink convertible sports car with the roof off
- Long blond and wavy hair with red ribbon
- Wet reflective pathway

For backgrounds:

- Pyramids in the desert
- Green mountain range with a calm lake
- Tall buildings full of windows
- Arizona's Grand Canyon
- Sunset at the beach

7. Choose your preferred variation from the properties window on the right.
8. Save your photo.

Expanding a photo

Unlike adding objects, you don't have to consider suggestions while utilizing Photoshop's Generative Fill function to expand the picture. Photoshop will automatically fill the extra canvas with an image that complements the original photo's surrounds.

Here's how to make your photo bigger:

- After importing your image into Photoshop, select the **crop tool** from the panel on the left.
- Extend your zoom to fill the frame with more of your photo.
- To resize the picture to the appropriate size, drag its corners or edge.
- Press **Enter** on the keyboard to save the dimensions.
- From the left side panel, choose the **Rectangular Marquee tool** and choose the blank space on your canvas. As an alternative, you can pick the image by selecting it and then use the contextual taskbar's inversion icon to flip the selection and pick the empty spaces.
- On the contextual taskbar, select the **Generative Fill** button.
- Don't fill in the prompt box.
- Decide which variation is your favorite. Photoshop provides you with multiple options instead of just one.
- (**Optional**) Adjust the picture as you see fit.
- Save the image to your desktop.

Removing an object

On top of adding new elements to the existing photo, Generative Fill lets you do the opposite and delete any element from the photo too. Here's how:

- **Open your photo.**
- Click on any of the selection tool icons in the left side panel (or hit a keyboard shortcut for the tool you feel like using). If it's a large object, it's recommended to use the Rectangular Marquee tool, as it avoids overly tight selections that may cause distortion. If, however, you want to remove objects from tight spaces, like a person from a group or an old box in the middle of a flower patch, use the Lasso tool for better accuracy.
- Select the object you want to remove from the photo.
- In the Generative Fill contextual taskbar, click on **Generative Fill**.
- Don't fill out the prompt box.
- Hit the **Generate** button to delete the selected object from the photo.
- Under the Variations section in the properties window on the right, pick your preferred edited version.
- Save the edited photo to your local storage.

CHAPTER THREE
GETTING STARTED WITH ADOBE PHOTOSHOP SYSTEM

The purpose of this chapter is to walk you through the basics of using Adobe Photoshop. It covers a variety of features of using the program, such as running Photoshop, navigating the home screen, becoming acquainted with the Photoshop workspace, and exploring the toolbar with its numerous tool groups and individual tools. The chapter looks into picking tools from the toolbar, working with those tools, understanding the tool settings available in the options bar, and using the status bar for a variety of activities. It explains how to use context menus, how to interact with panels, how to resize and manage them, and how to use undo and redo commands. The chapter concludes with a discussion of the history box, the management of editing stages, the customization of Photoshop settings, and the operation of cloud documents. In general, it offers users a complete introduction to the fundamental tools and functions included inside Adobe Photoshop.

LAUNCHING PHOTOSHOP

Launching Adobe Photoshop is a straightforward process, but the exact steps may vary slightly depending on your operating system (Windows or macOS).

Here are the general steps to launch Photoshop:

On Windows:
1. You can begin using Windows by clicking on the Start button, which is often found in the lower-left-hand corner of your screen.
2. Try searching for "**Photoshop**" by entering "**Photoshop**" or "**Adobe Photoshop**" into the search field and then pressing the **Enter** key.
3. Find the Adobe Photoshop symbol in the list of search results, and then click on it. To do this, use the arrow keys on your keyboard. After you begin Photoshop, it will automatically create a fresh working environment for you to use.

On macOS:
1. **Click on the Finder Icon:** The Finder icon looks like a smiling face and is usually located in your Dock at the bottom of the screen.
2. **Go to the "Applications" Folder:** In the Finder window, navigate to the "**Applications**" folder on the left sidebar.

3. **Find "Adobe Photoshop"**: Scroll through the list of applications until you find "Adobe Photoshop."
4. **Double-click on "Adobe Photoshop"**: Double-click on the Adobe Photoshop icon to launch the application. Photoshop will open and present you with a new workspace.

After launching Photoshop, you can initiate a new project or open an existing one by going to the "**File**" menu and choosing "**New**" or "**Open**." You can then start working on your photographs and other creative endeavors after you have done so.

GET ACQUAINTED WITH THE HOME SCREEN

After opening Photoshop, you will discover that you are brought back to the Home Screen. The Home Screen is broken up into multiple parts, each of which provides a unique set of settings and features, as follows:

- **Create New**: This part gives you the ability to begin a new project from scratch. There are several different document presets from which you can choose, including layouts for print, online, mobile, and other devices. To start a new document, you need just simply click on the preset you want to use.
- **Open**: This tab is where you can access previously saved Photoshop files or bring in new photos for use in the current project. You may search your computer for the file you wish to work on by clicking the "**Open**" button.
- **Recent**: The Recent section provides a list of the projects that you have most recently accessed. You may instantly access and continue working on your most recent files by selecting any of these thumbnails and clicking on them.
- **Learn**: The Learn area offers access to Adobe's many creative tools, as well as lessons and helpful hints. To improve your talents, you can go through tutorials that walk you through the steps, creative challenges, and stuff that inspires you.
- **Cloud Documents**: If you are using Adobe Creative Cloud, this area will enable you to access and manage your cloud documents, making it simple for you to work on your projects from a variety of devices. If you are not using Adobe Creative Cloud, you will not see this part.
- **New Features**: If you explore the New Features area of Photoshop, you can make sure that you are using the most recent features and advancements available. It draws attention to current enhancements and upgrades that have been made to the program.

Simply go to the "**Create New**" area to begin the creation of a new project. Choose a document preset that corresponds to the requirements of your project, or build a document that is unique to your needs by defining the size, resolution, and any other relevant options. If you want to continue working on a project that you have saved in the past, you will need to click on the "**Open**" area, then look for the file in the folders of your computer, and then click to open it. Expanding your knowledge of Photoshop can be accomplished with the help of the "**Learn**" section. Explore a variety of resources, including creative challenges, tutorials, and articles, to acquire new perspectives and skills. If you are using Adobe Creative Cloud, you can access and manage your cloud-based projects in a streamlined manner across all of your various devices by going to the "**Cloud Documents**" area. Keep an eye on the "**New Features**" area to be informed about the most recent improvements and new features that have been introduced to Photoshop. This can assist you in staying current with the ever-evolving capabilities of the program.

How to Turn Off the Photoshop Home Screen.

You're not feeling the main interface of Photoshop, are you? Turning it off is simple. Find out how it works, shall we?

- Navigate to the **Preferences** menu, then **General**.
- Find the option that says "**Disable Home Screen**," and then click on the box that's located to the left of it.

Restarting Photoshop will complete the process of turning off the home screen.

That sums it up well.

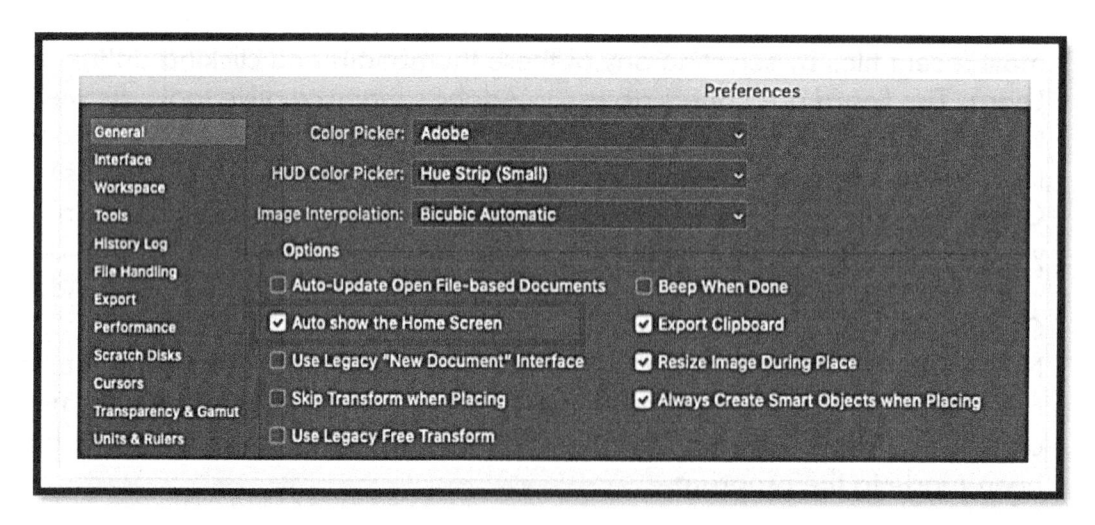

FAMILIARIZING WITH THE PHOTOSHOP WORKSPACE

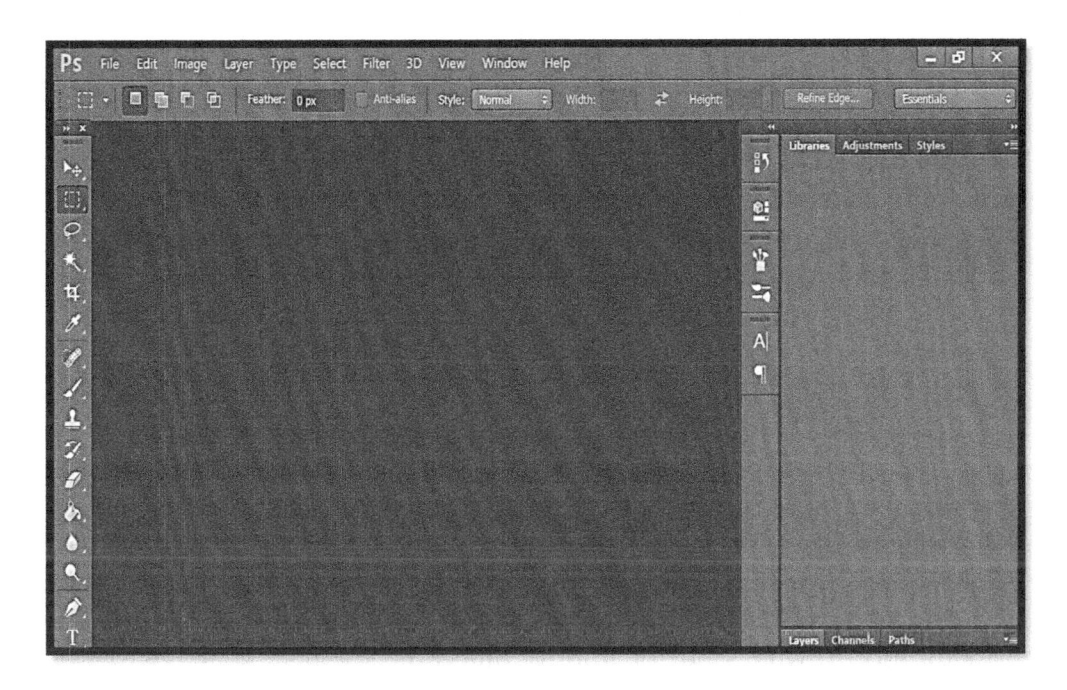

1. **Menu Bar:**
   - The Photoshop window's Menu Bar can be found at the very top of the program's main window. It has some different menus, such as the "**File,**" "**Edit,**" "**Image,**" **and** "**Layer**" menus, among others, and each of these menus grants access to a diverse collection of commands and settings.
2. **Application Bar (Windows) / Menu Bar (macOS):**
   - The Application Bar (on Windows) or the Menu Bar (on macOS) can be found at the top of your screen, respectively, and are located directly below the Menu Bar. It comes with a variety of options such as **Workspace, Tools,** and plenty more.
3. **The Options Menu:**
   - The Options Bar can be found just below the Menu Bar in the navigation bar. This bar's contents are dynamic and vary according to the tool or operation that is currently active; it provides choices and configurations pertinent to the chosen tool or activity.
4. **Tools Panel:**
   - The Tools Panel can be found on the left-hand side of the workspace. It provides a comprehensive set of tools that can be used for a variety of editing tasks, including selection, painting, and retouching, among others. To pick a tool, either clicks on it or use the shortcut keys on your keyboard.

5. **Window Document:**
   - The Document Window, which allows you to see and modify your photographs and projects, is located in the exact middle of the working area. You can have some documents open at once, each of which will be presented in a different tab inside the Document Window.
6. **Panels and Panel Groups:**
   - The right side of the workspace has a variety of Panels and Panel Groups for you to choose from. Access to various functions such as Layers, Adjustments, and History can be gained via the use of these panels. For better organization, you can choose which panels are shown and create panel groups.
7. **Status Bar:**
   - The Status Bar can be found at the very bottom of the workspace. This bar provides information about your project, such as the zoom level and the color mode.
8. **Workspace Layout:**
   - Photoshop's workspace can be laid up in a variety of ways to accommodate a wide range of tasks. You can tailor your workspace to certain processes by optimizing it with one of many different layouts, such as Essentials, Photography, or Painting, among others.
9. **Customization:**
   - The workplace can be personalized to reflect your tastes. This includes establishing personalized workplaces, moving panels, and preserving layout settings.
10. **Keyboard Shortcuts:**
    - You can complete tasks in a short amount of time with the help of Photoshop's large collection of keyboard shortcuts. Your productivity can be substantially sped up by being familiar with and making use of keyboard shortcuts.
11. **Contextual Menus:**
    - When you right-click (or Control-click on macOS) anywhere in the Document Window or any of the numerous panels, context-sensitive menus with the appropriate choices and commands are often shown.
12. **Zoom and Navigation Tools:**
    - Tools for zooming in and out, panning, and traveling inside your image can be found at the bottom-left corner of the Document Window.

13. **Document Tabs:**

- If you have more than one document currently active, you can navigate between them by using the tabs that are located at the very top of the Document Window.

Opening files

Instead of starting from scratch by creating a new blank image, you should most of the time start by opening an existing photo. You can open and edit pre-existing image files with Photoshop, including JPEG, PNG, and PSD (Photoshop document) files. **To open a file, go to the File menu and select Open.**

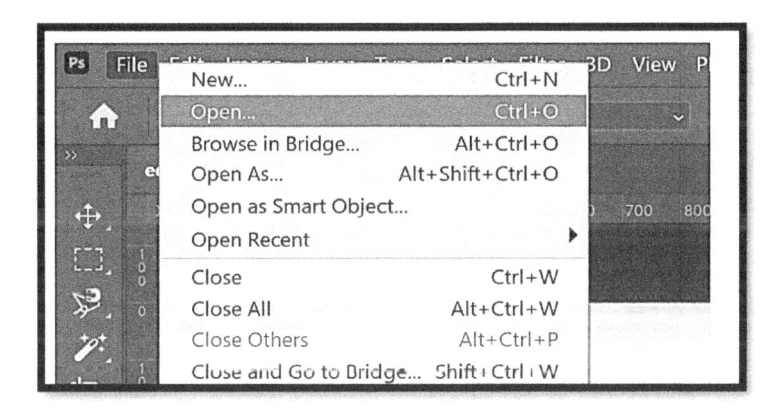

A dialog box will show up. Find the file you want to open on your computer, and then click the **Open** button when you're done.

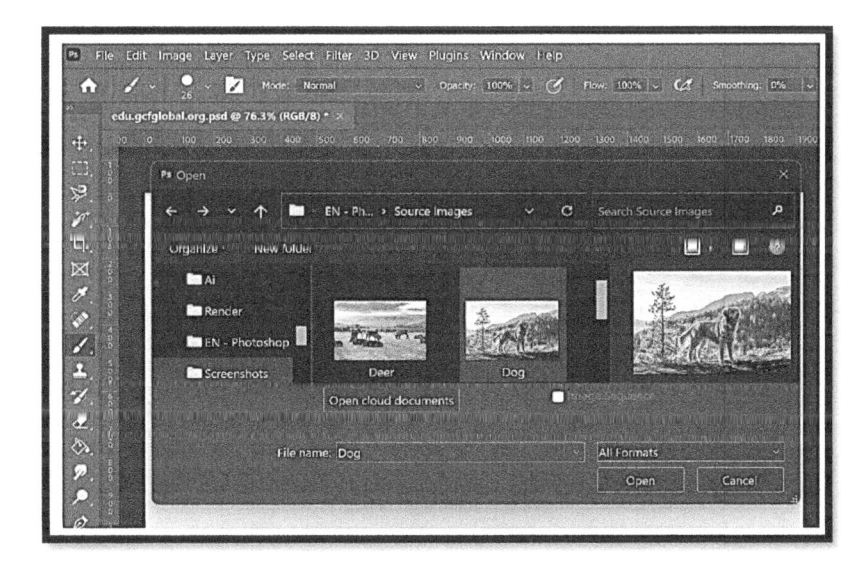

Photoshop will display the file when it's opened. If you don't already have Photoshop running, you can open the file by navigating to its location on your computer, right-clicking it, and selecting **Open With > Adobe Photoshop** from the context menu that appears.

EXPLORING THE TOOLBAR

Almost 70 options are available on the Photoshop toolbar, making it a potent collection of creative tools that can be used for a wide range of image editing and design tasks.

Now let's take a closer look at the layout and features of the toolbar:

1. Toolbar Layout: Finding and choosing the necessary tools is made simpler by the toolbar's intelligent organization, which is arranged in a logical order. You may promptly identify the appropriate tool for your assignment by sorting the tools based on their respective purposes.
- **Move and Selection Tools**: You can move and choose items in your image using the tools located at the top of the toolbar. These consist of the **Lasso Selection tools, the Move tool, and the Marquee Selection tools.**
- **Crop and Slice Tools**: These tools let you choose how to crop and slice your image after using the selecting tools.
- **Measurement Tools**: These tools help with accurate modifications by measuring angles and distances inside your image. The eyedropper and ruler tools are two examples.

- **Retouching and Painting Tools**: These tools are necessary for digital painting and image improvement. The Clone Stamp, Brush, Eraser, and Healing Brush tools are all part of this category.
- **Drawing and Type Tools**: The Pen, Custom Shape, and Text tools are examples of drawing and type tools that you can use to create shapes, pathways, and text.
- **Navigation Tools**: Lastly, you can zoom in, zoom out, and traverse your image using the navigation tools located at the bottom of the toolbar. With the aid of these tools, you can examine your work more closely and navigate the canvas more effectively.

2. **Hidden Tools:**
   - In the Photoshop toolbar, or any other Adobe program, if you see a little arrow to the lower right of a tool, it indicates that there are more "**hidden**" tool options. You can access hidden tools by clicking and holding on to them. Holding will cause a fly-out set of tools to display, allowing you to access every hidden tool beneath that specific tool. You can see that the hidden Quick Selection Tool is accessible by clicking and holding on to the Magic Wand tool in the example below.

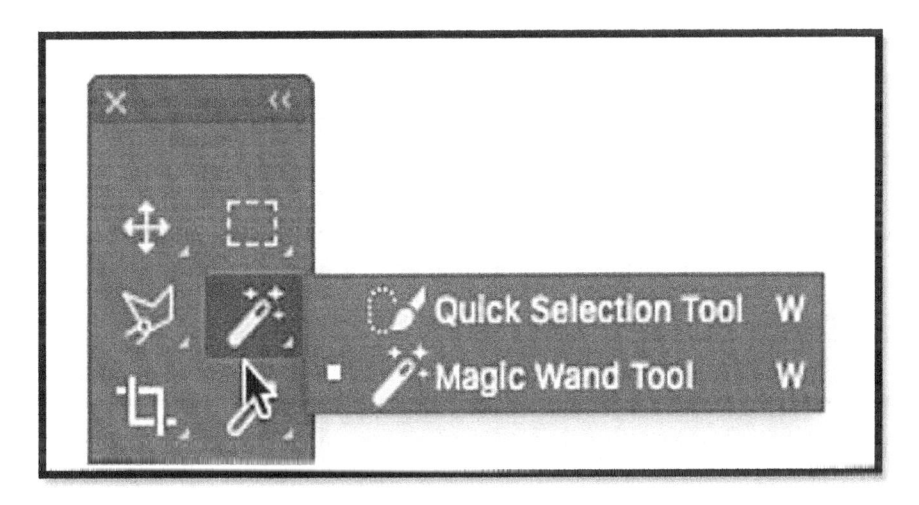

   - Holding down the Shift key while tapping the keyboard shortcut for the tool that shows in the tooltip will allow you to fast cycle among hidden tools. For example, you would press B to choose the first tool in the **Brush, Pencil, Color Replacement, and Mixer Brush** tool sets, then hold down Shift and hit **B** once again to cycle through that specific set of tools.

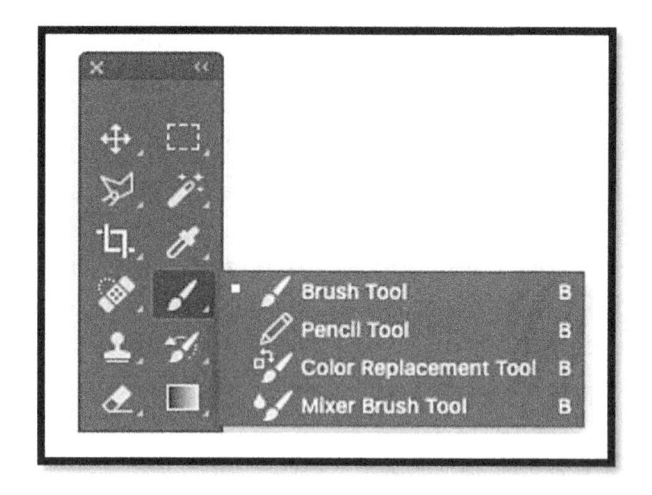

3. Tool Selection:
- All you have to do to choose a tool is click on its toolbar icon. Any tool will show a tooltip with its name and keyboard shortcut as soon as your cursor is over it. Your productivity can be greatly accelerated by learning these keyboard shortcuts, which allow you to swiftly move between tools without stopping your creative flow.

4. Customizing the Toolbar:
- Adobe Photoshop understands that every user has a different workflow. As a result, you can personalize the toolbar to your preference. You can rearrange the toolbar to your liking by dragging and dropping tools and groups in the "**Customize Toolbar**" dialog box. To accomplish this, choose "**Toolbar**" from the "**Edit**" menu. By organizing your workplace with this feature, you can put the tools you use most often close to hand.

SELECTION TOOLS GROUP

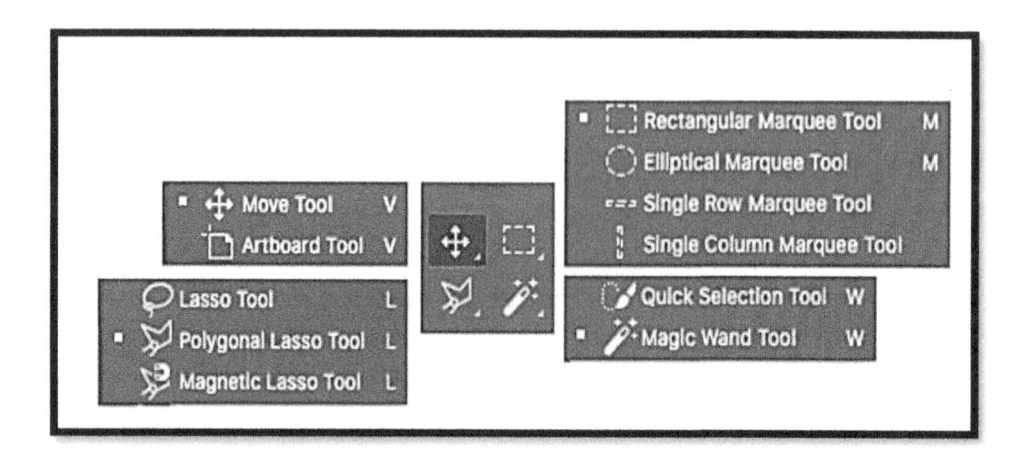

- **Move Tool (V):** You can pick and move layers or objects on your canvas with the Move Tool. It's one of your main tools for structuring your piece.
- **Artboard Tool (V):** This tool lets you create and edit artboards inside of your document. For online and app design, artboards are often used as virtual canvases contained inside a single document.
- **Rectangular Marquee Tool (M):** You can make square or rectangular selections with this tool. A selection can be made by clicking and dragging and everything within the selection can be changed or relocated.
- **Elliptical Marquee Tool (M):** This tool allows you to make circular or elliptical selections. It comes in handy while choosing spherical regions or things.
- **Single Row Marquee Tool:** This tool picks out a single row of pixels on the horizontal plane. It is useful for narrow choices when you just want a small horizontal strip.
- **Single Column Marquee Tool:** This tool chooses a single vertical column of pixels, much like the Single Row Marquee Tool.
- **Lasso Tool (L):** By drawing a circle around the region you want to choose, you can use the Lasso Tool to generate freeform selections. It's perfect for choosing asymmetrical shapes.
- **Polygonal Lasso Tool (L):** This tool allows you to make selections with well-defined edges. Click on it to create anchor points and make a polygonal selection.
- **Magnetic Lasso Tool (L):** This tool makes it simpler to make selections around intricate shapes by automatically snapping to the edges of items in your image.
- **Object Selection Tool (W):** This tool uses artificial intelligence (AI) to pick things in your image automatically. Photoshop will precisely pick and enhance an item that you can draw a rough outline around.
- **Quick Selection Tool (W):** This tool quickly chooses regions of your image that have a similar color or texture. It's excellent for making decisions quickly and precisely.
- **Magic Wand Tool (W):** With a single click, the **Magic Wand Tool** identifies regions that are similar in tone or color. To further narrow down the options, you can choose the tolerance level.

These selection tools are essential for a wide range of Photoshop tasks, including precise editing, object isolation, and intricate composition creation. You can improve the efficiency of your editing and design process by becoming proficient with these tools and realizing their potential.

CROP AND SLICE TOOLS GROUP

You can easily concentrate on key parts or optimize visuals for different uses by using the tools in Adobe Photoshop's Crop and Slice Tools Group to cut or isolate certain portions of your photos.

In this category, the following are the main tools:

1. **Crop Tool (C):** This tool allows you to resize or crop the image's canvas. By moving the cropping handles to indicate the region to be kept, you can crop the image to the desired area and hit **Enter**. With the use of this tool, you can prepare your photographs for certain output sizes or change the composition of your pictures.

2. **Perspective Crop Tool (C):** An improved version of the Crop Tool is the Perspective Crop Tool. It lets you change the viewpoint of an image in addition to cropping it. This works well for correcting distortion in angled photographs.

3. **Slice Tool (C):** The main uses of the Slice Tool are in web design and image slicing to speed up the loading of online pages. Slices of HTML are produced that can be exported and used online. When creating web layouts with many components, slices come in handy.

4. **Slice Select Tool (K):** After using the Slice Tool to create slices, you can choose and work with specific slices with the Slice Select Tool. This entails establishing web-specific features, connecting slices, and modifying slice features.

5. **Frame Tool (K):** This is a relatively recent tool designed to make working with pictures and graphics within frames easier. It offers a quick and easy method for positioning and adjusting graphics or pictures within pre-made frames or shapes.

MEASURING TOOLS GROUP

Adobe Photoshop has tools in the Measuring Tools Group that assist you in measuring and analyzing different elements of your photographs. These are particularly helpful tools for precise tasks, like documentation for science or architecture. **In this category, the following are the main measurement tools:**

1. **Eyedropper Tool (I):** This tool is very important for taking a sample of the colors in your image, even if it's not a typical measurement tool. You can click on any pixel to retrieve its color information, including RGB, CMYK, and hexadecimal values.

2. **Ruler Tool (I):** With this tool, you can measure areas, angles, and distances within your image. To measure certain sections or angles, you can drag the cursor around the image after setting a reference point. Depending on your selections, the tool shows measurements in pixels, inches, or other units.

3. **Count Tool (I):** You can use the **Count Tool** to monitor certain items or components in your image. The tool makes counting objects in a scene or components in a design simple by creating a numbered marker with each click.

4. **Notes Tool (I):** This tool can be useful for labeling and adding more information about your measurements and observations, even if its primary purpose is to add textual notes and comments to your image.

5. **3D Material Eyedropper Tool (I):** This is a specialist tool intended for use with the application's 3D models. It guarantees consistency and realism in your 3D designs by enabling you to sample and apply materials (textures and surface attributes) from one area of a 3D model to another.
6. **Color Sampler Tool (I):** This is a tool designed to show and extract color values from certain regions of an image. With the use of this tool, you can precisely measure and record the color information of different locations in your image.

For tasks requiring accurate measures, including quality control, scientific research, and architectural design, these measuring tools are quite helpful. They let you make defensible judgments based on precise measurements by enabling you to capture and store important information inside your photographs.

DRAWING & TYPE TOOLS GROUP

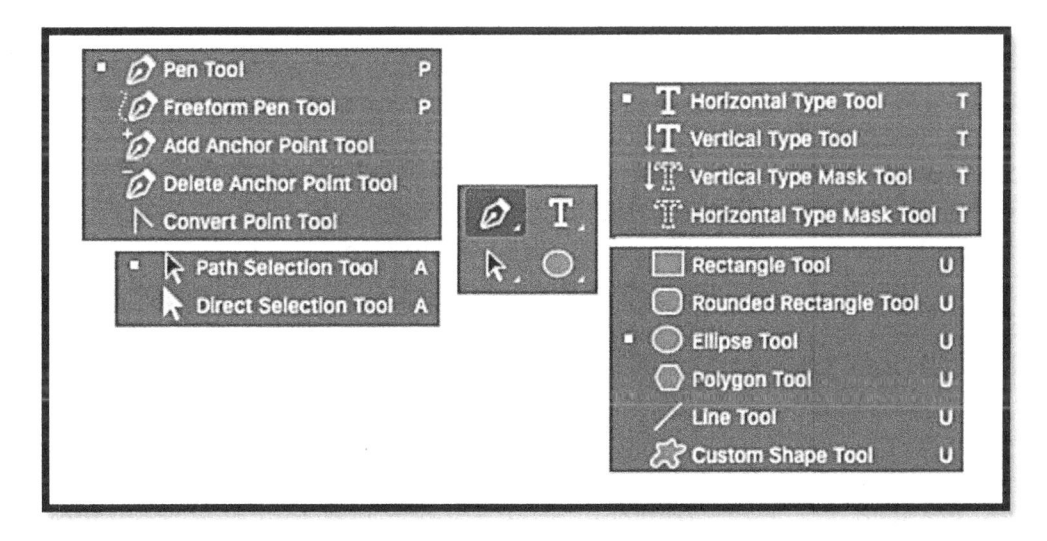

- **Pen Tool (P):** This multipurpose tool can be used to draw exact pathways and shapes. By setting anchor points and modifying their handles, you can draw straight lines and curves.
- **Freeform Pen Tool (P):** This tool allows you to create pathways much as with a pen or pencil. To design trails, it automatically joins and smoothes your strokes.

- **Curvature Pen Tool (P):** This tool adds control points automatically as you draw, making it easier to create smooth, curved paths.
- **Add Anchor Point Tool:** With this tool, you can modify existing pathways by adding anchor points. A path segment can be clicked to add a new anchor point.
- **Delete Anchor Point Tool:** You can eliminate anchor points from a path by using this tool. To remove an anchor point, click on it.
- **Convert Point Tool:** This tool allows you to convert corner points to smooth anchor points and vice versa. It helps change the kind of curvature that a path has.
- **Horizontal Type Tool (T):** This tool is used to add text that is horizontal to your canvas. You can enter and alter text characteristics such as fonts, sizes, and other customizations.
- **Vertical Type Tool (T):** This tool, which is similar to the Horizontal Type Tool, enables you to include vertical text—a prevalent feature in Asian languages—in your designs.
- **Vertical Type Mask Tool (T):** This tool combines selections with text. Using your input, it generates a vertical text selection.
- **Horizontal Write Mask Tool (T):** This tool generates horizontal text choices as you write, much as the Vertical Type Mask Tool does.
- **Path Selection Tool (A):** This tool allows you to choose and work with full pathways or shapes. With this tool, you can move, manipulate, and alter pathways.
- **Direct Selection Tool (A):** This tool lets you choose and modify specific handles and anchor points on a path.
- **Rectangle Tool (U):** To draw rectangular shapes, use the Rectangle Tool. With this tool, you can make filled or outlined rectangles.
- **Ellipse Tool (U):** This tool allows you to draw circular or elliptical shapes. Ellipses can be made with or without fill.
- **Triangle Tool (U):** Although this tool is not conventional, it can be used to draw triangles by using the Polygon Tool to draw polygons and setting the side count to three.
- **Polygon Tool (U):** Polygon with a predetermined number of sides can be created with this tool. You can draw shapes like triangles, pentagons, or hexagons that have different numbers of sides.
- **Line Tool (U):** You can draw straight lines using this tool. The length, location, and angle of the line can all be changed.
- **Custom Shape Tool (U):** This tool gives you access to some pre-made shapes, including stars, arrows, and more. You can choose shapes from a library and sketch them into your canvas.

These Photoshop tools are essential for a wide range of activities, from inserting and formatting text to generating intricate vector drawings. They provide you with the freedom to precisely and creatively create and alter aspects inside your photographs and designs.

NAVIGATION TOOLS GROUP

The tools and features in Adobe Photoshop's Navigation Tools Group are intended to make it easier for you to explore and work with your photos. These are the tools you need to move about the canvas, zoom in and out, and examine your work at various sizes.

The main elements of the Navigation Tools Group are as follows:

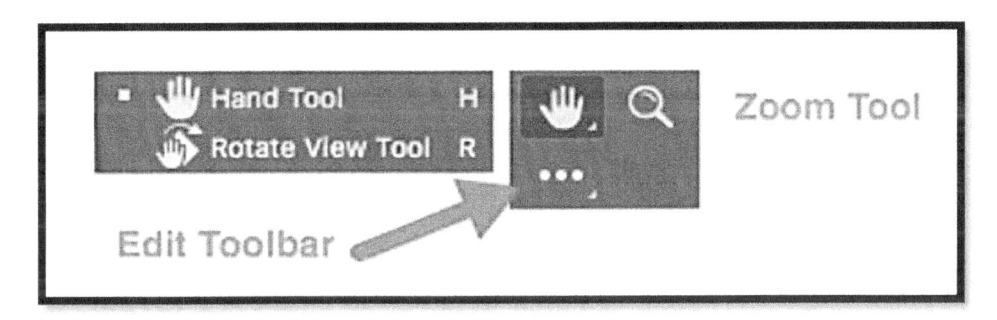

- **Hand Tool (H):** When your image is zoomed in beyond the viewable canvas area, you can use the Hand Tool to pan or move around it. To move the view inside the document window, use the Hand Tool to click and drag.
- **Zoom Tool (Z):** With this tool, you can enlarge or reduce the size of certain regions in your image. Using the Zoom Tool, click to enlarge an image; to zoom out, click while holding down the **Alt key** (or the **Option key** on macOS).
- **Rotate View Tool (R):** A useful tool that lets you temporarily flip your canvas' orientation so you can examine and work on your image from various perspectives. When working on projects that call for exact modifications or when you want to easily focus on certain portions of your image, this tool comes in handy.

RETOUCHING & PAINTING TOOLS GROUP

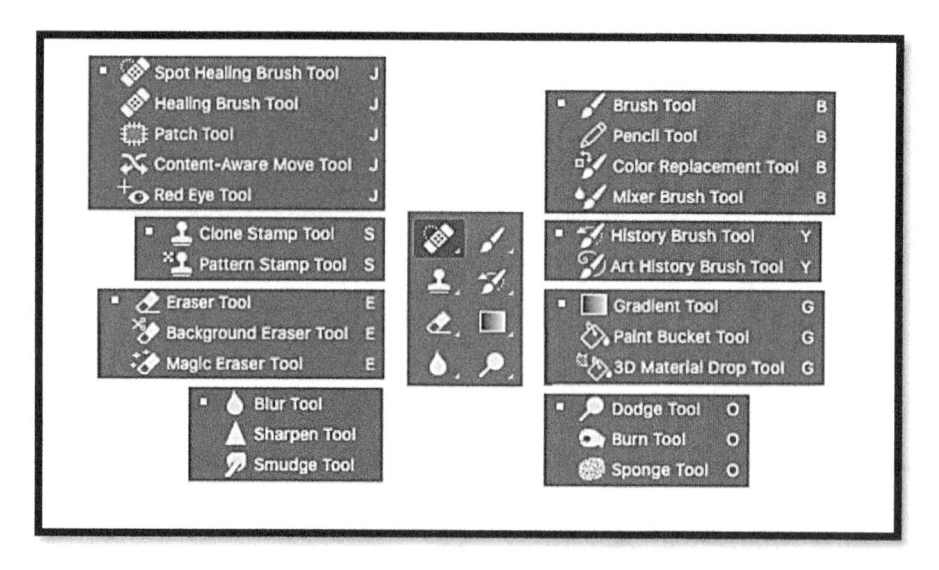

- **Spot Healing Brush Tool (J):** For quick and automated retouching, utilize the Spot Healing Brush Tool. It takes a sample of the surrounding pixels to automatically eliminate wrinkles, blemishes, and other minor flaws from your pictures.
- **Healing Brush Tool (J):** By painting over the problematic regions after sampling the source area, you can fix defects. For effects that seem natural, it combines the target area's color and texture with the source's.
- **Patch Tool (J):** For more thorough retouching, utilize the **Patch Tool**. You take a sample of a section from another region of the image and insert it in place of the troublesome area. The source and target regions are seamlessly blended with the Patch Tool.
- **Content-Aware Move Tool (J):** This tool uses content-aware technology to intelligently fill in the background while allowing you to move and expand items in your image.
- **Red Eye Tool (J):** This tool efficiently eliminates flash photography's red-eye effects. Just click on the red eyes and Photoshop will take care of the color correction on its own.
- **Brush Tool (B):** For producing artwork, adding color, and making fine changes, the Brush Tool is a useful painting tool. To personalize your strokes, it provides a large selection of brushes and settings.
- **Pencil Tool (B):** This tool produces pixel-perfect, hard-edged strokes, much like the Brush Tool. It helps produce intricate pixel art and clean lines.

- **Color Replacement Tool (B):** With this tool, you can alter the color of certain pixels in your image. The chosen color takes the place of the sampled color.
- **Mixer Brush Tool (B):** By blending and combining colors on your canvas, the Mixer Brush Tool replicates ancient painting methods. It works well for producing creative effects and realistic paint textures.
- **Clone Stamp Tool (S):** This tool lets you paint over an area of your image by duplicating a portion of it. It can be used to eliminate extraneous items, duplicate components, or correct flaws.
- **Pattern Stamp Tool (S):** This tool uses a chosen pattern as paint rather than colors. For your designs, you can make original patterns or choose from pre-made ones.
- **History Brush Tool (Y):** This tool lets you paint your way back to an earlier version of your image. It helps make specific edits or go back to a previous version.
- **Art History Brush Tool (Y):** This tool applies brush strokes that mimic several creative styles, such as impressionism or pointillism, to turn your image into an artistic depiction.
- **Eraser Tool (E):** This tool allows you to transparently erase or eliminate portions of your image. It can also be used to make accurate cuts and smooth transitions.
- **Background Eraser Tool (E):** This tool is meant to erase backgrounds from photographs that have intricate edges, including vegetation or hair.
- **Magic Eraser Tool (E):** This tool eliminates pixels by comparing them to the clicked region. It works well for eliminating broad, homogeneous color patches.
- **Gradient Tool (G):** This is a tool for creating progressive color or tone shifts. It can be used to give depth to your designs, apply gradient masks, and create gradients.
- **Paint Bucket Tool (G):** This tool applies a solid color or pattern to a chosen region. It's perfect for filling shapes or rapidly adding background colors.
- **3D Material Drop Tool (G):** Photoshop has 3D functionality with this tool. You can use it to add materials to three-dimensional objects in your creations.
- **Blur Tool:** This tool blurs and softens certain portions of your image. It works well for artistic blur effects, skin smoothing, and depth-of-field simulation.
- **Sharpen Tool:** By boosting contrast in certain regions of your image, the Sharpen Tool improves the sharpness and details. It works well for highlighting minute features.
- **Smudge Tool:** This is a tool designed to mimic the feeling of running your finger through wet paint. It's used to produce artistic effects or gentle, blending color transitions.

- **Dodge Tool (O):** This tool brightens and lightens certain regions of your image. It's used for exposure adjustment and highlight enhancement.
- **Burn Tool (O):** This tool makes some regions of your image look darker by darkening them. It's used to regulate exposure and enhance shadows.
- **Sponge Tool (O):** This tool allows you to desaturate or saturate certain colors in your image. It's helpful for selectively increasing or muting colors as well as color adjustments.

Using Adobe Photoshop, you can add creative effects to your designs, digitally produce artwork, and retouch and improve your photographs using these Retouching and Painting tools. You can use these tools to unleash your imagination and produce outcomes of professional quality, depending on the needs of your project.

SELECTING A TOOL FROM THE TOOLBAR

To select a tool, simply click on that tool in the Toolbar.

If you move your mouse over any tool in the menu, a tooltip will show up with the tool's name and the keyboard shortcut for it. As you learn Photoshop, this comes in very handy when you forget what a certain tool looks like. You should try to learn the shortcuts because they will make your work go so much faster. It's easy to remember some of the shortcuts, like **Z** for the Zoom tool or **E** for the Eraser. To use the tool, press the letter on the keyboard instead of clicking on it in the Tools Bar. You can switch between tools without taking your hands off the computer, which will make your work go much faster.

WORKING WITH THE TOOL PROPERTIES

Many useful settings and options in Adobe Photoshop's Properties Panel can help you make your designs look better, especially when you're working with many layers and elements at once. Depending on the type of layer or feature you chose in the Layers panel, this panel lets you view and change different properties.

These easy steps will get you to the Properties Panel in Photoshop:
- Open **Photoshop**.
- Find the "**Window**" menu in the menu bar at the top of the screen.
- Use the drop-down button to find "**Properties**."

Key Points about the Properties Panel

1. **Layer-Specific Controls:**
   - The Properties Panel gives you settings and options that are special to the layer you have chosen in the Layers panel. This behavior changes based on the type of layer you are working with, so you only see the properties that are important to you.
2. **Type Layers:**
   - The Properties Panel is where you can make changes to text when you pick a text (type) layer in the Layers panel. Formatting options for characters, paragraphs, text layout, and more can all be found in this panel. It's easier to change text this way since you don't have to switch between the Character and Paragraph boxes.
3. **Quick Actions:**
   - In the Properties Panel, you can now use **Quick Actions** on the Background layer and the pixel layers. Quick Actions are a group of useful tools that make it easy to do common tasks quickly. You can use Quick Actions to change the size of a picture, choose the **Crop Tool**, trim or rotate the frame, and even use tools like **Remove Background** and **Select Subject** right from the **Properties Panel**. This function makes things faster and easier by cutting down on the number of choices and screens that need to be opened.
4. **Shape Tools:**
   - The Properties Panel is also very helpful when you're working with shape layers. You can draw shapes on the screen and change how they look by using the **Live Shape Properties** in the Properties Panel. As well as changing shape properties like stroke, fill, and size, you can also precisely change and match shapes.
5. **Customizable Interface:**
   - You can change a lot about Photoshop's layout. You can order and set up panels in a way that works best for your process. This includes moving panels around, docking and undocking them, and grouping them as needed.
6. **Layer Filtering:**
   - If you have a complicated document with many layers, you can quickly find specific layers by using the searching options at the top of the Layers panel. These options let you search for layers based on their type, shape, or other properties.

HOW TO UNDERSTAND THE TOOL PROPERTIES IN THE OPTIONS BAR

Photoshop tools are adjustable, flexible, and can be changed to fit your needs. You can change tools to fit your needs and use them in different ways. Options can help you improve your picture editing or graphic design style in some ways, similar to how sub-tools work. In other words, you have options when it comes to using Photoshop tools. The menu bar is right above the options bar. It's a menu that runs across the screen and is on the left side by default. You may not see the options box. To get it back, on both macOS and Windows, go to the **Windows** drop-down menu and choose **Options**.

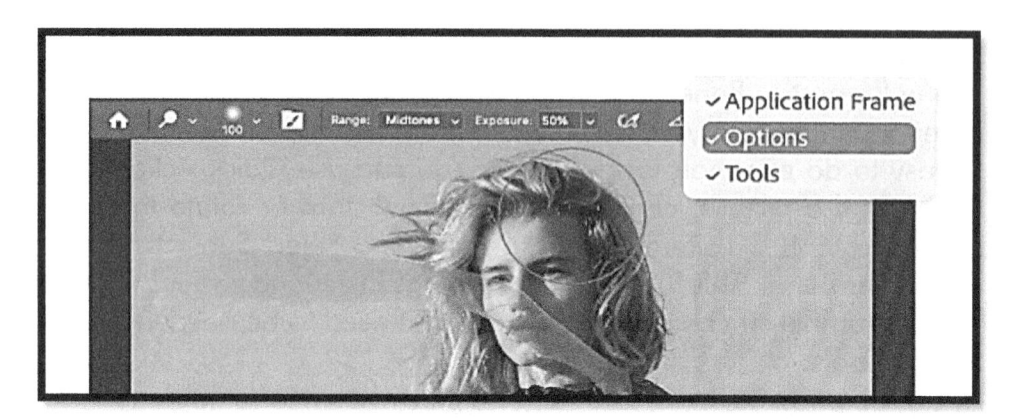

- **Tool-specific settings**: The **Options Bar** changes depending on the tool you've chosen. The options bar lets you change things like the brush tool's size and shape, as well as the color of the center and background. If you choose the type tool, the options bar lets you change the text's style, size, and position.
- **Hidden tools:** Each tool in the menu is shown by an icon, and there are a lot more tools that we can use than what we can see. If a tool icon has a small line in the bottom right corner, it means that there are more tools under it. To see these extra tools, right-**click (Windows)** or **Control-click (Mac)** on the button or click and hold on it.
- **Resetting options:** To get the options bar back to the way it was when you first opened it, choose a tool and **right-click (or Ctrl+click)** on it on a PC. You can reset the current tool to its original settings by clicking "**Reset Tool**" or "**Reset All Tools**" to reset all of them.
- **Moving options bar**: You can move it around your workspace by clicking near the Home icon on the left end of it and dragging it

USING THE STATUS BAR

The Status Bar is in the bottom left corner of the Photoshop window. You can choose what you want to know from this bar.

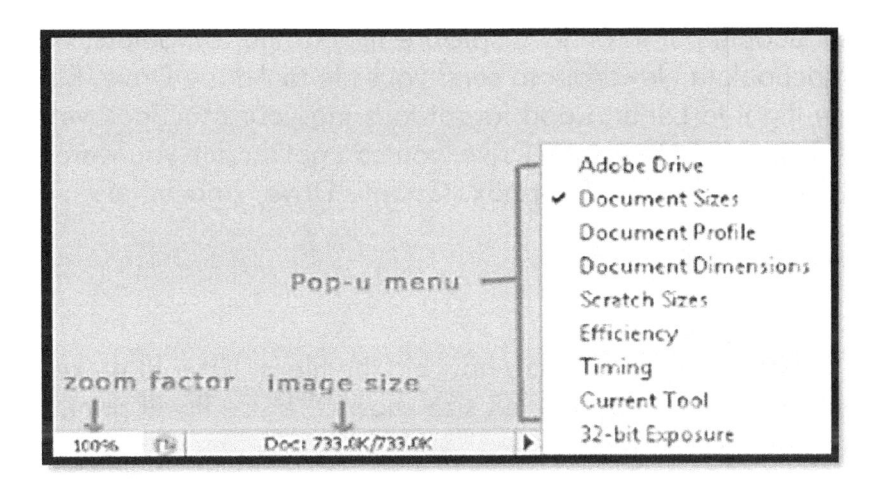

Zoom Factor

The zoom box shows how much you can zoom in on the present text. This tool lets you zoom in or out. To use it, double-click in the box, type in a number, and press **Enter**.

Figure out an image's width and height.

If you click and stay on the status bar, you can quickly see an image's width, height, channels, and quality.

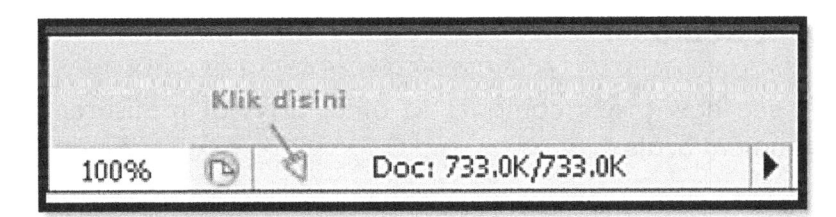

Some other information

When you click on the arrow that leads to the pop-up menu, you can see more options. These include **Document size** (dead view), **Document profile**, **Document Dimensions**, **Scratch Size**, **Efficiency**, **Timing**, **Current Tool**, and **Bit exposure**.

Adobe Drive

Probably, if you know what **Dropbox, Google Drive, Microsoft OneDrive**, etc. do, you can figure out what this one does from its name. Adobe Drive is a computer storage service that lets people who use Adobe products link freely across all of their devices. It lets people put the PSD or picture files on its computers. Now, let's say you used a MacBook in New York to send your file to Adobe Drive. But you had to catch an early flight to London and forgot to bring your MacBook with you. Don't be worried. If you sign in to Adobe Drive, you can get the file you were working on. Other cloud file services, like Dropbox, Google Drive, and others, use the same idea.

Document Size

It does what its name says: it tells you how big the file is. It might make you wonder why it shows two sizes. This page's left size shows the size it will print, and its right size shows the size it will save.

Document Profile

It shows the color profile of your image. It might now be very relevant to you until you are a hardcore photographer.

Document Dimensions

It tells you how big the picture is. This choice might not be useful for you if you have a ruler on **(Ctrl+R/Cmd+R)**. The sizes will be shown in "**pixels**" if your ruler is set to "**pixels,**" and "**inches**" if your ruler is set to "**inches**." First, turn on the ruler by going to **View > Rulers**. Then, right-click on the rulers and pick the unit you want to use.

Measurement Scales

If you want to see how pixels compare to other units of measurement, you can choose Measurement Scale.

Scratch Sizes

In this case, it tells you how much RAM and hard drive space Photoshop is using to show the open document. On the left is the amount of RAM that was used, and on the right is the amount of Hard Drive that was used.

Efficiency

I think you know what it means to be efficient. It means the same thing here as it does in the book. If Photoshop says it is working at 100% efficiency, it means it is going at its fastest speed. That means there are problems if it shows you less than that. You might need to add more RAM to fix it.

Timing

This number tells you how long Photoshop took to do the last thing. For instance, if the last thing you did was Gaussian Blur and it says "**0.3 seconds**," that means it took the Photoshop tool **0.3 seconds** to do Gaussian Blur.

Current Tool

It tells you which tool is currently active. It should tell you about the Brush **Tool** if you have it turned on.

32-bit Exposure

It lets you adjust 32-bit HDR images.

Save Progress

This shows you the save progress when you are saving your image or when Photoshop is saving the image automatically under its **Auto Recovery Feature**.

EXPLORING CONTEXT MENUS

Adobe Photoshop's context options are flexible and useful. They let you quickly access commands and options that are related to the tool, selection, or panel you are currently working with. These menus are different from the main options at the top of Photoshop.

They give you a way to work with your design and editing projects that is active and aware of your current situation.

1. Tool-Specific Context Menus:
   - The context options in Photoshop change based on the tool that is currently selected. When you right-click on a tool that is already chosen, a context menu with instructions and options that are specific to that tool shows up.

- If you right-click on the image while using the Eyedropper Tool, for example, the context menu will show you the way to sample and change colors.

2. **Accessibility of Context Menus:**
   - To see the context options for different tools, right-click on the page or your work area and pick the tool. When you do this, the context menu for the selected tool will appear.
   - When you open a context menu, you can click on the options and actions to move through them. You can press the Enter key on your computer or click somewhere outside the menu to close it.

3. **Panel and Dialog Box Context Menus:**
   - Context options aren't just for tools. There are also context options in some screens, chat boxes, and options bars. You can quickly get to the settings and functions that are useful for the panel or dialog box you're in by using these options.
   - For instance, the Layers panel has context options that let you do different things related to layers, like adding new layers, changing the styles of existing layers, and more.

4. **Pop-Up Sliders:**
   - Some settings in panels, dialog boxes, and options bars have pop-up buttons in addition to context menus. You can use these tools by clicking on the triangle icon next to a text box or number field.
   - If you click on the triangle, a pop-up slider will appear. You can change the setting by moving the slider handle. This makes it easier to see and understand how to change numbers.

5. **Toolbar Organization:**
   - It's important to know that Photoshop's toolbar is organized in a way that makes sense, with tools that are similar being grouped. An icon shows you what each tool is, and some tools hide other tools behind them.
   - If you see a small arrow in the bottom right corner of a tool icon, that means that that group of tools has more tools available. If you click and hold on the button, you can get to these extra tools.

The **Keyboard Shortcuts and Menus** window box does not have Context Menus. It is a window that you can get to by right-clicking on an open tool.

In this case, if we right-click on the image and choose the Eye Dropper Tool, we'll see the following menu:

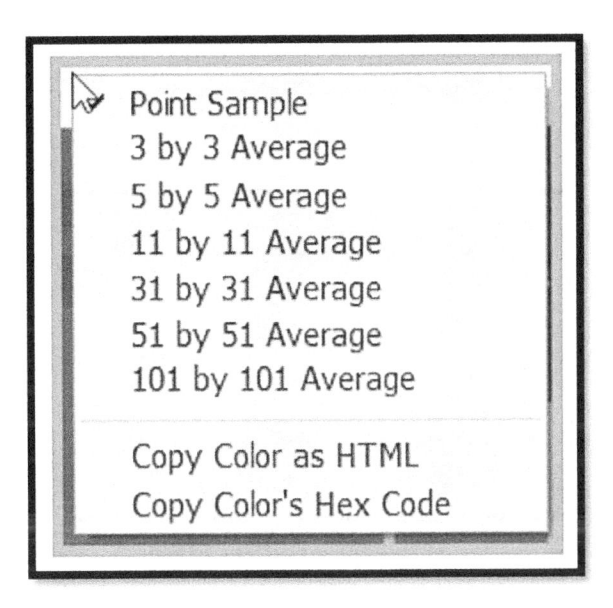

```
Point Sample
3 by 3 Average
5 by 5 Average
11 by 11 Average
31 by 31 Average
51 by 51 Average
101 by 101 Average

Copy Color as HTML
Copy Color's Hex Code
```

GETTING USED TO PHOTOSHOP PANELS

For each task, there is a different screen. One place where we work with layers in a text is in the **Layers panel**. The **Adjustments panel** is used to add an adjustment layer, and the **Properties panel** is used to set options for adjustment layers. In the **Color or Swatches panels**, we can pick colors. In the **Brush panel**, we can change a brush's size and how it works. With Photoshop's **History** box, we can even go back to a previous step in our process. Plus a lot more!

The Default "Essentials" Workspace

Before we start, let's make sure that the panels you have and the ones I have are the same. To do that, we'll quickly change the usual area in Photoshop. Which Photoshop panels are shown on your screen and how they are grouped depends on the location you choose. It comes with some areas that you can use, and you can even save your own. Photoshop's main work area is called the **Essentials workspace**. For now, you should stay in the Essentials area if you are new to Photoshop. The Essentials desk is a flexible area that can be used for a wide range of tasks. Let's make sure we're both in the Essentials area before we look at Photoshop's panels. We'll also make sure that the area is set to the way it normally looks.

Choosing the Essentials Workspace

To begin, we will pick the Essentials area. The two buttons can be found in the upper right part of the Photoshop screen. The rectangular button right next to the magnifying glass icon on the left opens Photoshop's new Search Bar. The square button in Photoshop is used to choose a workspace:

Click on the button to look at which of Photoshop's areas is open or to switch to a different one. You can choose from a list of areas at the top of the new page. There is a tick next to the name of the area that is currently being used. Essentials should be on by default. If it's not, click on it at the top of the list to choose it:

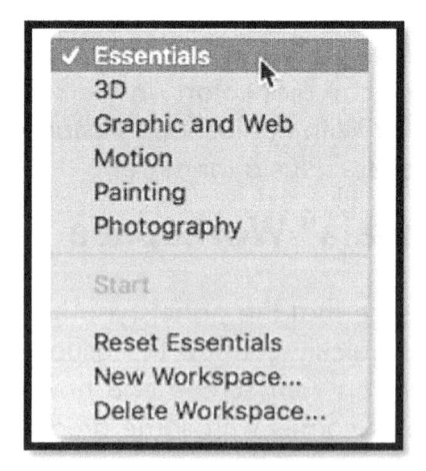

Resetting the Essentials Workspace

Now that the Essentials area is chosen, let's make sure that all of the panels are set to their original setup. Resetting the area is how we do that.

Pick Reset Essentials from the menu to start over with the Essentials workspace:

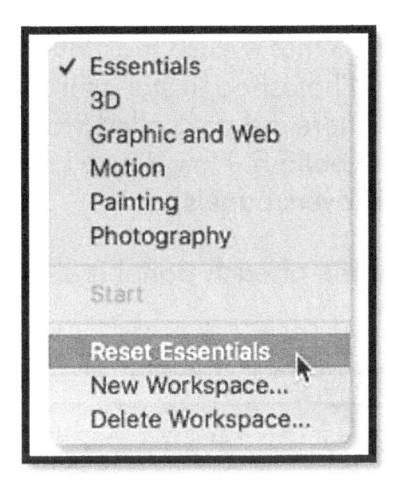

Working With Photoshop's Panels

The Panel Area

Now that the Essentials area has been changed and chosen, let's look at the Photoshop panels. In the panel area on the right side of the screen, the panels are shown in groups. When you first open Photoshop, there are three-panel columns. Now that there are more libraries, each one has its group on the far right. The main panel column is in the middle. This is where we find the panels we use the most. There is also a small second stack of panels on the left. **In the image, I made the rest of the interface darker to draw attention to the box on the right:**

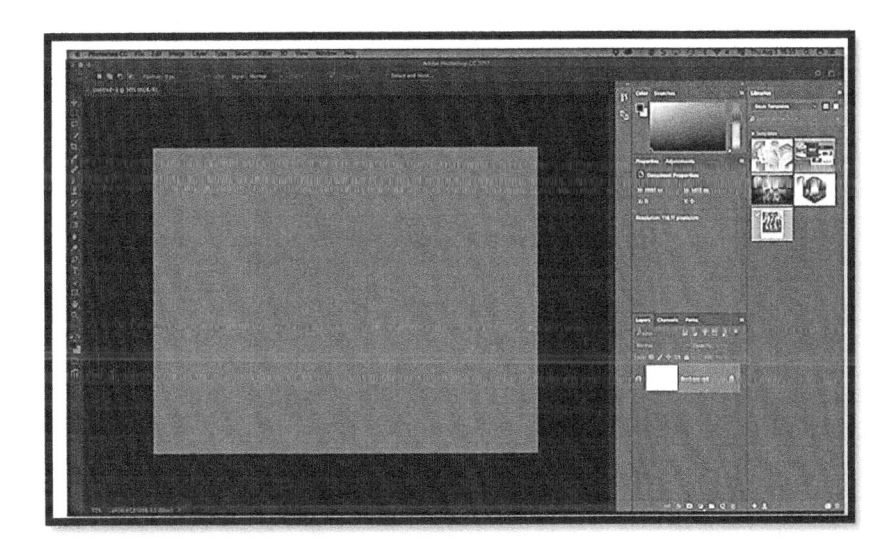

The Main Panel Column

These are the **Photoshop panels** that we use most often. They are in the main block in the middle. When we open Photoshop, it starts three screens by default. It's at the very top of the main column. There is a box called Properties below the Color panel. The Layers panel is at the very bottom. How do we know for sure that we're looking at the **Color, Properties, and Layers panels?**

We know this because the name of each panel is shown in a tab at the top of the panel:

Panel Groups

You can see that there are more panels in the column than just the Color, Properties, and Layers panels. This is an example of a tab that is to the right of the Color panel at the top. Along the side of the Properties screen is a tab called "**Adjustments**." The Layers panel is at the bottom right, and there are two more tabs there. These are **Channels and Paths**. Adobe needed a way to keep the panels from taking up too much space on the screen because Photoshop has so many of them. The answer was to put together groups of screens that were linked. There can be more than one separate panel in a panel group. In this way, more than one panel can fit inside of one panel. How do groups of people work? Take a look at the Color Panel. Because it says "**Color**" in the tab at the top, we know it's the Color panel. Another tab that says "**Swatches**" is right next to the "**Color**" **tab**. This other tab is for a panel that is grouped with the Color panel. Photoshop can only show one group of panels at a time. The other panels in the group stay hidden behind the open panel(s). The live screen is the one that is open in the group right now. The name of the active screen stands out more than the others, so we can tell which one is on.

Switching Between Panels in a Group

To navigate between the several panels that make up a group, click on the tabs. For instance, on the left, we can see that the **Color panel** is now active, but the **Swatches panel** is obscured by other content. On the right, I've clicked on the **Swatches** tab. This action brings up the Swatches panel while pushing the Color panel to the background of the window. To return to the **Color panel**, all I would have to do is click on the **Color panel's** tab:

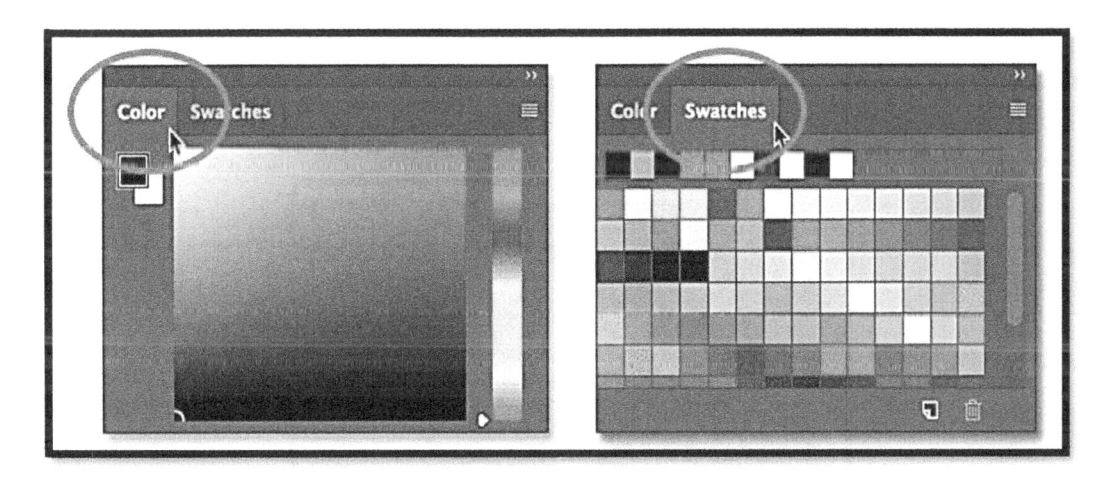

I'll proceed in the same manner with the Properties panel, which is presently active in a different group at the moment. Taking a look at the tabs, I can see that the **Adjustments panel** is tucked away in the sidebar. I'll click on the **Adjustments panel** tab when I want to transition to that panel. This toggles the visibility of the **Adjustments panel**, while the **Properties panel** remains hidden:

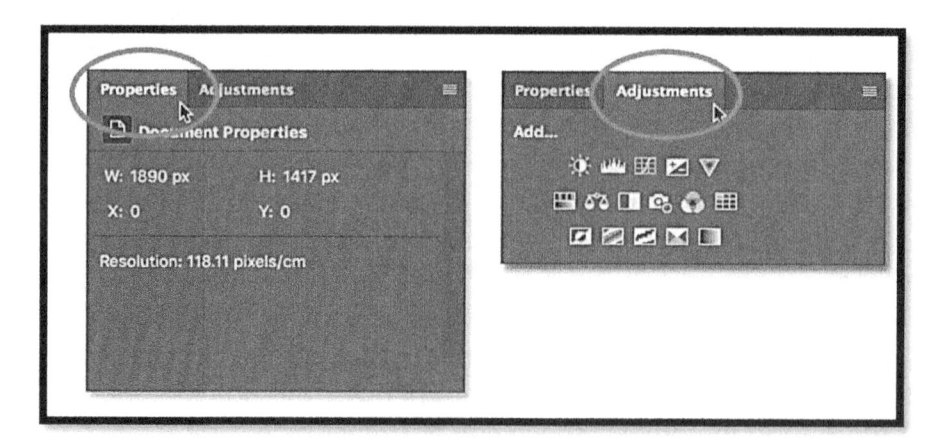

Changing the Order of Panels in a Group

Let's go over the steps to rearrange the sequence of the panels in a group. Take note that the Properties panel is shown first in the group, while the Adjustments panel is presented second after it. The layout you see there is the one that comes by default, but we can simply alter it. Simply clicking on a panel's tab will allow you to rearrange the panels that are included inside a group. After that, while keeping the **left mouse button** down, move the tab to the left or right. When you are ready, let go of the mouse **button** to allow the panel to fall into position. Here, I've selected the **Properties** tab by clicking on it to make it active, and now I'm dragging the panel to the right while keeping the mouse button down. I'll move it to the other side of the Adjustments tab:

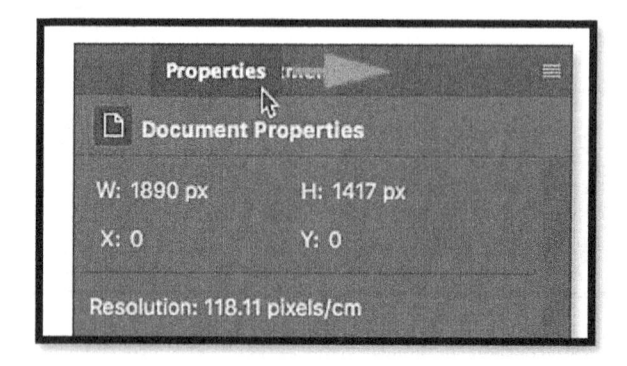

After you have moved the tab to the location that you choose, you can let go of the button on your mouse. Photoshop automatically moves the tab to its new location inside the group when it is closed. My Adjustments panel is now shown at the top of the group, followed by the Properties panel:

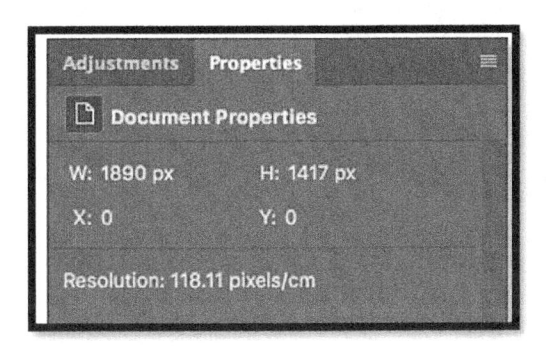

Moving Panels between Groups

Next, let's become familiar with the process of moving panels across different groups. What if, rather than just altering the order in which the panels appear inside a group, I wish to shift one of the panels to a new group entirely? Let's imagine, for instance, that I wish to transfer the Adjustments panel into the same group that houses the **Color and Swatches** panels. In this case, I would choose the **Group menu** option. Simply clicking on the panel's tab will allow you to shift it from one group to another. Then, while pressing the left mouse button, drag the tab inside the newly created group. It will seem like there is a blue highlight box around the group. When you let go of the panel's button in Photoshop, the program will place it in the location indicated by the blue box. **At this point, I'm going to move my Adjustments panel into the group that contains the Color and Swatches panel:**

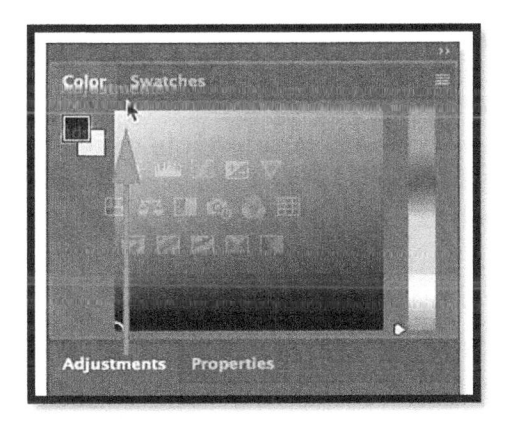

As soon as I let go of the **mouse button**, Photoshop moved the Adjustments panel to the same group as the Color and Swatches panels. Take note that the Properties panel is now located in its very own subgroup by itself:

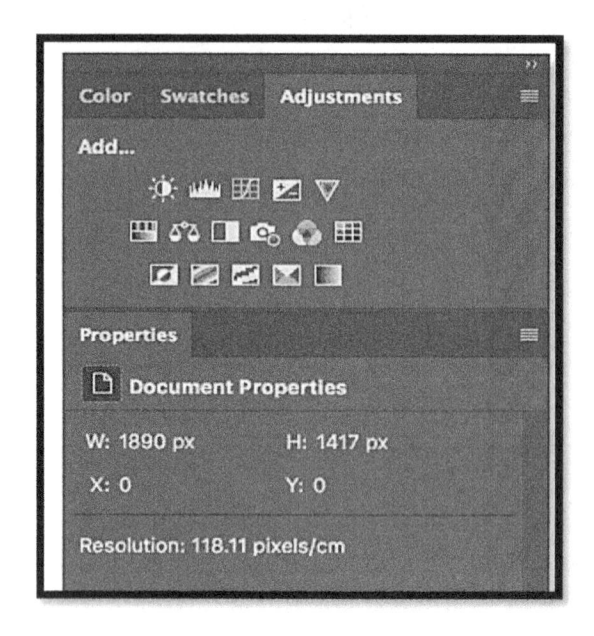

Creating New Panel Groups

In addition to the ability to move panels from one group to another, we can also build new panel groups in Photoshop. As we have just seen, I moved the Adjustments panel into a new group, which resulted in my Properties panel being left alone in its group by itself. However, we can truly form a new group by selecting any panel as our starting point. Holding down the mouse button while clicking on the tab of an existing panel group will cause the creation of a new panel group. The panel should then be dragged away from the group and dropped into a new position that is separate from any other group.

Consider the scenario in which I wish to segregate the Color panel so that it appears in its group. In addition, I would want the new group to be placed immediately on top of the Properties panel. To do this, I'll go to the Color panel and click on its tab. After that, while maintaining pressure on the left mouse button, I'll start dragging the tab down toward the Properties panel until a blue highlight bar emerges in the space between the two panels that are already there. You must take note of the fact that this time; we are searching for a highlight bar rather than a border:

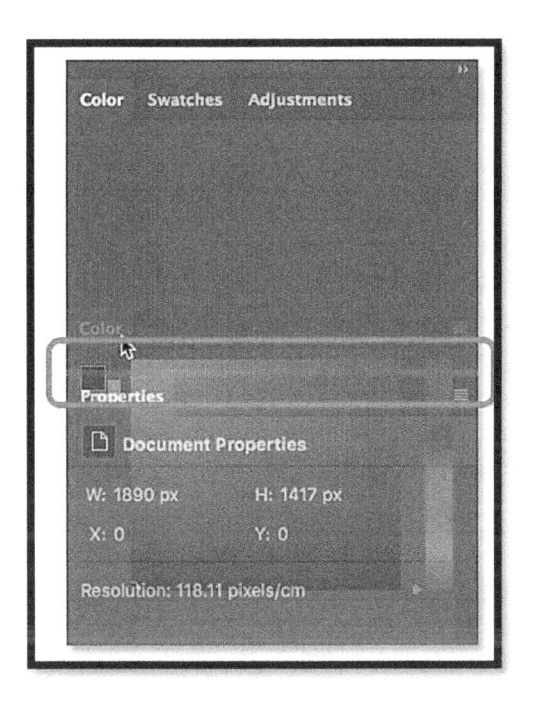

I'm going to let go of the mouse button as soon as the highlight bar appears. In Photoshop, the Color panel is separated into its group, which is located between the following two groups:

Collapsing and Expanding Panel Groups

Next, let's find out how to make the most efficient use of the space available in the panel area by collapsing and expanding the panel groups. A panel group can be temporarily collapsed such that just the tabs at the top of the group are visible. Because of this, there will be greater room for panels in the other groupings. Double-clicking on any tab inside a panel group will collapse all of the panels in the group. No matter the tab you were previously working in, this action will collapse all of the panels in the group. I've done a double-click on the Swatches tab in this area. This causes the Swatches panel and the Adjustments panel that is next to it to collapse so that just the tabs for those panels are shown. Take note of how the Color panel below them has increased in height to accommodate the additional space:

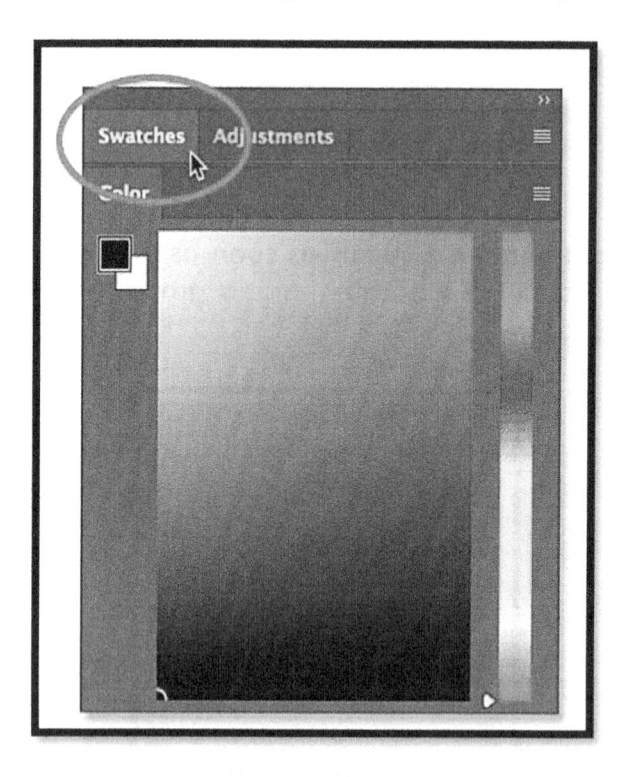

Simply make a single click on any of the tabs within the group that you want to expand after you have collapsed it to make the panels visible. I just gave the Swatches panel a single click over here, and as a result, it is now accessible once again. The Color panel that was located below the group has shrunk to the size it was before it was expanded. In conclusion, to collapse the panel group, you should double-click on a tab that you want to collapse.

To enlarge a tab, just make a single click on it:

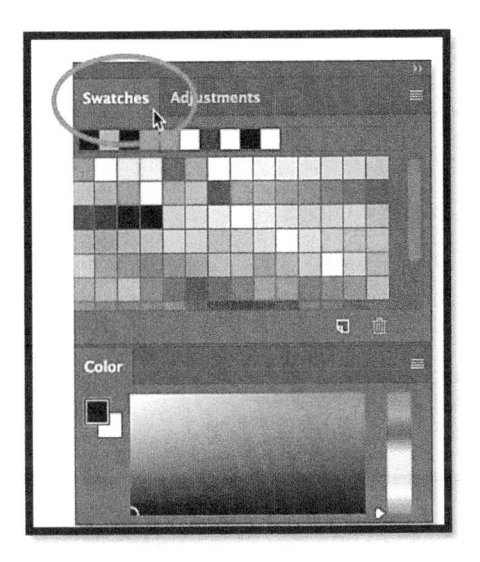

Closing a Single Panel

When working in Photoshop, in addition to collapsing and extending panels, we can also shut panels that we aren't now using. To shut only one of many panels inside a group, you must first choose the panel by clicking on its tab. Then, choose Close from the menu that appears when you click on the menu icon that is located in the upper right corner of the panel. I'll start by activating my Swatches panel by clicking on it. After that, I'll choose the "**Menu**" symbol. After that, choose the option to close the window.

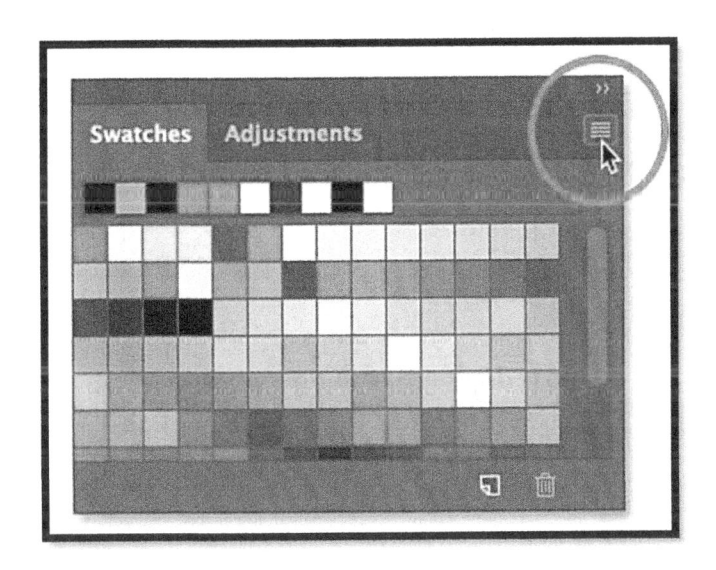

By clicking on the same menu button in the upper right corner, you will close a complete panel group rather than simply a single panel included inside the group. Then, from the menu, choose the option to Close Tab Group.

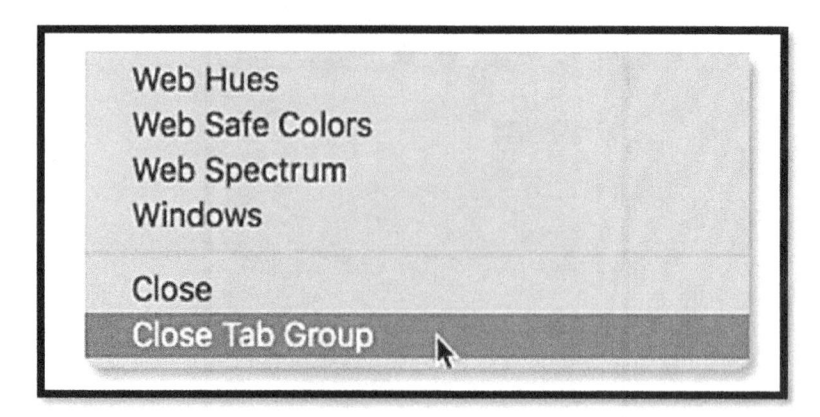

Closing A Panel or Group from the Tab

In Photoshop, you can also close a panel or panel group by right-clicking (on Windows) or control-clicking (on Mac) directly on the tab of the panel you want to close. Simply selecting "**Close**" from the menu will close only the panel by itself. Select **Close Tab Group** from the menu to close the whole panel group. On the Libraries tab, I have performed a right-click (on Windows) or control-click (on a Mac) here. In this instance, the Libraries panel is the only panel included inside the group; hence, selecting either **Close or Close Tab Group** will result in the group as **a whole being closed:**

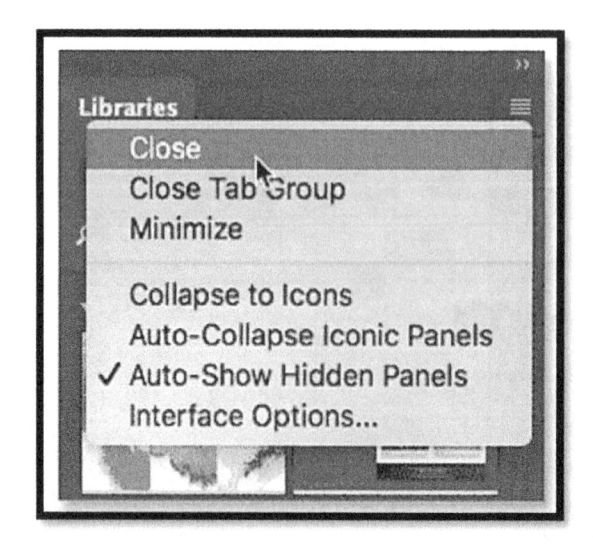

Opening Panels from the Window Menu

From the Window menu located in the Menu Bar that runs along the top of the screen, you can access any of Photoshop's panels. Clicking on the Window menu in Photoshop allows you to reopen a panel after you have closed it, as well as open any of the program's other panels. This action brings up a menu that, among other things, provides a comprehensive list of all of the Photoshop panels that are at our disposal. If there is a checkmark to the left of the name of a panel, it indicates that the panel is now open and being used on the screen.

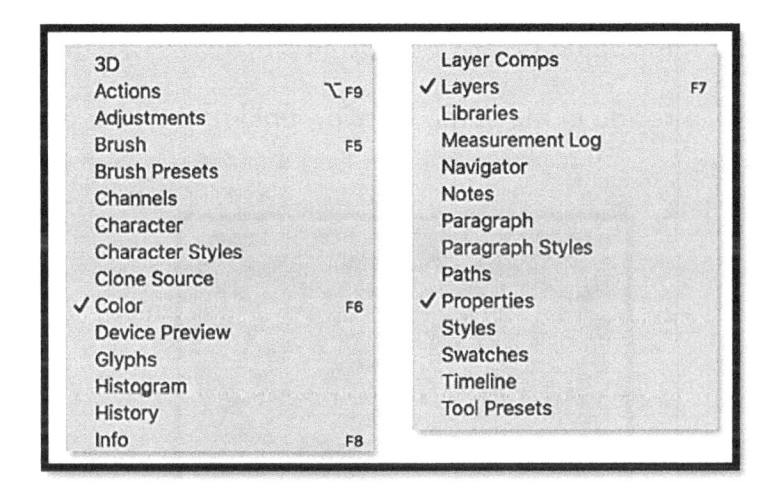

Simply clicking on the panel's name in the list will open any panels that are not currently visible (those that do not have a tick next to them). I'm going to pick the Adjustments panel to re-open it.

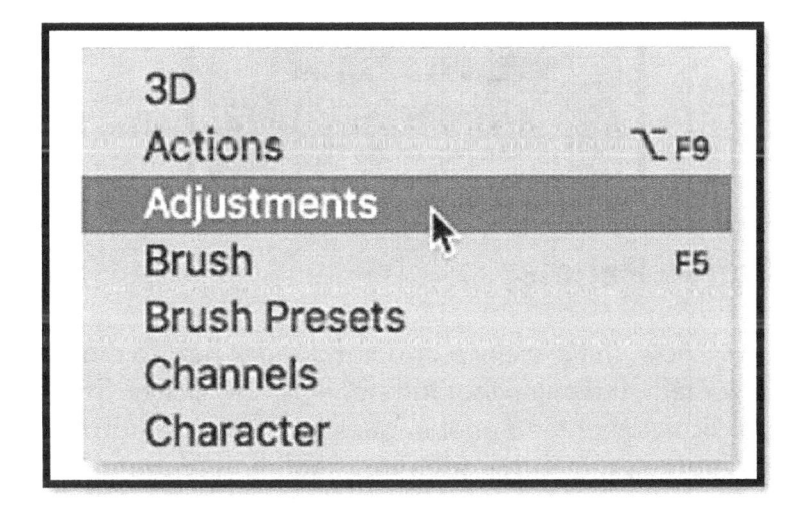

Photoshop's Sticky Panels

The Adjustments panel has been restored to its previous position at the very top of the main panel column, where it was held before I closed it. Also, take note that my Swatches panel has returned next to it in the same group, even though I did not choose the Swatches panel from the list of available panels. The reason behind this is that Photoshop remembers the panel configuration we used. In this particular instance, it recalled that my **Adjustments and Swatches** panels were organized together within a single group. And it recalled that their panel group was located above the Color panel that I was working on. All of the components of the Photoshop interface; including panels and groups have a sticky quality.

They will continue to reside in the same location until or until we decide to relocate them:

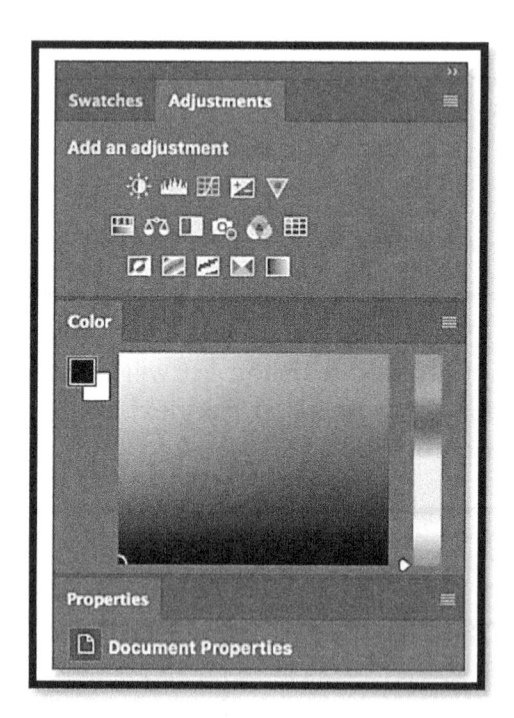

Open vs. Active Panels

As you should now know, the presence of a checkmark next to the name of a panel inside the Window menu indicates that the panel is now active. The checkmark, on the other hand, indicates that the panel in question is now the group's active panel. Other panels in the group may have openings as well. However, the checkmark will only be seen on the active panel inside the group. Take, as an example, a glance at the **Layers** panel. The Channels and Paths panels are bundled in with the Layers panel so that they are all accessible together.

The Layers panel, however, is the one that is now selected as the active panel in the group:

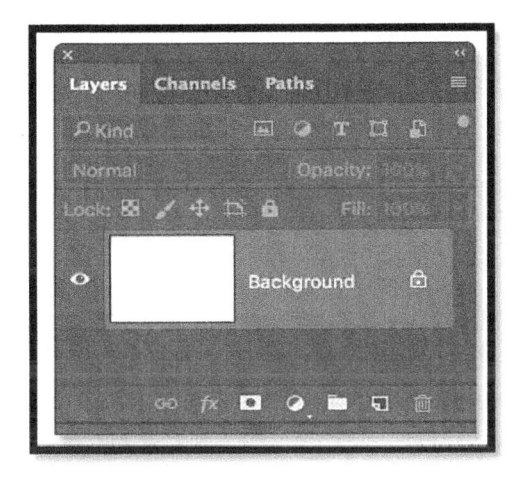

If we look at the list of panels that I have available under the Window menu, we can see that the Layers panel has been activated, as indicated by the presence of a checkbox next to its name. However, even though both the **Channels and Paths** panels are now shown on the screen, none one of them has a tick in them;

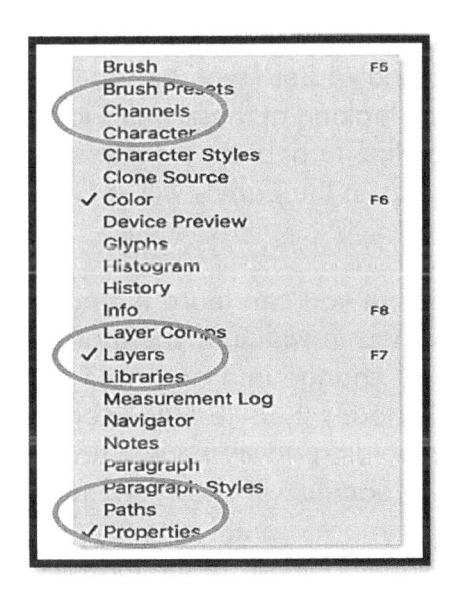

The Secondary Panel Column

Up until this point, we have been concentrating our efforts on the **primary panel** column. However, there is also a secondary column to the left of it. This second **column can at first seem to be a little bit confusing since, by default, the panels that are located in this column only display as icons:**

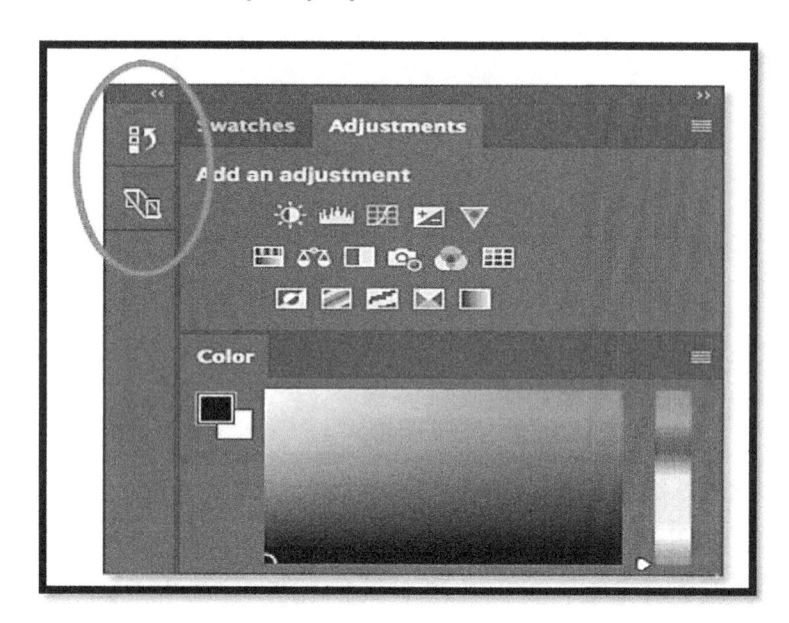

The History panel is located at the top of this second column in Photoshop, and the **Device Preview** panel is located just below it. Both panels are visible when you first open Photoshop. You could find yourself wondering, "**How are we supposed to know which panels they are just by looking at these weird icons?**" as a result of this. If you happen to have **Shown Tooltips** turned on in Photoshop's Preferences (it is turned on by default), then the names of the panels will show when you hover your mouse cursor over each icon.

This is just one of the ways that you can learn the names of the panels. However, there is a more efficient method in which, if you move your mouse cursor over the left side of the column, it will change into an arrow with two heads indicating the direction you should go. To modify the size of the column, first click on the edge of the column, and then while holding down the left mouse button, drag it out toward the left. The real titles of the panels will show next to their icons as you move the mouse around, which is a far more useful feature. When you have added sufficient space for the names to fit, you can let go of the mouse.

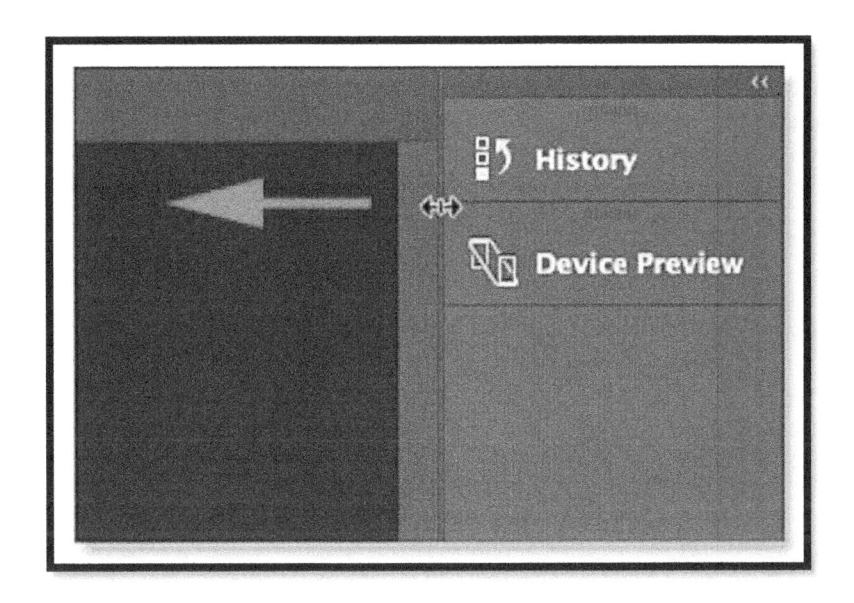

Expanding and Collapsing Secondary Panels

This secondary column can be put to good use by holding panels that are in use but do not need constant access to the open position. The icon view mode maintains access to these panels while preventing them from consuming important real estate on the screen. Either clicking on the panel's symbol or its name will cause it to expand to its full size. Here, I'm expanding the History panel by clicking on it:

To return the panel to its icon view mode, either click once more on the icon or name of the panel or click the little icon showing two arrows that is located in the top right corner of the panel:

Moving Panel Groups between Columns

In Photoshop, we can just as quickly transfer panels from one group to another as we can move them across columns. To transfer a panel from one column to another, you must first click and hold on the tab of the panel you want to move, and then drag the panel into the other column. When you let go of the panel's mouse button, the panel will drop to the location indicated by the blue box or bar that is highlighted. Imagine that I want to move the **Properties panel** that is now in the primary column to the secondary column. In addition, I would want it to be placed in the second column in its very own section by itself. To do this, I'll click and hold on the Properties tab at the top of the screen. After that, I will slide it across to the second column so that the blue bar displays exactly below the Device Preview panel:

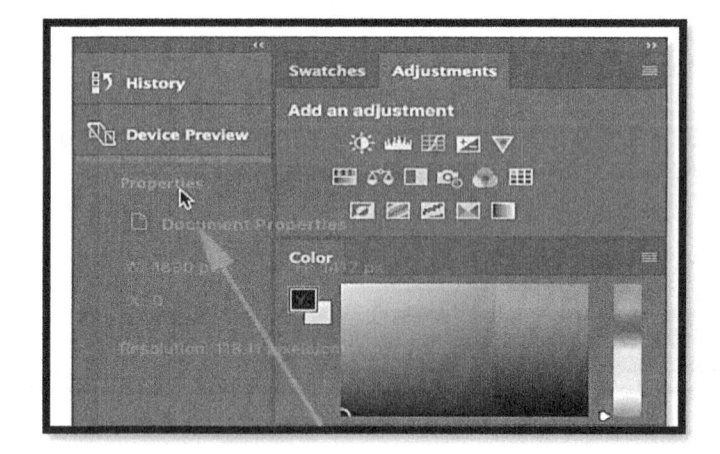

I'll let go of the button on my mouse, and you'll see that the Properties panel has moved into its group below the **Device Preview**:

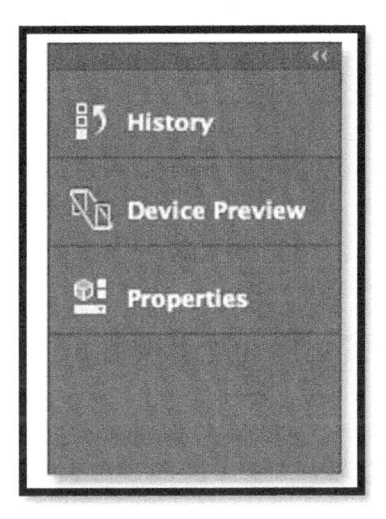

Following that, I want to move my Adjustments panel such that it is part of the same group as my Properties panel. I'll make some adjustments by clicking and holding the **Adjustments** tab in the main column. Then I'll drag it into the second column and over top of the Properties panel's tab so that the blue highlight box appears around the tab itself:

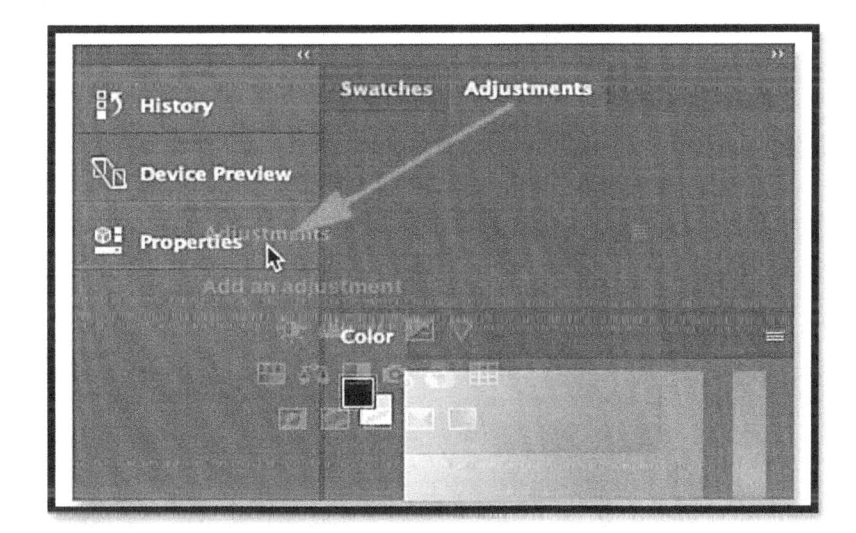

I'll let go of the mouse, and you'll see that both panels now belong to the same group in the second column.

61

MAKING IT RIGHT WITH UNDO AND REDO COMMANDS

It is certain that at some point throughout the process of working on a picture in Adobe Photoshop, you will find that you need to undo something that you have done inside the image. It is crucial to know how to go back in time and reverse previous actions, whether it is because you have made a mistake, changed your mind, or just need to fine-tune alterations you have previously done. It would seem like undoing changes in Photoshop is a straightforward process at first glance, but in reality, you can undo, go back, and update the changes you've made to your picture in a variety of different ways.

Edit-Undo (Control/Command + Z)

You can undo changes you've made to a project in Photoshop by going to the **Edit menu** and choosing the **Undo option**. This is the quickest and most straightforward method. You can make this process simpler and more productive by using the keyboard shortcut **Command-Z (Mac) or Control-Z (Windows)** to undo the most recent change you made.

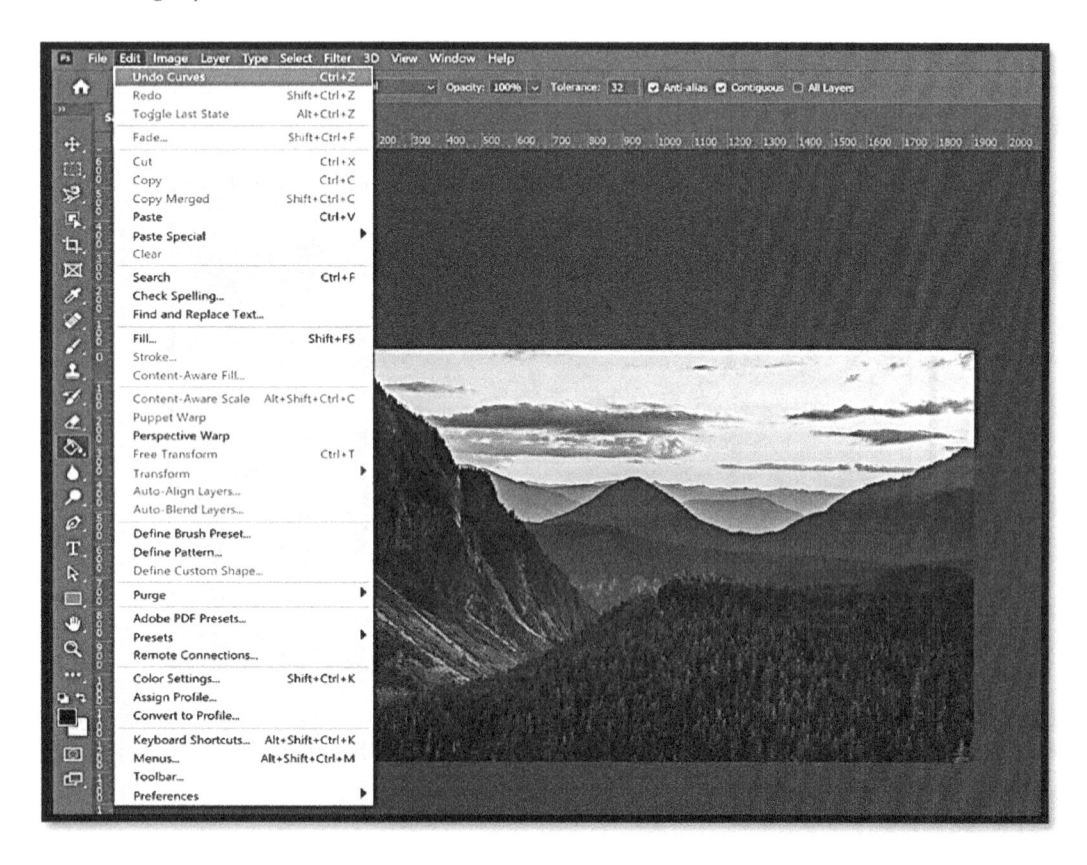

I'll let go of the button on my mouse, and you'll see that the Properties panel has moved into its group below the **Device Preview**:

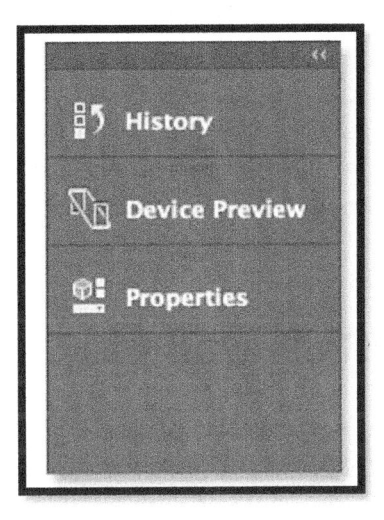

Following that, I want to move my Adjustments panel such that it is part of the same group as my Properties panel. I'll make some adjustments by clicking and holding the **Adjustments** tab in the main column. Then I'll drag it into the second column and over top of the Properties panel's tab so that the blue highlight box appears around the tab itself:

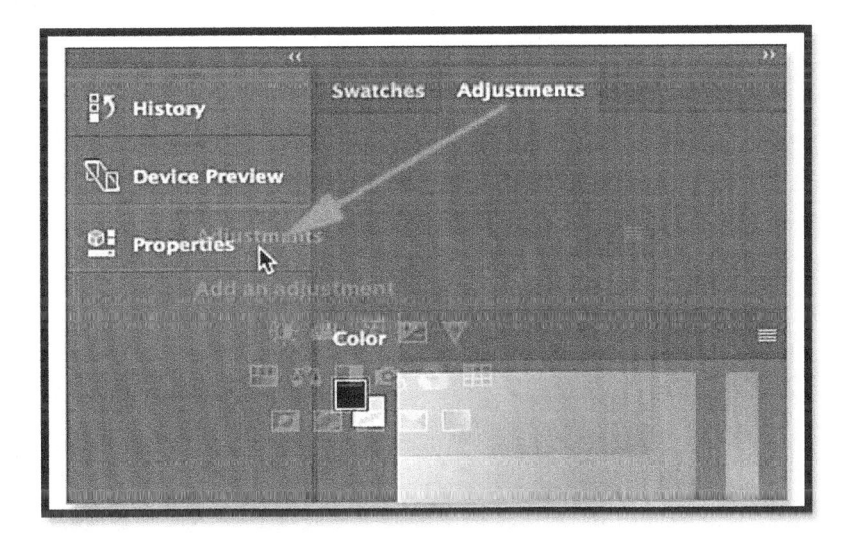

I'll let go of the mouse, and you'll see that both panels now belong to the same group in the second column.

MAKING IT RIGHT WITH UNDO AND REDO COMMANDS

It is certain that at some point throughout the process of working on a picture in Adobe Photoshop, you will find that you need to undo something that you have done inside the image. It is crucial to know how to go back in time and reverse previous actions, whether it is because you have made a mistake, changed your mind, or just need to fine-tune alterations you have previously done. It would seem like undoing changes in Photoshop is a straightforward process at first glance, but in reality, you can undo, go back, and update the changes you've made to your picture in a variety of different ways.

Edit-Undo (Control/Command + Z)

You can undo changes you've made to a project in Photoshop by going to the **Edit menu** and choosing the **Undo option**. This is the quickest and most straightforward method. You can make this process simpler and more productive by using the keyboard shortcut **Command-Z (Mac)** or **Control-Z (Windows)** to undo the most recent change you made.

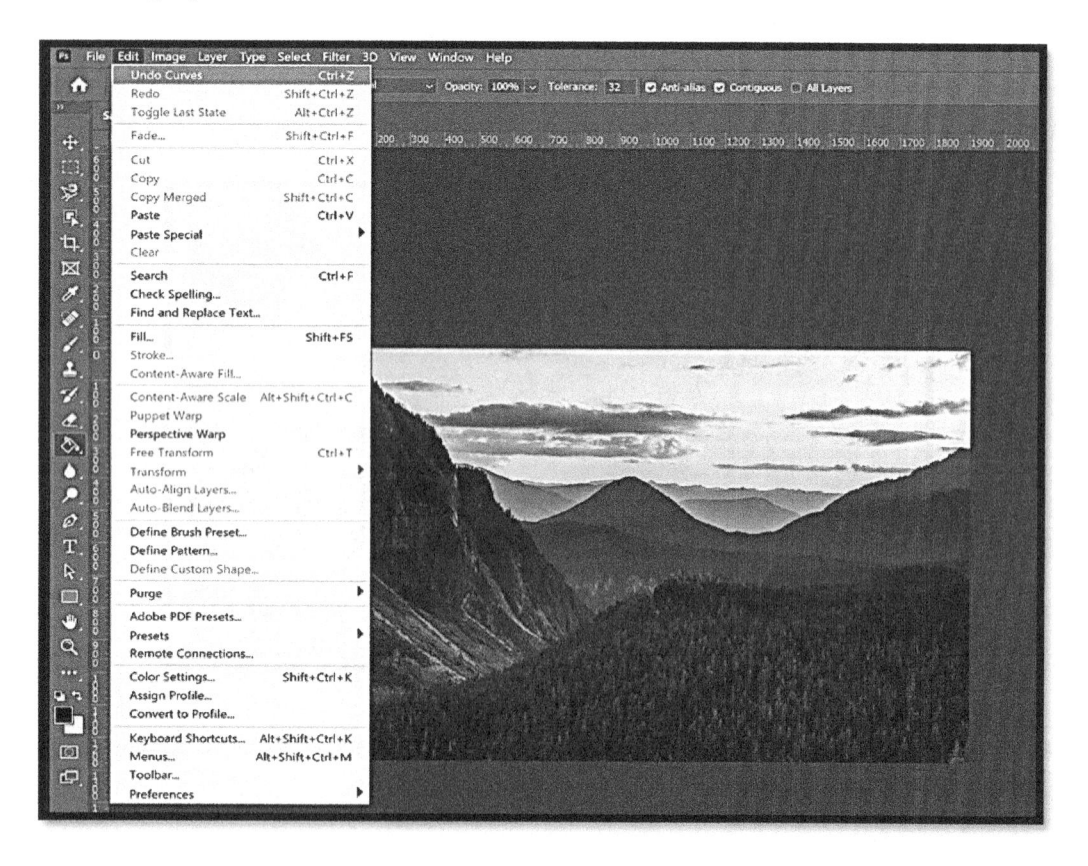

If you only ever learn one keyboard shortcut in Photoshop, it should be this one. It is fast and simple, and it is something that you will find yourself utilizing regularly. Going to the Edit menu to do an undo will cause a significant slowdown in your productivity. Having the ability to swiftly reverse changes by pressing **Control or Command Z** will save a significant amount of time, particularly when you are utilizing tools such as the Clone Stamp or Healing Brush tools.

Because this is pretty typical across the majority of major software products, you will likely already be familiar with both the keyboard shortcut and the location inside the **Edit** Menu. You will be able to revert the changes that you have made to your document if you keep selecting Undo (or by continually pressing **Command/Control + Z)**, as is the case with the vast majority of modern software products.

You also have the option to redo your previous undo action inside the Edit menu. Alternatively, you can use the keyboard shortcut **Shift + Control + Z (Windows) or Shift + Command + Z (Mac)** to redo the action. You also have the option to "**Toggle Last State**" in Photoshop, which enables you to rapidly analyze the impact that the most recent modification you made had on the picture as a whole. Toggle the effect of your most recent modification on and off by pressing **Control + Alt + Z (on Windows) or Command + Option + Z (on Mac),** respectively. This can also be done by switching between **Undo and Redo**, although utilizing keyboard shortcuts is a somewhat easier way to achieve the same result.

Legacy Undo Shortcuts

If you've been using Photoshop for a long time, you probably already know that in earlier versions of the program, the Undo command had a different purpose than it does in the most recent version of Photoshop. In previous versions, the Undo command performed the same actions that Toggle Last State does in the current version, and Adobe provided the option to step backward as a distinct command. In the current version, **Toggle Last State** replaces the Undo command. In the most recent version of Photoshop, the **Step backward** command performs the identical actions as the Undo command.

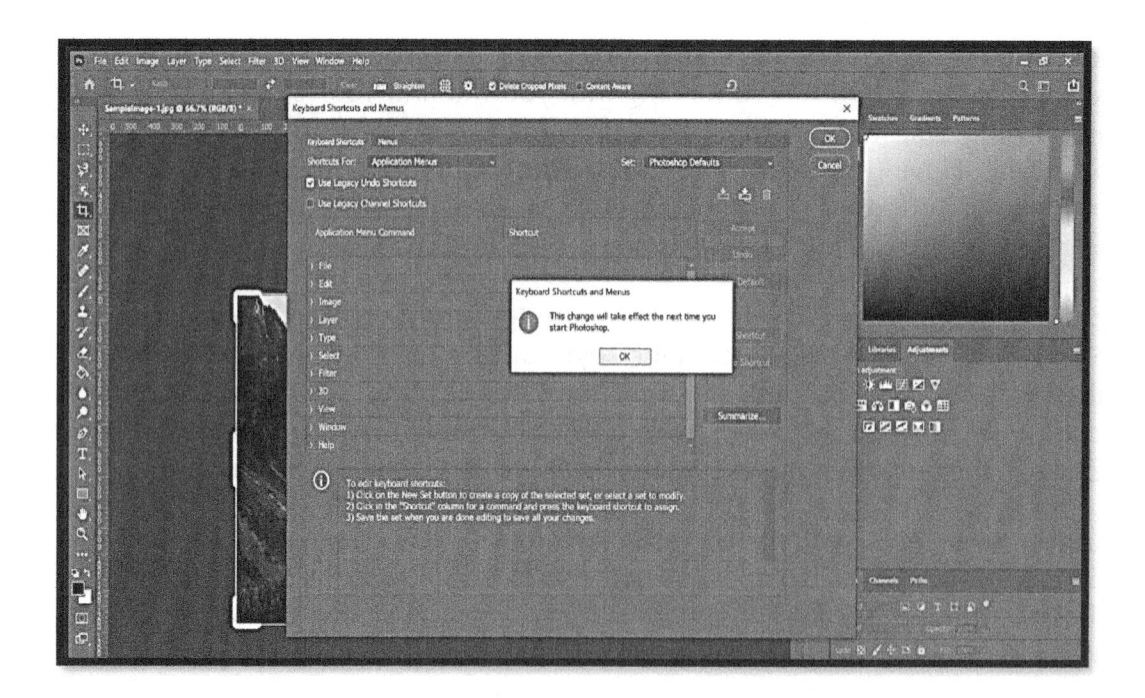

In Photoshop, two of the most useful undo capabilities for photographers are the option to turn the most recent change on and off and the capability to undo many changes at once (also known as stepping backward through the history states).

Adobe Engineers went back and forth over how the undo command was going to work in the beginning, but in the end, they decided to go with the toggle function. This decision came after some internal disagreement. But since almost every other modern software program offers an undo function that allows you to step backward multiple times, Adobe's decision to update the functionality to reflect modern standards makes sense. However, if you prefer the previous undo functionality, either because that is what you are used to or because it makes sense within your workflow then you have the option of setting your preferences to use the "**Legacy Undo Mode**".

Simply go to the Edit menu to activate the legacy undo feature. Click the **Keyboard Shortcuts** menu item, then click the "**Use Legacy Undo Shortcuts**" check box in the resulting dialog box. After that, Photoshop will need a fresh start from you. When legacy undo shortcuts are enabled, using **Command/Control + Z** will now turn on or off the most recent change you made. Using **Alt + Control + Z (Windows)** or **Command + Option + Z (Mac)** will now **Step Backward**, notwithstanding what the history shows.

ERASING EDITING STEPS WITH THE HISTORY BOX

It is almost guaranteed that at some time throughout the process of working on a photo in Adobe Photoshop, you will discover that you need to undo something that you have done inside the image. This realization is likely to come at some point in the middle of the process. It is crucial to learn how to go back in time and reverse earlier actions, whether it is because you have made a mistake, changed your mind, or just need to fine-tune alterations that you have previously done. At first look, it may seem that undoing changes in Photoshop is a basic procedure; but you can undo, rewind, and update the changes that you've made to your image in a variety of different ways. This is because Photoshop allows you to undo changes in some different methods. Moving forward and backward through your alterations can be accomplished in a manner that is more attractive to the eye if you make use of the History panel, which can be accessed by choosing **Window > History** from the menu bar. The **History panel** will present you with a rundown of all the changes you've made to the document.

You can go back to a particular modification that you made (for example, one that happened four steps ago) by choosing it in the History panel and then continue with your work from that point forward. You can quickly reverse the most recent change or two that you made to an image in Photoshop by hitting the Control or Command key in combination with Z (or by selecting reverse from the Edit menu). Both of these approaches are perfectly appropriate. When you need to make changes that go back more than a few steps, you should search in the History Panel for the option you're looking for. You can quickly access the History Panel by choosing **History** from the **Window** menu. This will bring up the panel for you. When compared to the other Photoshop panels, this one doesn't provide nearly as much of a challenge to comprehend. It provides a list of the history states, often known as the changes that you have made to the document that you are now working on.

Whenever you modify your photo while you are editing it, that alteration will be saved to the history. To revert your picture to an earlier version, all you have to do is click back on any change you've made in the image's history. If you need to reverse a large number of changes in a hurry, you can do it with a single click on the History Panel. This feature is convenient. The undo feature might be used to do this, but the History Panel is a far more time and effort efficient option.

Nevertheless, in addition to being a way that saves time when redoing several operations, the History Panel offers access to a few more capabilities that might be used. Right from this window, you can take pictures of your image at certain points in time as well as establish the history state for your History Brush. When you choose the camera icon in the History Panel, which is situated in the lower right-hand corner of the panel, your image is saved as a snapshot. A snapshot, in its most basic form, is a bookmark that records a particular time in the history of your image. It captures the scene exactly as it was at that instant. When you choose a snapshot with your mouse, the document will be reset to the state it was in at that particular instant. The **History Panel's Snapshots** can be found toward the very top of the panel. You have a very quick way to undo the results of multi-step modifications that you made to your image if you took photographs of it before you made those changes. If the results of those adjustments aren't to your satisfaction, you can use those photos to undo those changes.

Reviewing and analyzing the results of your picture modifications can be accomplished in a very time-efficient manner if you first photograph your work in its entirety and then use the mouse to go between the images. When you access the History Panel for the first time, it will automatically record the last 50 history states. Each click or brushstroke that you make creates a new history state. This is true whether you are painting, using the healing brush, or cloning, for example. Since each click or brush stroke represents a distinct history state, the number fifty is not as high as it may seem in this circumstance. By navigating to the **Edit menu** in Photoshop and choosing **Performance** from the drop-down menu, you will enable the program to remember more history states than it does by default. You should be aware, however, that increasing the number of history states will influence

Photoshop's speed (on the other hand, if you are running Photoshop on an older or slower system, you may want to reduce the number of history states to assist in improving Photoshop's performance). Taking snapshots can be useful for some reasons, one of which is the fact that they provide you the ability to roll back changes to a point in time that is farther in the past than the history panel would ordinarily permit.

It is vital to have a strong grasp of the fact that snapshots and historical states, in addition to the capability to undo past actions, are retained in the working memory of Photoshop and are not saved simultaneously with the file. It is also essential to understand that the capacity to undo prior actions is also stored in the working memory of Photoshop. When you close a photo or Photoshop, you will no longer have access to its historical state and will be unable to undo any changes that you may have made in the past.

History Brush

The History Brush is a tool that provides users with the ability to reverse modifications made to specific regions of their images. If you modify the brightness of your picture, for example, and you like the impact on the majority of the image but not in the sky, you can use the History Brush to undo the sky area of your image so that the adjustment is reverted to its previous state. Before you can use the History Brush, you will first need to choose how far back in your change history you wish to look. Within the History Window, there is a box located immediately to the left of each history state. When you click the checkbox next to the state in the history that you wish to restore, a brush symbol will appear.

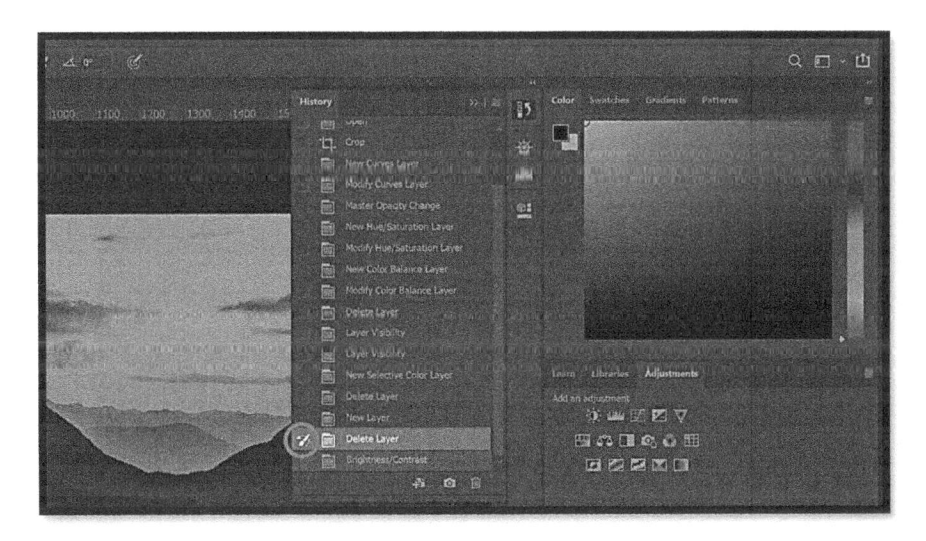

Then, from the Tool Panel, choose the history brush tool, and paint over the portion of the picture that you wish to reverse the previous change to. The **History Brush** is a brush tool, which means that you can modify its size, flow, opacity, and hardness, as well as how it blends.

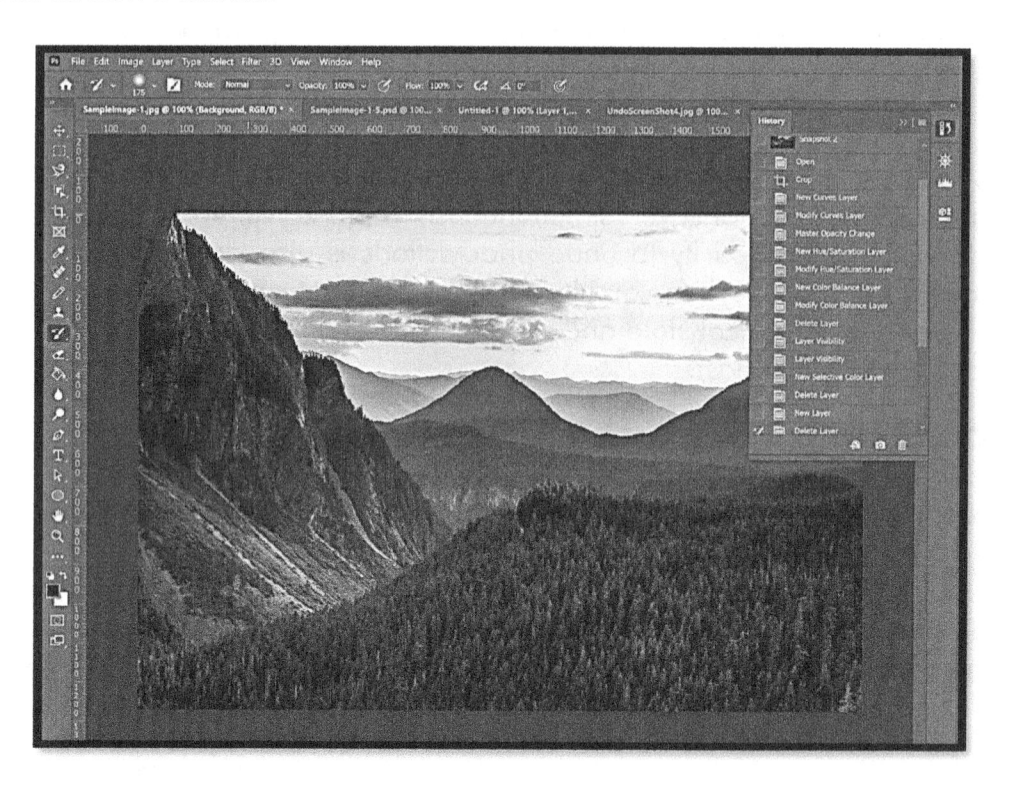

SETTING PHOTOSHOP PREFERENCES

The **Preferences panel** is where a wide variety of Photoshop options can be found, including those that affect the program's behavior, look, and overall performance. The Preferences panel in Photoshop has many more options than we could reasonably cover in a single guide, but that's good since the majority of the program's default settings are sufficient for most uses. We're only going to take a quick look at some of the Photoshop options that are important enough to pay attention to when you first begin learning the program. You can personalize Photoshop's user interface using a few of the available options. The contributions of others will quicken your process. And some assistance to ensure that Photoshop and your machine continue to function without a hitch.

How to Access the Photoshop Preferences

The Preferences panel in Photoshop is broken up into a few different areas. Where to begin? How about with the General category? On a Windows computer, the Preferences panel can be accessed by selecting **Edit** from the **Menu Bar** on the top of the screen. After that, choose **Preferences** from the menu at the bottom of the list, and after that, select General. To access the Photoshop menu on a Mac, which is what I am working with right now, go to the top of the Menu Bar. Click the **Preferences** button, and then click the **General** tab:

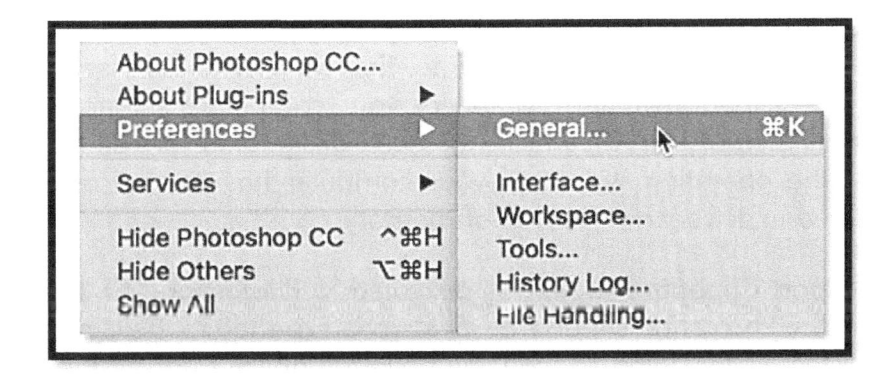

The Preferences Dialog Box

This brings up the dialog window where you can configure Photoshop's settings. The column on the left has a list of the several categories from which we can make our selection. The options that correspond to the category that is now chosen are shown in the primary area in the middle of the page. The General category is picked as the active one at the time. It is important to take note that Adobe included some new categories in the Preferences panel of Photoshop. These new categories include **Workspace, Tools, and History Log**.

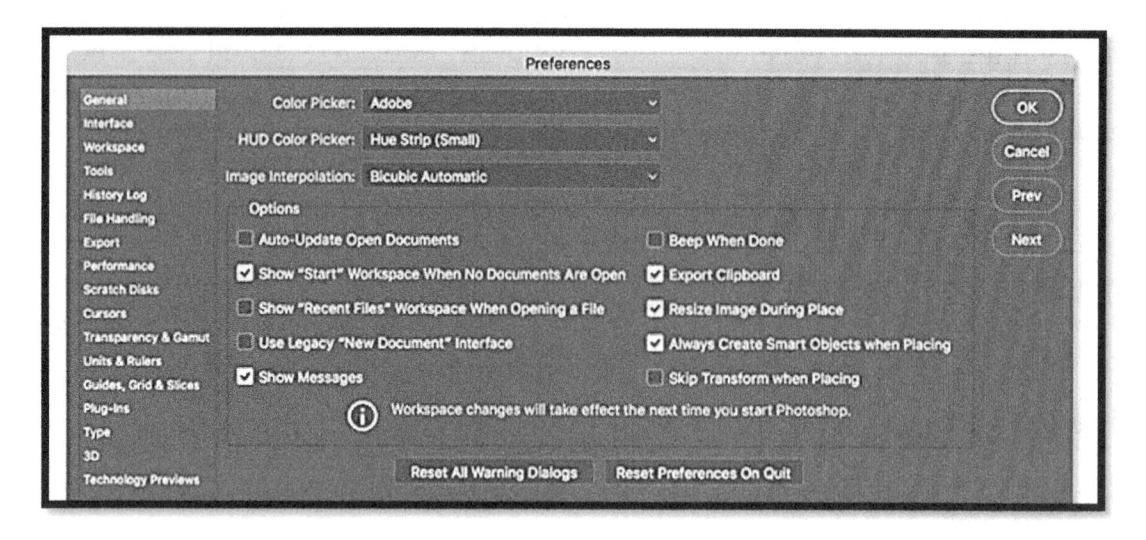

The General Preferences

Export Clipboard

The **Export Clipboard** setting, which can be located in the **General preferences**, will be the first one that we explore. The performance of your computer as a whole can be impacted by this setting. When we copy and paste photos or layers in Photoshop, the objects that are copied are saved to the clipboard that is included with Photoshop. The clipboard is the portion of your computer's memory, namely its random access memory (RAM), which has been designated for use by Photoshop. Additionally, the operating system of your computer has its very own clipboard, which is located in its very own region of memory.

When the "**Export Clipboard**" option is activated in Photoshop, all things that are now saved in the Photoshop clipboard will also be exported to the clipboard of your operating system. After doing so, you will have the ability to paste the objects that were copied into software, such as **Adobe Illustrator or InDesign**. However, the file sizes produced by Photoshop can be rather large. When you export massive files into the memory of your operating system, it can lead to errors and performance issues. "**Export Clipboard**" has its permissions enabled (checked) by default. Disabling (unchecking) this option on your computer will assist in keeping things operating smoothly. It is strongly recommended that you save the file in Photoshop even if you anticipate the need to export it from Photoshop and use it in another application. Then, launch the other software and load the file that you just saved:

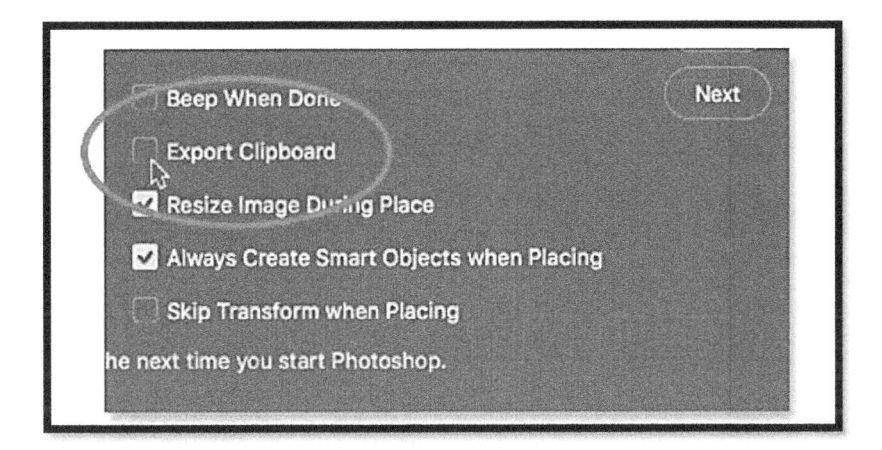

Interface Preferences

Next, let's take a look at a few of the options that are available to us so that we may personalize Photoshop's user interface. To access the Interface category, choose it from the menu on the left:

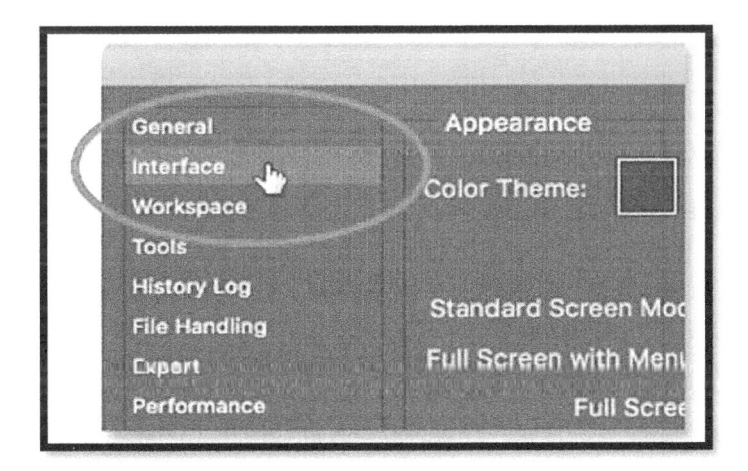

Color Theme

The first possibility that we will look into is the **Color Theme**. This feature allows you to change the color scheme used throughout Photoshop's interface. In this context, "**color**" refers to only the varying degrees of gray. Adobe provides us with a total of four unique color schemes to choose from. A swatch is used to symbolize each of the themes. The color scheme that is used by default is the second swatch from the left:

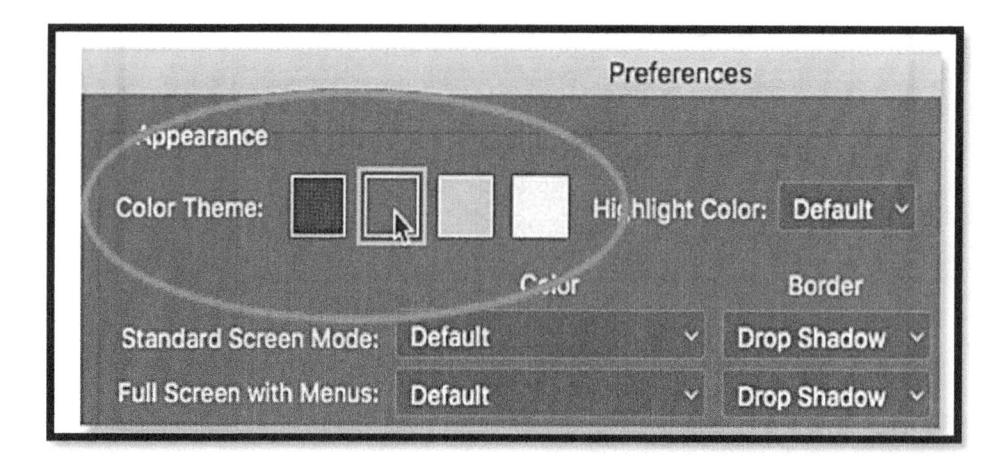

Simply clicking on the swatch of the color scheme you want to use will change it. There is one theme that is lighter than the default, as well as two others that are darker than the default. I'm going to go with one of the four themes that is the least weighty. It is important to note that the theme also determines the color of Photoshop's dialog boxes:

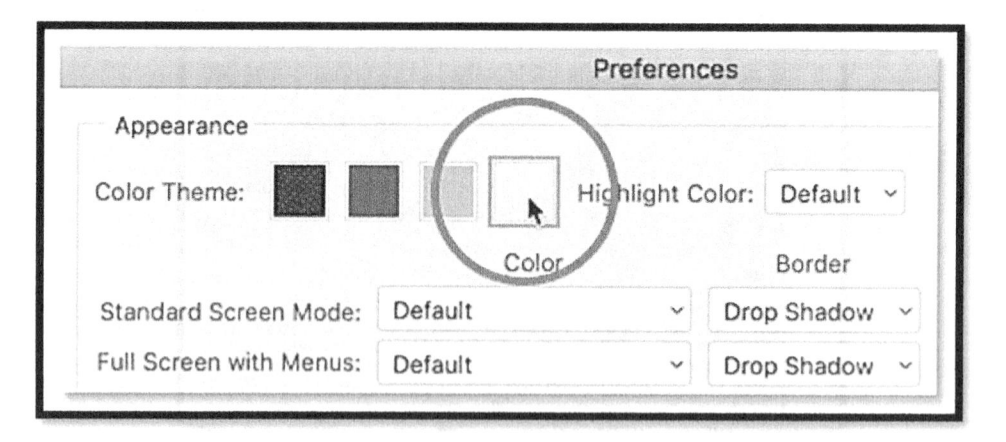

We can also notice that the UI of Photoshop has been simplified quite a bit here. The darker theme was chosen by Adobe with the thought that it would be less distracting, letting us concentrate more readily on the photographs we are editing. I feel the same way, which is why I don't mess with changing the theme. However, many like the simpler UI. Pick the subject matter that you feel the most at ease with.

At any moment, you can alter the color scheme of Photoshop by going to the Preferences panel:

How to Reset Photoshop Preferences

Step 1: Quit Photoshop
First, close off Adobe Photoshop. To exit an application using a Windows computer, go to the Menu Bar at the top of the screen, click **File**, and then choose **Exit**. On a Mac, choose "**Quit Photoshop**" from the **Photoshop menu** located in the menu bar by going to the top of the screen.
Step 2: Relaunch Photoshop While Pressing the Keyboard Shortcut
With Photoshop closed, press and hold **Shift+Ctrl+Alt (Win)** / **Shift+Command+Option (Mac)** on your keyboard and relaunch Photoshop the way you normally would.
Step 3: Delete the Photoshop Preferences File
A message will appear asking you to confirm whether or not you wish to remove the **Adobe Photoshop Settings** file just before Photoshop starts up. This is the file that contains your preferences. Make your choice. After that, Photoshop will launch with all of your options reset to their initial, factory settings:

WORKING WITH CLOUD DOCUMENTS

Cloud documents are a new document file format developed by Adobe that is native to the cloud and can be browsed online or offline straight from inside the Photoshop program. Documents stored in the cloud can be viewed from several devices, and the cloud will save any changes you make to them automatically.

You will get access to the following with Photoshop cloud documents:

- **Reliability**: Your adjustments are immediately updated and stored in Photoshop on the iPad. When working on a desktop, save your project as a cloud document so that you never have to worry about losing your work.
- **Mobility**: Access your cloud documents across devices - anytime, anyplace.
- **Quality**: Cloud documents are saved per layer, at full fidelity.
- **Access all your work:** You can simply discover all your cloud documents immediately inside Photoshop whether on your PC or iPad.

What is the difference between cloud documents and Adobe Creative Cloud Files?

Cloud document is the next generation of document files that are tailored for working on the move. You can effortlessly work smoothly across apps like Photoshop, XD, Fresco, and Aero utilizing cloud documents.

Your files enable you to save, save, and sync any file type in your Creative Cloud.

- While working with Photoshop on the iPad, you can save your work as a cloud document but not as a Creative Cloud File straight from inside the program.
- Cloud documents and Creative Cloud Files are kept in various places under your Creative Cloud account.
- Unlike cloud documents, PSDs stored as Creative Cloud Files are not native to the cloud and consequently do not have the same features as cloud documents.

Am I going to be forced to save my documents to the cloud in Photoshop?

On the desktop, you can always decide whether to save documents locally or to the document cloud. Until you tell it otherwise, Photoshop will remember how you last saved or opened your most recent document and will continue to provide you with that same experience. Using cloud documents is the standard workflow while using Photoshop on the iPad; however, to maintain compatibility with other apps, you can export your cloud documents locally as PSD, JPEG, PNG, or TIFF files.

Do cloud documents in Photoshop have anything to do with Lightroom photos?

Using the Lightroom top menu, choose a picture from Lightroom Classic or Lightroom Desktop, then open it in Photoshop on your desktop by choosing **Photo > Edit In > Edit in Adobe Photoshop**. This will allow you to work with Lightroom photographs in Photoshop on your iPad. Select **Save as a cloud document** while Photoshop is open on your desktop and your picture is visible. After that, Photoshop on the iPad will store your shot as a cloud document so you can access it anywhere at any time. You can export your cloud document into a Lightroom-compatible file type, such as a PSD or TIFF, and then import the shot back into Lightroom to see your Photoshop adjustments appear in your Lightroom collection.

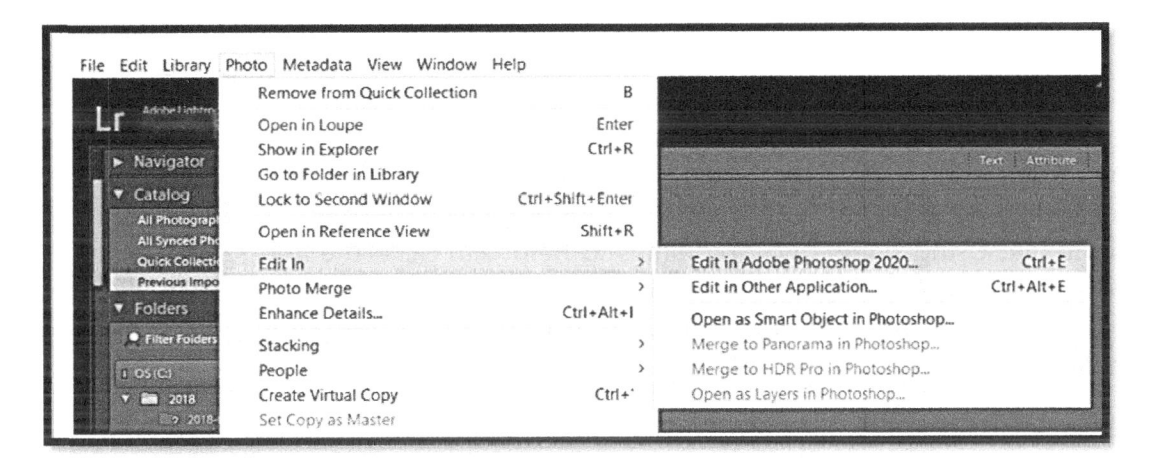

CHAPTER FOUR
ESSENTIAL REQUIREMENTS FOR IMAGE EDITING

The requirements that are essential to edit images in Adobe Photoshop are covered in this chapter. It starts by defining a pixel and how it can be used in image editing. In addition to examining how resolution can impact file size and the things to take into account when selecting the appropriate resolution for printing and screen display, the chapter also addresses image resolution and dimensions. The chapter also delves further into the differences between resizing and resampling photographs, including advice on whether and how to resample a picture to increase its file size or quality. It covers resizing the canvas, file compression, and selecting the right file formats (JPEG, PNG, TIFF, PDF, and Photoshop (PSD) formats) for various uses.

The chapter also discusses the rationale behind various file-saving practices, including saving an image as the original, copying, or saving a duplicate of the image file. Using rulers and guidelines to help with accurate image editing chores is also covered. All things considered, this chapter gives readers the basic skills and information they need to efficiently work with and prepare photographs in Adobe Photoshop for a variety of uses.

THE WORD PIXEL

Pixels, which stand for "**picture element**" in short, are the tiny units that comprise every computer image. A digital image is created from individual pixels, just the way a painting is created from individual brushstrokes. In Photoshop, the pixels are often too tiny to be seen when viewing an image at a regular zoom level (100% or less). Rather, what seems to be a continuous image with merging colors, textures, light and shadows, and other elements produces a scene that closely resembles one that would be seen in the actual world.

The Pixel Grid

As you zoom in close enough, generally over **500%**, you'll see that each pixel has a faint gray border around it. The purpose of Photoshop's Pixel Grid is to make individual pixels easier to see. You can disable the Pixel Grid if you think it's disturbing by selecting Show from the **Menu Bar's View** menu, then Pixel Grid. Simply pick it up once again to turn it back on:

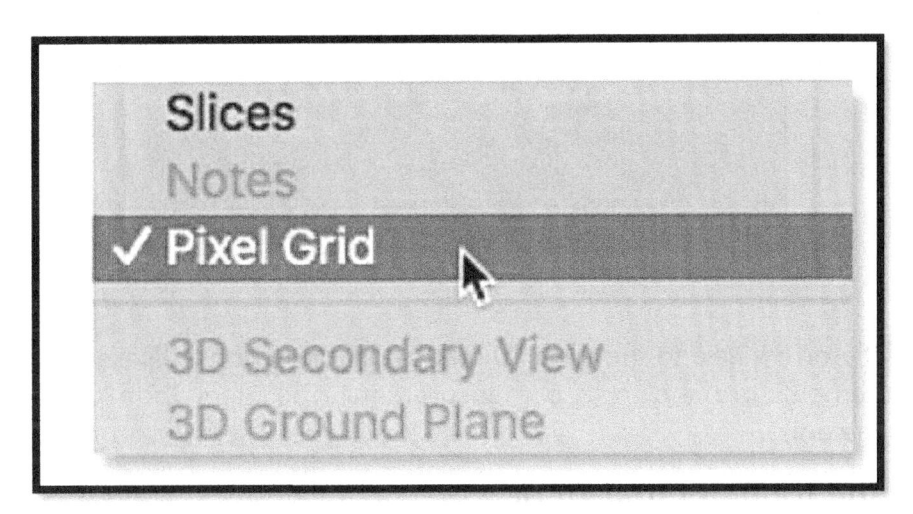

Zooming back out to view the image

Go to the display menu and choose **Fit on Screen** to display the complete image by zooming out from the pixels.

What is image size?

Now that we are aware that pixels are the microscopic color squares that comprise a digital image, let's examine a related subject: image size. The term "**image size**" describes an image's width and height expressed in pixels. Although it also refers to the overall amount of pixels in the image, what matters most is the width and height.

The Image Size dialog box

The Image Size dialog box in Photoshop is the best location to look for information about image size. Navigate to the Image menu and choose Image Size to open it.

The pixel dimensions

Pixel dimensions are the width and height of an image, expressed in pixels. We can see these measurements next to the term Dimensions, which is located toward the top of the dialog box.

The image width of 4509 pixels (px) and height of 3000 pixels are shown here:

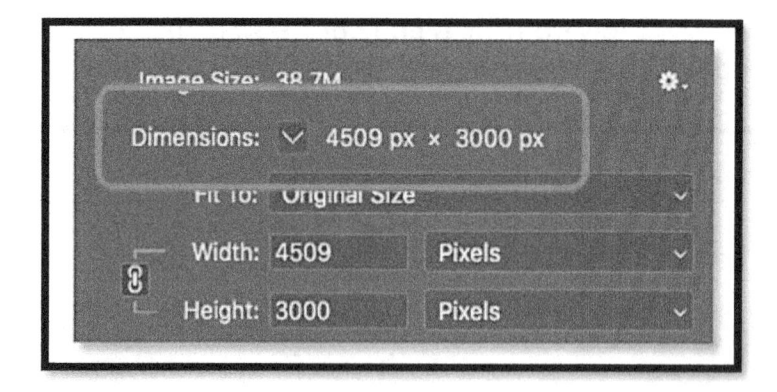

Click the little arrow next to the term "**Dimensions**" and choose **Pixels** from the list if the measurements are shown in a measurement type other than pixels, such as inches or percent.

Finding the total number of pixels

We just need to multiply the width and height numbers together to obtain the total number of pixels in the image. Thus, 4509 x 3000 = 13,527,000, or about 13.5 million pixels, in this instance. It's not necessary to know how many pixels there are in total. As we'll see when we look at image resolution next, however, as you get more adept at scaling photos, you'll discover that knowing the total number of pixels in advance will give you a fair sense of how big you can print the image.

WORKING WITH IMAGE RESOLUTION AND DIMENSION

What is image resolution therefore, given that all digital pictures are made up of small squares of color called pixels, and that an image's dimension is the sum of its pixels from top to bottom (the height) and left to right (the width)? Depending on the current image size, the image resolution determines how big or tiny the photo will print. It's critical to realize that image resolution alone influences the size of the image when printed. When looking at the image on screen, it makes absolutely no difference.

The Width, Height, and Resolution connection

The fields labeled Width, Height, and Resolution are located behind the word "**Dimensions**" in the Image Size dialog box.

Here, we can examine and modify the existing settings in addition to viewing them:

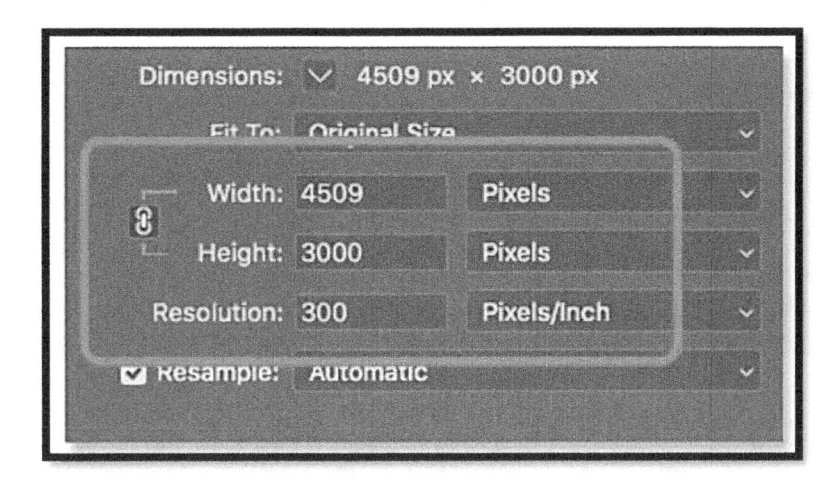

The Resample option

Before we continue, you will notice another important option called **Resample** if you check under the Resolution value. Additionally, Resample is on by default. When we look at how to resize photographs, we will learn all there is to know about the Resample option.

To put it simply, however, Resample enables us to alter the image's pixel count:

What would make you want to alter the pixel count? You can utilize Resample, often known as upsampling, to add extra pixels if the existing image size is insufficient to print your photo at the required size. Alternatively, you might use a tool called Resample, often known as downsampling, to lower the number of pixels in a picture if you want to send it to friends or post it online and the size is now too big. Again, when we look at how to resize images, we'll be learning everything about upsampling and downsampling. For now, uncheck Resample to turn it off and see how resolution impacts the image's print size.

Changing the print size, not the image size

You'll notice that the Width and Height values' measurement type changes as soon as you switch off Resample. I'm seeing the width and height in inches now, instead of pixels.

Furthermore, I'm now being informed that my image is 15.03 inches wide and 10 inches tall rather than 4509 pixels wide and 300 pixels tall:

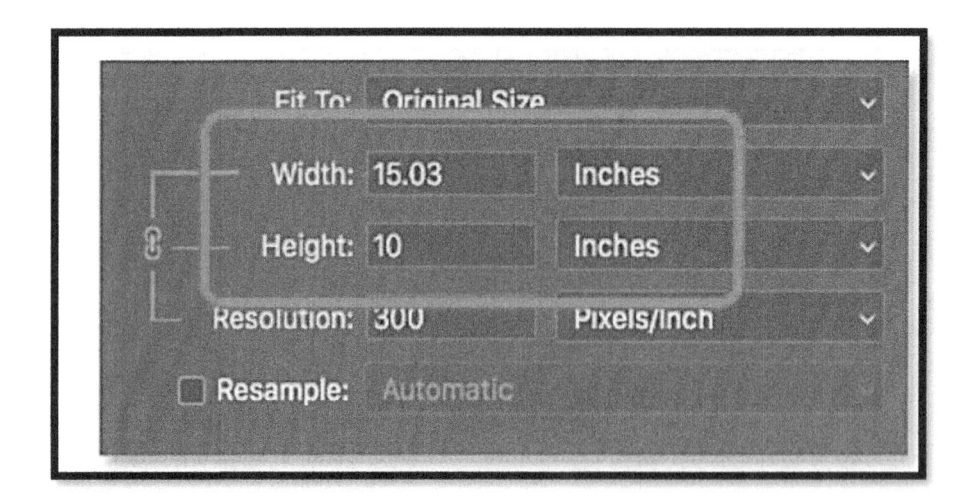

You'll note that Pixels is now grayed out and inaccessible if you click on the measurement type box for either the **Height or the Width**. This is because we are unable to alter the actual amount of pixels in the image when Resample is disabled. Print size is typically measured in inches (or centimeters, depending on where you are in the globe). All we can do is modify the size that the image will print.

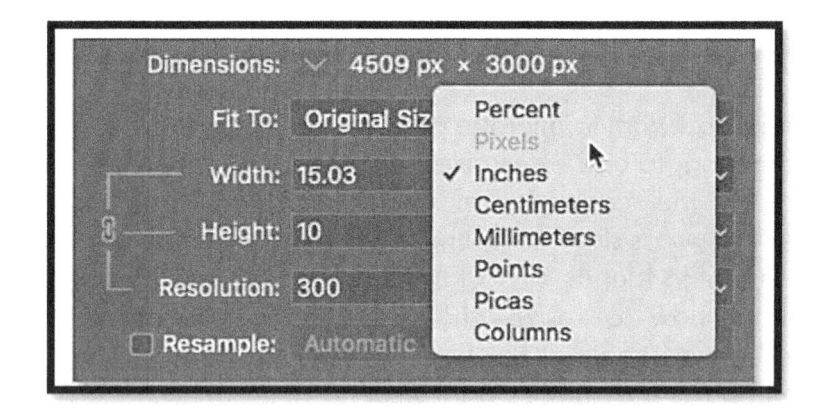

How does image resolution work?

By setting the number of pixels that will be crammed onto each inch of paper, both vertically and horizontally, resolution regulates the print size of an image. Because of this, the resolution value is expressed in terms of pixels per inch, or "**ppi**". The image can only have so many pixels, thus the more we jam them onto the paper, the smaller the image will print. For instance, I presently have my resolution set to 300 pixels per inch. This implies that every square inch of paper will have 300 of the image's pixels from the width and 300 from the height when I print it. 300 pixels may not seem like much these days. But keep in mind that the width and height add up to 300. Put otherwise, each square inch has 90,000 pixels, or 300 times 300.

Changing the resolution changes the print size

The image's pixel count remains constant when the resolution is altered, but the print size changes. It is evident that the pixel dimensions, which are 4509 x 3000 px, do not change when I reduce the resolution from 300 pixels per inch to 150 pixels per inch. However, both the height and the breadth rise. The width and height have increased since I'll only be able to fit half as many pixels per inch—both horizontally and vertically—onto the paper:

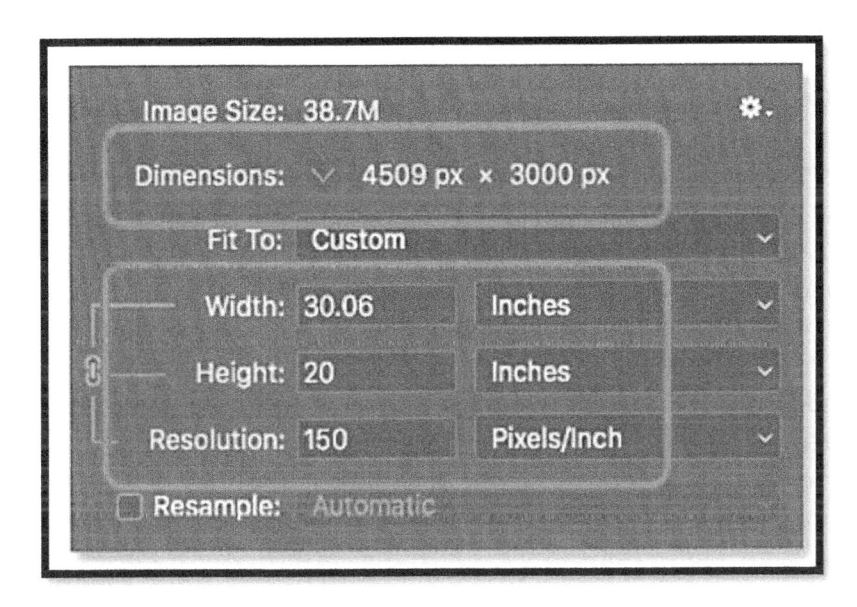

Changing the print size changes the resolution

Furthermore, because we're just altering the print size, adjusting the width or height will also alter the resolution. In actuality, all three variables (**Width**, **Height**, and **Resolution**) are connected when the **Resample** option that we previously examined is off. If you modify one, the others instantly change too. Photoshop automatically adjusts the Height value to 6.653 inches if I decrease the Width value to 10 inches, maintaining the image's aspect ratio.

Additionally, the Resolution number has risen to 450.9 pixels/inch because more pixels will need to be packed in to fit the complete image into the new, smaller print size:

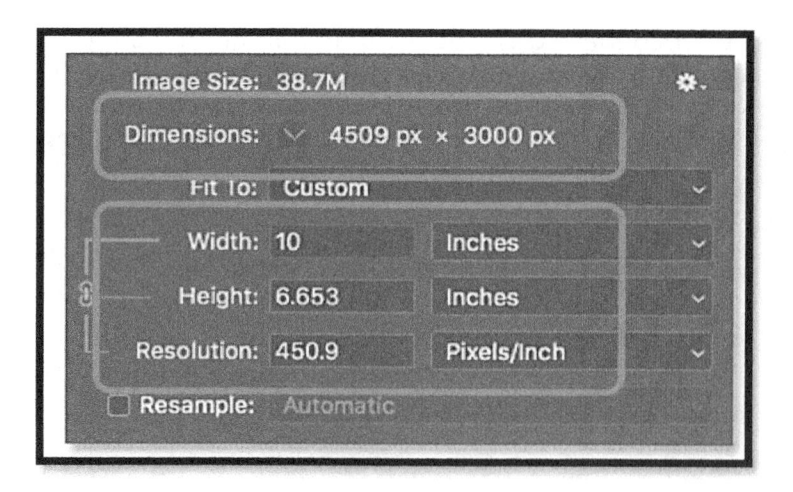

Does image resolution affect file size?

A prevalent misperception about image resolution is that it has some effect on the file size of the image. Many people think that you should reduce the resolution of a picture to reduce its file size before emailing it or posting it online. This is just untrue. The file size is completely unaffected by altering the resolution since it has no influence on the amount of pixels in the image. Looking at the number next to "**Image Size**" at the top of the dialog box, you should be able to see megabytes (**M**). For me, it is **38.7M**. The size of the image in your computer's memory is indicated by this number. A Photoshop image opens from your hard drive is uncompressed from the file format it was stored in, and is then put into RAM so you can work on it faster. The image's real, uncompressed size is shown by the value in the Image Size dialog box.

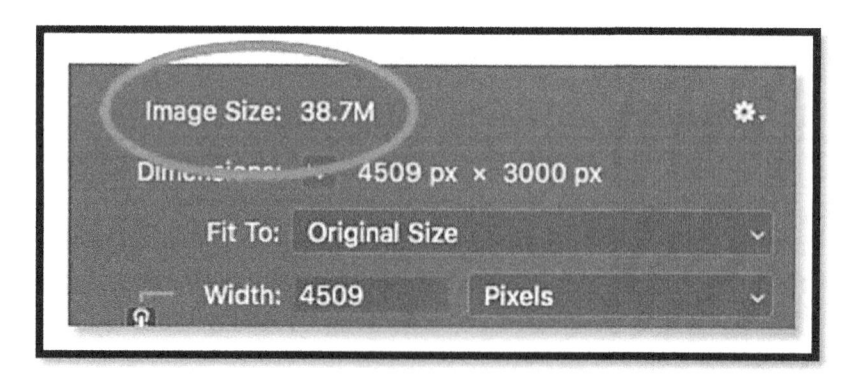

Lower resolution vs. file size

It's simple to demonstrate that the resolution of an image does not affect its size. Just pay attention to the size as you adjust the resolution. Whatever figure you choose for the resolution, the file size at the top will always stay the same as long as the Resample option is off, meaning you're not altering the number of pixels in the image. I've reduced the resolution down to 30 pixels per inch from 300 pixels per inch here. The print size has grown to a massive 150.3 inches by 100 inches since there are so few pixels on one inch of paper. However, despite this very low-resolution setting, the image's 38.7M memory size does not change:

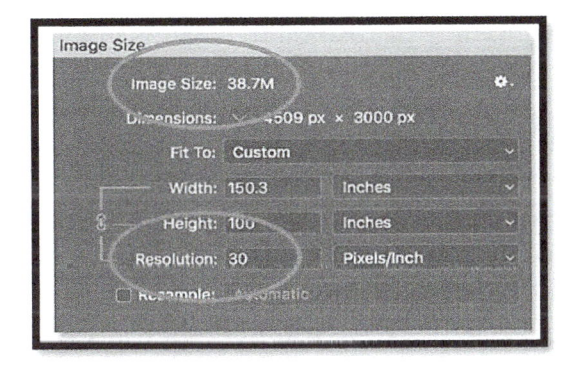

Higher resolution vs. file size

Here, I have fully set the resolution to 3000 pixels per inch. This again has little impact on the file size, which remains at 38.7M, but it does shrink the print size to only 1.503 inches × 1 inch. The only methods to lower an image's file size are to use the Resample option to decrease the image's pixel count, save the picture in a compression-enabled format (like JPEG), or do both. **The file size will not change only by changing the print resolution:**

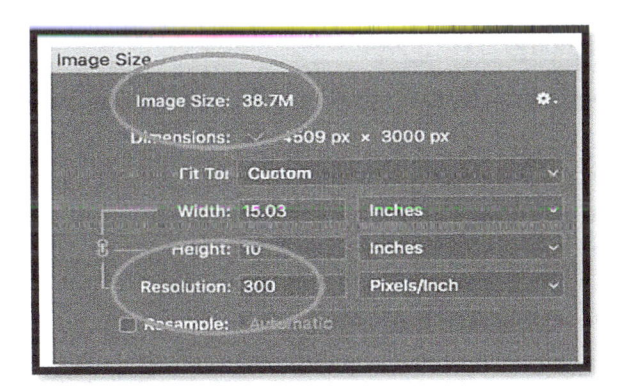

DIFFERENCE BETWEEN RESIZING AND RESAMPLING

Image resizing just modifies the document size—the size at which your image will print—while maintaining the same number of pixels in your image. The Pixel Dimensions, or the total amount of pixels in your image, are physically altered by **image resampling**. Whether you're resizing or resampling an image is controlled by the **Resample Image** option located at the bottom of the **Image Size** dialog box. You are resampling the image if the Resample Image is selected. You're just enlarging the image when it's left unchecked. When optimizing photos for the web, the Pixel Dimensions area of the Image Size dialog box is used to resize the images by altering the width and height settings. For printing, resizing images involves adjusting the width, height, and/or resolution settings in the Document Size section of the Image Size dialog box.

ADJUSTING CANVA SIZE

You can adjust the canvas's size for the first time when you start a new document. Keep in mind that this is not the same as just opening an image; when you do that, a new document with the canvas adjusted to the image size will open and the image will immediately display. Alternatively, you can choose **File > New** to start a new document. Alternatively, you can accomplish this by hitting **Command + N (Mac)** or **Control + N (Win)**.

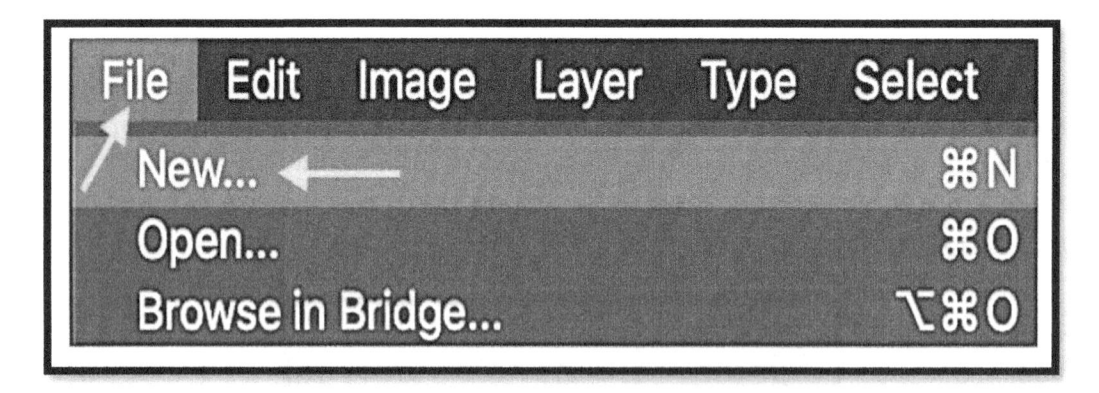

You can modify the size and color profile of the new project you are creating as well as other project-related settings by using the **New Document window** that will open.

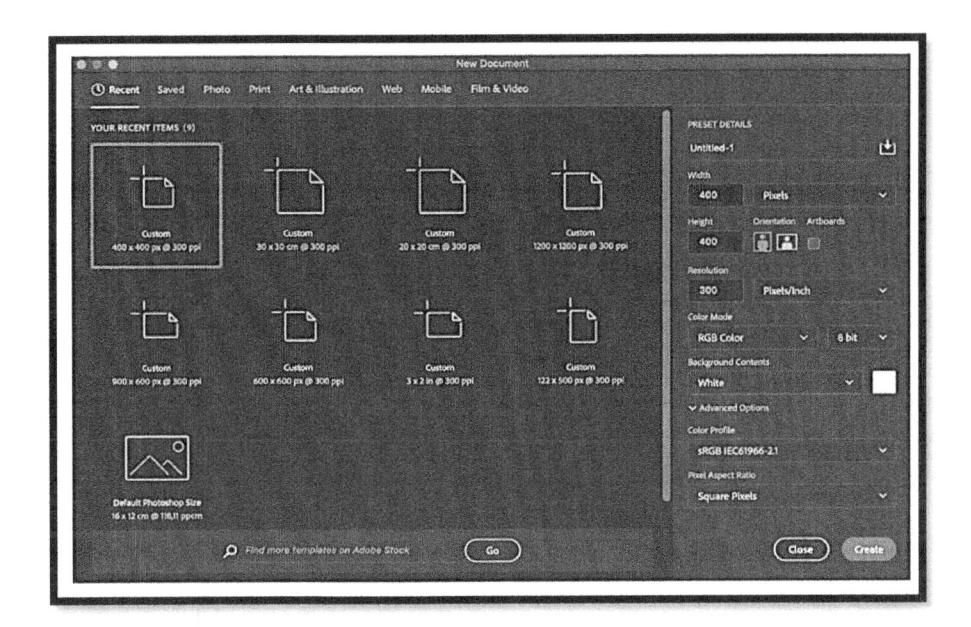

Either choose a predetermined canvas size from the tabs at the top or input your measurements in the section on the right.

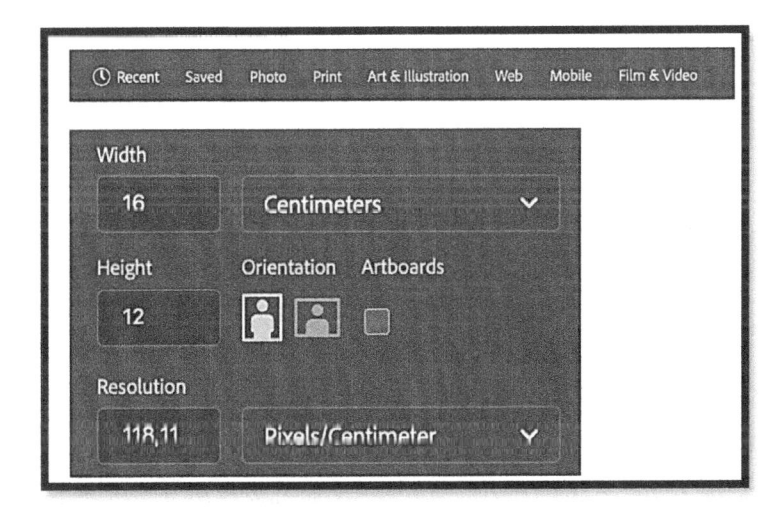

The canvas size will already be determined; it's probably the same as the one you've been using before. I suggest first deciding on the unit of measurement for your canvas to adjust the size. To do this, click the drop-down arrow next to each unit and choose your preferred unit from the list of options. You can enter the number of units you'd like the canvas proportions to fit in the Width and Height boxes after you've selected your preferred unit of measurement.

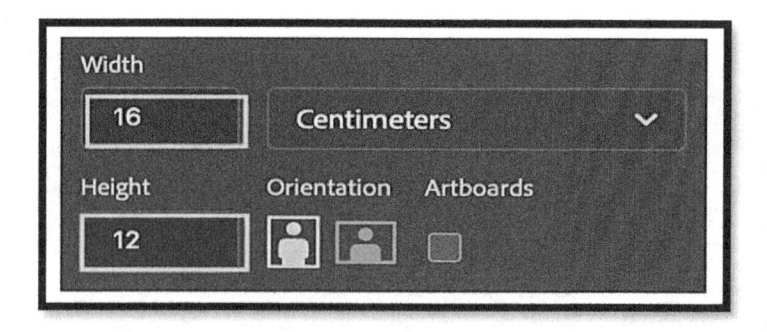

By selecting an option under **Orientation**, you can also specify whether you want your canvas to be oriented vertically or horizontally. When you're done, click **Create**, and your canvas with the specified dimensions will appear.

How to Change an Existing Canvas Size in Photoshop

You will find that while you work on a project, you really would want the canvas to be a different size. Maybe you have too much extraneous space, or you'd prefer additional room to add more components. Fortunately, you can simply resize your canvas as you work. When you adjust the canvas size while working, the image or items on the canvas will stay the same size, but the space on all four sides will vary. An image that fills the canvas will be cropped if the canvas size is reduced.

- Go to **Image > Canvas Size** to adjust the size while you're working. It will show the Canvas Size window.

Here, you can choose the unit of measurement and input a new size under New Size, and you'll see your canvas's existing measurements in the existing Size section. To make sure you're working in the same unit for both, changing the width unit will also alter the height unit and vice versa. Enter the desired value for your **Width and Height** in the fields after choosing the appropriate unit of measurement. You can input relative values in these fields by checking the **Relative** option. For example, if you type 3 next to Width, the size will rise by 3 units of the selected measurement. To reduce the size, use a negative value. The direction in which the new dimensions will be applied is determined by the Anchor settings. All four sides will see the same adjustments if you go with the default center setting. On the other hand, just the top right portion of the canvas will experience the size adjustments if, for instance, you choose the bottom left.

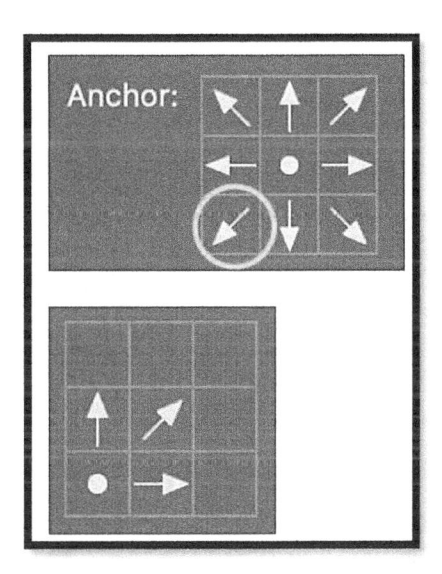

Click **OK** after you're satisfied. Your canvas will adjust to fit the new measurements that you have specified.

How to Change the Canvas Size on Export from Photoshop

Lastly, you can adjust the canvas's size when exporting your project. This is helpful if you want to have additional room around the borders of your image for printing, or if you need to put a border around your image.

- Go to **File** > **Export** > **Export As** when you're prepared to export your project.

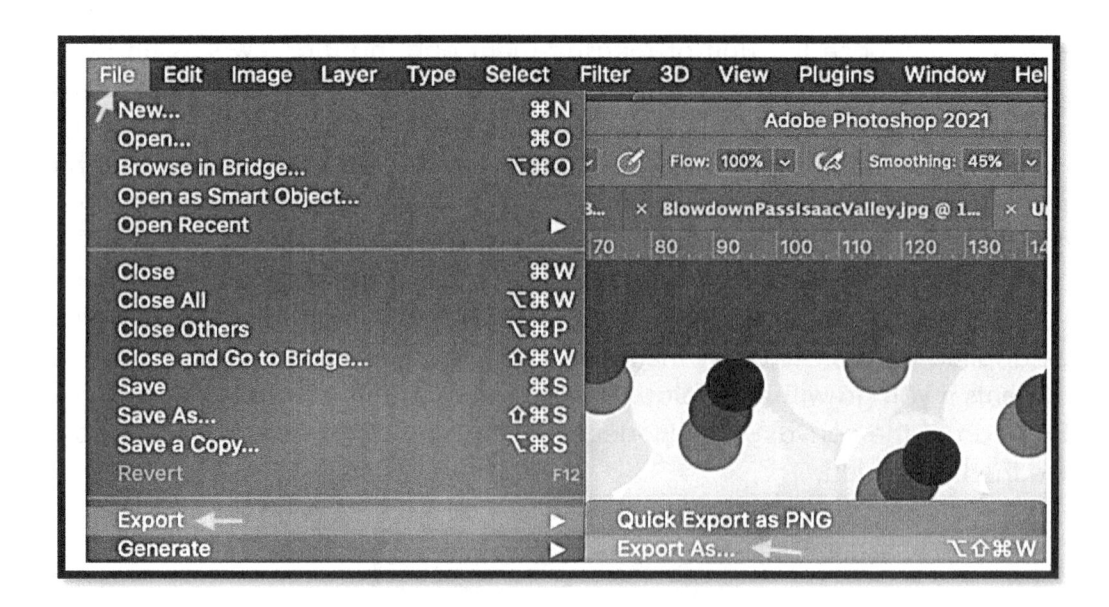

The Export As window will come up.

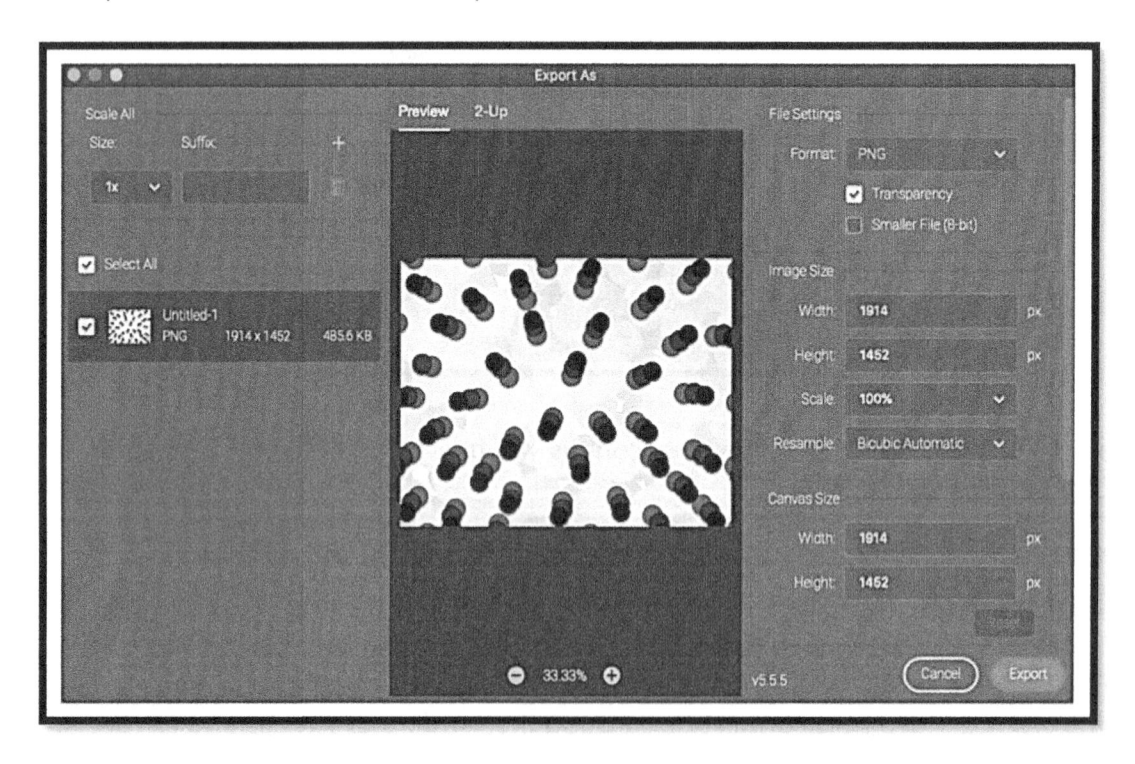

This window is where you can adjust and apply various settings upon the export of your project. Head to the Canvas Size area.

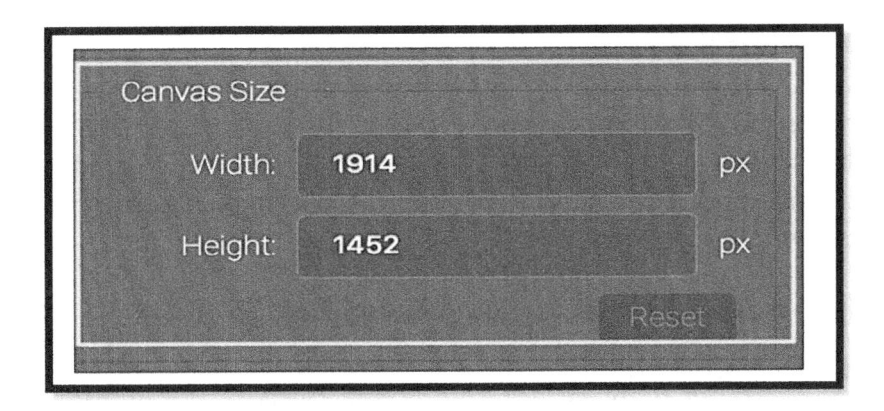

Here, you can change the project's width and height by typing it into the fields. You cannot alter the unit of measurement; it will always be in pixels. Additionally, you will need to input the numbers for **Width and Height**; they will not be connected, so you will need to enter them independently. Nevertheless, you can tell when it seems accurate since the preview will update as you input the data. You'll see that altering these values won't change the size of the image or artwork itself; rather, they will simply alter the canvas around your image or artwork.

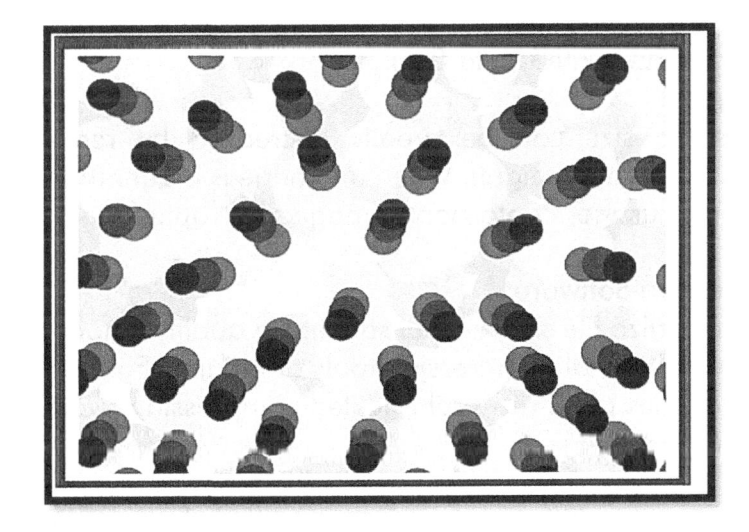

Remember that before exporting for printing, it's ideal to have an idea of the proportions you want to print in and to make sure your PPI (usually about 300 PPI) is high enough to show the project in a high-quality manner. Similarly, if you want to preserve memory, it's ideal to export for the web with a small file size; nevertheless, make sure your PPI is high enough for any particular digital display needs you may have. For digital usage, 72 PPI is usually sufficient.

FILE COMPRESSION

In Adobe Photoshop, "**file compression**" refers to the process of minimizing the size of image files while maintaining some degree of quality. Since smaller files need less storage space and travel faster over the internet, this is particularly helpful for sharing and saving photographs.

Photoshop has many techniques for compressing files:

1. **Saving as a Different Format:**
   - To compress a file in Photoshop, one of the most popular methods is to save it in a separate file format. As an example, you can save an image in a JPEG (Joint Photographic Experts Group) format, which minimizes file size without sacrificing acceptable image quality thanks to lossy compression. The JPEG compression level can be changed to manage the trade-off between file size and quality.
2. **Exporting for Web:**
   - You can explicitly optimize photographs for the web using Photoshop's "**Export As**" or "**Save for Web**" feature. This tool offers a real-time estimate of the final file size and allows you to preview the image at several quality settings and file formats (e.g., JPEG, PNG, and GIF).
3. **Resizing Images:**
   - An image's file size can be greatly decreased by reducing its physical dimensions (width and height). When an image is bigger than what is required for its intended usage, Photoshop's "Image Size" option can be used to resize it.
4. **Using Compression Software:**
   - To further minimize file size without sacrificing quality, Photoshop can be used in concert with external compression tools or plugins. For improved outcomes, these technologies often use sophisticated compression techniques.
5. **Batch Processing:**
   - You can utilize Photoshop's batch-processing features if you need to compress some photographs. This saves time and effort by enabling you to apply compression settings to numerous files at once.
6. **Adjusting Image Quality:**
   - You can regulate the amount of compression done by adjusting the quality setting when storing photographs in formats such as JPEG. While lower-quality settings result in smaller file sizes but may include compression artifacts, higher-quality settings provide bigger file sizes with greater image quality.
7. **Choosing the Right Format:**

- You can help minimize file size by choosing the right file format for your purposes. PNG files, for instance, work well for transparent pictures, whereas JPEG files work better for photos.

8. Using Layer Comps:
- You can utilize Layer Comps to generate alternative layer states and then export or save each comp individually, optimizing them for their intended usage if your Photoshop project has many versions or variants of an image.

It's important to remember that while file compression can greatly decrease file sizes, it may also cause some image quality degradation, particularly when lossy compression techniques are used. To achieve the ideal balance between file size and image quality, compression settings must be carefully chosen with the intended usage and audience in mind.

CHOOSING FILE FORMATS

Whether you're using Adobe Photoshop for print, online publishing, or other purposes, selecting the correct file format is crucial to reaching your unique objectives. Every file format has unique properties, functions, and ideal applications. Here's a detailed tutorial on using Photoshop to choose file formats:

JPEG (JOINT PHOTOGRAPHER EXPERTS GROUP)

When it comes to digital photography and graphics, one of the most popular and well-known image file formats is JPEG, which stands for Joint Photographic Experts Group. Photoshop users should be familiar with JPEG since it is the preferred format for a large number of print and web applications. This is a comprehensive Photoshop tutorial on JPEG:

JPEG Basics

1. **Compression Method:**
   - JPEG employs a lossy compression technique, which means that to minimize file size, some image quality is lost. The algorithm removes color information and features during compression that the human eye is unlikely to detect.

2. **Color Space:**
   - Color and grayscale photos are supported using JPEG. It mostly uses the RGB (Red, Green, Blue) color space, which is the industry standard for digital photographs, for color photos.

3. **Quality Levels:**
   - In Photoshop, you can adjust the compression level or quality when saving an image as a JPEG. Lower-quality settings boost compression, which reduces file size but may compromise image quality, whereas higher-quality settings preserve more image information but produce bigger file sizes.

Best Applications

1. **Web Graphics:**
   - For online graphics, such as photos and pictures for websites and social media, JPEG is the recommended format. Its excellent quality-to-size ratio makes it perfect for online viewing, and its modest file sizes speed up the loading of web pages.
2. **Pictures:**
   - JPEG is the common format used for digital photos taken with cameras and mobile devices. It is useful for saving and sharing images as it finds a balance between file size and image quality.
3. **Print Graphics:**
   - JPEG is not the best format for high-quality print work, but it can be utilized for certain print projects (like flyers and posters) if the quality setting is changed to account for file size.

JPEG Compression Settings

1. **Quality Slider:**
   - You can modify the quality slider in Photoshop when saving an image as a JPEG. Larger file sizes are associated with higher quality settings (e.g., 80% to 100%), which provide greater image quality. worse settings (such as 60% or less) result in smaller files but worse image quality.
2. **Progressive VS Baseline:**
   - Baseline and Progressive are the two encoding techniques that JPEG provides. While Progressive JPEG loads in many passes, presenting a low-resolution version initially and progressively enhancing it, Baseline JPEG loads from top to bottom. Progressive JPEG provides a more aesthetically pleasing loading experience, making it ideal for online usage.

3. **Subsampling:**
   - JPEG further reduces file size by using chroma subsampling. Compared to 4:2:0 subsampling, color information is lost in 4:2:2 subsampling but is retained at a higher quality level. Choose 4:4:4 subsampling for important image quality, even if it produces bigger files.

Image Artifacts

1. Compression Artifacts:
- Notable artifacts can be introduced by JPEG compression, particularly when quality settings are lowered. Blocky patterns, color bleeding, and a loss of fine detail are typical artifacts. Intense compression can make these aberrations more noticeable.

JPEG Optimization in Photoshop

1. Save for Web:
- Photoshop has a function called "**Save for Web**" that helps JPEG photos become optimized for the web. This lets you adjust settings, see the projected file size, and preview the image at various quality levels.
2. **Delete Metadata**:
- If you want to further minimize file size and safeguard privacy, you might think about deleting extra information (EXIF data) from JPEG photographs before storing them online.

PNG (PORTABLE NETWORK GRAPHICS)

PNG, which stands for Portable Network Graphics, is a raster image format that was developed as an open standard to replace the older and less versatile GIF format. It was first introduced in 1996 and has since become one of the most popular image formats on the web.

Key Features of PNG

1. **Lossless Compression**: The PNG compression technique does not lose any image data in the process of compressing an image. This makes it perfect for pictures like graphics, logos, and photos when maintaining quality is crucial.
2. **Transparency**: Images with soft edges, partial transparency, and anti-aliased edges are all possible with PNG's capability for alpha **transparency**. For web designers and graphic artists who have to produce graphics with asymmetrical proportions or gentle transitions, this function is very crucial.
3. **Support for a Wide Range of Color Depths**: PNG can handle pictures with a color depth of 48 bits true color or as basic as 8 bits grayscale. Because of its adaptability, it works well with a wide range of images and photos.
4. **Metadata**: PNG files enable the storing of textual data, sometimes referred to as metadata. This can include the image's written description as well as creator and copyright information.

5. **Interlacing**: PNG allows for **interlacing**, which allows the image to load gradually and show a lower-resolution version of the image before the complete image loads. This can enhance the online image viewing experience for users.

Benefits of PNG

- **High Quality**: PNG is the recommended format for high-quality photos because of its lossless compression, which guarantees that image quality is maintained.
- **Transparency**: Image production with changeable transparency is made possible by the alpha channel support, which is essential for digital art and web design.
- **Broad Compatibility**: PNG files can be used for some things since they are extensively supported by image editing programs, web browsers, and other apps.
- **Textual Information**: For credit and documentation, it is helpful to have the option to incorporate textual information directly into the image file.
- **Compression Efficiency**: PNG files have far higher compression efficiency than other lossless formats like BMP, although often bigger than JPEGs, a popular lossy format.

Working with PNG in Photoshop

1. **Making PNGs:** Photoshop lets you convert existing pictures to PNG format or start from zero when creating new PNG files. In Photoshop, you can choose PNG as the file format when you save an image.
2. **Editing Transparency**: Working with PNG pictures is a great fit for Photoshop's layer-based editing system. To produce intricate image compositions and regulate transparency, you can create and modify layers.
3. **Transparency Masks**: Photoshop provides tools for the creation and refinement of transparency masks, which let you carefully, control the transparency of various areas of an image.
4. **Export Options**: You can adjust the PNG settings, including the compression ratio, interlacing, and metadata inclusion when you export an image from Photoshop.
5. **Batch Processing**: Working with big collections of PNG pictures is made efficient by Photoshop's capabilities for batch processing.
6. **Plugins and Filters**: PNG pictures can be creatively enhanced and modified using Photoshop's vast collection of plugins and filters.

7. **Text & Typography**: Photoshop is useful for designing graphics with textual components since you can add and edit text on PNG images.

TIFF (TAGGED IMAGE FILE FORMAT)

One popular file format used in Adobe Photoshop and other image editing programs is **Tagged Image File Format (TIFF)**. Professionals in the area of digital photography, such as photographers and graphic designers, really appreciate the many beneficial features and capabilities it provides.

Now let's explore TIFF's function in Adobe Photoshop:

1. **High-Quality Image Storage**
   - TIFF is well known for its superb image storage capabilities. Because it uses lossless compression, no image data is lost in the process of being stored. Because of this characteristic, TIFF is the recommended format for storing high-resolution Photoshop digital artwork and images.
2. **Color Depth Flexibility:**
   - Using Adobe Photoshop and TIFF together, users may deal with pictures in 8-bit, 16-bit, and 32-bit color depths per channel. Because of its versatility, it's the perfect option for expert image alteration, allowing for accurate color correction and editing.
3. **Transparency and Layers:**
   - Layers and transparency, two essential components of Photoshop's sophisticated image editing features, are supported by TIFF. is made possible via layers, which let users work on different parts of an image independently before seamlessly combining them.
4. **Compatibility:**
   - Adobe Photoshop TIFF files are very compatible with other programs, so you can share and utilize your modified photographs in a variety of settings. TIFF guarantees cross-application compatibility whether you're working with other designers or need to utilize your photos in multiple projects.
5. **Lossless Editing Workflow:**
   - In Photoshop, you can use a lossless editing method while dealing with TIFF files. Thus, you can save any edits you make to the image without worrying about the quality being lost. For experts who must preserve the greatest degree of image authenticity throughout the editing process, this is essential.
6. **Versatile Usage:**

- Photoshop-created TIFF files can be used for online graphics as well as high-quality print manufacturing. TIFF's versatility in terms of resolution and color depth guarantees that your final output will fit your exact needs, whether you're generating an image for a massive billboard or a website banner.

7. Professional Printing:
- The TIFF integration in Adobe Photoshop is very useful for professional printing. Because TIFF files can hold high-quality, CMYK color-separated images—which are necessary for precise and colorful printed materials—many print shops and publishing firms choose them.

8. Archival and Preservation:
- When preserving digital photos, TIFF is the recommended format, particularly for photographs of artistic or historical importance. You can use Adobe Photoshop to produce TIFF files that are suited for long-term archival storage since they capture every aspect of your work.

PDF (PORTABLE DOCUMENT FORMAT)

The widely used and adaptable Portable Document Format (PDF) has revolutionized the creation, sharing, and viewing of digital documents. Because of its special characteristics and capabilities, PDFs have become an essential component of many sectors, including commerce, education, publishing, and government.

Let's examine PDF in more depth:

1. Universal Compatibility:
- Because PDFs are platform-independent by nature, they can be read and viewed without the need for special software on almost any device or operating system. Because of its widespread compatibility, PDF is now the preferred format for exchanging and distributing documents.

2. Fixed Layout:
- A document's layout, formatting, fonts, and visuals are all preserved in PDFs precisely as intended by the author. The uniform presentation of the article on various devices and screen sizes is guaranteed by this set arrangement.

3. Text and Image Integration:
- Multimedia components like movies and hyperlinks, as well as text, photos, and vector graphics, can all be effortlessly integrated into PDFs. They may thus be used for a variety of content types, ranging from simple text documents to intricate presentations and interactive forms.

4. Security Features:
- Digital signatures, encryption, and password protection are just a few of the strong security features that PDFs provide. Because of these characteristics,

users can manage who has access to, can change, or can print their documents—making PDFs appropriate for sensitive and private data.

5. **Interactive Elements:**
   - Interactive components like buttons, bookmarks, hyperlinks, and forms are supported in PDFs. The generation of interesting and user-friendly papers, interactive forms, and multimedia-rich presentations is made possible by this interaction.

6. **Compact File Size:**
   - PDFs can be adjusted to have reduced file sizes, which makes them appropriate for email attachments and online distribution. Because of this compression, the document's quality is not affected, making PDFs a useful tool for document sharing without compromising on quality.

7. **Accessibility Features:**
   - PDFs can be produced with accessibility in mind, guaranteeing that people with impairments can read them. Text-to-speech capability, image alt text, and a logical reading sequence are just a few of the features that make PDFs inclusive and accessible.

8. **Print-Ready Format:**
   - The printing industry uses PDFs extensively because they can hold color profiles, high-resolution photographs, and other print-specific settings. Because they guarantee that printed documents exactly resemble their digital versions, PDFs are necessary for publishing and printing professionally.

9. **Archival and Long-Term Preservation:**
   - A modified variant of the PDF format called PDF/A is intended for the long-term preservation of documents. It is appropriate for digital archives and libraries since it has characteristics that guarantee that materials that have been preserved can be accessed and displayed correctly for many years.

10. **Editing and Conversion:**
    - Although the main purpose of PDFs is to be seen and shared, they can also be altered and converted to other forms with the help of specialist software. When required, users may alter the content of PDF files using Adobe Acrobat and other third-party applications.

PHOTOSHOP (PSD)

Adobe Systems created the Photoshop (PSD) file format, a proprietary file format, for use with Adobe Photoshop, its main image editing program. It is generally acknowledged as one of the most complete and adaptable image file formats out now, especially for professional digital artists, photographers, and graphic designers. The ability to handle numerous layers, channels, and masks makes the

PSD file format distinctive and enables intricate image compositions as well as non-destructive editing.

I'll go into detail about the characteristics, benefits, and typical applications of the PSD file type here.

- **Layer Support**: Support for layers is one of the key characteristics of PSD files. Layers are discrete components that can be individually altered, changed, and arranged inside an image. Examples of these components include text, shapes, and pictures. The layer-based method offers a great deal of versatility in the creation and modification of intricate compositions. Intricate designs are possible since each layer can have its blending modes, opacity settings, and layer effects.
- **Alpha Channels and Transparency**: PSD files also include alpha channels and transparency. This implies that portions of an image can be fully translucent; enabling a smooth transition into other images or backgrounds. Further transparency data can be stored in alpha channels, giving artists more exact control over image masking and compositing.
- **Smart Objects**: A potent Photoshop tool that lets you incorporate one or more layers as a single, non-destructive object inside a PSD file is Smart Objects. When dealing with intricate patterns or wanting to make alterations without sacrificing image quality, this tool comes in handy.
- **Editable Text and Vector Graphics**: PSD files allow for editable text and vector graphics, which makes them ideal for designing scalable designs without sacrificing quality. Even after adding text and vector shapes to a PSD file, you can change them.
- **High-Resolution photographs**: PSD files created in Photoshop are renowned for the ease with which high-resolution photographs can be handled without noticeably sacrificing image quality. They may thus be used for print design and professional photography.
- **Layer Comps**: In a single PSD file, Layer Comps lets you store and switch between various layer visibility and placement settings. This is useful for producing many mockups or design variants in a single document.

Common Use Cases

- **Graphic Design**: The preferred format for graphic designers is PSD files. Web graphics, logos, posters, brochures, and other visual items are made using them.
- **Image Editing**: Photoshop PSD files are used by photographers to enhance and edit photos. Layer-based editing offers fine-grained control over modifications.

- **Digital Art**: To produce intricate, multi-layered artwork, digital artists use PSD files. PSD is perfect for digital painting and drawing since it allows you to work with brushes, textures, and other effects.
- **Web design**: PSD files, which can be translated into HTML/CSS code, are often used by web designers to develop website layouts and templates.
- **Print Design**: PSD files are often used for print design tasks, such as creating magazines, flyers, and business cards. Print materials will seem crisp and colorful thanks to the high resolution.

DIFFERENT MOTIVES FOR SAVING FILES DIFFERENTLY

SAVING THE IMAGE AS THE ORIGINAL

- Choose **Save, Save As, or Save a Copy** from the File menu.
- When choosing a save command, you can decide to save to Creative Cloud or save to your PC.
- If you choose **Save As**, click **Save** after selecting a format from the Format menu, providing a filename and location.

SAVING IMAGE TO DUPLICATE THE IMAGE FILE

- Start by opening the image you want to copy.
- Choose **Duplicate** from the Image option at the top.
- You can click OK to name your copied image in the dialog box that displays.
- The copied image will show up in a new project tab, and you can use Photoshop's top bar to navigate between the new and original projects.
- Don't forget to often save your work to prevent losing any modifications. By selecting File > Save or File > Save As, you can do this.

If you want to duplicate a layer within the same image:

- Select the layer you want to duplicate.
- From the top menu, select **Layer > Duplicate Layers > OK**.
- Alternatively, you can use the keyboard shortcut **Command+J (Mac)** or **Ctrl+J (Windows)**.

SAVE A COPY

- Go to the **File** menu at the top of the screen.
- Select **Save a Copy**.

- In the dialog box that appears, choose a format from the Format menu, and specify a filename and location.
- Click **Save**.
- Please note that if you're having trouble saving files in certain formats like JPG, make sure you have "**Enable legacy "Save As"**" checked in **Preferences** under the File Handling tab. If you're still having issues, you might want to try resetting your preferences or reinstalling Photoshop

WORKING WITH THE RULERS AND GUIDES

You can quickly and simply enhance the compositions of your works by making use of the grids, guides, and rulers that are available in Photoshop. You can go to **Menu > View > Rulers** in Photoshop to display rulers in your document, or you can simply use the keyboard shortcut **CMD+R (Mac) or CTRL+R (Windows)** instead. They do not appear while printing or exporting a document, which is a convenient benefit when it comes to presenting printed files and exported files on screen.

They also enable you to align visual elements and put components at regular intervals. At some point in the course of every designer's creative process, the use of rulers and grids is almost certain to become an indispensable tool, regardless of whether they are being put to use to concentrate a single component or to align hundreds of items inside a piece.

How to Display Rulers in Photoshop

Setting up Photoshop such that it displays rulers that we can use to position our guides will take place with a document or image open. To use this feature, go to the **View menu** and choose **Rulers (control + R on Windows; command + R on Mac)**.

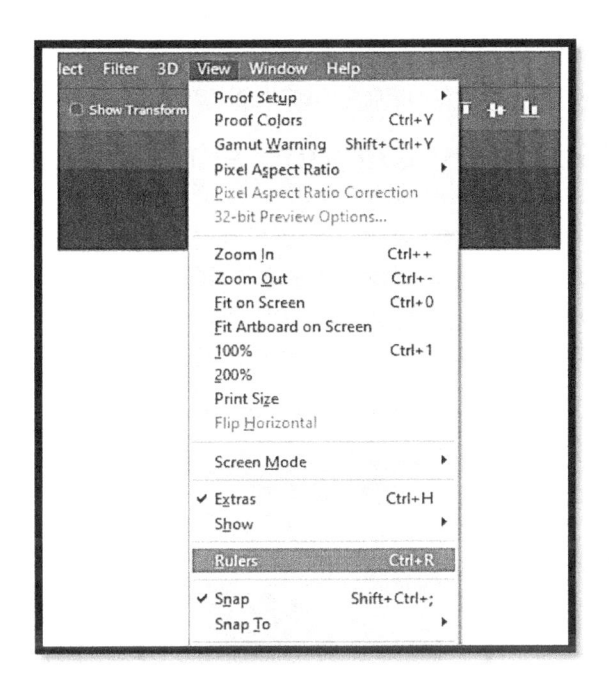

How to Change Unit / Increment of Your Rulers

Right-clicking on either the horizontal or vertical ruler will bring up a dropdown menu from which you can choose the desired unit of measurement. Doing so will alter the current unit of measurement.

You can also alter the unit of your Rulers by going into your **Preferences** and selecting the appropriate option. You can make your selection by going to **Menu > Edit > Preferences > Units & Rulers** and using the drop-down menu there.

How to Add a Guide Lines in Photoshop

After you have the rulers set up, you can go on to the next step, which is to add a new guide. To do this, click and drag from either of the rulers (the one on top to create a horizontal guide, or the one on the side to create a vertical guide). When you click and drag your mouse in a certain direction across the screen, the pointer will change into a double arrow. You just need to let go of the mouse button to position the guidance exactly where you want it. When you are attempting to align text, for example, to have the borders of each line be in the same location, adding guides can be quite helpful. Guides can also be used to help align images. For instance, we have displayed how you would wish to bring in guides at the vertical line at which you would want each line of text to finish in the image that can be seen below. You can find this demonstration.

You can resize elements or move them closer to the appropriate guides by referring to them, and doing so will guarantee that all of the objects are aligned properly.

Reposition a Guide by Clicking and Dragging

If you make the decision that you want to relocate a guide to a different place, then we can reposition it by making use of the relocate Tool, which is symbolized by the icon that is located below. After that, all you have to do is click on the guide you wish to relocate and then drag it to the new location.

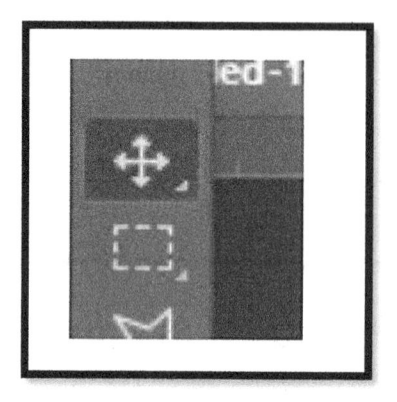

How to Lock Your Guides in Photoshop

When you're working on a document that has guides on it, it can be unpleasant when you keep mistakenly shifting the guides out of position instead of the pieces of the piece that you're attempting to move. You can fix this problem by going to **View** and selecting **Lock Guides**. This will prevent you from mistakenly moving the guides while you are working on other parts of your document.

How to Delete a Guide in Photoshop

If you wish to get rid of a single guide, you can do it by clicking on the guide, dragging it with your mouse, and then letting go of it when it is positioned above one of the rulers. To get rid of all of the guides that are now present in your document, pick **View > Clear Guides** from the menu bar. This will clean up your workstation and give you the option of either starting over with new guides or working without them altogether.

Snap Objects onto Guides or Grids

You can make the guides or grids in your document work like magnets by turning on Snapping. This will enable items to, in effect, be attracted to the guides. This will help you to get the most out of the guides and use them to their full potential. To do this, choose View > Snap from the menu that runs along the very top of the screen. Pick **View > Snap To** if you want to pick explicitly what your objects snap to, and then choose the required items from the dropdown menu that appears after you make that selection.

How to Create a Grid in Photoshop

In addition to serving as guides, grids are a very helpful method for aligning the many visual components that go into making up a composition. They are often used by designers, particularly because they make it possible to apply the rule of thirds to a composition. You can see, for instance, how a grid can be helpful when reviewing the composition of images, both landscapes and portraits, by looking at the example that is provided below.

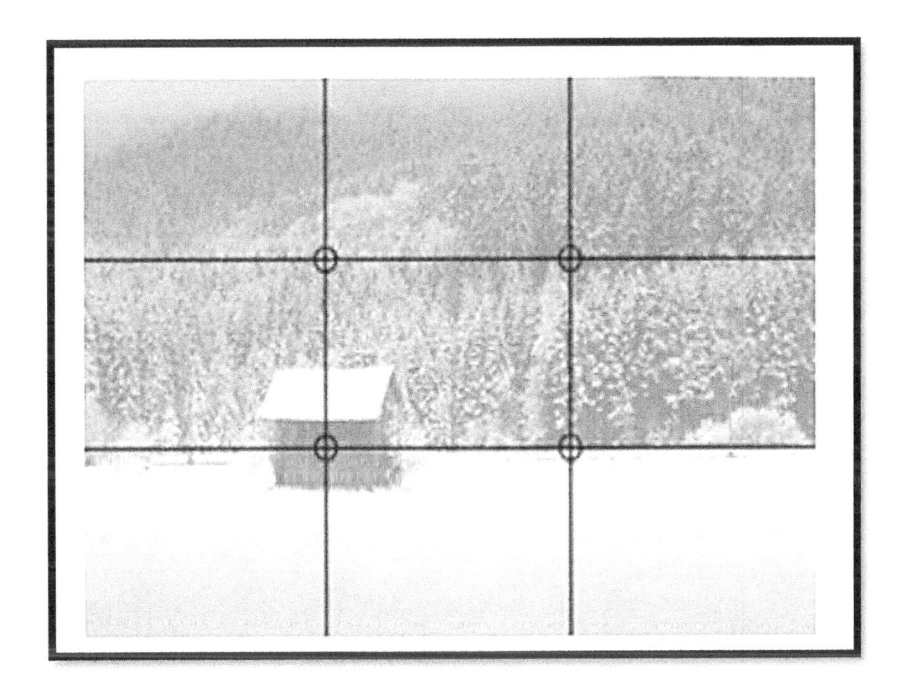

Go ahead and pick **View > Show > Grid (Ctrl +'[Win] / Cmd +'[Mac])** from the menu bar that runs along the top of the screen in Photoshop. This will allow you to build a grid in the program.

How to Change Your Grid Layout

If you choose this, a grid with an inch between each line and four subdivisions will be added to your working area automatically. If you deselect this, the grid will be removed. In the Preferences Window, we can alter the appearance of our grid.

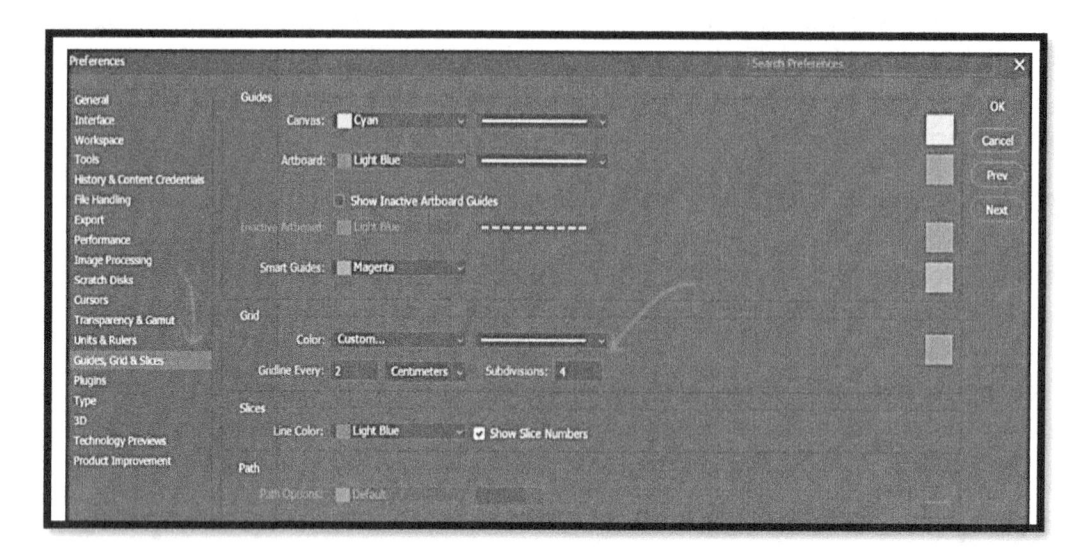

Now that the window is open, you can adjust the attributes of your grid depending on how you wish to organize the area you have available to work in. If at any time you decide that you would rather not see the grid, you can temporarily deactivate it by selecting **View > Show > Grid** again.

Change Photoshop Ruler to Inches

One problem that a large number of users come into often is that the default setting of the ruler units is to utilize pixels. For people who are more comfortable working in inches, the need to frequently translate measures between the metric and imperial systems can be an annoyance. Changing the ruler units in Photoshop from pixels to inches is a straightforward technique that, if followed, can help users save time and avoid unnecessary difficulties.

Step 1: Accessing Preferences

The Preferences dialog box has to be opened before we can modify the ruler units that are used in Photoshop. While you are on the main interface, simply pressing "Ctrl + K" on your keyboard (or "Command + K" on a Mac) is one of the simplest ways to accomplish this task. There are other ways to accomplish this task as well.

You can also select "Edit" from the top menu bar, then "**Preferences**," and then "**Units & Rulers**" from the menu.

Step 2: Selecting Units & Rulers

There will be tabs at the top of the Preferences dialog box, each one indicating a different category of settings that can be adjusted. Find the option labeled "Units & Rulers" and then pick it.

Step 3: Choosing Inches

After you have navigated to the **Units & Rulers** options category panel, look for the "**Rulers**" section. There, you will find a drop-down menu that allows you to select the unit of measurement that you want your rulers to be displayed in. In this particular scenario, we will select inches as the preferred unit of measurement for our rulers. Is it that easy? Now, every other figure that was specified would be displayed in inches, and this includes the grids as well.

Tip: For those who regularly work with specific measurements other than inches, such as millimeters or points, Photoshop also provides options for working with those units of measurement. Simply repeat Step 3, but this time **select 'mm'** from the unit drop-down list rather than '**in**'.

Step 4: Select the OK button

After making the necessary adjustments to the ruler options in Photoshop by selecting the appropriate measurement system, such as "inches," you are virtually finished. Just scroll down to the bottom of this category panel and click the "**OK**" button.

Common FAQs about Changing Photoshop Ruler to Inches

There is a good probability that you are familiar with Adobe Photoshop, whether you are a designer, a graphic artist, or simply an average person who enjoys playing around with different photos. It is common knowledge that this piece of software has been very influential in the creative industries and has served as the instrument of choice for a great deal of work that is image-related.

One of the challenges that often arise for customers is the have to adjust or configure their rulers in inches, which can be fairly challenging, particularly if this is your first time carrying out the task.

Q: How do I change my Photoshop ruler from pixels to inches?

To begin, launch Photoshop and choose the file you want to edit. When you click on "**Image**" in the top menu bar and then pick "**Image size**," a window will emerge in front of you that display the dimensions of the document as well as its resolution. This can be done regardless of whether your measurement units are currently set up as pixels or inches. You can pick between other units such as pixels, inches, millimeters, centimeters, etc., under the "**Units**" section, which is located under the "**Document Size**" heading in the "**Preferences**" menu. Select **Inches**, and then click the **OK** button.

Q: Why would I need to change my ruler unit from pixels to inches?

Changing the unit of measurement on your ruler to inches will help you get a better idea of how big or tiny the final printed version of your document will be. Since the majority of printers utilize standard dimensions based on inches (such as 8 by 10 prints), this also helps enhance accuracy when working with high-quality print materials. In addition, if you plan on digitally sharing your images with people who are not familiar with pixels, it makes more sense to display measurements using units that are more familiar to them. This is because people are more likely to understand the meaning of the displayed measurements.

Q: What is DPI and how does it relate to changing rulers into inches?

Dots per Inch (abbreviated as DPI) is a measurement used to describe the quantity of information that can be produced by a printer. Changing rulers from millimeters to inches may at times necessitate changing image resolution to optimize it for printing at various DPI settings. For instance, if you want to print a high-quality photo that includes minute details, you will need to adjust the resolution so that there is sufficient data per inch of printable space (more dots equals a higher DPI). This can be done by clicking the "**Settings**" button in the "**Print**" menu. This indicates that you should take into consideration the image resolution before switching the units of measurement on your ruler from pixels to inches.

Q: What am I doing wrong? I've tried switching the unit of measurement on my ruler to inches, but it hasn't worked out so far.

If you are using an older version of Photoshop, check to see that you have the most recent release installed because it is possible that it will not behave correctly. In addition, make sure that the settings are correct and that you have chosen the appropriate options, such as selecting "Inches" rather than "Pixels" or any other option in the measurement section under the "Units" heading. You can also try restarting Photoshop or even your entire computer before attempting again just to make sure that everything is refreshed.

Pros and Cons of Using the Inch Measurement System in Photoshop

One of the most important talents that you need to learn if you want to work as a graphic designer is the ability to grasp the many measuring systems that are used in design software such as Photoshop. Although many measuring systems are in use in different parts of the globe, the inch and the pixel are two of the most popular ones.

Pros

1. Inches are a unit of measure that is internationally recognized and can be readily comprehended by everyone. Inches are a common unit of measurement, so it's likely that even if you're not used to working with digital equipment or software, you still have at least a basic understanding of how it's done.
2. Scaling and Proportions: When it comes to print production, using inches as the unit of measurement enables more precise and proportionate scaling, since it is standard practice for printing services to demand that measurements be presented in inches.
3. When it comes to print design, inches give precise measures, which is ideal since many printers work with sheets that are 8.5 by 11 inches (or A4 size), which are standard paper sizes that ensure uniformity throughout printed papers.

Cons

1. If your project requires non-standard measurements that fall outside of the typical U.S. paper sizing system, such as tabloid/ledger-size papers or

international posters and banners, then the inch system becomes less ideal. This causes numerous conversion steps between metric and imperial units, which could be time-consuming. Converting between metric and imperial units can be difficult.
2. The difficulty with using fixed dimensions such as inches is that they often lead to stiff compositions rather than flexible ones. This makes revision procedures more labor and time-intensive when they are required.
3. Because online displays show pictures using pixels rather than using physical measures, this results in a mismatch when compared to print productions, which in turn creates an inconsistent design when moving offline or print assets into online media channels.
4. Using further higher numeric values leads to superior level accuracy when working on items such as digital graphics where nuances matter much; yet, it restricts itself when only able to note by fractions, when occasionally genuinely requiring decimal notation instead. This lack of precision is a problem when working on objects where subtleties matter considerably.

Before you switch the ruler in Photoshop to inches, these are the top five things you need to know.

You must be acquainted with the issues that come with utilizing Photoshop rulers because of your profession as a graphic designer. It is essential to modify the parameters of the ruler so that they correspond to the specifications of the project you are working on. This will allow you to create detailed and accurate drawings. Before you go ahead and adjust the ruler settings from pixels to inches, there are a few things you need to make sure you take into consideration first. Before you go and change the ruler in Photoshop to inches, here are the top five things you need to know first.

1. The Difference between Pixels and Inches

When converting from pixels to inches, the first thing you need to be aware of is the difference in scale between the two units of measurement. Points on a computer screen are referred to as pixels, but inches are units of measurement for actual space. Therefore, whether developing a print project or a tangible product such as a poster, brochure, or business card, it is recommended practice for the dimensions and assets inside your Photoshop artwork/designs be set up in inches rather than pixels.

2. Resolution Matters

Adjusting the ruler in Photoshop from pixels to inches requires you to also take into account the resolution scale and size for relevant printing shapes and sizes offered by your printer device. Not all printers accept the same sizes, so you need to be sure that at the very least your printer can handle the size you need. If you can commit these specifics to memory, you will be able to avoid such headaches in the future.

3. Typefaces & Font Size

When designing print projects or materials such as brochures or magazines, etc., consideration of the typefaces that will be used should also be given attention; typically, printed fonts can reduce much finer due to their tiny resolutions at a microscopic level, which can be more noticeable once printed/delivered back from the printers end later on. Therefore, while scaling font types during image conversions in Photoshop, be sure that this process is not overlooked throughout the editing or creation workflow stages.

4. The Transitions Involved

It is important for users who switch measure modes (for example, from pixels to inches) to become comfortable with how everything changes render-wise as well. Since foreground and background color schemes can shift when switching to new modes, it is critical that you manually adjust these colors and elements in your design if necessary.

5. Modes Supported by Your Hardware

In the end, it is essential to determine whether or not the hardware system you are using supports the unit of measurement that you want to use (inches in this instance). The majority of contemporary computer equipment and software are intended to function with inches as a unit of measure, but this is not always sufficient. As a result, validating driver intelligence for accuracy and correct printing is something that should be verified whenever new implementations take place; this is true even within processes that are constrained by time constraints.

How Does Changing the Ruler Unit Affect Your Final Design Output?

You are a skilled designer, thus you are aware of the fact that each component of your design can affect the result. Finding out how to utilize the ruler unit properly can be the deciding factor between producing something that seems amateurish and producing something that looks like a polished masterpiece. Although some people may assume that the ruler unit is simply a minor feature, this is not the case. If you've ever questioned how altering your ruler unit impacts the end product of your design, the following information should answer your questions:

1. Your Design Process Is Directly Influenced By The Ruler Unit

Changing the unit that your ruler measures in can have a huge impact on the result of your design in some ways, one of the most crucial being how it molds the whole creative process. If you are someone who generally works in inches or millimeters but suddenly switches over to working in pixels or points, you will find it difficult to maintain track of size consistency across various aspects such as shapes and typography in your work. If there are infographics or charts involved in the creation of marketing materials, then this inconsistency might affect more than just the visual appeal. This is because the positioning of graphical components such as charts and graphs with text or explanations will change depending on the marketing material.

2. Different Projects Call for Different Units

The kind of project you're working on is a significant consideration that, in addition to determining how you should go about developing a design project that makes use of correct measurements, also plays a significant role in determining which ruler unit is the most appropriate for you to use. For instance, if you're going to be generating digital visuals like website designs or social media postings that will mostly be seen on screens, you should specify the sizes in pixels.

On the other side, projects involving physical printing need die-exact measurement, which is where millimeter units come in useful. Other projects may include numerous formats concurrently, which require multiple units at a parallel scale range for each format.

3. Working more efficiently through familiar units

The fact that identical equivalents are recorded differently inside multiple systems, such as the fact that one inch is approximately equivalent to 25 millimeters, is yet another manner in which transitioning between different ruler systems has a detrimental impact on designs and, yes, even productivity.

CHAPTER FIVE
GETTING STARTED WITH DRAWING ON PHOTOSHOP

The purpose of this chapter is to walk you through the fundamentals of drawing in Adobe Photoshop. It starts by describing the difference between bitmap pictures and vector graphics, focusing on how the two types of graphics process and display image data differently. After that, the chapter dives into the idea of paths, outlining what they are as well as their relevance in the process of producing accurate and modifiable objects in Photoshop. It covers things like generating shapes using the Pen Tool, which includes drawing both straight lines and curved pathways, among other things. In addition to this, it offers instructions on how to make complicated designs by combining straight and curved pathways.

In this chapter, one of the most important skills that will be addressed is drawing a path from a picture, which entails making use of reference photographs to trace or replicate shapes. In addition, the chapter details the process of converting a path into a selection and applying that selection as a mask to a layer. This is an essential method for isolating and modifying certain parts of an image. This chapter is intended to serve as an introduction for users who wish to begin drawing and making shapes in Adobe Photoshop. It will cover fundamental drawing tools and methods, such as the Pen Tool and path modification, among other topics.

BITMAP IMAGES

Bitmap pictures are made up of a grid of individual pixels, where each pixel is a small square or dot of color. Bitmap images can be saved in a variety of formats, including JPEG, GIF, and PNG. The arrangement of these pixels and the way they interact with one another provide the overall visual look of an image. Changing the size of a bitmap image can result in a loss of image quality owing to pixelation or blurriness. Bitmap images are resolution-dependent, which means that they have a certain number of pixels. In all practical respects, a raster image created in Photoshop and saved in the Bitmap color setting constitutes line art with sharp edges. It gets rid of the anti-aliasing effect that artwork normally has, leaving a rough and jagged edge. Because a visual example is the most effective method of communicating the concept of anti-aliasing, I have provided one below.

The image on the left does not use anti-aliasing, which means the edges of the image have not been smoothed down in any way. The image on the right has been anti-aliased, which indicates that the computer has softened the contrast between the foreground and background colors by blending the sharp edges. This was accomplished by taking the color of the item and the background and averaging the results.

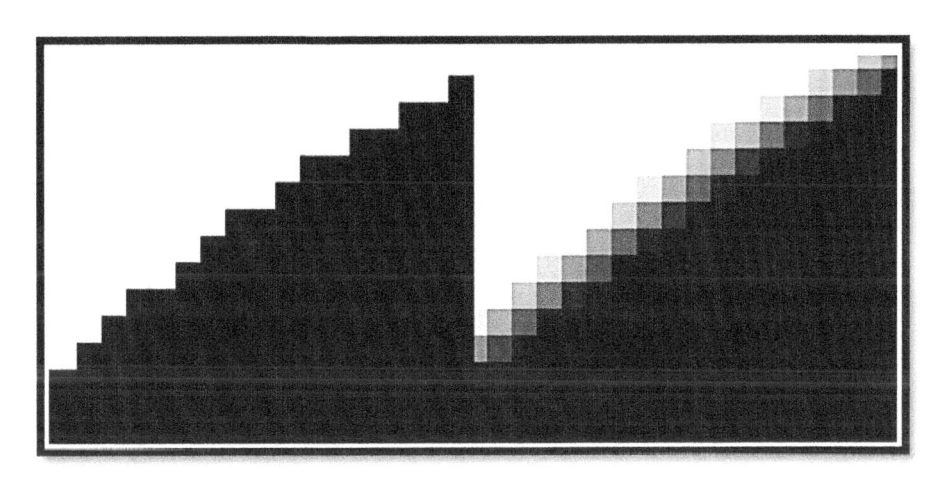

When you create a bitmap image (not to be confused with the BMP file format used by Windows), you are generating a crisp, print-ready image; yet, there are several limitations associated with this kind of image. In a document, it can only ever appear as a single color, and for it to have a smooth appearance when printed, the resolution has to be exceedingly high (1200 DPI, real size). When the image's resolution is poor, the edge of the picture will begin to seem jagged. When there is no other vector graphic option available, people often resort to using the bitmap color mode. Instead of recreating the design in Adobe Illustrator, it will be easier for you to scan the existing graphic and make a bitmap TIFF file from it, for example, if you have been provided a logo that is just one color and is printed on the letterhead. Because the bitmap color mode does not support anti-aliasing, images that are transformed to this format maintain their transparent backgrounds.

Bitmap Image Exercise

Playing around with the Median and Levels tools in Photoshop will allow us to illustrate one method for enhancing 'organic' text such as a signature. Launch Photoshop and open the file. If you double-click the magnifying glass, the view will default to "**Actual Pixels**," which is the option that displays the image with the least amount of jagged edges. The signature passes muster when seen digitally, but it won't cut it when printed. If this is imported into Quark or InDesign without any changes, it will have a fuzzy appearance with a white background block.

Simply go to the IMAGE menu and choose the IMAGE SIZE option to bring up the following dialogue box:

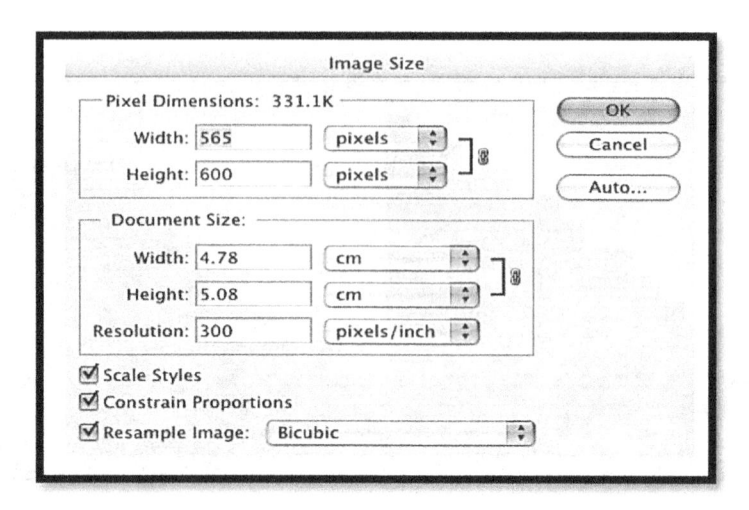

The actual dimensions are 4.78 centimeters by 5.08 centimeters, and the resolution is 300 dots per inch (DPI). After increasing the width to 10 millimeters at a resolution of 1200 dots per inch, we will convert this to line art (as a bitmap image). To begin, raise the size by entering '10' into the WIDTH field and '1200' into the **RESOLUTION** field. To access Actual Pixels, either double-clicks the magnifying glass or go to the **VIEW** menu and choose **ACTUAL PIXELS**. The image will seem somewhat like this when you do so:

It needs some kind of cleaning. Navigate to the **LAYERS** palette (shown further down). Select **LEVELS** from the submenu that is found under **ADJUSTMENT LAYERS** (which is marked in yellow). Because we want our edits to be non-destructive, we are making them using adjustment layers rather than applying the **LEVELS** option from the **IMAGE** menu under **ADJUSTMENTS** rather than **LEVELS**. This ensures that even if we make a mistake, the original image will not be changed. In the process of retouching images, this is a best practice that should always be followed. Always be sure to save the original, layered PSD file in addition to the final, "**flattened**" image. Therefore, go to the option for adjustment layers and pick **LEVELS**. Move the slider for the white triangle to the left, and then move the slider for the black triangle to the right. If you continue to do this, you will see that the image borders are becoming more defined (provided that the PREVIEW box is ticked).

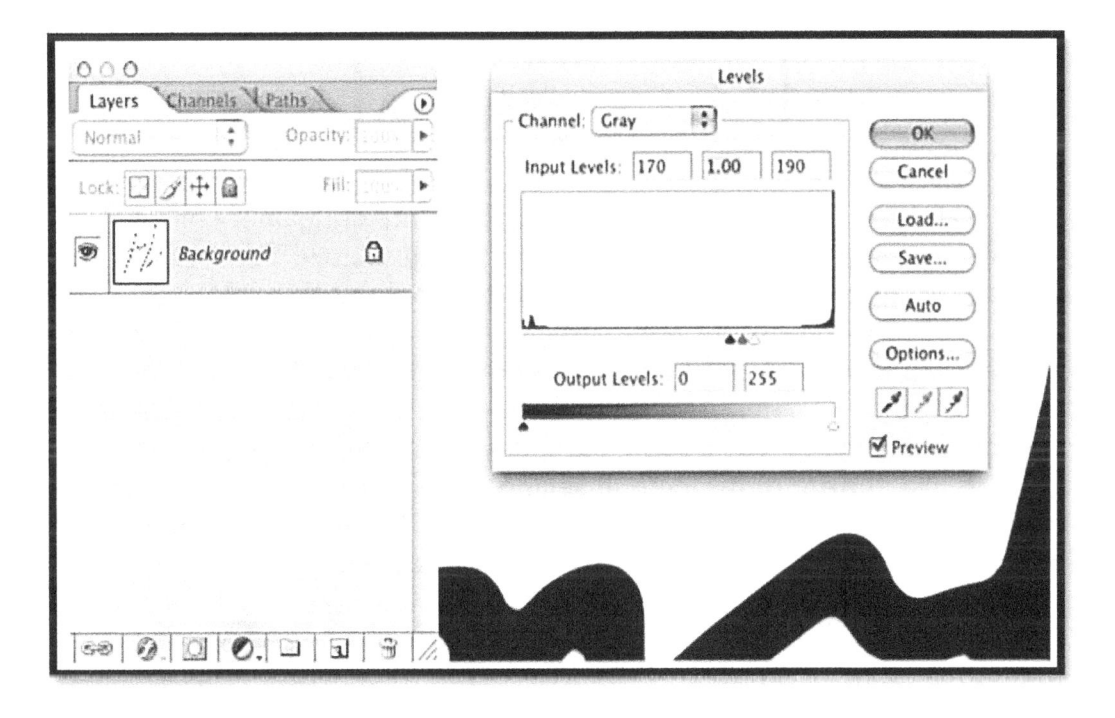

However, the edges are still pretty '**jittery**' at this point in the process. To begin, we will need to apply a filter. Remove the adjustment layer and start again. Because the filters are '**destructive**,' we will first make a copy of the background layer before applying the effect to it. This will ensure that the original image is not altered in any way. To create a duplicate of the background image, just drag it over the '**New Layer**' button located at the very bottom of the palette. To find the median, go to **FILTERS > NOISE**. Move the radius slider to a setting of around 10 pixels.

Launch the **LEVELS** adjustment layer once again and bring the white and black sliders closer together, as demonstrated in the image below. You will see that the edge is beginning to take on a more defined and polished appearance. It is now necessary for us to turn off the anti-aliasing. At this point, you could convert the image directly to Bitmap, but there is still one more adjustment layer that has to be applied if you want the end output to be as fantastic as it possibly can be. Make a selection for **THRESHOLD** in the submenu of the Adjustment Layers menu. If you do nothing and just leave it at the default setting, all anti-aliasing will be turned off. This is the location where you will store your layered PSD file. After that, you should flatten the image using the **LAYER/FLATTEN IMAGE** command.

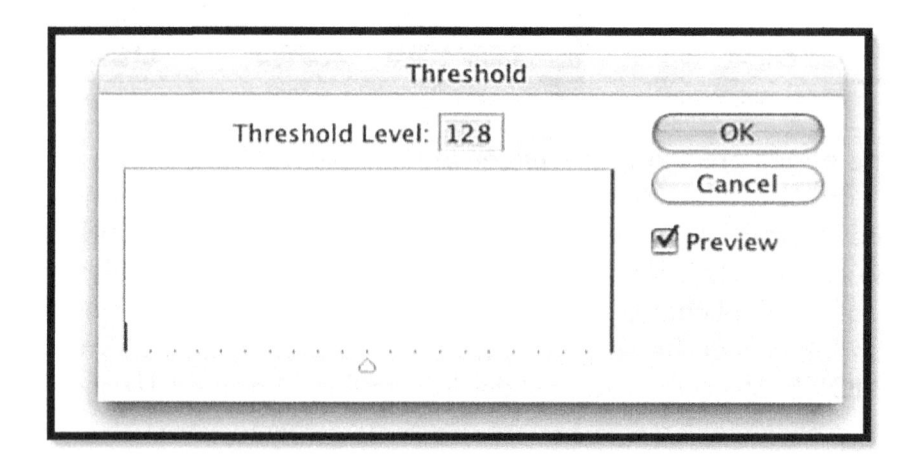

Click the OK button, choose **IMAGE/MODE/BITMAP**, and ensure that both the input and output resolutions are set to **1200DPI**. Finally, save the image using the **TIFF** file type.

VECTOR GRAPHICS

Raster images, also known as bitmap images, are made up of pixels, which stay the same size as you zoom in and out of an image. This means that blowing up these images or zooming in can cause pixelation because the pixels become more visible. Vector graphics are digital designs that remain sharp at any size. Two-dimensional digital images are either rasters or vectors. Vector images, on the other hand, are made up of geometric polygons and colors; and since mathematical equations are used to create them, they can adapt to remain crisp and clean at any scale, making them popular assets in graphic design and digital arts. Typically, logos, typefaces, and icons are all examples of vector graphics.

When to use vector images.

Vectors are an excellent format for any image that has to alter size, such as logos and graphics that need to look nice in some situations. The same design could appear on business cards, T-shirts, coffee mugs, and billboards, so the logo must maintain its integrity no matter where it's shown.

When to use raster images.

Creating an image out of hundreds upon thousands of pixels means that you can show off light, shadows, color, and contrasts in a more precise manner than you can with the equations that make up vector images. Digital photographs and paints are examples of raster graphics. Raster images are excellent at holding detail. Raster graphics include digital photos and paintings.

The path to vectors

In general, Photoshop works with raster images, whereas Adobe Illustrator is the Adobe Creative Cloud application of choice for creating vector art. In either app, the edges of a vector image can be delineated by a path, which can be thought of as a line with anchor points at both ends. Defining paths on an image is an important part of the process of going from raster to vector in Photoshop.

Why go from raster to vector?

You will need to convert an existing photo or illustration into a vector in Photoshop if you want to make a scalable logo from it. This is also a useful task if you want to create simplified image files that can be used with a laser engraver or cutting machine to create precisely cut pieces of vinyl or other materials.

How to turn a raster image into a vector image in Photoshop.

If you are working in Illustrator, you can use the Image Trace function to vectorize an image in a very short amount of time. However, if you are working in Photoshop, you will need to follow these steps to convert from pixels to scalable vectors. You will need to simplify the image and add paths that specify where the vector starts and finishes. In the end, each shape that makes up your new vector image can only be one color. This means that to convert the thousands of colored pixels in a photograph into a vector, you must first simplify your image into one foreground color and one background color, such as black and white. After the image has been converted, you can choose a new color for each piece that makes up your new vector image. Converting multicolored photographs is more difficult (but not impossible) than converting a single-color illustration or graphic.

Pick an image and give it a try with these steps:

1. Open your image.

Import the image you want to vectorize into Photoshop.

2. Select the part of the image you want to vectorize.

Using the right selection tool, choose the portion of the image that you want to be vectorized. Make use of the Rectangular Marquee tool if you want to choose a rectangular region. Use the Magic Wand tool if you want everything to be a certain color. Use the Select topic command if you just want to vectorize the topic of the image that you are working with.

3. Add a Threshold layer.

Using the Layers panel, create a new **Threshold layer**, and from the panel's **Create** menu, pick **Create New Fill or Adjustment layer**. This will turn your selection into a single-color image. You move the slider to set the threshold, and every pixel that has a brighter tone than the one you chose will become white, while any pixel that has a darker tone will become black.

4. Select Tonal Areas with the Color Range Command.

Make a selection that includes all of the pixels in an image that has a color that is the same by using the **Color Range command**. Depending on whatever portion of the picture you want to vectorize, you will need to choose all of the white or all of the black in the image. Select Color Range by going to the Select menu. Make a selection of either the black or the white region by using the Eyedropper tool.

5. Convert your selection into a path.

To establish a tolerance value for your path, right-click anywhere within your selection, and pick the **Make Work Path** option from the context menu. The amount that your path should adhere to the outlines of the selection is determined by something called a tolerance value. When the tolerance value is increased, the path will correspond to the selection more exactly.

6. Create a solid color layer.

Create a new Fill layer or Adjustment layer by going to the Layers panel and selecting the appropriate button. Make your selection using the menu and choose Solid Color. On top of the Threshold layer sits this new layer, which is responsible for defining the form of the vector. It can be colored in any way that you choose.

7. Save the Vector Image as an SVG file.

Select **SVG file** from the menu that appears when you right-click on the layer. You now have a file that is in vector format.

Bitmap and vector graphics strengths and weaknesses

- In most cases, the file size of a bitmap graphic is much more than that of a comparable vector graphic.
- The resolution of a bitmap image may change its appearance. When you expand a bitmap graphic, it will take on a pixelated appearance. Its characteristics lose their clarity and become hazy as the size of the object is reduced. Because the shapes of vector images are rebuilt to account for variations in resolution, this cannot occur with these types of graphics.
- It is simple to modify vector graphics because the shapes included inside them can be ungrouped and changed separately. When vector graphics are

accessed in applications that do not comprehend the rendering languages in which they are stored, it might be challenging to edit or even show the vector drawings.

For instance, whereas numerous drawing tools for Mac OS can easily view and edit PICT files, very few are capable of doing anything at all with WMF files. The vast majority of painting programs, on the other hand, can open a wide variety of bitmap graphic file types.

- You can convert one sort of bitmap file into another kind of bitmap file with ease. A vector drawing can also be converted into a bitmap if necessary. However, the process of converting a bitmap design into an actual vector graphic is quite challenging. Even converting one kind of vector graphic to another (for example, PICT to WMF) is a challenge due to the complexity of the format.
- Vector graphics are not suitable for pictures with a high level of complexity, such as digital photos.

WHAT KNOWLEDGE DO YOU HAVE OF PATHS?

Although Photoshop is not a program that is primarily based on vectors, it does have several vector-based tools and capabilities. The most important one is called Paths. Paths are essentially vector-based line drawings, to put it another way. A path can be constructed using any number of line segments that are linked together at anchor points. These sections of line can be straight, curved, or a mix of the two in any way that best suits the design. It is necessary for there to be an opening for there to be a path. Because of this, each anchor point must be linked to a different anchor point.

How does path work?

There is one significant benefit of using paths. Because they are built on vectors, they will maintain their crispness and clarity regardless of the size at which they are shown. You can receive the same high level of detail and clarity regardless of the size or resolution of the image. Another benefit of using Paths is that it enables you to design your one-of-a-kind shapes. There are certain built-in shapes included with Photoshop, but there are many more shapes available that you could find more helpful. When you have finished making a path in the form of a shape that you may wish to use again in the future, you can store that path. As a result, you can reuse it anytime you want and scale it to the size you need without experiencing any quality loss or distortion. It is always accessible as a path.

How is Paths Utilized?

Paths offer a variety of different practical uses that, when used properly, can make your artwork seem to be of a much higher quality. Bezier Points are used rather often by graphic designers for a variety of purposes, including but not limited to: making text follow a curve or construct a circle; accurately separating objects from backgrounds; and stylizing type for creative typography. For the creation of logos and other visuals that, in the course of future projects, may need to be scaled to a variety of different sizes, it is an excellent tool. As a result of the tool's ability to convert freehand drawings into accurate vector-based pictures that can be edited and scaled to the user's specifications, digital artists will also find the tool to be useful. **You can make paths in a few different methods, including:**

- **With the pen tool**: Draw lines with anchor points at the ends to make a path.
- **With the shapes tool**: Use the Paths option to turn any shape into a path.
- **Create as a path**: You can purposefully create a path using either the pen tool or the shapes tool.
- **Convert to a path**: You can convert an existing image, graphic, or even text into a path.

You can do anything that you can do with other components, including setting a fill color for the path, as well as the color and weight for the path's stroke. Paths are likely one of the tools of Photoshop that is utilized the least and is misunderstood the most, but it is a tool that you should consider adding to your armory because of the potential benefits that it can provide. If you aren't currently using this function, you should give it a go.

An example path

Here's a typical path in Photoshop.

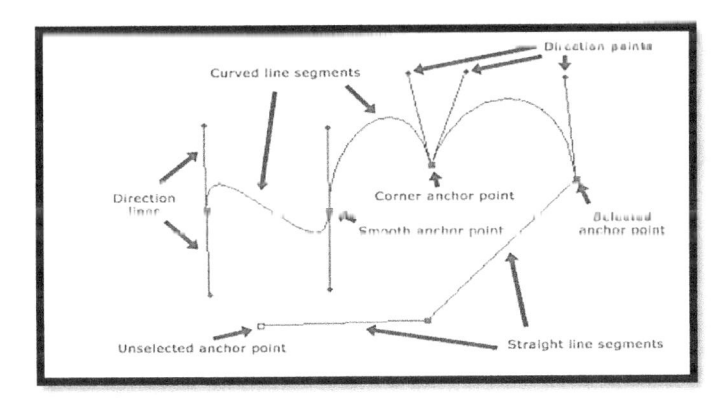

You are going to see that the path is made up of a few different line segments as well as anchor points. The actual components of the path, known as line segments, include straight lines and curved lines. Anchor points are moveable points that are located at the ends of the line segments. They allow you to alter the location of the lines as well as the form they take.

Types of line segments

There are two types of line segments:

> - **Straight line segments.** These are the ones that are the least difficult to sketch and comprehend. You'll notice that there are no direction lines or direction points associated with the segments of a straight line.
> - **Curved line segments.** These are the ones that are going to test you! The direction lines and direction points that you can see in the figure that is shown above are what determine the form of each curve. More to come on these in a moment.

Types of anchor points

Also, there are two types of anchor points:

> - **Smooth anchor points.** A smooth anchor point is created when the curves on either side of an anchor point enter and depart the point at the same angle. In other words, there is a seamless transition from one curve to the next across the place where the two curves meet. You can see that this particular sort of point has two direction lines that are perpendicular to one another (i.e., 180 degrees apart) by looking at the image above.
> - **Corner anchor points.** The transition from one curve to the next sometimes takes place at a point that signifies a dramatic shift in direction. In addition to this, it is used when coupled to one or two straight lines. Observe that the direction lines on the corner anchor points of the figure are not spaced 180 degrees apart (or that there are no direction lines at all in the case of the straight line segments).

About path components

In addition to that, let's take a glance at the path components. One or more path components can make up the whole of a path. A sequence of segments and anchor points make up each component. In addition, each component stands alone and is unique from the others; in other words, they are not connected in any way.

The following is an example of a path that has three separate path components:

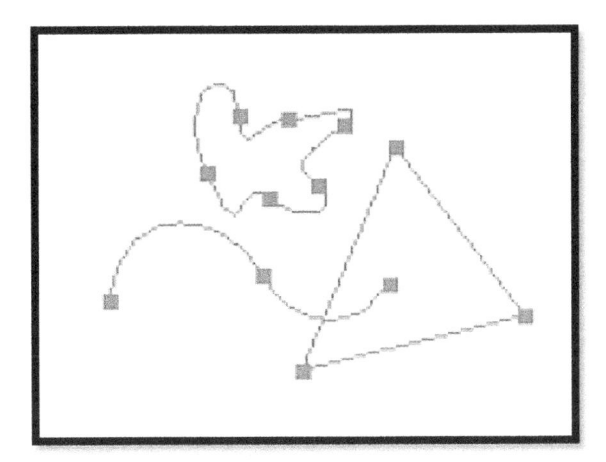

It is important to keep in mind that the components of a path do not have to be closed paths; instead, they can include endpoints like the wavy line in the example above. It is important to keep in mind that the wavy line and the triangle, although they overlap one another, are not connected and are thus considered to be different path components.

CREATING A SHAPE USING THE PEN TOOL

- Launch Adobe Photoshop and start a new document. Pick the Pen Tool from the toolbar that is located on the left side of the screen.
- Click on the location on the canvas where you wish to begin sketching your shape. This will result in the creation of what is known as an **"anchor point."**
- After that, all you have to do is click and drag your mouse along the path that you wish to go.

As you continue to do this, you will see that a line is beginning to take shape. This particular line is known as a "path."

- Continue to design the form you desire by clicking and dragging the mouse until you have it. After that, let go of the mouse button.
- Simply clicking on the first anchor point that you made will allow you to finish off your shape. This will **"close"** off your form and bring the path to a successful conclusion.

And that brings us to the end of our discussion! After some practice, using the **Pen Tool** in Photoshop to draw various shapes is a task that can be accomplished with relative ease.

DRAWING STRAIGHT LINES

Let's begin with the method that requires the least amount of effort. To begin, create a new document that is about 500 pixels by 500 pixels in size so that you have enough room to work. Then, in the Tools panel, pick the **Pen** tool to continue. Now use the mouse to click on the appropriate places on your page. You'll see that the initial anchor point that you wanted to install has been set. Make a new click after moving the mouse. You've just finished creating the first part of your line, which now has two anchor points at either end.

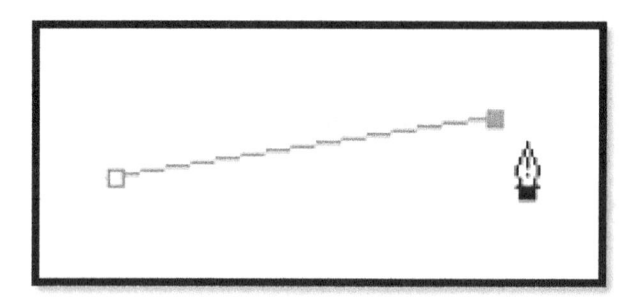

Make a couple more clicks across the document you're working on. You'll see that each click results in the addition of a new anchor point and a new section of straight line.

Quick tip: *Select the* **Rubber Band** *option (under the* **Pen Options** *drop-down in the options bar) to see where the line is going to be placed before you place it. This is especially useful for beginners, as it enables you to see exactly what's happening!*

Your path seems to be clear at this point. This indicates that it has a beginning and an end, but no other points of connection in between. To build a closed path, drag the mouse cursor over the initial point you generated and you'll see the Pen tool pointer changing to show an 'o' next to it:

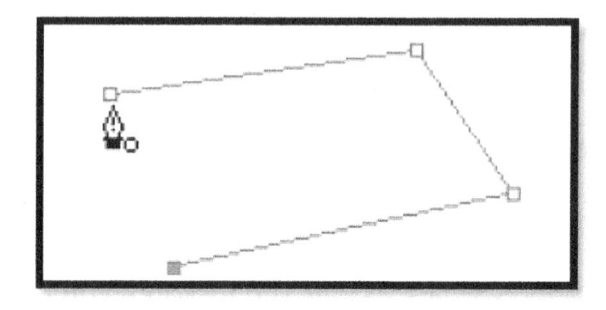

Now click with the mouse, and you'll see that you have now created a complete shape – **a** *closed path*. Well done!

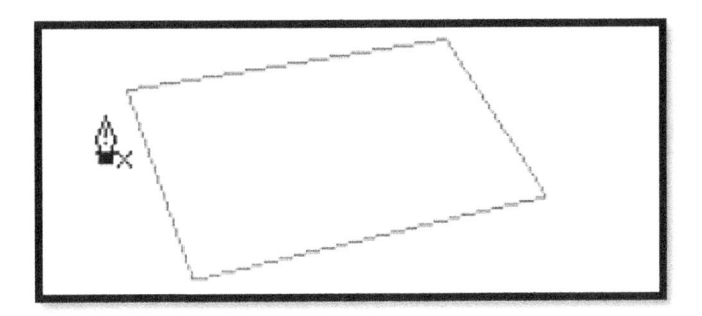

Deleting your path

The path that you have just made has been saved in a short-term path that is known as the Work Path. So that we can start again with a clean slate, let's erase this path. Click on the **Paths tab** in the Layers palette to bring up the list of available paths. Now drag the *Work Path* to the trash can icon.

DRAWING CURVED LINES

To create a curve, first choose the **Pen tool**, then click anywhere in your document, and then drag the mouse in the general direction you want the curve to go.

For this particular example, try moving the mouse in an upward manner on the page:

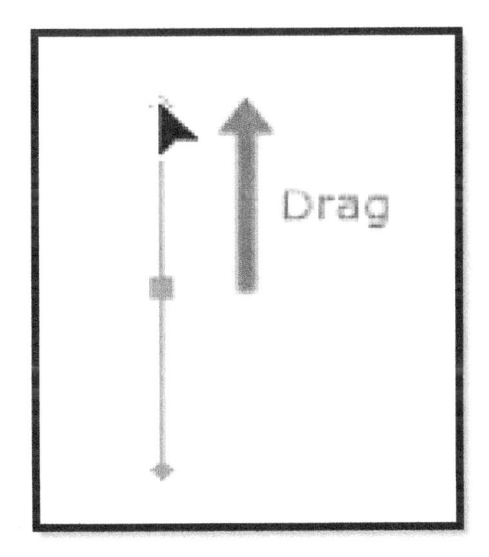

As you drag, you'll see that two direction lines and direction points are generated as a result.

These determine the contour of the curve that you are going to generate and include:

- The path that the new curve will take is going to be determined by the direction that the lines are going in.
- The amount of impact that this anchor point will have on the curve is determined, in part, by the length of the lines. When the line grows longer, the curve will be "**pulled**" closer to the line to an increased degree.

Experimenting with the direction lines is the most effective approach to get an understanding of how they work.

Now, give the process of generating a new anchor point a go by clicking the mouse to the right of the anchor point you already have and dragging it downwards:

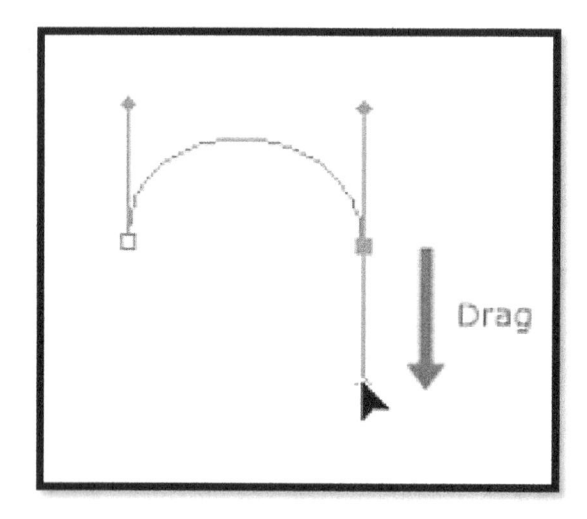

You've just added a second anchor point, and as a result, you've made a curve that connects the two of them! Take note that you dragged in an upward direction from the first anchor point and that you dragged in a downward direction from the second anchor point. This moves up from the first point, then down when it reaches the second point, and follows the path of the curve while doing so. If you carried the object upwards from the second anchor point as well, what do you think would happen? Test it out! (You can decide to erase the Work Path and begin the process all over again.)

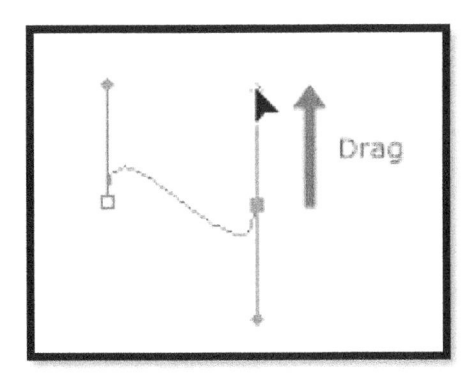

This time, the curve can be seen to rise upwards towards the second point, and as it does so, it reverses its direction. Therefore, the curve will continually attempt to go in the direction that you pull it! Until you feel comfortable with the method, hone your sketching skills by creating a few curves similar to these and dragging them in a variety of directions.

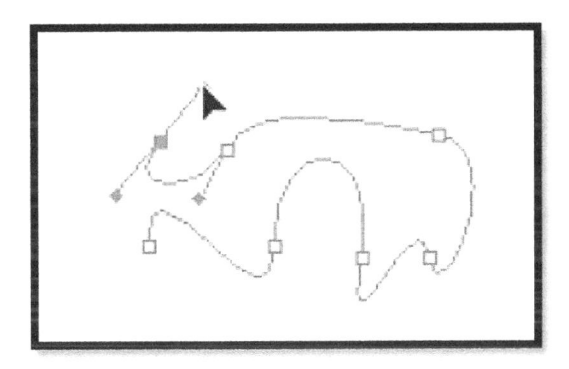

Switching between curves and lines

When designing a path, it is common practice to include both straight and curved lines in the final product. Making the transition between the two is simple. Simply clicking with the mouse to create some straight lines is a good place to start:

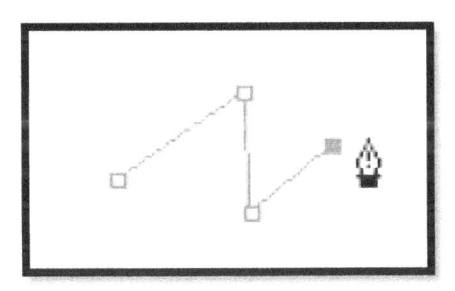

To switch to sketching a curve, click and drag with the mouse to place the end point of the curve:

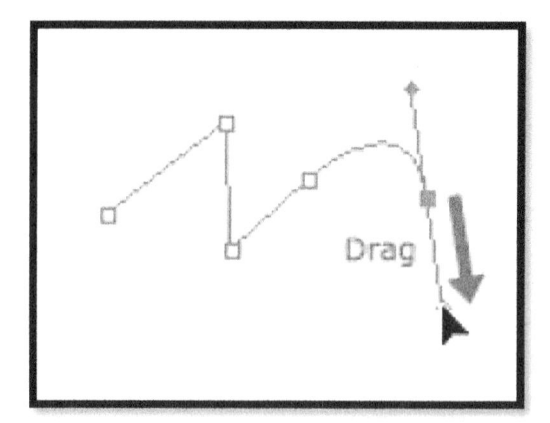

Create the anchor point of your last curve by clicking rather than clicking and dragging (in other words, build a corner point) to return to drawing a straight line. This will allow you to go back to drawing a straight line.

Then use the left mouse button to click on the location where you want the straight line to terminate:

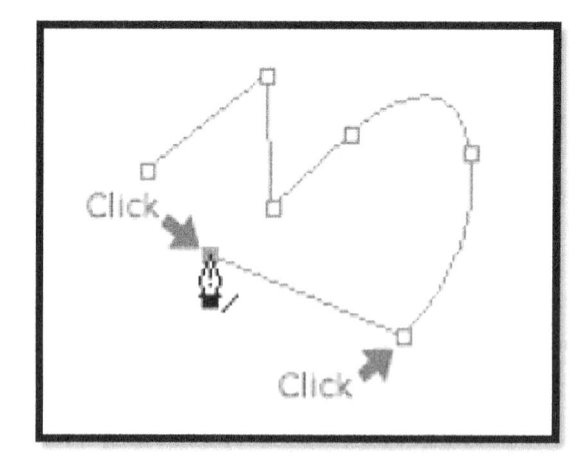

Continuing paths

If you come back to a path that you have previously left unfinished and you want to continue adding to it, you can do so by dragging the Pen tool over either end of the path until it changes into the "**Pick up Path**" cursor:

"Pick Up Path" Cursor

It is important to note that you cannot pick up a closed path using this method; nevertheless, you can add and remove points on the closed path, as well as drag points about, to obtain the new form you want. A path that has been closed can also be reopened.

The Freeform Pen tool

You can rapidly draw out your path using the Freeform Pen tool that is available. It is not particularly exact, and it often does not set anchor points where you would ideally want them to be, but it is simple to use, which is a positive for those who are just starting in this field.

To utilize this tool, you must first choose it from the icon labeled "Pen Tool" in the Tools palette:

Then all you have to do is click and drag with the mouse to create your path. As soon as you let go of the mouse button, the path will be produced. Changing the value in the **Curve Fit box** in the options bar will allow you to customize the number of anchor points produced by the **Freeform Pen tool**. This can be done by clicking on the box. The greater the number, the fewer anchor points and path segments will be constructed; however, the resulting path will also be less precise. The Magnetic checkbox in the options bar can be used to make the Freeform Pen tool behave similarly to the Magnetic Lasso tool. This can be done by simply clicking the checkbox. After that, the tool will automatically conform to the contours of the shape you're sketching around.

SKETCHING A PATH FROM A PHOTO

Step 1: Select the Picture You Want to Use

Your very first step should be to choose the photograph that will serve as the basis for the Photoshop path-creation process that you will later use. I'm going to go forward with that particular image.

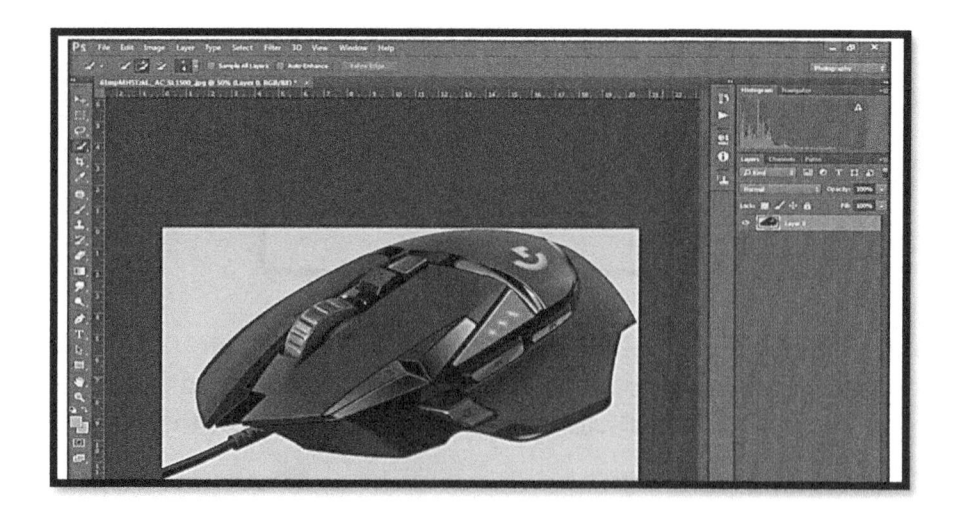

The background in the image isn't in the finest shape, which gives the object a shadowy effect overall. We are going to get rid of this background that is not appropriate for our purposes by using the path-building approach. Go to the "**File**" option at the top of the screen, then choose the image from which you want to remove the inappropriate background. After that, choose the **Pen Tool** from the menu on your left. Check to see if the most fundamental layer has been unlocked. Have you completed the task already? You should go to the second step at this point.

Step 2: Choose Your Starting Point and Create Path

Now, we're going to select a starting point that looks convenient. For our sample image, it seems like the bottom section would be a better point to start with.

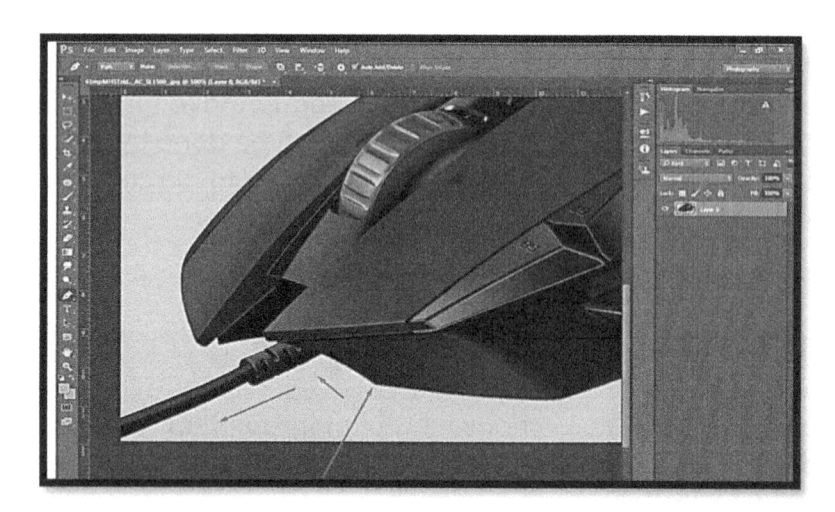

If it appears like it would be easier to do so, you can alternatively begin from the top of the page. Nevertheless, you can begin designing Photoshop paths from any point you choose as long as you make sure to cover the whole object.

Step 3: Customizing Clipping Path

When working with photos, it is simpler to generate paths for objects that have a straight form. On the other hand, constructing a path across curved terrain can be challenging for you. There is no reason to be concerned about it. By moving your mouse in a certain direction, you can create paths for the bending region. Additionally, you can tailor the newly constructed path by using the "**ALT" and "CTRL**" keys.

To add additional anchor points to the path that is being generated, press the "**CTRL**" key on your keyboard. On the other hand, a designer can adjust the course of the path by holding down the "**ALT**" key while adjusting.

If you are just starting, you can have some trouble when you try to create paths for complex objects. You can obtain help from Photoshop path designers by using the **Clipping Path Service**. This service is available to you. On the other hand, let's go to the fourth stage and figure out how to preserve a path.

Step 4: Save Your Path

You may need to construct many paths for a single photograph at times. In such a scenario, you need to save your path before beginning the process of building numerous paths. By selecting this option, you can store your path.

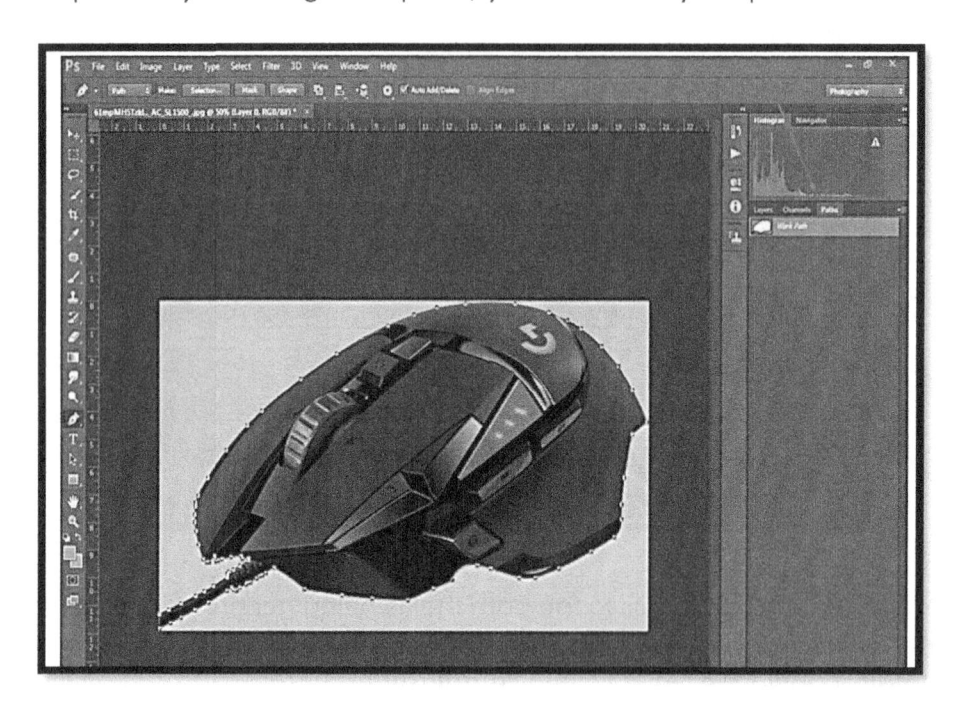

You can save your path by doing nothing more complicated than double-clicking on the work path option in the menu that appears. Are you happy with that arrangement? Okay, let's go on to the next step.

Step 5: Turn the Clipping Path into Dotted Lines

A clipping path has been applied to our object at this point, so it is protected from unwanted changes. We need to right-click with the mouse and then choose "**Make Selection**" from the menu that appears. When you click this button, the feather radius option will be brought up on your screen. We are not going to deviate from the goal of zero.

Step 6: Erase Unsuitable Background

As we have selected the product, we should press "**CTRL + SHIFT + I**" to reverse the selection. Following that, the whole background will be covered with dashed lines. You can erase the unsuitable background of your image easily by pressing the "**Delete**" key. Also, you can select "**Layer via Cut**" to cut your product on a transparent background.

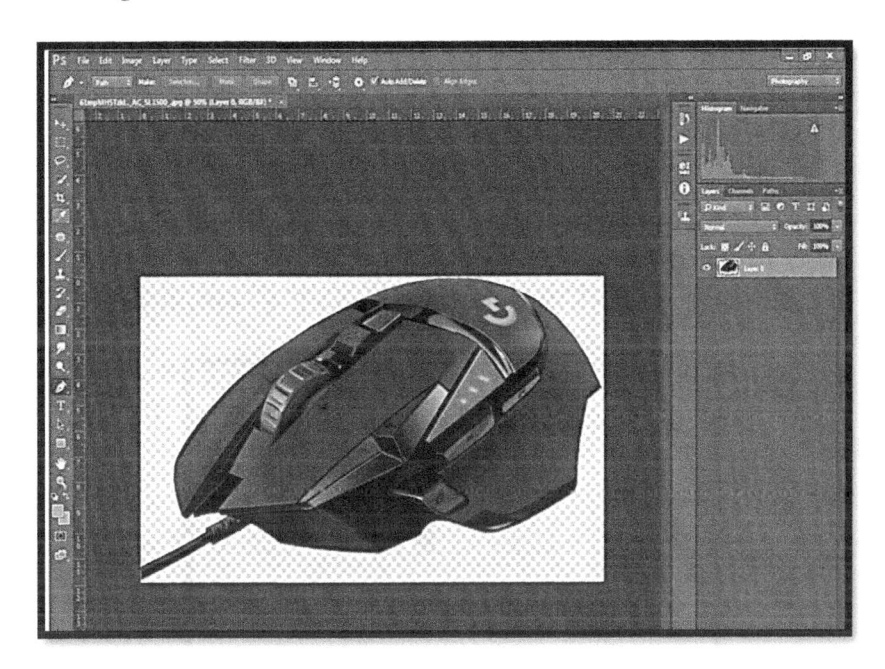

That's the outcome. Following that method, you will be able to create paths from images. While creating a clipping path in Photoshop, you should be careful about maintaining accuracy. Otherwise, you could lose details of your objects.

Editing Paths in Photoshop

Now that you know how to make paths, we'll go over the several ways in which you can modify a path after you've already created it. You can "**fine-tune**" the lines and curves of your path in this manner until they are exactly as you want them to be. This will allow you to change the shape of your path.

Selecting paths

In this section, we will examine the many methods in which you can pick your paths, or sections of your paths, for the sake of editing.

The Path Component Selection tool

This tool allows the user to pick a complete path component in a very short amount of time. This is helpful in many situations, such as when you wish to resize or relocate a component of a path. The tool can be found in the **Tools panel**, just below the symbol depicting a black mouse pointer:

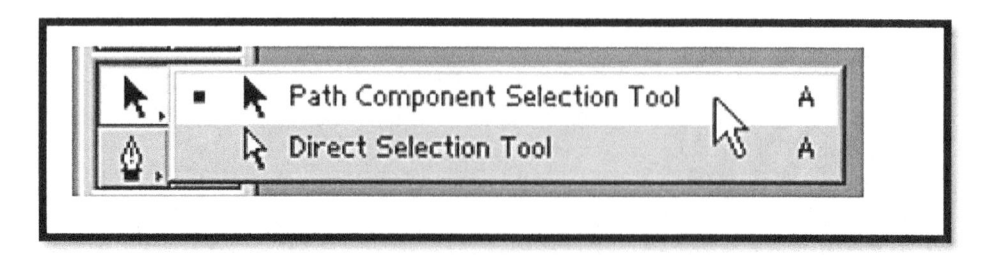

To select a component, just click anywhere in or on the component:

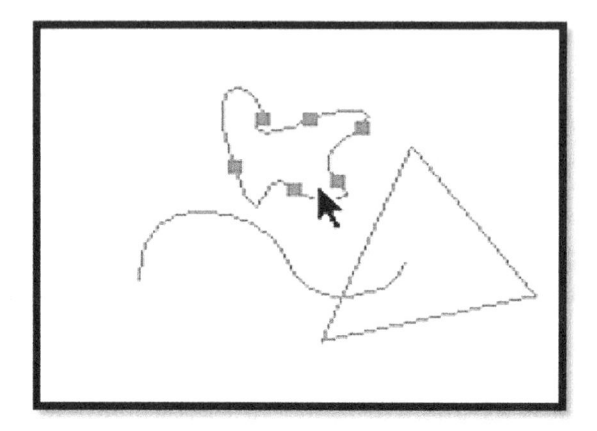

To select many components at the same time, you can also click on more than one component while holding down the Shift key, or you can click and drag a marquee. To deselect all components, you can either use the Path Component Selection tool to click on an empty part of your page or use the Esc key on your keyboard.

The Direct Selection tool

In the Tools palette, the Direct Selection tool is located just under the **Path Component Selection** tool popup. This can be accessed by clicking on the arrow next to that window. Utilizing this tool, you can pick specific portions of a path as well as anchor points for customization.

Simply clicking on the section you want to choose will choose it:

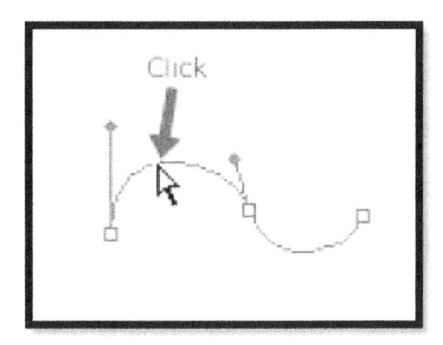

To select an anchor point, click on the point:

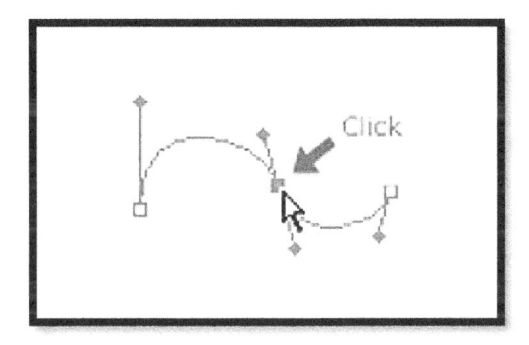

You can also click and hold the **Shift key** while clicking on several segments or points, or you can click and drag a marquee to pick many items at the same time. To deselect all of the segments and points in your document, you can either use the **Esc key** on your keyboard or click on an empty part of the page using the **Direct Selection tool**.

Some handy shortcuts

- While using the **Direct Selection tool**, you can briefly activate the Path Component Selection tool by holding down the **Control key (Windows) or the Command key (Mac)** while clicking with the mouse.
- You can also use the Direct Selection tool from any of the other drawing tools by holding down the **Control key (on Windows) or the Command key (on Mac)** while clicking with the mouse. At the same time using the Pen tool to create new path components, comes in extremely handy for selecting and altering already created path components.

> By hitting **Shift and A** simultaneously, you can switch between the Direct Selection tool and the Path Component tool.

Let's take a look at how to modify path components and segments now that you understand how to pick them individually.

Modifying path segments

Becoming an expert with the Pen tool requires you to have the skill to move and rearrange path segments with pinpoint accuracy. You will be able to design any shaped path with a high degree of accuracy if you know and understand how the shape of path segments can be varied. This knowledge is required to create a path. Therefore, you must pay close attention! You will need to make use of the Direct Selection tool to modify a path segment. Holding down the Control key (Windows) or the Command key (Mac) allows you to activate this tool while you are drawing with the Pen tool. This is the simplest method to engage this tool.

Moving straight segments

It is simple to relocate straight parts. Simply use the Direct Selection tool to click on the portion of the image you wish to relocate, and then drag it with the mouse:

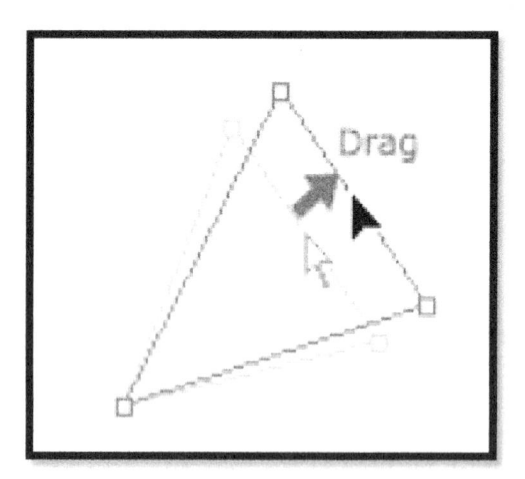

Moving curved segments

To move a curved segment, you must first use the Direct Selection tool and click on the part you want to move. After that, you have to pick both of the segment's anchor points by clicking on them while holding down the **Shift key**:

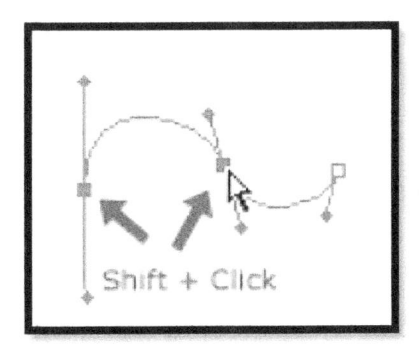

After you have picked both of the anchor points, click on the curve, and then drag it to move it around:

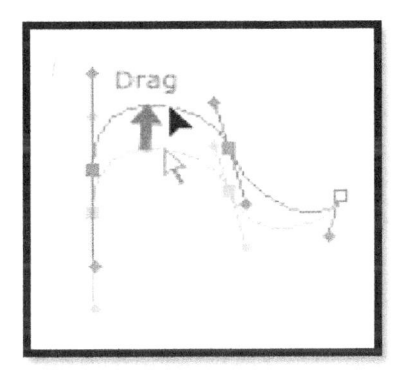

Take note of the fact that the only thing you are doing here is shifting the location of the curved segment; you are not modifying its shape (although the shape of the adjacent curve will shift to accommodate the new curve's position).

Reshaping curved segments

There are two distinct approaches to reforming the shape of a curved section. The first method simply condenses or elongates the curve, without altering the shape of the segments that are located on either side of it. The second method is making adjustments to the direction lines at an anchor point to modify the shape of the segments that are located on either side of the point.

Technique 1. Shrinking and stretching

If you want to reduce the size of a segment or increase its length, you must first click on the segment using the Direct Selection tool, and then make sure that none of the segment's anchor points are chosen, or that only one anchor point is selected (if both are selected, the segment will simply be moved). You can deselect the anchor point (or points) as needed by clicking on them while holding down the Shift key. After that, choose the curve by clicking on it, and then drag it to the desired size using your mouse.

Technique 2. Altering the direction lines

You can alter the shape of the curves on each side of an anchor point by dragging the direction lines at the point while holding down the shift key. Simply putting in some practice is going to be your most effective tool for mastering this. To modify a direction line, use the Direct Selection tool to choose the direction point at the line's end, then click and drag the direction point in the desired direction.

Performing edits on the anchor points

Altering the curves and direction lines of your path, as seen above, is just one of the many customization options available to you. You can also alter the sort of anchor point used along your path. This gives you the ability to fashion a pathway into any shape you can imagine! The Convert Point tool can be found in the Tools Palette under the Pen Tool. This tool will be used to perform the majority of the modifications that need to be made to anchor points.

Tip: If you are working with the Pen tool and want to swiftly pick the Convert Point tool, you can do so by holding down the **Alt key (on Windows) or the Option key (on Mac)** while you make your selection.

Converting from a corner point to a smooth point

Clicking on the point with the Convert Point tool and dragging away from the point will cause the direction lines to show, which will allow you to change a corner anchor point into a smooth anchor point.

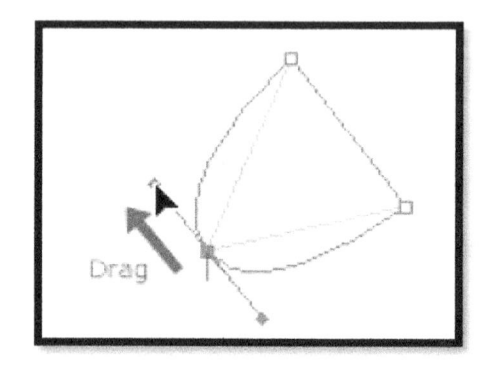

Converting from a smooth point to a corner point

There are three various kinds of corner points that you can make, which enables you to generate curves and lines in a variety of shapes.

Making a corner point without direction lines

You just need to make one click with the Convert Point tool on the anchor point you want to convert to transform a smooth point into a corner point that does not have any direction lines. After the direction lines have been removed, you will be left with a corner point that is flanked by two segments of straight line on each side.

Making a corner point with direction lines

To convert a smooth point into a corner point with direction lines, or to make a corner with curves as opposed to a corner with straight lines, use the Convert Point tool to click on either one of the direction points and then drag the point around until you achieve the required shape. This will generate a corner with curves rather than a corner with straight lines.

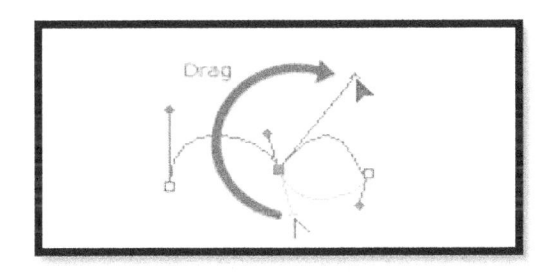

Take note that you have now "broken" the direction lines so that they function independently of one another. Due to this, you now have two curves that enter and exit the points at quite different angles (a corner). Compare this to the first version of the smooth point, in which the direction lines moved simultaneously and were rotated 180 degrees from one another, and the curves went smoothly through the point.

Making a corner point with only one direction line

In addition to this, it is possible to build a corner point using a single-direction line. This will result in the segment on the side of the point that contains the direction line becoming a curve as it leaves the point, while the segment on the other side of the point that does not have the direction line will become a straight line as it leaves the point (although it may curve at the other end if it's traveling towards a smooth anchor point). You can quickly flip from curves to straight lines and vice versa at any anchor point if you are familiar with this approach. Extremely practical! To create a corner point with a single direction line, all you have to do is use the Convert Point tool to drag the undesirable direction point into the anchor point until it vanishes. This will allow you to produce a corner point with only one way line. You may delete a direction point by selecting it, holding down the mouse button, and dragging it until it is on top of the anchor point.

Dragging anchor points

You can naturally alter your paths by dragging anchor points in different directions. Make sure that the point that you wish to move is chosen by using the **Direct Selection tool** (you can use the Shift+click combination to pick several points, or you can click to deselect points as needed). Then all you have to do is click and drag on a point! Working with all of these tools to alter path segments and anchor points is something you should practice since having these abilities is essential to developing high-quality paths.

Reopening and joining path components

If you have previously closed a path component (by clicking on the first anchor point with the Pen tool to complete the loop), you can later re-open the path by using the Direct Selection tool to pick one of the path segments (by clicking on it), then hitting the **Delete key.** This will allow you to re-open the component that you had previously closed. You can also combine two distinct path components into one by joining them together, provided that all of the components are open. To begin, choose the **Pen tool** from the toolbox and then click on the endpoint of the first path to indicate where you want the join to begin. Then, choose the location at the end of the second path where you want the join to terminate by clicking there. After that, your path's components will be merged into a single continuous component.

CHAPTER SIX
GETTING STARTED WITH TYPE

This chapter covers a variety of topics related to using type in Photoshop. It starts by outlining the main categories of functions connected to text. producing point type for simple text, enhancing text look using clipping masks and shadows, producing text along a path for curved or bespoke shapes, warping text for creative effects, and developing paragraph type for more organized and prepared text layouts are just a few of the topics covered in this chapter. All things considered, this chapter provides a thorough overview of text manipulation in Photoshop, including both fundamental and sophisticated methods.

MAJOR GROUPING OF PHOTOSHOP TEXT

Graphic design and picture editing in Adobe Photoshop both heavily rely on text. Text is often utilized to produce visually striking images, add visual features, and communicate information. Photoshop text can be broadly grouped into many important regions, each with a specific function and a range of modification choices. **Let's take a closer look at these main categories of Photoshop text:**

1. Text Tools:
   - **Horizontal Type Tool:** You can generate horizontal text in your document with this tool. You can begin typing in the document by clicking anywhere.
   - **Vertical Type Tool:** This tool lets you generate vertical text and is similar to the Horizontal Type Tool.
   - **Horizontal Type Mask Tool:** This tool helps create text-based masks since it makes a selection in the shape of your text.
2. Text Properties:
   - **Character Panel:** Photoshop's Character panel offers customization choices for each character's look. You can change the tracking, kerning, font, size, and other settings.
   - **Paragraph Panel:** This panel allows you to manage the text paragraphs' indentation, alignment, and spacing.
   - **Paragraph and Character Styles:** Text formatting can be saved as styles for simple reuse throughout your work.
3. Text Effects:
   - **Layer Styles:** Photoshop provides a variety of layer styles, such as drop shadow, bevel and emboss, outer and inner glow, and more, that can be applied to text layers to produce a variety of effects.

- **Blending Modes**: To create distinctive visual effects, text layers can be merged with underlying layers using various blending modes.
- **Warped Text**: You can warp text to apply different distortions, such as an arch, bulge, or flag, or to form shapes.

4. **Text on Path**:
   - **Path Text Tool**: Use the Path Text Tool to write text along a path or shape. You can utilize pre-existing shapes as paths or create your unique path.

5. **Text Masking**:
   - **Clipping Masks**: Text can be used as a mask to reveal or hide portions of an underlying image or layer. This is often used in creative compositions.

6. **Text Transformation**:
   - **Free Transform**: You can use the Free Transform tool to scale, rotate, or distort text layers.
   - **Warp Transform**: The Warp Transform option allows you to bend, twist, or distort text for unique effects.

7. **Text Filters**:
   - **Filter Effects**: Photoshop offers a variety of filters that can be applied to text layers, including blur, sharpen, distort, and stylize filters.

8. **Text Export**:
   - **Rasterize Text**: You can rasterize text layers to convert them into pixels, making them part of the image. This is useful for certain effects and transformations.
   - **Export Options**: When saving or exporting your Photoshop document, you have control over how text is preserved or flattened for different output formats.

9. **3D Text**:
   - **3D Text**: Photoshop supports 3D text, allowing you to create and manipulate text in a three-dimensional space.

10. **Text Presets**:
    - **Text Presets and Libraries**: Photoshop provides various text presets and libraries that include pre-designed text styles, making it easy to apply ready-made text effects.

CREATING A POINT TYPE

For any point text area to load properly in the Design Editor, it must have a consistent format. The first font style is applied to the full text and the other styles are disregarded if several font styles are applied to a layer of that type.

In Photoshop, to make a point text layer:

- Select either the Horizontal Type Tool or the Vertical Type Tool from the Tools panel after selecting Type Tool.
- Type some text and click where you want it to appear. Press enter to start a new line.
- When you're done, click **Done**.

Point text can be changed to paragraph text. To do this, choose Convert to Paragraph Text from the context menu when you right-click a point text layer. Click **Toggle text orientation** in the **Options** Bar to switch between horizontal and vertical orientation.

Paragraph Text

Unlike point text, paragraph text has boundaries. Paragraph text can be loaded into the Design Editor as either basic bounded text or rich formatted text. While basic confined text only supports one style per layer, the rich formatted text allows for several font styles in a single layer along with extensive paragraph formatting. The editor treats paragraph text as rich-styled text by default.

In Photoshop, to make a paragraph text layer:

1. Select either the Horizontal Type Tool or the Vertical Type Tool from the Tools menu after selecting Type Tool.
2. Enter some text after dragging to form a boundary rectangle. Press Enter to open a new paragraph.
3. When you're done, click **Done**.

Point text can be created from paragraph text. Right-click a paragraph text layer, and then choose ** **Convert to Point Text**** to do this. You can also change point text into paragraph text in the same manner. Click **Toggle text orientation** in the Options Bar to switch between horizontal and vertical orientation.

CREATING A CLIPPING MASK AND APPLYING A SHADOW

One typical method for giving an image or graphic depth and dimension in Adobe Photoshop is to create a clipping mask and apply a shadow.

This is the method you can follow step-by-step:

1. **Open Your Images:**
   - Open the image you want to apply the shadow to.
   - Place the desired shape or picture over the original image to be used as a clipping mask. Make sure you have it on a different layer. For this, you can use a shape, text, or any other element.

2. **Create a Clipping Mask:**
   - To create a clipping mask, choose the layer that contains the element you want to utilize.
   - From the context menu, choose "**Create Clipping Mask**" after right-clicking on the layer. Alternatively, you can use the keyboard shortcut **Ctrl+Alt+G** (Windows) or Cmd+Option+G (Mac).

By doing this, the top layer will be clipped to the shape and only be visible in the portion of the shape that is below it.

3. **Apply a Shadow:**
   - Verify that the clipped layer—the one to which you want to apply the shadow—is selected.
   - Click the "**Layer**" option at the top, pick "**Layer Style**," and then click "**Drop Shadow**." By doing this, the Layer Style dialog box will appear.
   4. **Modify the Shadow Settings:**

You can change the shadow settings in the Layer Style dialog box to get the appropriate result. Among these settings are:

- **Blend Mode:** Select how the shadow combines with the layers below. The most common default option is "**Multiply**."

- **Opacity**: Modify the shadow's transparency.
- **Angle**: Determine the angle at which the shadow is projected by the light source.
- **Distance**: Find the distance between the object and the shadow.
- **Size**: Adjust the shadow edge's blurriness or softness.
- **Color**: If necessary, alter the shadow's color.

Play around with these settings until you get the desired shadow effect.

5. Click **OK**:

To apply the shadow to your clipped layer, click the "**OK**" button in the Layer Style dialog box if you're happy with your shadow settings. That is all! With Photoshop, you've successfully made a clipping mask and given an element a shadow. This method can be used for many effects and is particularly beneficial for picture compositing and design tasks.

CREATING TYPE ON A PATH

Find the "**Pen Tool**" on the Photoshop toolbar, or hit "**P**" on your keyboard to open it. You may give your text unique paths using this tool. Now, draw the path you want your text to follow using the Pen Tool. To generate curved segments, drag and click to establish anchor points. Any path or shape you like can be created. After drawing your path, use the keyboard shortcut "T" or choose the "**Type Tool**" from the toolbar. After that, drag your mouse over the path you made until a text cursor with a wavy line appears.

The text pointer will follow the path you created when you click on it. Proceed to type your text now. The text will flow naturally as you follow the path. Using the options bar at the top of the screen, you can change the text's font, size, color, and other features. By using the "**Direct Selection Tool**" (the white arrow) from the toolbar, you can edit the text on the path. To tweak the look of the text, you can use this tool to shift certain anchor points on the path or change the distance between letters. You can utilize the "**Warp Text**" option to further alter how your text looks on the path. To do this, choose "**Warp Text**" from the Layers panel by performing a right-click on the text layer. This is where you can shape and resize the text to suit your layout. After you are happy with the way your text appears on the path, choose "**File**" > "**Save**" or "**File**" > "**Save As**" to save your Photoshop project. If you want to utilize your design outside of Photoshop, you can also export it in several forms, including JPEG or PNG.

WARPING TEXT

Text Warp Defined

Text warp, to put it simply, is the act of twisting or bending a word or set of words into a certain shape. This specific technique is often used to improve the visual appeal of designs and modify text inside a certain shape or area. Text warping, for instance, can be used in a design that has text around a circle. Aside from that, you can twist and deform your text to fit within a certain shape—perhaps a rectangle with restricted space.

Warp and Distort Text in Photoshop?

Thus, we will now begin discussing how to use Photoshop to warp and distort text. Using Photoshop, applying warp effects to your text is quite quick and straightforward. The nicest thing about using Photoshop's warp feature is that it provides a wide variety of warp effects, so you can customize your design to your heart's content.

1. Open Photoshop and Type Your Text

Start by opening Photoshop and making a new background layer with the size you want. After that, type the text you want to distort. You can also choose an appropriate background layer color and alter it.

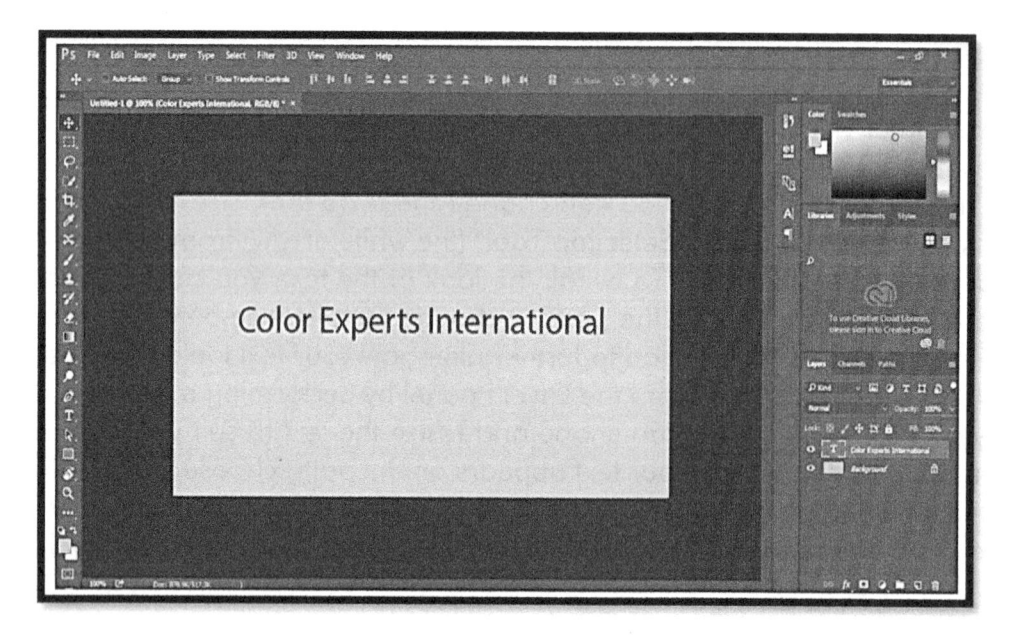

2. Warp Your Text

Go to the menu bar now and choose the "**Type**" option. Several things will appear immediately. From the list of objects, choose "**Wrap Text**."

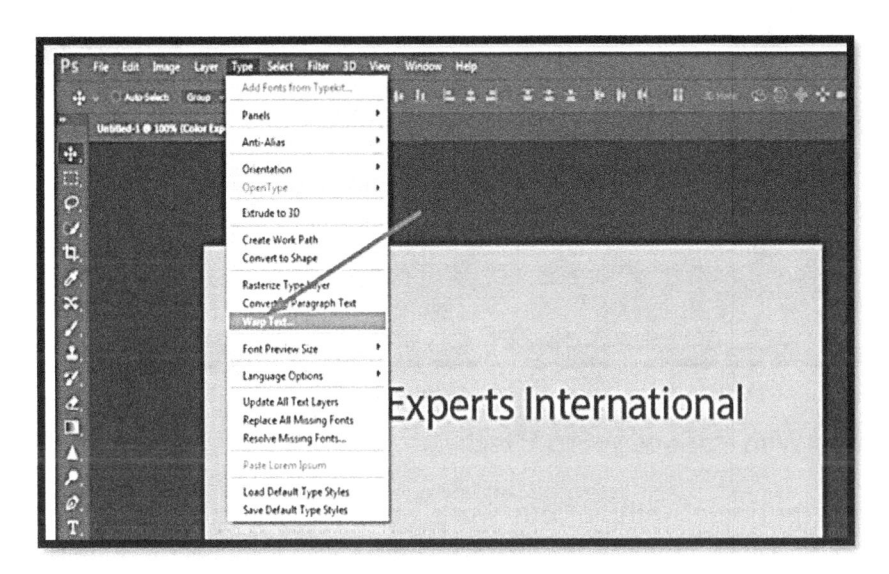

After that, a little window will appear right away. A list of warping effects will then show up. Any of the warp effects can be selected to fit your design requirements.

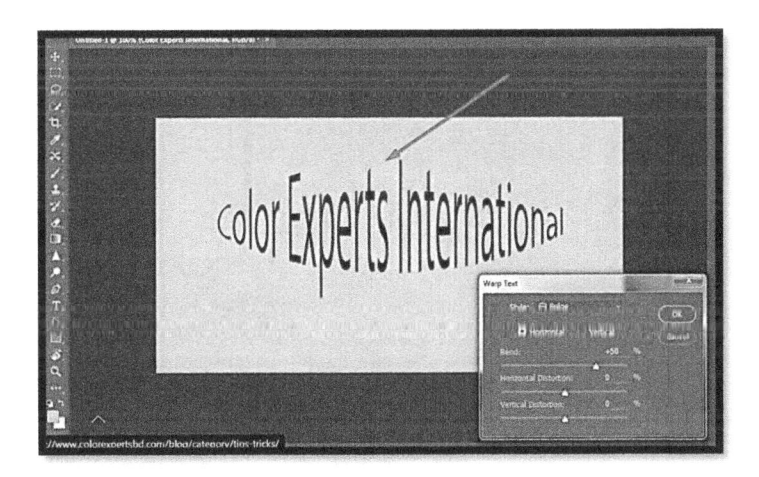

3. Modify Your Warp Text

Numerous more parameters, including **Bend, Horizontal Distortion, and Vertical Distortion**, will be shown in the window. You can change and fine-tune your warp text by dragging the sliders.

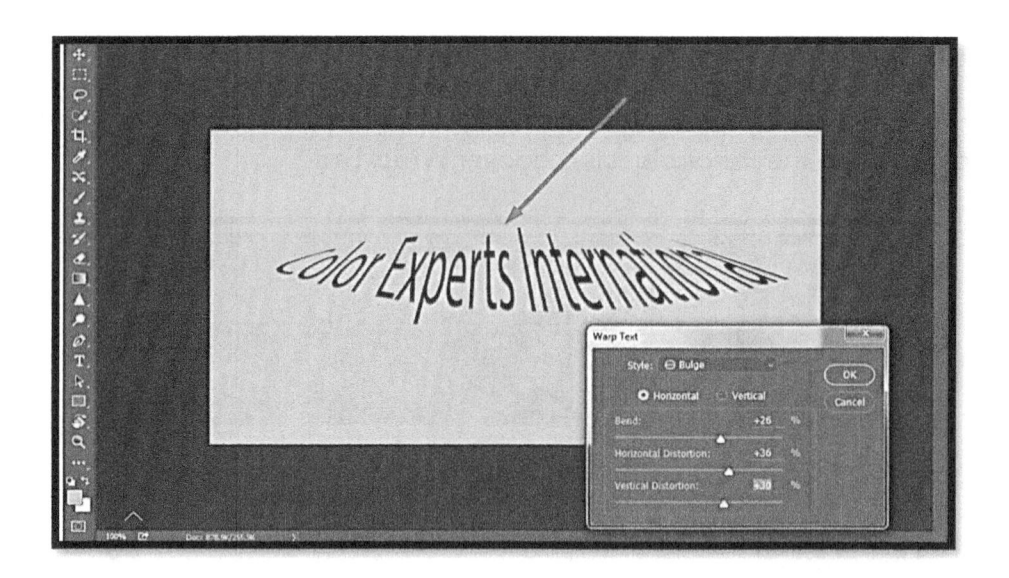

4. Play Around With Various Warp Effects

Proceed and experiment with various warp effects such as arc, arch, fisheye, flag, wave, and so on to see how they seem. After that, you can decide which warp effect is ideal for your design.

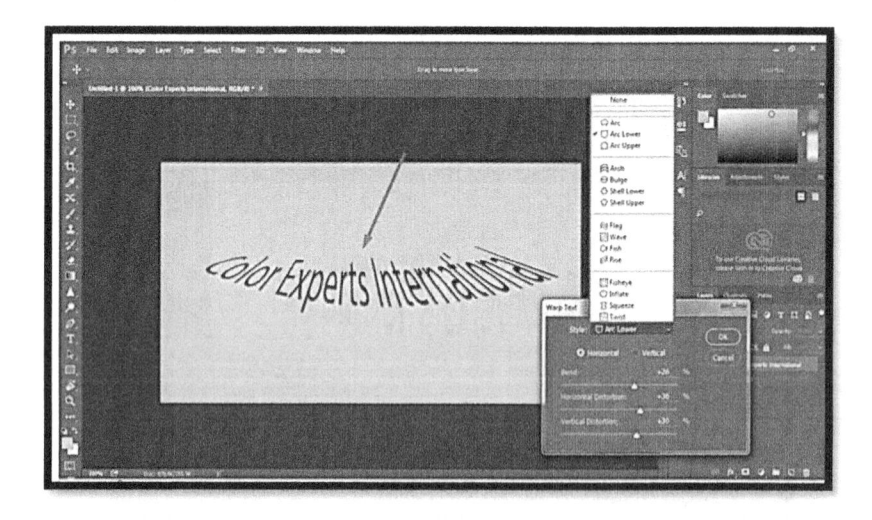

5. Edit Warp Text Live

To alter the text live, just choose the already-warped text. Double-click the text layer in your layer panel to do that. You can then remove the current text and enter a new one that will appear in a distorted shape.

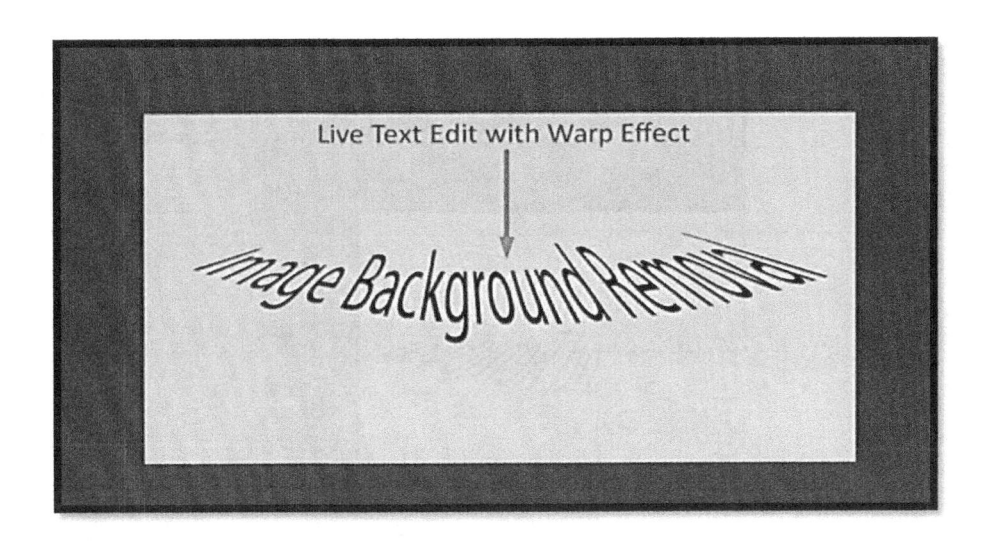

6. To distort, rasterize the twisted text

Now that you have finished bending the text, it is necessary to rasterize it so that it can be distorted. The bent text cannot be distorted without rasterization.

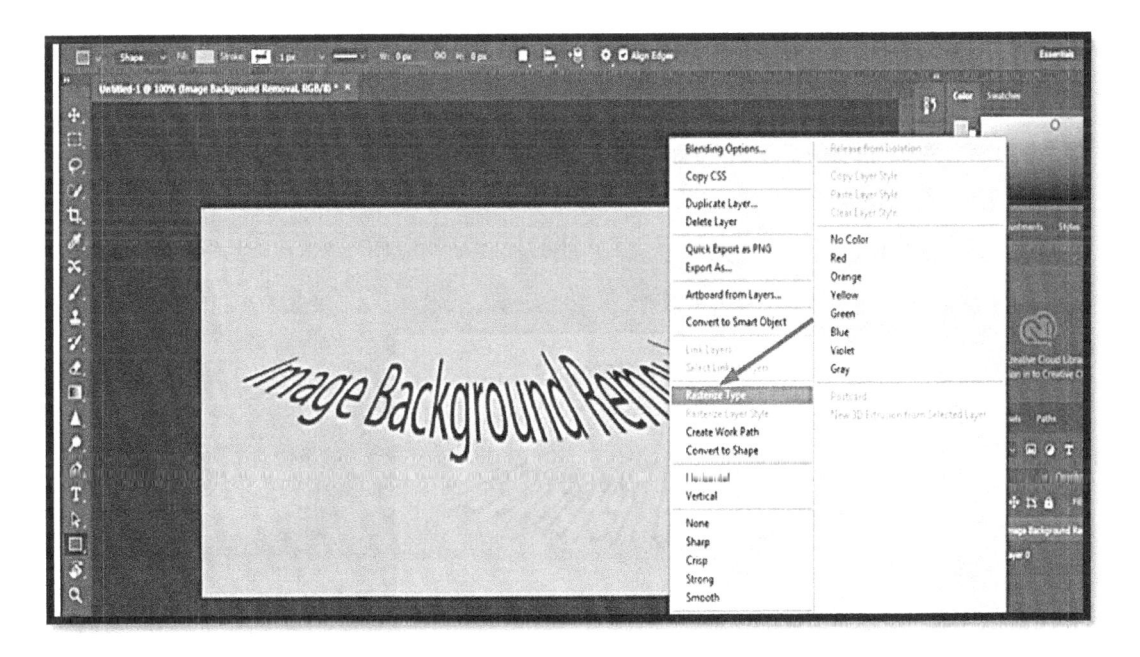

7. Distort the Warped Text

Proceed to the "**Edit**" menu and choose "**Transform**" now. Next, choose "**Distort**" from the item list.

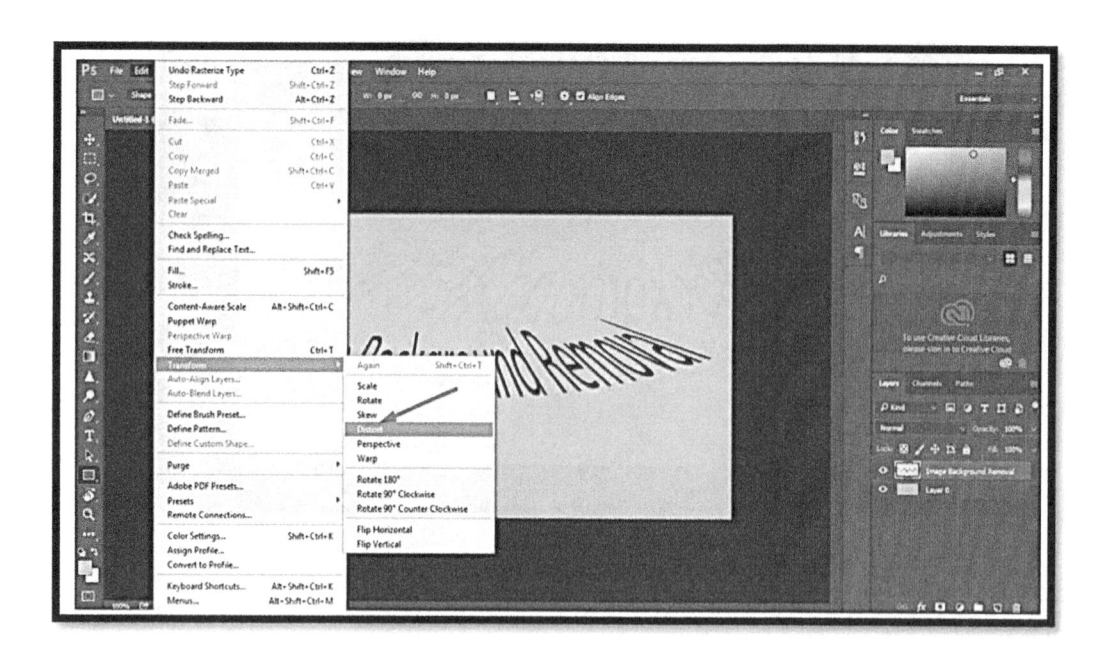

8. Text Warped and Distorted

You can now begin to twist and distort the text to suit your needs. By using the distortion effect, you can make the text fit into any shape.

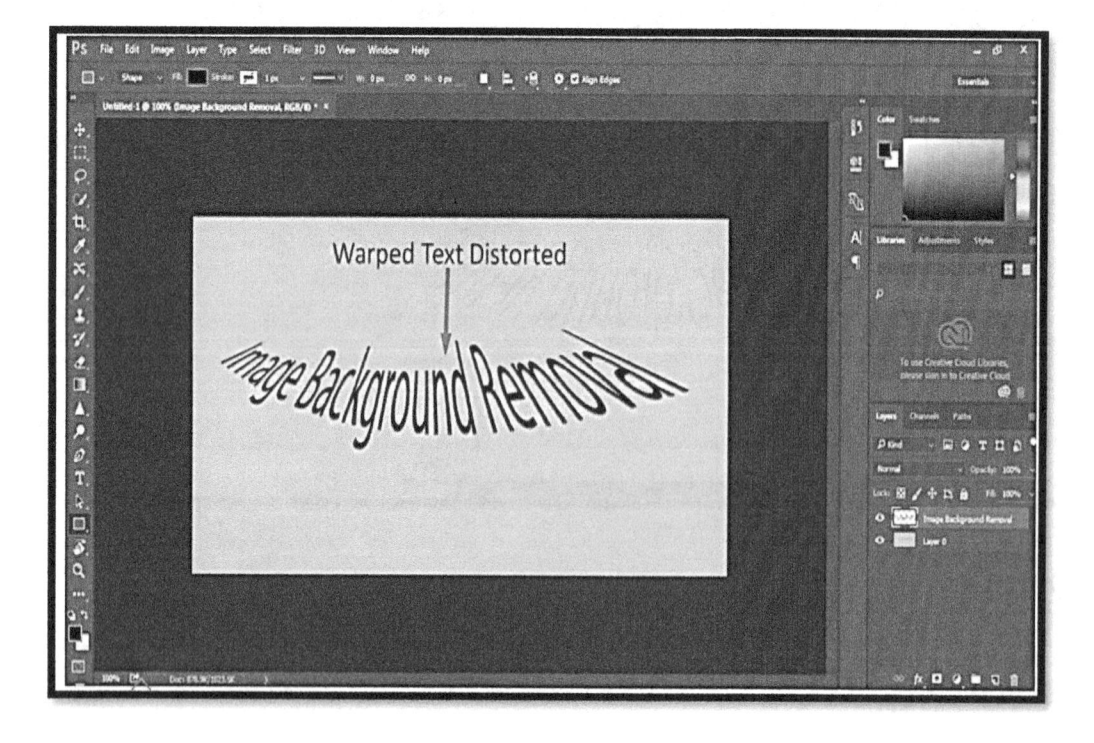

CHAPTER SEVEN
UPDATED SHORTCUTS COMMAND

This focuses on Photoshop's improved keyboard shortcuts. It includes a broad range of shortcut categories, such as layer shortcuts for working with layers, edit shortcuts for manipulating content, command shortcuts for general actions, select shortcuts for making selections, view shortcuts for adjusting the view and display settings, and tool shortcuts for rapidly accessing and utilizing different Photoshop tools. This chapter gives readers useful tips on how to use keyboard shortcuts to expedite their workflow and improve their efficiency while using Photoshop.

List of modifier keys

On a computer keyboard, modifier keys are keys that can be used in conjunction with other keys to carry out certain tasks or change how other keys behave. These keys are often seen on most computer keyboards and are essential to some different software programs.

These are a few typical modifier keys:

- **Shift**: On keys with two symbols written on them, the Shift key is used to access the top symbols and type capital characters. It may also be used in conjunction with other keys to initiate other features.
- **Ctrl (Control)**: The Control key, which is often shortened to "Ctrl," can be used alone or in conjunction with other keys to execute some keyboard shortcuts. Keyboards running Mac OS X and Windows often have it.
- **Alt (other)**: Frequently denoted as "Alt," this key allows you to access other uses for other keys, such as typing special characters or bringing up menus in software programs.
- **Option (Mac)**: The Option key on Mac keyboards performs the same function as the Alt key on Windows keyboards. It's utilized to get access to different functionalities and characters.
- **Command (Mac)**: Exclusive to Mac keyboards, the Command key is often indicated by the ⌘ sign. On macOS, it serves as a modifier key for some keyboard shortcuts and system functions.
- **Fn (Function)**: On certain laptop keyboards, the Function key, denoted by the letter "**Fn**," is used to access unique features or shortcuts, such as adjusting screen brightness or managing multimedia playing.

- ❖ **Windows Key (Windows):** The Windows key, which is often symbolized by the Windows logo or the ⊞ **key**, is a keyboard shortcut that opens the Windows Taskbar, opens the Start menu, and activates some system shortcuts.
- ❖ **Option/Alt Gr (On Some International Keyboards):** To access special characters and symbols unique to that keyboard layout, press the extra Alt key on some international keyboards that are designated "**Alt Gr**" or "**Option**".
- ❖ **Caps Lock:** Using the Caps Lock key, you can switch between entering letters in uppercase and lowercase on the keyboard. When Caps Lock is engaged, all letters written will be capitalized until it is released.
- ❖ **Num Lock:** Some keyboards include a numeric keypad that can be used as navigation keys or as a numeric keypad. To utilize it, press the Num Lock key.
- ❖ **Scroll Lock:** Although its functionality is not often used in contemporary applications, the Scroll Lock key was traditionally employed to regulate the scrolling behavior in certain programs.
- ❖ **Insert (INS):** Frequently shortened to "Ins," the Insert key allows users to switch between the overtypes and insert modes and can alter the behavior of other keys, especially in text editing software.
- ❖ **Print Screen (PrtScn):** This key copies what is currently on the screen or in the active window to the clipboard. Some keyboards have the labels "**PrtScn**" or "**PrtSc**."

When used with other keys, these modifier keys can significantly improve the efficiency and utility of keyboard and computer interactions. They are extensively utilized in many different programs and operating systems and are an essential component of keyboard shortcuts.

NOTE: The shortcuts shown below can be customized to your tastes. The actions that you can do in Photoshop have these preset shortcut keys. You can, however, alter them to suit your tastes. Use the keyboard keys **Alt + Shift + Control + K (Windows)** or **Option + Shift + Command + K (Mac)** to do that, or choose **Edit > Keyboard keys**.

CREATING YOUR KEYBOARD SHORTCUTS

It's simple to start: just launch **Photoshop**, and choose **Edit > Keyboard Shortcuts**. It is toward the bottom of the list, so you'll need to scroll down or use the shortcut, which is **Alt + Shift + Control + K (Win)**, or **Option + Shift + Command + K (Mac)**.

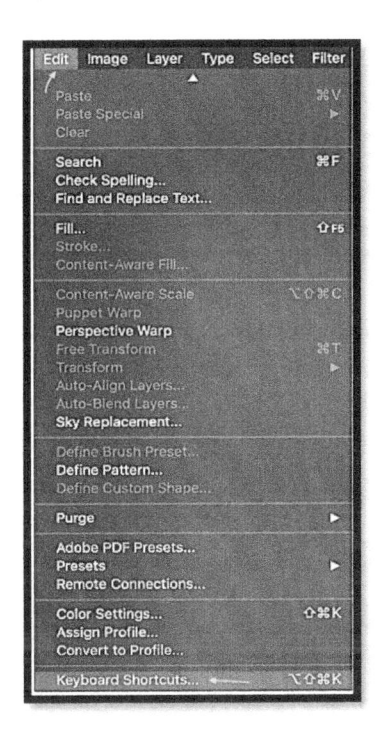

The **Keyboard Shortcuts and Menus** window will open.

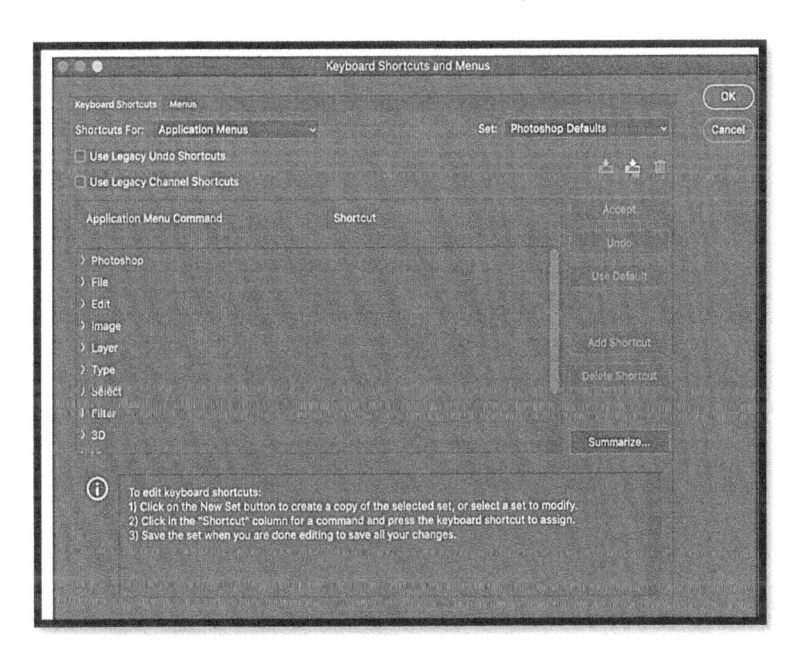

This will prompt you to choose the kind of shortcut you want to create in the "Shortcut For" area at the top of the window.

> Keyboard Shortcuts   Menus
> Shortcuts For: Application Menus
> ☐ Use Legacy Undo Shortcuts

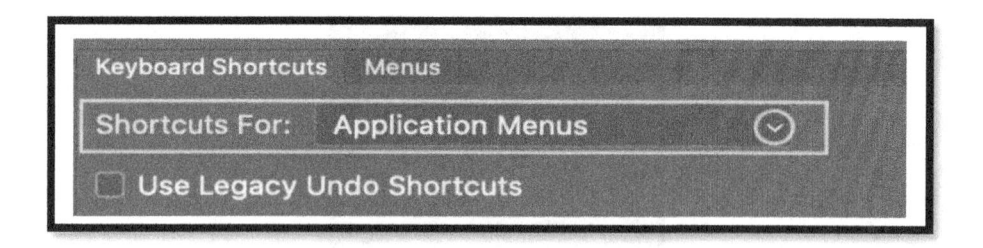

After you click the down arrow, all of the accessible shortcuts will be shown to you. The Photoshop application window has several menu options that you can choose from: the Application Menus, which are the menu options at the top; the Panel Menus, which are the various panels that you can access; the Tools, which are the options on the left vertical toolbar; and the Taskspaces.

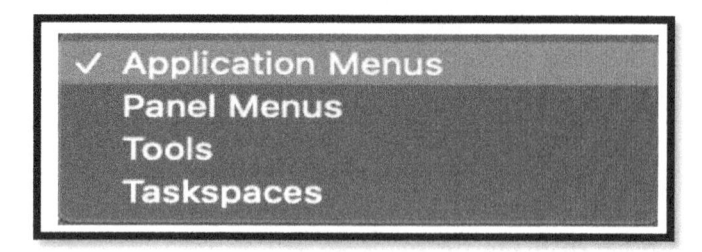

> ✓ Application Menus
> Panel Menus
> Tools
> Taskspaces

Select the one for which you want to create a shortcut. The many options for which you can build a shortcut will show up in the table below after you've chosen a shortcut type. **For example, I would see the following table if I attempted to create a shortcut for one of the Application Menu options:**

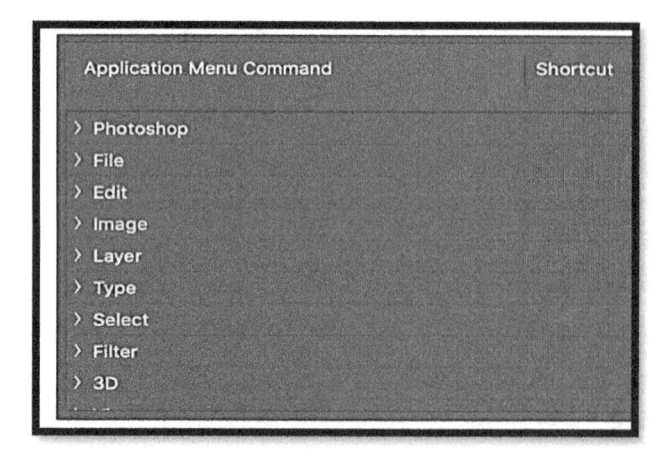

Application Menu Command	Shortcut
> Photoshop	
> File	
> Edit	
> Image	
> Layer	
> Type	
> Select	
> Filter	
> 3D	

You will see any accessible shortcuts on the right for the Menu Command, which is the command that is shown on the left. You will see that a considerable number of commands, including those located under the File tab, already have shortcuts.

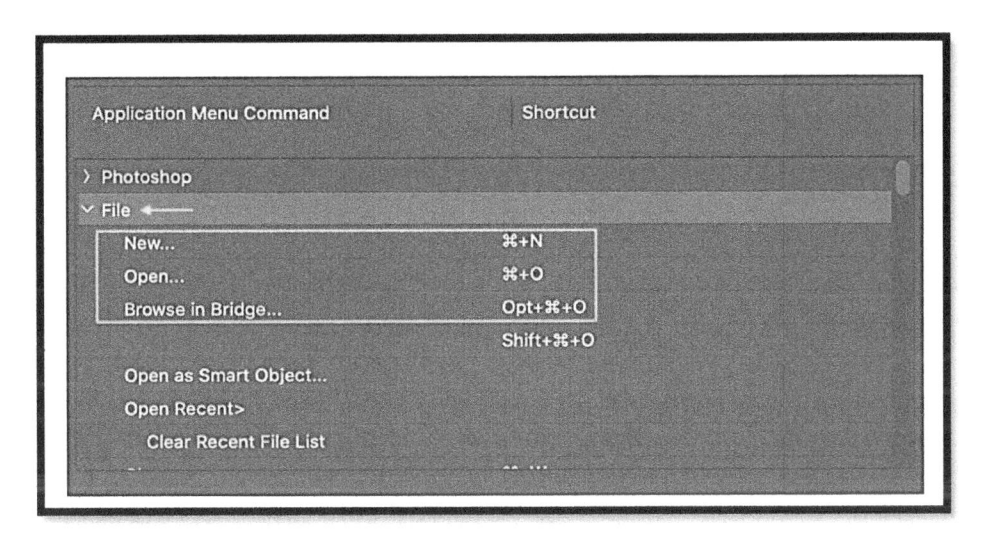

Application Menu Command	Shortcut
> Photoshop	
∨ File	
New...	⌘+N
Open...	⌘+O
Browse in Bridge...	Opt+⌘+O
	Shift+⌘+O
Open as Smart Object...	
Open Recent>	
Clear Recent File List	

To create a shortcut, find and click the tab containing the command you want to make a shortcut for. To rapidly adjust my image's brightness and contrast, I would choose the Image tab, then swiftly scroll down to locate the Brightness/Contrast area under the Adjustments heading. I would use this as a shortcut. A new box named "**shortcut type**" will appear in the right column when you pick the command for which you want to create a shortcut. You can now type the shortcut you want to use to access the Brightness/Contrast settings. As you would typically do while working, press the corresponding keys on the keyboard and enter the keyboard shortcut.

Note: You must press one of the F keys in addition to the Control (Win) or Command (Mac) key for menu shortcuts to function. The "**Tools**" abbreviation is also a letter that can stand alone.

To see how to utilize the Brightness/Contrast shortcut, on a Mac, press and hold the Control key in addition to the Command key, or on a PC, press and hold the Control key in addition to the Windows key. You'll see that shortcuts have previously been used several times. A yellow triangle will appear next to the command and a warning stating that the key is already in use will appear if you attempt to enter a shortcut that is already being used for another command.

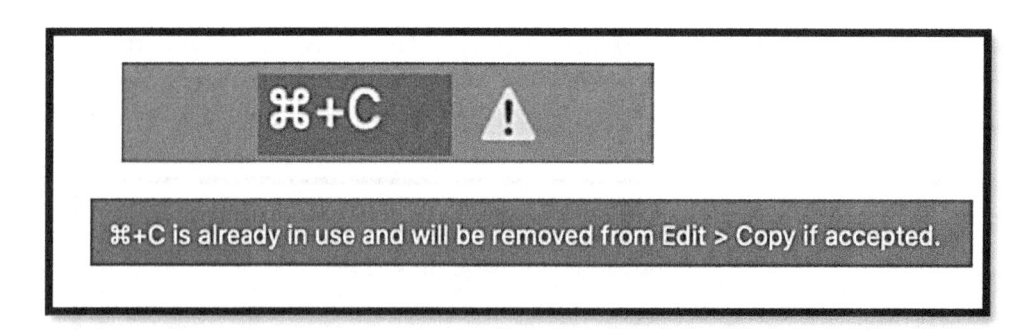

⌘+C is already in use and will be removed from Edit > Copy if accepted.

This keyboard shortcut will remain unutilized if you continue to use it for this command. As long as you accept that the other command will be overridden, you can keep using the shortcut. For this reason, I advise you to replace shortcuts only for instructions that you use seldom, if at all. You can locate the shortcut you want to remove and hit the **Delete** key on your keyboard if you have any that you no longer need. I wouldn't advise doing this with too many shortcuts, however, since you never know when one of them could come in useful. This will free up the shortcut so that it can be utilized in another context. You can assign a keyboard shortcut after you have made the necessary customizations. Click Accept to confirm the shortcut, and then click OK to close the window and return to the workspace.

It's time to test your shortcut when you've completed making it. I will utilize those keys since I already have a shortcut set up by hitting **Control + Command + B (on a Mac) or Control + Windows + B (on a Windows PC)**. Every time I use my shortcut, the **Brightness/Contrast** adjustment is successfully triggered, and the window opens when I hit the shortcut. This proves that I can use the shortcut without risk. You may now create as many shortcuts as you like to improve the efficiency and simplicity of your workflow.

EDIT SHORTCUTS

The "**Edit**" menu in Photoshop encompasses a wide array of essential functions, and knowing the keyboard shortcuts for these commands can save you time and make your editing process smoother. **Let's explore some of the most commonly used "Edit" menu shortcuts in Photoshop:**

1. Undo and Redo:
    - **Ctrl + Z** (Windows) or **Command + Z** (Mac): This shortcut allows you to undo your previous action.
    - **Ctrl + Shift + Z** (Windows) or **Command + Shift + Z** (Mac): To redo an action that you've undone.

2. **Cut, Copy, and Paste:**
    - **Ctrl + X** (Windows) or **Command + X** (Mac): Cut the selected item.
    - **Ctrl + C** (Windows) or **Command + C** (Mac): Copy the selected item.
    - **Ctrl + V** (Windows) or **Command + V** (Mac): Paste the copied or cut item.
3. **Deselect:**
    - **Ctrl + D** (Windows) or **Command + D** (Mac): Quickly deselect any selected area or object.
4. **Free Transform:**
    - **Ctrl + T** (Windows) or **Command + T** (Mac): Activate the free transform tool, allowing you to resize, rotate, and skew layers.
5. **Transform Selection:**
    - **Ctrl + T** (Windows) or **Command + T** (Mac) followed by **Enter**: Transform the selected area or object within a layer.
6. **Fill:**
    - **Shift + F5**: Opens the Fill dialog, enabling you to fill selections or layers with a color or pattern.
7. **Content-Aware Fill:**
    - **Shift + Backspace** (Windows) or **Shift + Delete** (Mac): Access the Content-Aware Fill dialog for advanced retouching and object removal.
8. **Keyboard Shortcuts:**
    - **Ctrl + Alt + Shift + K** (Windows) or **Command + Option + Shift + K** (Mac): Open the Keyboard Shortcuts dialog to customize and view existing keyboard shortcuts.
9. **Preferences:**
    - **Ctrl + K** (Windows) or **Command + K** (Mac): Quickly access the Photoshop Preferences dialog to customize various settings.
10. **Purge:**
    - **Alt + Ctrl + Shift + R** (Windows) or **Option + Command + Shift + R** (Mac): Purge undos, clipboard, or history states to free up memory.
11. **Cut to New Layer:**
    - **Ctrl + Shift + J** (Windows) or **Command + Shift + J** (Mac): Cut the selected area or object to a new layer.
12. **Keyboard Shortcuts for Menu Commands:**
    - If you want to see the keyboard shortcut for a specific menu item, press **Ctrl** (Windows) or **Command** (Mac) and hover over the menu item. The corresponding shortcut key will be displayed next to the menu item.

These keyboard shortcuts are invaluable for speeding up your editing process in Photoshop. By memorizing and integrating them into your workflow, you can work more efficiently, reduce the need to navigate through menus and maintain a seamless creative experience.

IMAGE SHORTCUTS

This menu contains various functions for manipulating and enhancing your images.

Here's a list of keyboard shortcuts for common tasks found in the "Image" menu:

1. Image Size:
    - **Alt + Ctrl + I** (Windows) or **Option + Command + I** (Mac): Opens the Image Size dialog for resizing images.
2. Canvas Size:
    - **Alt + Ctrl + C** (Windows) or **Option + Command + C** (Mac): Access the Canvas Size dialog to change the image canvas dimensions.
3. Rotate Canvas:
    - **R** (Windows/Mac): Enables the Rotate Canvas tool. Hold down **Shift** while rotating for 15-degree increments.
4. Trim:
    - **Alt + Ctrl + C** (Windows) or **Option + Command + C** (Mac) followed by **T**: Opens the Trim dialog to automatically remove excess transparent pixels.
5. Reveal All:
    - **Alt + Ctrl + 0** (Windows) or **Option + Command + 0** (Mac): Fits the image on the screen while revealing all hidden areas.
6. Adjustments:
    - **Ctrl + L** (Windows) or **Command + L** (Mac): Opens the Levels dialog for adjusting image tonal values.
    - **Ctrl + M** (Windows) or **Command + M** (Mac): Access the Curves dialog to fine-tune image contrast.
    - **Ctrl + B** (Windows) or **Command + B** (Mac): Opens the Color Balance dialog for adjusting the image's color balance.
7. Desaturate:
    - **Shift + Ctrl + U** (Windows) or **Shift + Command + U** (Mac): Converts the image to grayscale (removes color).
8. Invert:
    - **Ctrl + I** (Windows) or **Command + I** (Mac): Inverts the colors of the image.

9. Auto Tone, Contrast, and Color:
    - **Shift + Ctrl + L** (Windows) or **Shift + Command + L** (Mac): Automatically adjusts the image's tone levels.
    - **Shift + Ctrl + C** (Windows) or **Shift + Command + C** (Mac): Automatically adjusts image contrast.
    - **Shift + Ctrl + B** (Windows) or **Shift + Command + B** (Mac): Automatically adjusts the image's color balance.
10. Apply Image:
    - **Alt + Ctrl + Shift + I** (Windows) or **Option + Command + Shift + I** (Mac): Opens the Apply Image dialog for blending image channels.
11. Calculations:
    - **Alt + Ctrl + Shift + K** (Windows) or **Option + Command + Shift + K** (Mac): Opens the Calculations dialog for complex channel blending.
12. Match Color:
    - **Shift + Ctrl + B** (Windows) or **Shift + Command + B** (Mac) followed by **M**: Opens the Match Color dialog for matching image colors.
13. Variations:
    - **Ctrl + Y** (Windows) or **Command + Y** (Mac): Opens the Variations dialog for adjusting image colors and tones.
14. Image Rotation:
    - **Alt + Ctrl + Shift + R** (Windows) or **Option + Command + Shift + R** (Mac): Rotates the entire image canvas.
15. Duplicate Image:
    - **Ctrl + Alt + Shift + D** (Windows) or **Command + Option + Shift + D** (Mac): Creates a duplicate of the current image.
16. Image Mode:
    - **Alt + Shift + Ctrl + I** (Windows) or **Option + Shift + Command + I** (Mac): Opens the Image Mode submenu for changing the color mode of the image.

These keyboard shortcuts for the "Image" menu in Photoshop will help streamline your editing process and make it more efficient. Whether you're resizing images, adjusting colors, or performing other image-related tasks, these shortcuts will save you time and effort, allowing you to focus on your creative work.

FILE SHORTCUTS

Efficiently navigating through the "File" menu in Adobe Photoshop is crucial for managing your projects, opening and saving files, and performing various file-related tasks.

Here's an extensive list of keyboard shortcuts for common functions found in the "File" menu:

1. **New File:**
    - **Ctrl + N** (Windows) or **Command + N** (Mac): Opens the New Document dialog to create a new file.
2. **Open File:**
    - **Ctrl + O** (Windows) or **Command + O** (Mac): Opens the Open dialog for selecting and opening an existing file.
3. **Open as Smart Object:**
    - **Shift + Ctrl + O** (Windows) or **Shift + Command + O** (Mac): Opens a file as a Smart Object.
4. **Open Recent Files:**
    - **Ctrl + Alt + O** (Windows) or **Command + Option + O** (Mac): Opens the Open Recent submenu to access recently opened files.
5. **Close File:**
    - **Ctrl + W** (Windows) or **Command + W** (Mac): Closes the current file. Use **Ctrl + Shift + W** (Windows) or **Command + Shift + W** (Mac) to close all open files.
6. **Save File:**
    - **Ctrl + S** (Windows) or **Command + S** (Mac): Saves the current file.
7. **Save As:**
    - **Shift + Ctrl + S** (Windows) or **Shift + Command + S** (Mac): Opens the Save As dialog to save the current file with a new name or in a different format.
8. **Save for Web:**
    - **Alt + Shift + Ctrl + S** (Windows) or **Option + Shift + Command + S** (Mac): Opens the Save for Web dialog for optimizing images for web use.
9. **Revert to Saved:**
    - **F12**: Reverts the current file to the last saved version.
10. **Place Embedded:**
    - **Shift + Ctrl + Place** (Windows) or **Shift + Command + Place** (Mac): Places an external file into the current document as an embedded object.
11. **Export As:**
    - **Alt + Shift + Ctrl + W** (Windows) or **Option + Shift + Command + W** (Mac): Opens the Export As dialog for exporting images in various formats.
12. **Export All:**

- **Alt + Shift + Ctrl + S** (Windows) or **Option + Shift + Command + S** (Mac): Exports all open files.
13. **Generate Image Assets:**
    - **Shift + Ctrl + Alt + S** (Windows) or **Shift + Command + Option + S** (Mac): Converts layers into image assets for web and app development.
14. **Automate:**
    - **Alt + Ctrl + F** (Windows) or **Option + Command + F** (Mac): Opens the Automate submenu for batch processing and other automation tasks.
15. **Scripts:**
    - **Alt + Ctrl + F** (Windows) or **Option + Command + F** (Mac) followed by X: Opens the Scripts menu to run Photoshop scripts.
16. **File Info:**
    - **Alt + Shift + Ctrl + I** (Windows) or **Option + Shift + Command + I** (Mac): Opens the File Info dialog for adding metadata to the file.
17. **Close and Go to Bridge:**
    - **Ctrl + Alt + O** (Windows) or **Command + Option + O** (Mac) followed by B: Closes the current file and opens Adobe Bridge if installed.
18. **Page Setup:**
    - **Shift + Ctrl + P** (Windows) or **Shift + Command + P** (Mac): Opens the Page Setup dialog for setting up printing options.

These keyboard shortcuts for the "File" menu in Photoshop will help you efficiently manage your files, save your work, and access various file-related functions with ease. Whether you're starting a new project, opening existing files, or exporting your creations, these shortcuts are invaluable for a smoother and more productive workflow.

LAYER SHORTCUTS

Layer menu shortcuts in Photoshop are essential tools for streamlining your workflow and enhancing your efficiency when working on complex image editing projects. These keyboard shortcuts provide quick access to various layer-related functions, allowing you to manipulate layers, blend them, and manage your composition more effectively.

Creating and Selecting Layers

1. **New Layer**: To create a new layer, you can use the shortcut **Ctrl+Shift+N** (Windows) or **Cmd+Shift+N** (Mac). This opens the New Layer dialog box, where you can customize layer properties.
2. **Duplicate Layer**: Quickly duplicate a selected layer by pressing **Ctrl+J** (Windows) or **Cmd+J** (Mac). This is handy when you want to make copies for different edits.
3. **Select All Layers**: To select all layers in your document, use the shortcut **Ctrl+Alt+A** (Windows) or **Cmd+Option+A** (Mac).

Layer Blending Modes

4. **Blending Modes**: Adjust layer blending modes using shortcuts. First, select the Move tool (**V** key) and then press **Shift** and the plus or minus key to cycle through the blending modes. For example, **Shift++** to move forward and **Shift+-** to move backward through the blending modes.

Layer Opacity

5. **Layer Opacity**: You can change the opacity of a selected layer by typing a number between 0 and 9 on the keyboard. For example, **5** sets the opacity to 50%.

Layer Visibility

6. **Toggle Layer Visibility**: To quickly toggle the visibility of a selected layer on and off, press the **/** (forward slash) key.

Layer Locks

7. **Lock Layers**: Lock layers to prevent accidental changes. Use **Ctrl+2** (Windows) or **Cmd+2** (Mac) for locking transparency, **Ctrl+3** (Windows) or **Cmd+3** (Mac) for locking position, and **Ctrl+4** (Windows) or **Cmd+4** (Mac) for locking all layer attributes.

Layer Groups

8. **Create Layer Group**: To create a new layer group, press **Ctrl+G** (Windows) or **Cmd+G** (Mac) when you have one or more layers selected. This helps in organizing your layers into folders.

9. **Collapse/Expand Layer Group**: Use **Alt+[** (Windows) or **Option+[** (Mac) to collapse a layer group and **Alt+]** (Windows) or **Option+]** (Mac) to expand it, making it easier to manage complex compositions.

Layer Masking

10. **Add Layer Mask**: Add a layer mask to the active layer with **Alt+Click** (Windows) or **Option+Click** (Mac) on the layer mask icon at the bottom of the Layers panel.
11. **Disable/Enable Layer Mask**: Temporarily disable or enable a layer mask by pressing **Shift+Click** on the layer mask thumbnail in the Layers panel.

Layer Styles

12. **Layer Style Dialog**: Open the Layer Style dialog for a layer by double-clicking the layer or using **Alt+Double-Click** (Windows) or **Option+Double-Click** (Mac) on the layer.

Layer Alignment

13. **Align Layers**: To align selected layers, use **Ctrl+Shift+V** (Windows) or **Cmd+Shift+V** (Mac) to open the Align Layers dialog box, where you can choose alignment options.

Layer Linking

14. **Link Layers**: Link or unlink layers together by selecting the layers and using **Ctrl+L** (Windows) or **Cmd+L** (Mac).

Layer Opacity and Fill

15. **Opacity and Fill Dialog**: To access the Opacity and Fill dialog for a selected layer, press **Shift+Click** on the layer's opacity or fill value in the Layers panel.

These layer menu shortcuts in Photoshop can significantly expedite your editing process and help you maintain a well-organized workflow. By incorporating these shortcuts into your daily Photoshop usage, you'll become a more proficient and efficient digital artist or photo editor, ultimately saving you time and effort in your creative endeavors.

SELECT SHORTCUTS

Select menu shortcuts in various software applications, including Photoshop, are essential for efficiently choosing and manipulating different elements within your project.

Basic Selection Tools

1. **Marquee Selections**: Photoshop provides two main marquee selection tools. To access these, press **M** to activate the Marquee tool, and then use **Shift+M** to toggle between the Rectangular Marquee (**M**) and Elliptical Marquee (**Shift+M**) tools.
2. **Lasso Selections**: To access the Lasso tool and its variations, press **L** to activate the Lasso tool, and then use **Shift+L** to cycle through the Lasso tool options, including the Polygonal Lasso (**Shift+L**) and Magnetic Lasso (**Shift+L**) tools.
3. **Magic Wand Selection**: The Magic Wand tool is handy for selecting areas with similar colors. To select it, press **W**. You can also cycle through the Quick Selection tool (**Shift+W**) and the Object Selection tool (**Shift+W**) using this shortcut.

Advanced Selection Tools

4. **Select Subject**: Quickly select the main subject of an image by pressing **W** and then using the **S** key to activate the Select Subject command. This leverages Adobe Sensei's AI to intelligently identify the subject.
5. **Select and Mask**: To refine selections and work on the fine details, press **W** and then **Shift+M** to open the Select and Mask workspace. This allows for precise selection adjustments, feathering, and more.

Selection Modification

6. **Add to Selection**: To add to an existing selection, press **Shift** and hold while using any of the selection tools (Marquee, Lasso, Magic Wand, etc.).
7. **Subtract from Selection**: To subtract from an existing selection, press **Alt** (Windows) or **Option** (Mac) and hold while using any of the selection tools.
8. **Intersect with Selection**: To intersect a new selection with an existing one, press **Shift+Alt** (Windows) or **Shift+Option** (Mac) and hold while using any of the selection tools.

Select All and Deselect

9. **Select All**: Quickly select the entire canvas by pressing **Ctrl+A** (Windows) or **Cmd+A** (Mac).
10. **Deselect**: Remove an active selection by pressing **Ctrl+D** (Windows) or **Cmd+D** (Mac).

Select Menu Commands

11. **Inverse Selection**: Invert the current selection by pressing **Shift+Ctrl+I** (Windows) or **Shift+Cmd+I** (Mac).
12. **Modify Selection**: Access the Modify menu by pressing **Ctrl+Shift+M** (Windows) or **Cmd+Shift+M** (Mac). This menu offers options to expand, contract, feather, and more.
13. **Color Range**: Open the Color Range dialog for selecting specific colors within an image by pressing **Alt+Shift+Ctrl+O** (Windows) or **Option+Shift+Cmd+O** (Mac).

These select menu shortcuts in Photoshop empower you to efficiently create and manipulate selections, saving you time and allowing for more precise edits in your digital artwork or photo editing projects.

VIEW SHORTCUTS

View menu shortcuts in Photoshop provide quick access to various display options and tools that help you navigate and view your work more efficiently. These shortcuts allow you to customize your workspace and toggle different view settings. Below, you'll find an extensive list of view menu shortcuts in Photoshop:

Zooming In and Out

1. **Zoom In**: Zoom in on your document by pressing **Ctrl** and the **+** key (Windows) or **Cmd** and the **+** key (Mac). You can also use the **Z** key to activate the Zoom tool and then click to zoom in.
2. **Zoom Out**: Zoom out from your document by pressing **Ctrl** and the **-** key (Windows) or **Cmd** and the **-** key (Mac). In addition, you can use the **Z** key to activate the Zoom tool and then **Alt** (Windows) or **Option** (Mac) while clicking to zoom out.
3. **Fit to Screen**: Fit your document to the screen by pressing **Ctrl+0** (Windows) or **Cmd+0** (Mac).
4. **100% Zoom**: Set your view to 100% by pressing **Ctrl+Alt+0** (Windows) or **Cmd+Option+0** (Mac).

Navigation and Panning

5. **Hand Tool**: Access the Hand tool, which allows you to pan around your document, by pressing the **H** key.
6. **Rotate View Tool**: Rotate your view by pressing **R**. You can use this tool to temporarily rotate your canvas for easier drawing or editing.

Screen Mode

7. **Full-Screen Mode with Menu Bar**: Toggle between full-screen modes with and without the menu bar by pressing **F**.
8. **Standard Screen Mode**: Switch to standard screen mode by pressing **Shift+F**.
9. **Maximize Screen Mode**: Go into maximize screen mode by pressing **F** twice in quick succession.

Rulers, Grids, and Guides

10. **Show/Hide Rulers**: Show or hide rulers along the top and left sides of your document by pressing **Ctrl+R** (Windows) or **Cmd+R** (Mac).
11. **Show/Hide Grid**: Show or hide the grid over your document with **Ctrl+'** (Windows) or **Cmd+'** (Mac).
12. **Show/Hide Guides**: Toggle visibility of guides with **Ctrl+;** (Windows) or **Cmd+;** (Mac).

Extras

13. **Show/Hide Extras**: Display or hide extras like the selection edges and other overlays by pressing **Ctrl+H** (Windows) or **Cmd+H** (Mac).

Snap To

14. **Snap To**: Enable or disable snapping to guides, grids, or other elements by pressing **Shift+Ctrl+;** (Windows) or **Shift+Cmd+;** (Mac).

Timeline (for Animation)

15. **Toggle Timeline**: If you're working with animations, you can toggle the Timeline panel with **Alt+Shift+Ctrl+T** (Windows) or **Option+Shift+Cmd+T** (Mac).

Screen Mode for Multiple Monitors

16. **Full Screen with Menus (Secondary Monitor)**: When working with multiple monitors, you can toggle full-screen mode on the secondary monitor with **F** (when your mouse pointer is on the secondary monitor).

TOOL SHORTCUTS

1. **Move Tool (V)**: Press "V" to select the Move tool, which allows you to move and arrange layers.
2. **Marquee Selection Tool (M)**: Press "M" to select the Marquee selection tool, which includes the Rectangular Marquee Tool and the Elliptical Marquee Tool.
3. **Lasso Tool (L)**: Press "L" to select the Lasso tool, which includes the Lasso, Polygonal Lasso, and Magnetic Lasso tools.
4. **Magic Wand Tool (W)**: Press "W" to select the Magic Wand tool, which allows you to select areas based on color and tone.
5. **Crop Tool (C)**: Press "C" to select the Crop tool, which is used for cropping and straightening images.
6. **Eyedropper Tool (I)**: Press "I" to select the Eyedropper tool, which is used to sample colors from an image.
7. **Brush Tool (B)**: Press "B" to select the Brush tool, which is used for painting and drawing.
8. **Clone Stamp Tool (S)**: Press "S" to select the Clone Stamp tool, which is used for duplicating parts of an image.
9. **Eraser Tool (E)**: Press "E" to select the Eraser tool, which is used for erasing parts of an image or a layer.
10. **Gradient Tool (G)**: Press "G" to select the Gradient tool, which is used to create gradient fills.
11. **Bucket Fill Tool (G)**: The Paint Bucket tool shares the same shortcut as the Gradient tool. To switch between them, press "Shift + G."
12. **Blur Tool (R), Sharpen Tool (R), Smudge Tool (R)**: Press "R" to select the Blur, Sharpen, or Smudge tool. These tools are grouped under the same shortcut key.
13. **Pen Tool (P)**: Press "P" to select the Pen tool, which is used for creating vector paths.
14. **Text Tool (T)**: Press "T" to select the Text tool, which is used for adding text to your images.
15. **Hand Tool (H)**: Press "H" to select the Hand tool, which allows you to pan around the image when zoomed in.

16. **Zoom Tool (Z)**: Press "Z" to select the Zoom tool, which lets you zoom in and out of your image.
17. **Pen Tool (P) Options**: When you have the **Pen Tool** selected, pressing "**Ctrl**" (Cmd on Mac) temporarily switches to the **Direct Selection Tool** (white arrow), and pressing "**Alt**" (Option on Mac) temporarily switches to the **Convert Point Tool** (hollow arrow).
18. **Brush Size**: You can change the brush size on the fly by using the "[" (left bracket) and "]" (right bracket) keys."[" makes the brush smaller, and "**]**" makes it larger.

19. **Brush Hardness**: To adjust the brush hardness, use the Shift key in combination with the "{" (left curly brace) and "}" (right curly brace) keys. "{" decreases hardness, and "}" increases it.
20. **Rotate Brush**: When using the Brush or Clone Stamp tool, you can rotate the brush by using the arrow keys. The "Shift" key in combination with the arrow keys will rotate the brush in 15-degree increments.
21. **Cycle through Tools**: To cycle through tools within the same group, hold down "Shift" and press the keyboard shortcut for the tool. For example, "Shift + J" will cycle between the various tools in the Healing Brush group.

COLOR AND SWATCH SHORTCUTS

Color and swatch shortcuts in Photoshop can significantly enhance your workflow efficiency and help you create visually appealing designs with ease. Photoshop offers various shortcuts and tools to manage colors and swatches, allowing you to work more effectively.

Let's delve into some of the essential color and swatch shortcuts in Photoshop:

1. **Eyedropper Tool (I):** The Eyedropper tool is a fundamental color-picking tool. Press 'I' to select it, and then click on any area in your image to sample the color.
2. **Foreground and Background Colors (D/X):** Press 'D' to reset your foreground and background colors to the default black and white. Press 'X' to swap between them.
3. **Color Picker (Alt + Click):** To open the Color Picker and choose a custom color, press 'Alt' and click anywhere in your image.
4. **Brush Tool Opacity (Number Keys):** You can change the opacity of the Brush tool by pressing a number key (e.g., '1' for 10% opacity, '5' for 50%, and '0' for 100%).

5. **Brush Tool Flow (Shift + Number Keys):** To adjust the flow of the Brush tool, hold 'Shift' and press a number key (e.g., '1' for 10% flow, '5' for 50%, and '0' for 100%).
6. **Swatches Panel (F6):** Open the Swatches panel by pressing **'F6'** or going to Window > Swatches. Here, you can manage and organize your color swatches.
7. **Create a New Swatch (Alt + Click):** To add the current foreground color as a new swatch, hold 'Alt' and click on a space in the Swatches panel.
8. **Load Swatches (Click the Swatch Panel Menu):** Click on the menu icon in the Swatches panel to access options like loading, saving, or resetting swatches.
9. **Delete Swatch (Drag to Trash Icon):** You can remove a swatch by clicking and dragging it to the trash icon at the bottom of the Swatches panel.
10. **Gradient Map (Ctrl + Shift + G):** Apply a Gradient Map adjustment layer by pressing 'Ctrl + Shift + G.' this allows you to map a gradient to the tonal values in your image.
11. **Color Balance (Ctrl + B):** Adjust the color balance of an image using 'Ctrl + B' to bring up the Color Balance dialog.
12. **Hue/Saturation (Ctrl + U):** Modify the hue, saturation, and lightness of colors with 'Ctrl + U' to open the Hue/Saturation dialog.
13. **Color Picker Shortcuts (Double-click Foreground/Background Color):** Double-clicking the foreground or background color in the toolbar opens the Color Picker dialog.
14. **Eyedropper Tool Options (Right-click):** Right-click with the Eyedropper tool to access options like **Sample Size and All Layers**.
15. **Quick Mask Mode (Q):** Enter Quick Mask mode with 'Q' to create selections using brush strokes, which can then be converted into a regular selection.
16. **Selective Color (Image > Adjustments > Selective Color):** Access the Selective Color adjustment to fine-tune the colors in your image.
17. **Color Range Selection (Select > Color Range):** Use **'Select > Color Range'** to make selections based on specific colors in your image.
18. **Save Swatch Library (Swatches Panel Menu):** Save custom swatch libraries by going to the Swatches panel menu and selecting "Save Swatches."

By mastering these color and swatch shortcuts in Photoshop, you can streamline your design process, work more efficiently, and achieve precise control over the colors in your images and projects. Experiment with these shortcuts to find the most efficient workflow for your specific needs.

Clear shortcuts from a command or tool

1. Select **Keyboard Shortcuts** under **Edit**.
2. Choose the command or tool name whose shortcut you want to remove from the Keyboard Shortcuts dialog box.
3. Choose **Delete Shortcut**.

Delete a set of shortcuts

1. Select **Keyboard Shortcuts** under **Edit**.
2. Select the shortcut set you want to remove from the Set pop-up menu.
3. To close the dialog box, click the **Delete** symbol and then click **OK**.

View a list of current shortcuts

You can export the shortcuts currently in use to an HTML file that you can see or print using a web browser.

1. Select **Keyboard Shortcuts** under **Edit**.
2. From the Shortcuts For menu, choose a shortcut type: **Application Menus, Panel Menus, or Tools**.
3. Select "**Summarize**."

IMPORTING/EXPORTING KEYBOARD SHORTCUTS

- Select the **Keyboard Shortcuts** option from the **Edit** menu.
- Press the "**Load**" button to import a keyboard shortcut collection.
- Find and choose your keyboard shortcut file by navigating to its stored place.
- To import the file, click "**Open**".

Your keyboard shortcuts will be imported and operational after completing these procedures.

EXPORTING KEYBOARD SHORTCUTS IN ADOBE PHOTOSHOP

- Select the **Keyboard Shortcuts** option from the **Edit** menu.
- Press the "**Save**" button to export a keyboard shortcut collection.
- Give your keyboard shortcut file a name and choose a storage place.
- To export the file, click "**Save**".

Your keyboard shortcuts will be stored in a file that you can share with other users or import into another version of Adobe Photoshop after you has finished these procedures.

HOW TO RESET TO THE DEFAULT SHORTCUT IN ADOBE PHOTOSHOP

To get started, choose **Edit > Keyboard Shortcuts** from the top menu bar to open the Keyboard Shortcuts dialog box. A list of all the different keyboard shortcuts available in Photoshop will be shown to you. Finding the shortcut whose default settings you want to modify is the next step. Next, click the "**Reset to Default**" button at the bottom of the dialog box.

CHAPTER EIGHT
EDITING WITH CAMERA RAW EDITOR

This chapter explores modifying photographs in Photoshop using the Camera Raw editor. It begins by outlining the benefits of the several raw file formats over JPEG photos. The chapter explains to readers that using Camera Raw photos rather than JPEGs is advantageous. After that, it walks users through the process of opening a picture in the Camera Raw editor and presents them with the panel-based interface. The chapter describes how to choose an Adobe Raw profile for the picture and covers the Basic panel, which is used to change image tone. Additionally, readers will learn how to save their Camera Raw adjustments as new files and how to sharpen photographs using the Detail panel. The chapter ends with instructions for adjusting saturation and white balance in the Camera Raw editor, giving readers a thorough rundown on how to use this potent tool for picture editing.

UNDERSTANDING VARIOUS RAW FILE FORMATS

RAW files are a type of file in Photoshop that holds raw or very lightly processed image sensor data. Since they haven't been processed and can't yet be changed or printed, they are referred to as "raw."

There are three main categories into which RAW file formats usually fall:

- **Uncompressed RAW**: Although these files are the biggest, editing them might go more quickly.
- **Lossless compressed RAW**: No quality degradation occurs despite the files being lower in size.
- **Compressed RAW** (also known as "**lossy compressed**"): These are the smallest RAW files; nonetheless, there could or might not be a noticeable quality change.

Photoshop can open most of the RAW file types that each camera manufacturer provides, such as **Nikon's.NEF, Canon's.CR2, and Sony's.ARW**. A RAW file opened in Photoshop will open in **Adobe Camera Raw (ACR),** one of Photoshop's most useful features that allow you to work with RAW files before opening them in Photoshop. This entails changing the white balance, exposure, contrast, and a host of other settings. Do not forget to save a copy of your picture in Photoshop format (PSD) to maintain access to all Photoshop capabilities (layers, effects, masks, and more).

Save in Large Document Format (PSB), Photoshop Raw (only for flattened images), TIFF (up to 4 GB), or DICOM format for files greater than 2 GB.

DO I NEED CAMERA RAW IMAGES INSTEAD OF JPEG IMAGES?

For photographers of all skill levels, the decision of whether to shoot in JPEG or Camera RAW is a recurring challenge. Both formats have benefits and drawbacks, and as a photographer, your unique requirements and tastes will ultimately determine which format is best for you. We will examine the distinctions between JPEG and Camera RAW files here, as well as the situations when each format works best and the reasons you would choose one over the other.

Recognizing JPEG and RAW from Camera

Before exploring the rationale behind selecting one format over the other, it is essential to comprehend the basic distinctions between Camera RAW and JPEG.

1. **Camera RAW:** This raw, uncompressed picture format records all of the data that your camera's sensor gathers without sacrificing any information.
   - Compared to JPEGs, these files usually have a bigger size and more data.
   - Specialized software, such as **Adobe Lightroom or Capture One**, is required to edit and convert Camera RAW data into other formats.
   - Because there is a plethora of data, they provide more freedom in post-processing, enabling more extensive alterations without sacrificing quality.

2. **JPEG:** JPEG is a compressed picture format that reduces file sizes by discarding some image data during the compression process.
   - JPEGs don't need any further processing and are ready to use right out of the camera.
   - They can be printed, shared online, and used for regular photography.
   - Because of lossy compression, which can result in quality deterioration when performing substantial modifications, JPEGs offer limited post-processing flexibility.

When to Choose Camera RAW Images

1. **Post-Processing Control:** Camera RAW is the best option if you want total control over your photos during the post-processing stage. With little loss of picture quality, exposure, color balance, and sharpness may all be adjusted because of the abundance of data that was collected. For professional

photographers who need the utmost accuracy in their work, this is extremely crucial.
2. **Dynamic Range**: In instances with great contrast, Camera RAW comes to the rescue. With the ability to record a wider dynamic range, information in both highlights and shadows can be preserved. For landscape and architectural photographers, who often work in difficult lighting circumstances, this is useful.
3. **Color Accuracy**: Camera RAW is better if you need exact color accuracy. More color information is included in RAW files, which facilitates the correction of color casts and allows you to create the precise tones you want.
4. **Retouching and Corrections**: Camera RAW helps photographers, especially portrait photographers, to more precisely edit skin tones and repair defects without sacrificing picture quality.
5. **Future-Proofing**: The capacity to review and rework your RAW files guarantees that your photos remain current and relevant using the newest editing methods as camera technology advances.

When to Choose JPEG Images

1. **Convenience**: For casual photographers who want to record moments without the burden of post-processing, JPEGs are a handy option. They can be used, shared, or printed right away.
2. **Smaller File Sizes**: JPEGs have a much smaller file size than RAW files, which is good news for anyone worried about storage capacity. They are thus appropriate for occasions when you take plenty of pictures.
3. **Speed**: JPEGs write to your camera's memory card more quickly, which can be advantageous for shooting subjects that move quickly, such as animals or sports.
4. **Everyday Photography**: JPEGs are often more than enough if you mostly use your camera to capture candid moments, family get-togethers, or trip images.

In the end, the decision between Camera RAW and JPEG photographs comes down to your own tastes and photography ambitions. The question of whether you should use Camera RAW photos rather than JPEG photographs cannot be answered in a generalized way. Instead, think about your desire to spend time post-processing and the context of the shot. Shooting in Camera RAW has several advantages for professional photographers, particularly for those who need exact control over their photographs. However, JPEGs could be a more sensible option for enthusiasts, novice photographers, and those who value portability and reduced file sizes. Ultimately, each format has a role in the world of photography, and by knowing its advantages and disadvantages; you can choose the best format for your needs both technically and creatively.

OPENING IMAGES IN THE CAMERA RAW EDITOR

Just as with any other picture file type, you can open a raw file with Photoshop. The raw file opens in the Camera Raw interface rather than the default Photoshop workspace, which is the difference. To open the picture in Photoshop Camera Raw, double-click on it. Photoshop shouldn't be open. It will start on your PC and open the Camera Raw window.

Alternatively

This can be accomplished by selecting Open with > Adobe Photoshop CS6 from the menu when you **Ctrl + Click (Mac) or Right-Click (Windows)** on the file. If Photoshop isn't already open, this will launch it, followed by the Camera Raw window. Originally designed to handle raw images, Camera Raw can be opened by double-clicking on a raw image on your computer, which will instantly load the image in Camera Raw and start Photoshop.

Open images in Photoshop Camera Raw from Photoshop or Bridge

This procedure looks too easy, however, in addition to the earlier one for opening photos in Photoshop Camera Raw. A raw, JPEG, or TIFF file can be opened straight from Adobe Photoshop or Bridge. Regarding Adobe Bridge To save a raw, JPEG, or TIFF picture, click it once, then use **Ctrl + R on Windows or Cmd + R on a Mac.** Or In the Content panel, choose a picture, then select **File > "Open in Camera Raw."**

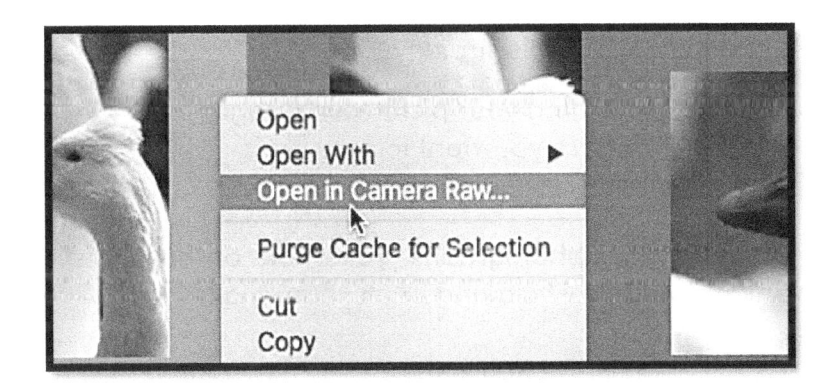

- Open Adobe Photoshop by navigating to the **File** menu and selecting **Open As**. Look through your directories to locate the desired JPEG or TIFF pictures.
- After selecting the desired file by clicking on it, click Open after changing the bottom-right pop-up option to Camera Raw.

For Mac users, choose **Open** from the File menu in Photoshop. The **Open dialog box** shows up. Look through your directories to locate the desired **JPEG or TIFF pictures**. Click the desired file. It will indicate JPEG (or TIFF if you choose a TIFF file) in the Format pop-up option at the bottom. Click on that menu and select Camera Raw. Once you click the Open button, Camera Raw will open and your picture will be shown.

How to Make JPEGs and TIFFs Always Open In Camera Raw

Although having to clearly state that you want to open your photos in Camera Raw is tedious, you can set it as the default for the next operations. That being said, photographers should use this instead of graphic designers.

1. Select **Edit** > **Preferences** > **Camera Raw (Windows)** or **Photoshop** > **Preferences** > **Camera Raw (Mac)**.
2. Select **Automatically Open All Supported JPEGs** and **Automatically Open All Supported TIFFs** under **JPEG and TIFF handling** at the bottom of the Camera Raw Preferences dialog box, respectively.
3. Select "**OK**." Keep in mind that you won't see this change until you launch Photoshop again.

In Camera Raw, you can open numerous files from Bridge or Photoshop at once and make the same modifications to many files at once. You can do a lot of work in a short amount of time using this strategy.

1. Open the folder containing your pictures in Bridge.
2. **Shift + Click** each picture you want to see.
3. Select **File** > **Open** With In Camera Raw.

Camera Raw opens for your photographs. Take note of the film strip on the left. You may alter any picture by just clicking on its thumbnail.

GETTING ACQUAINTED WITH CAMERA RAW EDITOR WINDOW

Once you open a raw image, it will automatically open in the Camera Raw Editor window. This window consists of several key sections and tools:

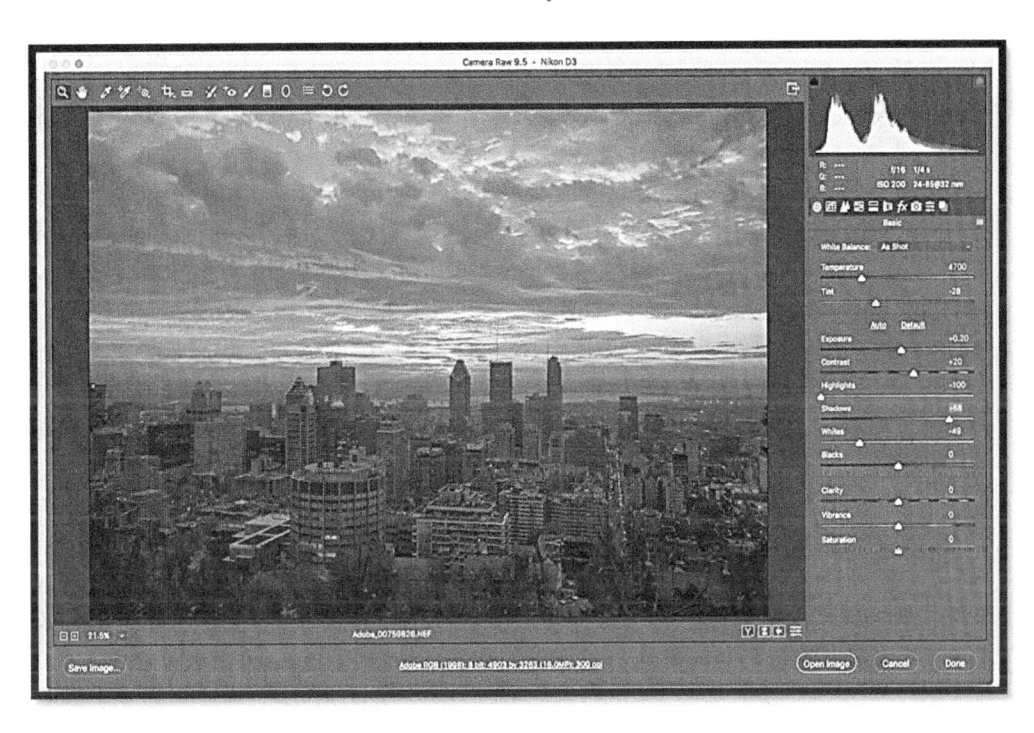

1. **Image Preview**: In the middle of the Camera Raw Editor window is where you'll see a preview of the raw image you're working with. You can zoom in and out of the picture by using the zoom slider or keyboard shortcuts such as the **+ and -** keys on your keyboard. When the picture is zoomed in, you can pan around it with the Hand tool.
2. **Basic Panel**: The Basic panel can be found on the right hand side of the screen. This panel allows you to make important modifications to the exposure, contrast, highlights, shadows, whites, blacks, clarity, vibrance, and saturation of the image. Utilizing these sliders, you will be able to make global alterations to the tonal and color properties of your picture.
3. **Tone Curve Panel**: The Tone Curve panel is located immediately below the Basic panel in the interface. The contrast and tonal distribution of your picture can both be fine-tuned here using the unique tone curves that you generate. The Point Curve option provides very fine-grained control over certain tonal ranges.

4. **Detail Panel**: The Detail panel is where you can make adjustments to the lens corrections, noise reduction, and sharpening of the image. There are sliders for the amount, the radius, the detail, the masking, and the noise reduction. You can efficiently improve the image's sharpness and minimize noise with the assistance of these tools.
5. **HSL/Grayscale Panel**: The **HSL/Grayscale panel** gives you the ability to adjust the hue, saturation, and luminosity of each color channel in your picture so that the colors come out exactly as you want them to. By choosing the Grayscale option, you can also utilize it to transform the picture into a black-and-white representation.
6. **The Split Toning panel**: This allows you to apply color tints to the highlights and shadows of your picture. This panel can be found under the Adjustment tab. This can provide one-of-a-kind color effects as well as improve the overall atmosphere of your shot.
7. **Detail Panel**: The Effects panel includes settings for post-crop vignetting, grain, and dehazes. This panel can also be accessed via the Detail panel. By making these modifications, you get more control over the entire appearance and sensation of your image.
8. **Camera Calibration Panel**: The Camera Calibration panel in Adobe Camera Raw gives you the ability to fine-tune how the program interprets the colors and tones in your raw picture depending on the profile of your camera. It can be especially helpful for ensuring color rendering that is consistent across a variety of camera types.
9. **Presets and Snapshots**: The Presets and Snapshots panels can be found on the left side of the Camera Raw Editor window. This is where you can access them. You may get your picture off to a rapid start by applying some predetermined modifications that are provided to you by the presets. You can save several copies of your adjustments using snapshots, which makes it easier to compare them.
10. **Histogram and Toolbar**: The histogram, which offers a visual depiction of the image's tonal distribution, can be found at the top of the Camera Raw Editor window. You can access a variety of editing tools, such as the Crop tool, the Straighten tool, and others, from the Toolbar that is located below the histogram.
11. **Applying Edits**: Once you have finished making modifications in the Camera Raw Editor, you can apply them to your picture by selecting the "**Open Image**" button to launch Photoshop and open the image that has been changed. Alternatively, you can click the "**Done**" button to store the changes you've made to the raw file as metadata. This will enable you to make more adjustments to the picture at a later time without compromising its quality.

GETTING FAMILIAR WITH THE BASIC PANEL

The Basic panel includes crucial options for altering a variety of crucial settings, including exposure, contrast, tone, and color balance, among other important parameters. By playing around with these modifications and being familiar with the effects they have on your pictures, you will be able to make more educated judgments about the editing process, which will result in an overall improvement in the quality of your photographs.

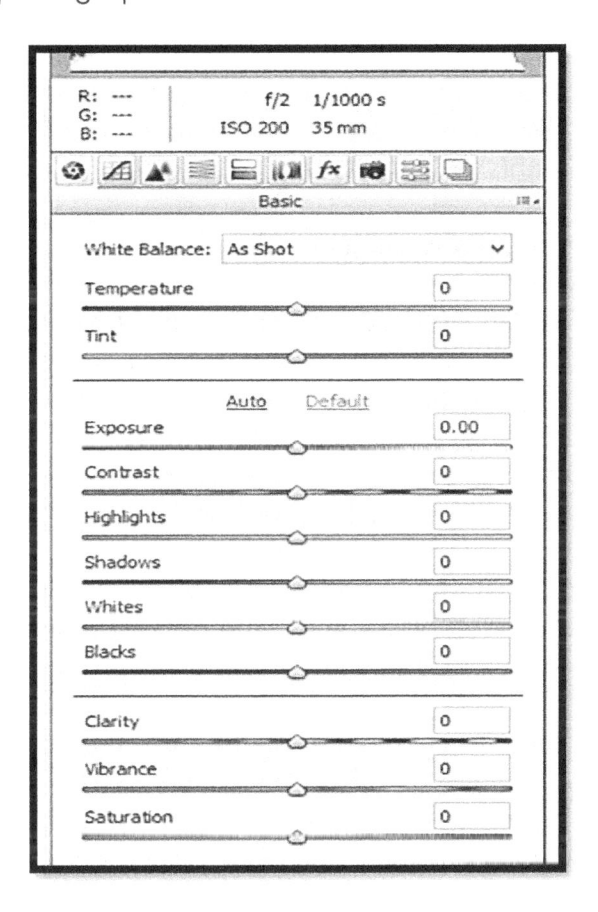

1. Accessing the Basic Panel
When you load a raw picture in Adobe Photoshop, the Basic panel in Camera Raw will automatically show as one of the major panels on the right-hand side of the Camera Raw Editor window. This allows you to access the Basic panel in Camera Raw.
2. Exposure:
- **Exposure Slider**: The Exposure slider gives you control over the overall brightness or darkness of the picture you are working with. When the

exposure is increased by moving the slider to the right, the resulting picture is brighter; when the exposure is decreased by sliding the slider to the left, the resulting image is darker.

3. Contrast:
   - **Contrast Slider**: The Contrast slider allows you to modify the degree to which the highlights and shadows in your picture vary in brightness from one another. The contrast can be increased by sliding the slider to the right while decreasing it can be accomplished by moving it to the left.

4. Highlights
   - **Highlights Slider**: The Highlights slider focuses on the regions of your picture that are the brightest. Moving it to the left will restore information in highlights that have been overexposed, but moving it to the right will lessen the amount of detail in highlights.

5. Shadows
   - **Shadows Slider**: The Shadows slider allows you to adjust how much darkness is present in your picture. By sliding it to the right, shadow detail and brightness are both increased, whilst moving it to the left creates a more dramatic effect by increasing the depth of the shadows.

6. Whites and Blacks:
   - The white slider allows you to alter the pixels in your picture that are the brightest. The Blacks slider allows you to adjust the pixels that are the darkest. It can be used to fine-tune the brightest parts without affecting the exposure as a whole.
   - Adjusting the Blacks slider will affect the pixels in your picture that are the darkest. It gives you the ability to set the darkest point without affecting the exposure all the way through.

7. Clarity
   - **Clarity Slider**: The Clarity slider increases the contrast between midtones, which makes edges and textures look more distinct. Moving it to the right improves the picture's clarity, whilst moving it to the left causes the image to become more blurry.

8. Vibrance and Saturation
   - **Vibrance Slider**: The Vibrance slider increases the intensity of colors in your picture that are less saturated while safeguarding colors that are already saturated.
   - **Saturation Slider**: The Saturation slider has an equal influence on all of the colors in your picture. If you move it to the right, the overall color intensity will rise, but if you move it to the left, the saturation will decrease.

9. Temperature and Tint

- **Temperature Slider**: The Temperature slider gives you the ability to modify the amount of warmth or coolness that your picture has. If you move it to the right, you'll get a warmer tone (with more orange), while sliding it to the left will give you a cooler tone (with more blue).
- **Tint Slider**: The Tint slider allows you to fine-tune the color balance of your picture by adjusting the ratio of green to magenta. If you move it to the right, you'll get more magenta, and if you move it to the left, you'll get greener.

10. **Auto Button**:
    - When you click the Auto button, Adobe will automatically assess your picture and apply some fundamental alterations based on the algorithms that it has developed. Even while it can be a speedy starting point, it is still necessary to manually fine-tune your adjustments to get the best possible outcomes.

11. **before and After Views**:
    - **Preview Toggle**: The Preview toggle, which can be found at the very top of the Camera Raw Editor window, allows you to see the modified version of the picture alongside the original.

12. **Applying Edits**:

After altering the sliders in the Basic panel, you can apply the changes by selecting the "Open Image" option to open the picture that has been altered in Photoshop. This will bring up the image after it has been edited. Alternatively, you can click the "Done" button to store the changes you've made to the raw file as metadata. This will give you the ability to make more alterations in the future.

13. **Presets**:

The Basic panel also gives you the option to store your modifications as presets. These presets can then be applied to other pictures to give them a uniform appearance or used as a jumping-off point for subsequent edits that are comparable.

SELECTING AN ADOBE RAW PROFILE

1. **Open Your Image**: To begin, launch Adobe Camera Raw and open the raw image you want to edit. You can do this by choosing "File" > "Open" and then browsing to the location of your picture file. You can also right-click on the picture file you want to edit, and then choose "Open in Camera Raw."
2. **Open the Profile Panel**: Find the "Profile" panel within the Camera Raw application's main interface. In most cases, it will be located on the right-hand side of the screen. If the panel is not visible, you can access it by selecting the "Profile" item in the navigation bar.
3. **Look through the Preset Profiles**: You will automatically be presented with a list of Adobe's built-in profiles when you launch Adobe Photoshop. These

profiles are arranged in several categories, some of which are "**Adobe Color**," "**Adobe Landscape**," "**Adobe Portrait**," and others. Simply expanding a category and showing you the profiles it contains require you to click on it.

4. **Preview Profiles**: Simply hovering your mouse pointer over a profile will allow you to get a preview of how that profile will change your picture. The adjustments that are made to your picture by each profile will be shown in real time as a thumbnail of your image. This gives you the ability to evaluate many profiles side-by-side to choose the one that works the best with your picture.

5. **Pick a Profile**: Once you have located a profile that enhances the aesthetics of your picture, you can click on it to apply it to your shot. To find the profile that works best for your particular picture, you can always swap between them.

6. **Make More Refinements to Your Edits**: After you have chosen a profile, you can make more adjustments to your picture by utilizing the many editing tools and sliders that are available in Adobe Camera Raw. You may obtain the appearance you want by adjusting the exposure, color balance, and sharpness, as well as a wide variety of other factors, using these tools.

7. **Save your Image**: Click the "**Open Image**" option if you are pleased with the changes you have made to your image. This will open your photo in Photoshop, where you can continue refining your image by making use of the vast editing possibilities offered by Photoshop.

ADJUSTING IMAGE TONAL USING THE BASIC PANEL

When you choose Auto in the top-right corner of the **Edit panel**, Camera Raw analyzes the picture and adjusts the tone settings in accordance with its findings. You can also apply automated settings in a granular fashion to each tone control. Double-clicking an individual slider in the Basic panel, such as Exposure or Contrast, while holding down the Shift key will cause an automated change to be made to that particular slider. Simply double-clicking the slider will cause the various tone controls to revert to their default settings. When you choose to have **Camera Raw** automatically change the tone, any prior modifications made in other tabs, such as the Tone Curves tab's fine-tuning of the tone, are not taken into account. Because of this, it is recommended that automated tone adjustments be applied first, if they are to be applied at all, to get a preliminary estimate of the ideal settings for your picture.

If you take great care when shooting and make a conscious effort to capture images with varying exposures, you probably do not want to destroy your hard work by making automated tone changes afterward. You can, on the other hand, always test selecting Auto and then undo the modifications if you don't like how they turned out. This option is always available to you. The image settings that are now active in Adobe Bridge will be used by the previews. In the Camera Raw options, find the section labeled "**Default Image settings**," and then pick the radio button labeled "**Apply Auto Tone Adjustments**." Doing so will include automated tone adjustments into the default image settings. Keep an eye on the end points of the histogram as you make modifications, or use the previews of the shadow and highlight clipping to guide your work.

- To manually modify a tone control, either move the slider, type a number into the box, or pick the value in the box and hit the **Up or Down** arrow key depending on which direction you want to go.
- Double-clicking the slider control will bring the value back to its initial state.

PV referred to in the brackets below is Process Version.

- **Exposure (All):** Adjusts the overall brightness of the photograph. Adjust the slider until the picture is the required brightness and the photo appears fine. Exposure settings are given in increments that correspond to camera aperture values (fstops). A +1.00 adjustment is equivalent to opening the aperture 1 stop. Similarly, a 1.00 adjustment is equivalent to narrowing the aperture 1 stop.
- **Contrast (All):** Adjusts visual contrast, mostly impacting midtones. When contrast is increased, the middle-to-dark picture parts darken and the middle-to-light image areas lighten. As contrast is reduced, the visual tones become inversely influenced.
- **Highlights (PV2012):** Adjusts the brightness of picture highlights. Drag to the left to restore "blown out" highlight details and darken highlights. To enhance highlights while reducing clipping, drag to the right.
- **Shadows (PV2012):** Adjusts the dark regions of a picture. To deepen shadows while reducing clipping, drag to the left. To lighten shadows and retrieve shadow details, drag to the right.
- **Whites (PV2012):** Modifies the white clipping. Drag to the left to decrease highlight clipping. To enhance highlight clipping, drag to the right. (Increased clipping can be beneficial for specular highlights, such as those seen on metallic surfaces.)
- **Blacks (PV2012):** Adjusts the clipping of blacks. Increase black clipping by dragging to the left (map more shadows to pure black). To decrease shadow clipping, drag to the right.

- **Blacks (PV2010 and PV2003):** Controls which picture values are assigned to black. Moving the slider to the right increases the number of dark spots, giving the appearance of enhanced visual contrast. The impact is most noticeable in the shadows, with considerably less variation in the midtones and highlights.
- **Recovery (PV2010 and PV2003):** This feature attempts to restore information from highlights. Camera Raw can recover some features from places where one or both color channels have been clipped to white.
- **Fill Light (PV2010 and PV2003):** Attempts to restore shadow details without enhancing blacks. Camera Raw can recover some features from regions where one or both color channels have been cut to black. Fill Light works similarly to the shadows component of the Photoshop Shadow/Highlight filter or the After Effects Shadow/Highlight effect.
- **Brightness (PV2010 and PV2003):** Adjusts the image's brightness or darkness, similar to the Exposure attribute. When you move the slider to the right, Brightness compresses the highlights and stretches the shadows rather than cutting the picture in the highlights or shadows. The easiest method to utilize this control is to first establish the entire tone scale by adjusting Exposure, Recovery, and Blacks before adjusting Brightness. Because large Brightness changes can cause shadow or highlight clipping, you should correct the Exposure, Recovery, or Blacks properties after altering Brightness.

FINE-TUNE CURVES

After making modifications to the picture's tone in the Basic panel, you can use the settings found in the Curve drop-down of the Edit panel to fine-tune the image. Alterations that were made to the image's tonal scale are shown by the curves. The tone values that were present in the picture when it was first captured are shown along the horizontal axis as the "**input values**."

Black values are located on the left, while lighter values go toward the right down the axis. The tone levels (output values) that are being altered are shown along the vertical axis, which begins with black at the bottom and progresses upwards to white at the top. If a point on the curve goes upward, the output is a brighter tone, and if it moves downward, the tone that is produced is darker. If the line is straight and 45 degrees, this shows that there have been no changes to the tone response curve and that the input values and output values are identical.

Adjusting the values of certain tonal ranges in a picture is made easier with the aid of the Parametric Curve. The regions of the curve that are influenced by the highlights, lights, darks, or shadows region attributes are determined by where the split controls that are located at the bottom of the graph are set. The features of the middle region, known as Darks and Lights, have the most significant impact on the portion of the curve that is located in the center. Both the Highlights and Shadows characteristics have a predominant influence on the extremes of the tonal spectrum.

1. **To adjust tone curves, do any of the following:**
   - To adjust the **highlights, lights, darks, or shadows** of the image, use the respective sliders in the **Parametric Curve**. By sliding the area divider controls along the horizontal axis of the graph, you can either make the curve sections that the sliders impact more expansive or more restrictive.
   - To use the Point Curve, drag a point around on the curve. The Input and Output values are going to be presented underneath the tone curve as you move the point around. Using the Refine Saturation slider, you can also make adjustments to the saturation.
   - Using the "**Parametric Curve Targeted Adjustment**" tool, drag it into the picture after selecting it from the menu. The Highlights, Lights, Darks, or Shadows curve area can be adjusted using the Parametric Curve Targeted Adjustment tool depending on the values in the picture that you pick.

SHARPENING IMAGE WITH THE DETAIL PANEL

The sharpening capabilities of Camera Raw are just remarkable. The luminosity (also known as lightness or brightness values) of your picture is altered when you sharpen it using Camera Raw; nevertheless, the color is unaffected, so you should not see any unexpected color changes. But when it comes to sharpening, should you utilize Camera Raw? The answer is yes, but only if you don't plan on making many changes to the picture in Photoshop. If you want to conduct a significant amount of editing in Photoshop, you should save sharpening until the very end of the process (after you have finished resizing and touching up the image).

It is not recommended that you sharpen the picture using both of these apps, at least not the whole image. In Camera Raw, sharpening is a global operation, which means that it impacts the whole picture. It is also a procedure that is at least somewhat automated: the picture is sharpened the moment you open it in Camera Raw unless you turn off the automatic sharpening option. If you allow Camera Raw to sharpen your picture, after the image is in Photoshop you will need to practice local or selective sharpening to prevent over-sharpening it. If you let Camera Raw sharpen your image.

The sharpening settings are located on the Detail tab. These adjustments modify the image's edge definition. When applying local sharpening, the Adjustment Brush tool and the Graduated Filter tool make use of the Radius, Detail, and Masking parameters respectively. You can choose whether the sharpening effect is applied to all of the photographs or just the previews by using the option found in the Camera Raw options called "**Apply Sharpening to.**"

Note: The **Open Options Dialog** button can be found in the toolbar. Clicking this button will allow you to access the options from inside Camera Raw.

1. Zoom the preview image to at least 100%.
2. In the Detail tab, adjust any of these controls:
   - **Amount**. This parameter functions in the same manner as the Amount slider found in the Unsharp Mask dialog box; it determines the degree to which the image has been sharpened. If you set it to 0, there will be no sharpening of any kind, and if you set it to 150, there will be an excessive amount of sharpness. To see whether or not this makes a difference, try setting it to 40 and toggling the Preview checkbox at the top of the Camera Raw window between off and on (while ensuring that the zoom level is set to 100 percent).
   - **Radius**. This slider determines the size of the details that are sharpened while using Camera Raw. If your photograph has a great deal of minute detail, you should keep this setting at 1. You can increase this option to 1.5 if your photograph does not include many details; if you are feeling very daring and insane, you might increase it to 2.
   - **Details**. Using this slider, you can alter the amount of information that is brought out by Camera Raw (how much it accentuates the borders of the image). If you have a picture that has a lot of features and textures, such as rocky terrain, a close-up of a tree, or a fancy-schmancy structure, turn this option up (to around 90), so that it's at its maximum. This slider has a range of 0 to 100; the best setting for most photographs is somewhere around 40; nevertheless, you should experiment to find out what looks nice.
   - **Masking**. You have complete control over which parts of your picture Camera Raw sharpens thanks to this option. If you set it to 0, Camera Raw will sharpen the whole image; if you set it to 100, it will just sharpen the edges that have a high degree of contrast. If you use this option, it will be somewhat similar to putting a layer mask on a sharpened layer in Photoshop; however, the masking will be done automatically instead of manually. The only drawback to using this option is that you can't see whether it's making any effect at all.

The answer is to move the slider while holding down the **Option key (or the Alt key on a PC)** to get a preview of the regions that will be sharpened. When you do that, your whole picture will seem white; but, as you move the slider to the right, you will begin to see sections of the image that are black. Keep dragging until all of the essential edges in your picture are white so that they can be sharpened, but remember that only the white regions will be sharpened and not the black portions.

- **Luminance.** This option allows you to manage the amount of grayscale noise that Camera Raw attempts to remove from your picture by "**smoothing**" the pixels in a manner that is similar to blurring. To lessen the appearance of grains and splotches in your photograph, first, ensure that the zoom level is set to at least one hundred percent, and then move the slider to the right. For instance, a value of 25 should give a decent combination of noise reduction and picture quality, but you'll need to experiment with your photographs to find the optimal level for you.
- **Luminance Detail.** This slider determines how much smoothing Camera Raw applies to grayscale noise in the more detailed sections of a picture. It also influences the luminance noise threshold. To keep more of the information and to reduce the amount of noise reduction applied to specific regions, drag it to the right. When working with photos that have a lot of noise, dragging it to the left can make a smoother image and apply more noise reduction (however doing so can wipe away information, so be careful about that). The **Luminance Detail** is pre-configured to have a value of 50 rights out of the factory.
- **Luminance Contrast.** Using this option, you can preserve the contrast of the picture. You may move it to the right to keep the contrast and texture, or you can move it to the left to throw caution to the wind and create an image that is smoother and less noisy. This slider comes out of the factory with a value of 0.

NOTE

If the Luminance slider is set to zero, both the **Luminance Detail and Luminance Contrast** sliders will also be muted since they are reliant on the Luminance slider. Activating the other two requires increasing the Luminance setting first.

- **Color.** If your picture contains a lot of color noise (weird specks of color), which can happen if you shoot in incredibly low light or at a high ISO (the light-sensitivity level on your camera), drag this slider to the right to have the Camera Raw attempt to eliminate the specks. This can happen if you

shoot in really low light or at a high ISO (your camera's light sensitivity setting). In most cases, a figure of 25 will perform an acceptable job.
- **Color Detail**. Using this slider, you can adjust the color noise threshold of the picture. If you drag it to the left, you can get rid of additional color specks; but, doing so can cause the color to leak into other regions. If your picture has a lot of narrow, detailed, high-contrast sections of color (also known as edges), move the slider to the right to reduce the amount of noise reduction applied to the image.

TIP

Zoom in to 100 percent or more and then hold the Option key (Alt on a PC) while dragging the sliders in any of Camera Raw's sharpening options. This will allow you to see what is happening with those parameters. Your image becomes grayscale, which reveals which parts of the picture Camera Raw is modifying (although it's difficult to make out any changes while you're playing about with the Radius setting). The most helpful parameter is called **Masking**, and if you hold down the Option (Alt) key while you adjust it, you will see what seems to be an edge mask that outlines precisely which aspects of your picture Camera Raw is sharpening and which aspects are covered up by the mask.

SAVING CAMERA RAW EDITS AS NEW FILES

Save Your Edits as a DNG (Digital Negative) File

- You can choose to save your edited picture as a DNG file to preserve your non-destructive edits and have more flexibility for making future adjustments. The open standard for raw picture files developed by Adobe is called **DNG**.
- Within the ACR interface, choose the "**Save Image**" option to save the file in a DNG format.
- In the "**Save Options**" menu, make sure that the "**DNG**" file format is selected.
- If you want to change the file's name, choose a new folder to save it in and give it a new name.
- To create the edited DNG file, click the "**Save**" button on the toolbar.

Save Your Edits as a TIFF or PSD File

- You can save your edited picture as a TIFF (Tagged picture File Format) or PSD (Photoshop Document) file if you prefer a file format that is widely accepted and preserves all editing modifications.

- In the "Save Options" window of ACR, enter the following:
  - Make sure that "**TIFF**" or "**Photoshop**" is selected as the format.
  - Choose a destination folder and give the new file a name before continuing.
  - If you want to make sure that this software is compatible with other programs, make sure that the "**Maximize Compatibility**" box is checked.
  - Activate the "**Save**" button on your browser.

Save Your Edits as a JPEG for Sharing

- If you intend to share your edited image on the web or with others, you can save it as a JPEG (**Joint Photographic Experts Group**) file.
- In the "Save Options" dialog in ACR:
  - Choose "**JPEG**" as the format.
  - Adjust the quality slider to determine the level of compression (higher quality means larger file size).
  - Select a destination folder and enter a new filename.
  - Click the "**Save**" button.

Organize Your Edited Files

- After you have finished editing your photographs, it is a good idea to arrange them in a logical folder structure on your computer so that they are simple to find and retrieve when necessary.

CORRECTING THE WHITE BALANCE IN THE CAMERA RAW

In Adobe Camera Raw (ACR), adjusting the white balance can be done in one of three distinct ways: using the Temperature and Tint sliders; selecting a white balance preset from the drop-down menu; or using the White Balance tool. But before we get into these various ways, let's talk about the difference between RAW and JPEG in terms of how the white balance is handled. When you load a RAW picture in ACR, it will initially show the white balance selection that you made in the camera. However, there is a White Balance preset drop-down box where you can truly choose your white balance after the fact. When you shoot in JPEG, the white balance preset you choose in your camera is baked into the picture. Because of this, the drop-down menu will only include the option to select "**Auto**" as a white balance preset.

Because of this, there is a common misconception that the white balance of JPEG photographs cannot be altered; however, this is not the case. You can make adjustments to it by utilizing the Temperature and Tint sliders, as well as the White Balance tool (which, to be honest, are the tools that I use the most). However, it is not a myth that white balance modifications appear better when conducted on RAW photographs as opposed to JPEG files; you can try this for yourself. JPEG images have a lossy compression format. Make sure that your camera is set to shoot in RAW + JPEG mode before you go out to take pictures the next time. Locate a photograph with an incorrect white balance, use Adobe Camera Raw to adjust the white balance of both photos, and then evaluate the differences between the two.

USING THE PRESETS

Okay, let's go back to really adjusting the white balance, shall we? We'll begin by using the defaults since doing so will either make adjusting your white balance as simple as clicking a button or, at the absolute least, provide you with a solid foundation from which to build when making more adjustments. To begin evaluating the results, choose "**Auto**" from the "**As Shot**" drop-down option that appears once you click it. If it seems correct to you, and there's a good likelihood that it will, then you can consider the job finished. If the appearance is off, you should cycle through all of the presets until you find one that fixes the problem. If you can't find one that's spot on, choose the one that comes the closest to what you want and make it your starting point. If you can't find one that's spot on, select the one that looks the most like what you want.

USING THE TEMPERATURE & TINT SLIDERS

Adjusting the white balance is as simple as moving any of these two sliders closer to the hue you choose. Because Adobe included a color gradient behind each of these sliders, you can see which direction to drag to acquire the color you desire. This makes the process simpler than it first seems. For instance, if you believe your picture appears a bit too bluish (cold), you can make it seem more yellow (warmer) by dragging the Temperature slider to the right. This will change the color of your image. When you look at those color gradients, you can see that the picture will seem warmer if you move the slider farther to the right. Even though the numbers that are shown on the Temperature slider are in Kelvin degrees, which is the standard method used to measure the color temperature of light, this is an entirely visual decision on your side; you should stop moving the slider when the picture seems to be the appropriate level of warm.

Also, if you choose a White Balance preset and then change either the Temperature or Tint slider, the preset menu will now show Custom, which simply indicates that you began with a preset and then adjusted it. This happens when you move any of the sliders. By the way, there is no "**International Committee of White Balance**" that will evaluate the decision you make; rather, you decide on the white balance that you think will look the best for what it is that you are attempting to produce. When you're performing commercial product photography, when the color of the thing needs to be correct for sales reasons, that's when your decision becomes essential since it's the only time it matters. During the shoot, you would utilize a color checker or gray card to create a bespoke white balance in your camera if this were the case.

USING THE WHITE BALANCE TOOL

Because it is simple and I can test out a variety of various white balances in a short amount of time, this is my preferred method for adjusting the white balance. To use it, first choose the White Balance tool from the toolbar (or press the letter I on your keyboard), and then click on an area of your picture that should be gray. The setting will be applied immediately. When you tell ACR that "**This area right here is supposed to be neutral gray**," it will eliminate any yellow, blue, or other tints from that area so that it truly becomes gray, which will fix all of the colors in your picture. In an ideal situation, you should seek for anything to click on that is a very light gray (not white), but if there isn't anything gray in the picture, you should attempt to pick a hue that seems to be neutral. I clicked on the back of the bride's dress in the photograph that is now shown here.

If you accidentally click on the incorrect part of the picture, you'll notice it right away since the color will look bad (see the example below). If that does happen, you can just try clicking on a new spot to continue. In most cases, you'll be able to discover a white balance that suits your preferences with just a few mouse clicks. If you can't get the color just right, go as near as you can and then use the Temperature and Tint sliders to adjust it; for instance, if it seems a little too blue, simply move the Temperature slider to the right a little bit and you're done. If you can't get the color just right, come as close as you can and then use the sliders.

Tip: I don't mind experimenting with various white balance settings since it's simple to start over from scratch. This is one reason why I don't mind doing so. If things start to seem strange, just double-click directly on the White Balance tool located at the top of the toolbar, and it will restore everything to the settings that were in place when the photo was taken with the camera.

FROM START TO FINISH

The majority of the time, adjusting the white balance is the very first thing that I do in ACR. This is because if the color is significantly wrong, it is so distracting that I am unable to concentrate on anything else. When it comes to setting the white balance, I typically only have to make use of one or two of the three available ways (presets, **Temp/Tint sliders**, and the WB tool). First, decide if your white balance needs adjusting at all—" **If it isn't broke, don't fix it.**" If you think it needs fixing, look for something that's supposed to be gray, click on it with the White Balance tool, and you're probably done (it might take two or three clicks in nearby areas to find one you like).

If you cannot find a clear spot to click, use the presets found in the White Balance drop-down box to adjust the settings. If even one of them looks decent, you may consider the job done. If not, choose the one that seems to be the most similar to the appearance you desire, and then use the Temperature and Tint sliders to adjust it to your liking. In most cases, the only thing you will need to do is adjust the Temperature slider by dragging it to the left to make the picture colder or to the right to make it warmer.

CORRECTING SATURATION IN CAMERA RAW

By altering the parameters for Clarity, Vibrance, and Saturation in the Basic panel, you can vary the color saturation of any color. (The parameters in the Color Mixer panel can be used to modify the saturation of a particular color palette.)

- **Clarity**: This gives a picture more depth by enhancing the local contrast; this effect is most pronounced in the midtones of the image. This option functions similarly to an unsharp mask with a big radius. When using this option, it is recommended that the zoom level be increased to 100% or higher. To get the most out of the effect, first turn the setting up till you see halos appearing along the edge details of the picture. After that, turn it down just a little bit.
- **Vibrance**: Adjusts the saturation in such a way that clipping is reduced to a minimum when color intensity approaches its maximum. This option modifies the saturation of all colors with a lower saturation while having a lesser impact on the colors with greater saturation. Additionally, vibrancy prevents the saturation of skin tones from becoming too extreme.

- **Saturation**: This feature allows you to adjust the degree to which each color in the picture is saturated, ranging from -100 (monochrome) to +100 (twice the saturation).

CHAPTER NINE
GETTING ACQUAINTED WITH COLOR MODE

The goal of this chapter is to introduce readers to Photoshop's color modes. It begins by answering the issue of which color mode to use for a particular project, outlining the distinctions between popular color modes like RGB and CMYK as well as the appropriate applications for each. Additionally, the chapter discusses the concepts of calibration and profiling, which are critical to maintaining color constancy and accuracy in digital photographs. Converting an RGB picture to CMYK mode is one of the main topics discussed; this is crucial for getting ready images for printing. It details the procedures and things to think about before converting. Finally, the chapter offers instructions on how to save photographs as Photoshop PDF files, which can help share and print among other things. The information in this chapter gives readers the tools they need to handle photos in various contexts and choose color modes wisely.

WHICH COLOR MODE SHOULD I CHOOSE?

When it comes to choosing the right color mode in Photoshop, your decision should be based on the specific requirements of your project. Photoshop offers several color modes, each with its own characteristics and ideal use cases.

Different color modes

1. RGB mode (millions of colors)
2. CMYK mode (four-printed colors)
3. Index mode (256 colors)
4. Grayscale mode (256 grays)
5. Bitmap mode (2 colors)

Depending on the number of channels in a color model, the color mode, also known as the picture mode, controls how colors mix. File size and color detail vary depending on the color mode used. For example, to save file size without sacrificing color fidelity, choose RGB color mode for photos in emails or the web and CMYK color mode for photographs in full-color print brochures.

RGB Color mode

Using the RGB paradigm, Photoshop RGB Color mode gives each pixel an intensity value. Each RGB (red, green, and blue) component of a color picture has an intensity value between 0 (black) and 255 (white) in 8 bits per channel image. A vivid red color, for instance, has a B value of 50, a G value of 20, and an R value of 246. A neutral gray color results when the values of the three components are equal. The outcome is pure white when all component values are 255 and pure black when all component values are 0. Three colors, or channels, are used in RGB graphics to replicate colors on screen. The three channels correspond to 24 (8 bits x 3 channels) bits of color information per pixel in 8 bits per channel pictures. The three channels can reproduce up to 16.7 million colors per pixel using pictures that are 24 bits in size. Even more, colors can be reproduced per pixel in 48-bit (16 bits-per-channel) and 96-bit (32 bits-per-channel) pictures.

The RGB model is not just the default mode for newly created Photoshop pictures, but computer displays also utilize it to show colors. This indicates that Photoshop transforms a CMYK picture to RGB for on-screen display while working in color modes other than RGB, like CMYK. Despite being a common color model, RGB can represent a wide variety of colors, depending on the application or display device. Photoshop's RGB color mode changes based on the working space configuration you choose in the Color Settings dialog box.

CMYK Color mode

Every pixel in the CMYK mode has a percentage value allocated to it for each process ink. Process ink colors are allocated smaller percentages to the lightest (highlight) colors and larger percentages to the darkest (shadow) hues. Bright red, for instance, may have 2% cyan, 93% magenta, 90% yellow, and 0% black. Pure white is produced in CMYK pictures when the values of each of the four components are 0%. When creating an image for process color printing, use the CMYK mode. The process of converting an RGB picture to CMYK separates the colors. It is preferable to edit an RGB picture in the beginning and convert it to CMYK after the process if you start with an RGB image. You can mimic the results of a CMYK conversion in RGB mode by using the Proof Setup instructions, all without altering the original picture data. CMYK mode can also be used to work directly with scanned or imported CMYK pictures from high-end computers.

Despite being a common color model, CMYK's precise color representation can vary based on the press and printing circumstances. Photoshop's CMYK color mode changes based on the working space configuration you choose in the Color Settings dialog box.

Lab Color mode

The human perception of color serves as the foundation for the **CIE L*a*b* color model (Lab)**. All of the colors that a person with normal eyesight perceives are described by the numerical values in Lab. Lab is regarded as a device-independent color model since it specifies the appearance of a color rather than the quantity of a specific colorant required for a device (such as a monitor, desktop printer, or digital camera) to create colors. Color management systems typically convert a color from one color space to another by using Lab as a color reference. A lightness component (L) in the Lab Color mode can have a value between 0 and 100. The b component (blue-yellow axis) and the component (green-red axis) in the Adobe Color Picker and Color panel can have values between +127 and −128.

Photoshop, Photoshop EPS, Large Document Format (PSB), Photoshop PDF, Photoshop Raw, TIFF, Photoshop DCS 1.0, or Photoshop DCS 2.0 are among the formats in which lab photos can be stored. Lab photos in the 48-bit (16 bits per channel) format can be saved as TIFF, Photoshop, Photoshop PDF, Photoshop Raw, or Large Document Format (PSB).

Grayscale mode

Images in grayscale mode use various tones of gray. There can be up to 256 shades of gray in 8-bit graphics. In a grayscale picture, each pixel has a brightness value between 0 (black) and 255 (white). The number of shades in a picture is much more in 16- and 32-bit images than in 8-bit ones. In addition, grayscale values can be expressed as percentages of black ink coverage, where 0% represents white and 100% represents black. The working area option that you provide in the **Color Settings** dialog box determines the range that is used in grayscale mode.

Bitmap mode

Bitmap mode represents an image's pixels using one of two color values: black or white. Because they have a bit depth of 1, pictures in bitmap mode are referred to as bitmapped 1-bit images.

Duotone mode

Using one to four bespoke inks, the duotone mode produces monotone, duotone (two colors), tritone (three colors), and quadtone (four colors) grayscale graphics.

Indexed Color mode

Up to 256 colors can be produced in 8-bit picture files using the Indexed Color mode. Photoshop creates a color lookup table (CLUT) that saves and indexes the colors in the picture when it converts to indexed color. The application selects the nearest color or applies dithering to mimic the color using the available colors if a color from the original picture is absent from the database. Indexed color can shrink files while keeping the visual quality required for websites, multimedia presentations, and the like while having a smaller color palette. In this mode, there is little editing accessible. To do substantial editing, you need to switch to RGB mode momentarily. Photoshop, BMP, DICOM (Digital Imaging and Communications in Medicine), GIF, Photoshop EPS, Large Document Format (PSB), PCX, Photoshop PDF, Photoshop Raw, Photoshop 2.0, PICT, PNG, Targa®, or TIFF are among the formats in which indexable color data can be stored.

Multichannel mode

Images in multichannel mode are helpful for specialty printing since each channel has 256 levels of gray. Photoshop, Large Document Format (PSB), Photoshop 2.0, Photoshop Raw, or Photoshop DCS 2.0 are the formats in which multichannel mode photos can be stored.

When converting photos to Multichannel mode, the following rules are applicable:

- Layers are unsupported and therefore flattened.
- Color channels in the original image become spot color channels in the converted image.
- Converting a CMYK image to Multichannel mode creates cyan, magenta, yellow, and black spot channels.
- Converting an RGB image to Multichannel mode creates cyan, magenta, and yellow spot channels.
- Deleting a channel from an RGB, CMYK, or Lab image automatically converts the image to Multichannel mode, flattening layers.
- To export a multichannel image, save it in Photoshop DCS 2.0 format.

UNDERSTANDING CALIBRATION AND PROFILING

Fundamental ideas in digital image and color management, especially with Adobe Photoshop, are calibration and profiling. These procedures guarantee the accuracy and consistency of the colors you see on your display, print, or see on other devices.

Here's a summary of what calibration and profiling in Photoshop mean:

1. **Calibration:**
   - **Monitor calibration:** This procedure entails modifying your computer monitor's settings to get the most accurate color output. Ensuring that the colors on your screen correspond with the real colors in your photographs is the aim. Typically, monitor calibration involves gamma, brightness, contrast, and color temperature adjustments.
   - **Printer Calibration:** Calibration refers to setting your printer's settings so that the colors it prints correspond to the colors you see on your calibrated display. For jobs involving color accuracy and good printing, this is extremely crucial. It might be necessary to load or build printer profiles for certain materials and inks.

2. **Profiling:**
   - **Monitor Profiling:** You must create a monitor profile after calibrating your display. This profile explains the many settings that affect the color display on your monitor. To test your monitor's color properties, you can use hardware and software equipment like spectrophotometers and colorimeters. Photoshop (and other programs) can display colors on that monitor more accurately thanks to the generated profile.
   - **Printer profiling:** This technique, which is similar to monitor profiling, entails building a profile of your printer that describes the color reproduction capabilities. To make these profiles, you can use a color target along with profiling software or hardware. These profiles are used by Photoshop to correct the color in your photos so they print correctly.

3. **Working Space:**
   - In Photoshop, you work with color spaces like sRGB, Adobe RGB, or ProPhoto RGB. These spaces define the range of colors available for editing. Profiling and calibration ensure that your monitor and printer can accurately represent the colors within these working spaces.

4. **Soft Proofing:**
   - After calibration and profiling, you can use Photoshop's soft proofing feature to simulate how your images will look on different devices, such as when printed on a specific printer or viewed on a different monitor. It helps you make adjustments to your images to maintain color accuracy.

5. **ICC Profiles:**
   - ICC (International Color Consortium) profiles are files that contain information about the color characteristics of devices like monitors, printers, and scanners. Photoshop uses these profiles to translate colors between devices accurately.

In summary, calibration makes sure that your monitor and printer display colors accurately, while profiling creates profiles that describe how these devices handle colors. Using these profiles, Photoshop can accurately map and adjust colors to ensure consistency across different devices. Proper color management, including calibration and profiling, is crucial for professional photography, graphic design, and printing work.

CONVERTING RGB IMAGE TO CMYK MODE

Step 1: Save a Backup of Your Work

Making a backup copy of the original design in advance is crucial since switching between color profiles can alter the appearance of your work and you might not be able to go back to it later.

- To save your document as a CMYK option, select **File > Save As**.
- After saving your work, you can go to the following step.

Step 2: Flatten All Layers

Before converting to CMYK, you must flatten your layers if the document you're working with has a lot of layers, tweaks, smart objects, and other effects. If you don't, there's a chance that changing color profiles will unfavorably alter your design. Go to **Layer > Flatten Image to flatten** your layers. Next, make sure there is only one flattened layer by checking your Layers panel:

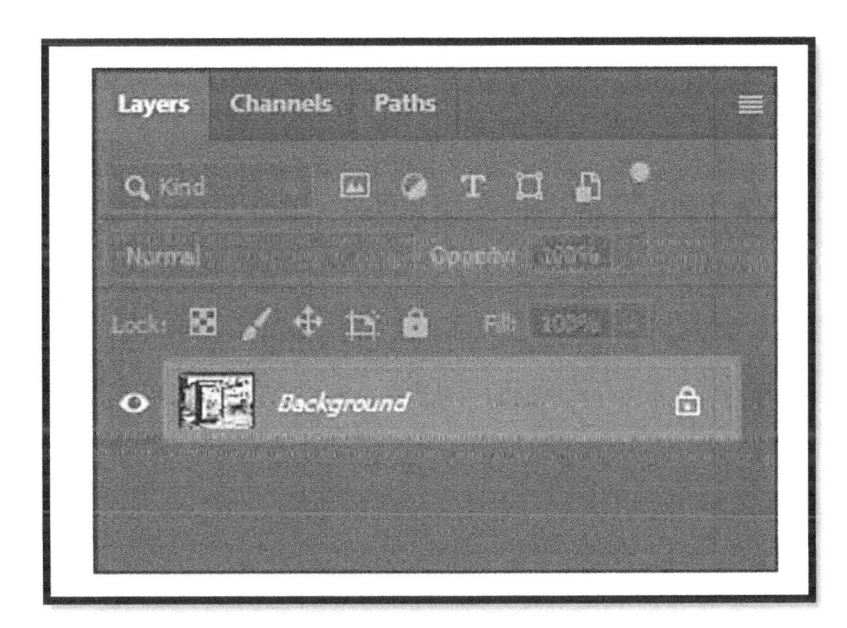

Step 3: Change the Document Color Profile

All you need to do now is select **Edit > Convert to Profile** to bring up the Convert to Profile menu to convert RGB to CMYK:

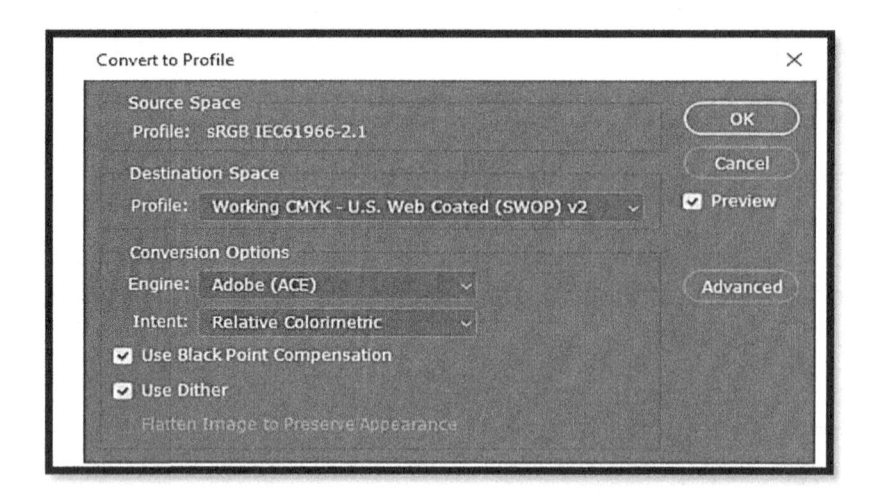

The "**Source Space**" area will be at the top of the Convert to Profile menu. This shows the color profile that your document is now using. It is **sRGB IEC61966-2.1** in this case. The color profile you want to switch to is represented by the second menu option from the top, "**Destination Space**." The dropdown menu will open up a large selection of color profiles for you to select from:

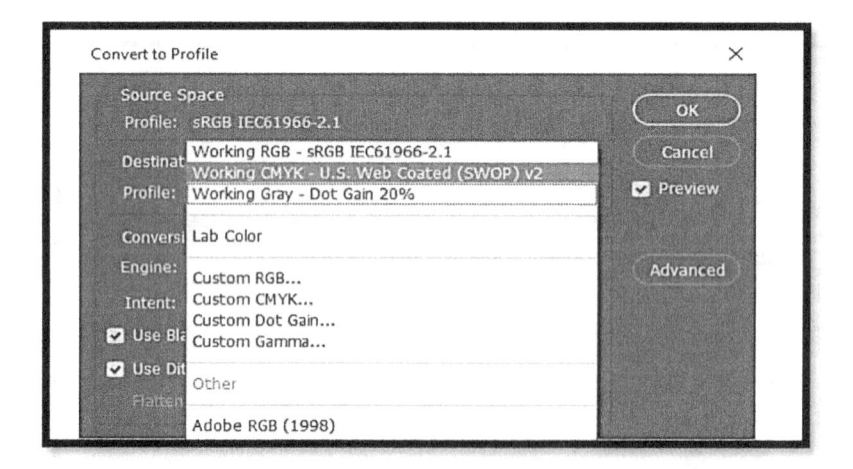

Make careful to choose the particular color profile that your print shop requests. If not, select the **"Working CMYK – U.S. Web Coated (SWOP) v2"** default CMYK profile and click **OK** to make the modifications.

A CMYK color profile will now be integrated into your Photoshop document, and you can confirm this on the document's tab:

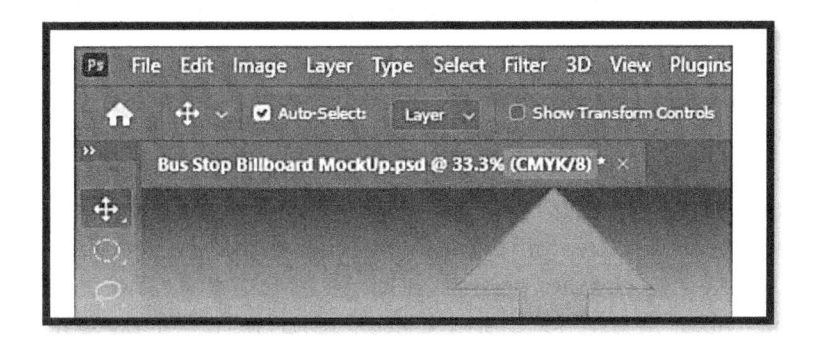

Precautions

It should be remembered that your design will almost certainly look different in Photoshop if you convert from RGB to CMYK. Unfortunately, other than possibly adding some adjustment layers to modify some of the colors, there isn't much you can do to fix this. The best defense against this issue is to start with your document in CMYK color mode. In some way, having to make these adjustments retroactively will inevitably lead to unfavorable outcomes.

SAVING YOUR IMAGE AS PHOTOSHOP PDF

- Click **Save As** after selecting File from the menu bar.
- To view this list of format options, select the **Save as type box** in the menu that appears.
- Then choose **Photoshop PDF**.
- Check the **As a Copy** option near the bottom if you want to be able to use Photoshop to continue working with the original file.
- Select **Save**.
- There will be another menu before the document saving. When saving a PDF, many options will make the document better suitable for a certain purpose.
- To open this dropdown menu, click in the **Adobe PDF Preset** box located near the top section. Select the relevant preset (e.g., Smallest File Size for online use, Press Quality for professional printing, High-Quality Print for home printing) according to your needs.
- Verify that the option labeled Preserve Photoshop Editing Capabilities is ticked if you wish to be able to edit the PDF file afterward. Uncheck this option to reduce the file size that you wish.

CHAPTER TEN
FINE ART PAINTING WITH THE MIXER BRUSH

This chapter covers Photoshop techniques for fine art painting, with a particular emphasis on using the Mixer Brush tool. It starts by going over how to pick a suitable workstation and adjust the brush settings for digital painting. It explains the subtleties of using brushes and wetness settings, assisting readers in comprehending how to manipulate paint flow and replicate conventional painting methods in a digital environment. The chapter spends a large amount of time explaining to users how to use the Mixer Brush to blend colors in a way that is both realistic and expressive while creating digital paintings. It walks users through the process of making and saving personalized brush presets, enabling artists to customize their tools to suit their unique demands and artistic tastes. If you are interested in using Photoshop's Mixer Brush tool to create high-art paintings, this chapter offers insightful advice and helpful strategies.

CHOOSING A WORKSPACE AND SELECTING BRUSH SETTINGS

Choosing a Workspace

- Open an image.
- **Select > Select and Mask** is the option.
- On a Mac, press **Cmd+Option+R**; on Windows, press **Ctrl+Alt+R**.
- Turn on a selection tool, like Lasso, Magic Wand, or Quick Selection.
- In the **Options** box, select **Select and Mask**.

Choosing the Brush Settings

- In the options bar, select a painting or editing tool and click the Brush pop-up menu.
- Pick out a brush.
- On the **Brush Settings** panel, you can also choose a brush.
- Click **Brushes** in the panel's upper-left corner to see the loaded presets.
- Modify the preset brush's settings.

Recall that you can design brushes with multiple ways to apply paint to images. You can make a custom brush tip from a portion of an image3, choose an already-existing preset brush, or use a brush tip shape. To customize how the paint is applied, select settings from the Brush Settings panel.

WORKING WITH BRUSHES AND WETNESS OPTIONS

One of the main tools used in painting is the brush. It operates by applying color with strokes, just like a conventional drawing tool would. It's in the normal toolbar, and the letter B is the default shortcut for it. To utilize the Brush Tool, first add a shaped mark to a layer. Then, if you keep pressing the mouse button or the pen on a tablet, multiple marks will be added until you remove the pressure, forming a stroke. Photoshop's Paint Tool's primary settings include **Brush Tip Shape, Blending Mode, Opacity, and Flow.** Before adjusting the advanced settings, you must comprehend those ideas. There are multiple presets, or ready-to-use predefined brushes, included with Photoshop.

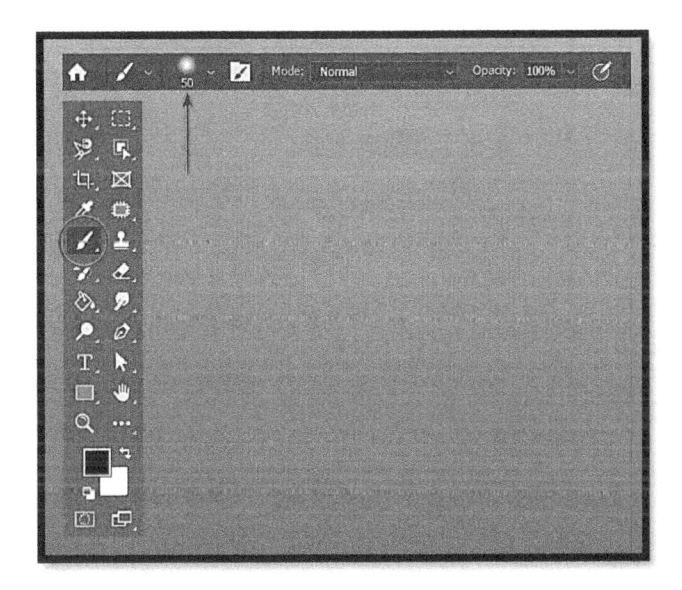

The Basics

Brush Tip

The Paint Tool in Photoshop has this most basic setting. You may change how the Brush Tool adds color to a Photoshop document by adjusting the Brush Tip settings. Upon selecting the Brush Preset Picker from the default Options Panel, some pre-installed presets will become visible.

You can easily change two crucial values on a lot of the presets:
- Size affects how big or little the brush tip is. The **[key and] key** are the standard shortcuts for increasing and decreasing. As an alternative, you can

dynamically adjust the brush size by using **Control-Option-Click** on a Mac or **Alt-Right-Click** and **Drag** on a Windows computer.
- The border strength of the brush tip is affected by its hardness. A boundary that is 100% accurate and 0% soft is indicated.

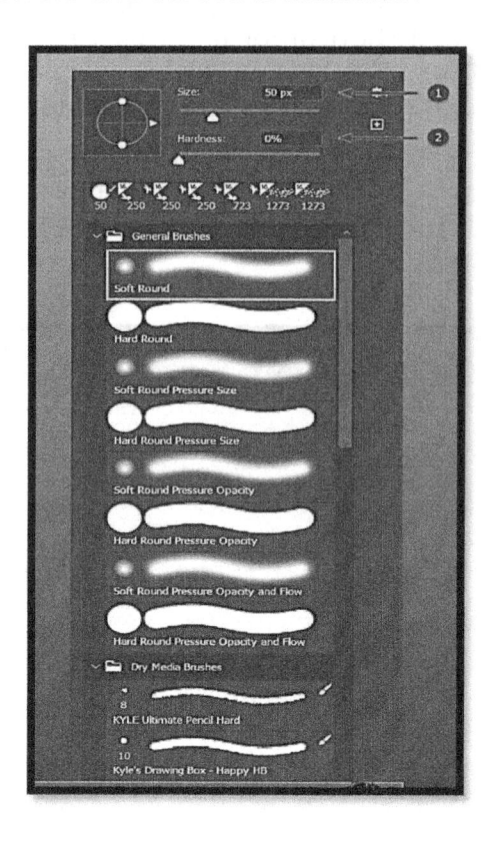

Foreground Color

The Foreground Color setting, located at the bottom of the Tools toolbar, determines the color that the brush tip applies. In Photoshop, click the Foreground Color and select a new color with the Color Picker to alter the brush's color.

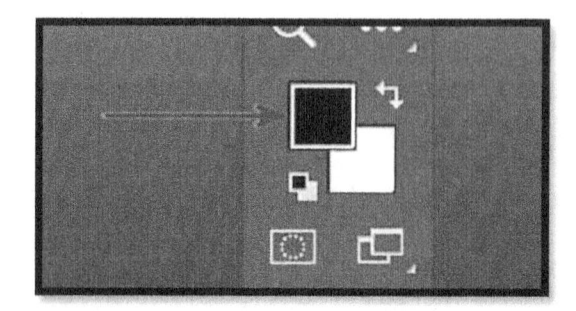

Brush Preset Picker Contextual Menu

The Brush Preset Picker menu has some helpful tools, such as **New Brush Preset, New Brush Group, Delete Brush,** and **Rename Brush.**

The Preset Picker panel then offers many options for how the list of brushes is displayed; a few examples of these are shown below. Additionally, you can simply manage the brush list by adding new brushes or loading, storing, and replacing existing brushes. You can even append pre-existing brush collections.

Brush Modes

You can select a Blending Mode for the stroke each time you paint with the Brush Tool. You can alter the way a brushstroke interacts with the pixels behind it by using a Blending Mode. Give a few of them a try.

Modes: Behind, Clear, Normal, and Dissolve

Let's go over a few of the fundamental brush modes.

1. **Normal Mode**, which leaves the color exactly as it is, is the first option on the list.
2. The **Dissolve Mode** introduces some noise near the brush stroke's edge.
3. **Behind Mode** paints behind an existing stroke, even if they are both on the same layer.
4. Next, select **Clear Mode**. Similar to the Eraser tool, the "**Clear**" blend mode makes the pixels you paint on transparent.

Although most of the blending modes' names do a passable job of explaining what they do, it's still preferable to browse through them and experience the various blending modes for yourself!

More Blending Modes

The Blending Modes listed below are identical and can be used on layers as well. You can view some applications and blending mode samples below. They can be used to add color (**Darken, Multiply, Overlay**) or light (**Lighten, Color Dodge, Linear Dodge**) to objects. Here is a lot for you to try out. You never stop learning about Blending Modes in Photoshop, no matter how long you've been using it.

Opacity

An opaque stroke has a 100% opacity value, indicating complete color, whereas a more transparent stroke has a smaller proportion.

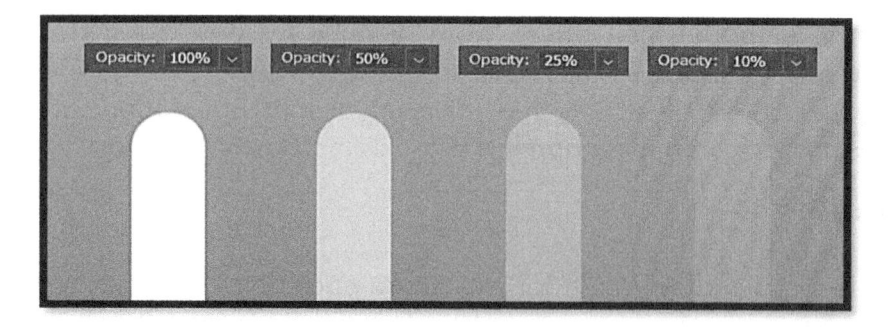

Flow

The paint application speed is adjusted by the Flow setting. More paint will accumulate in the same area with each brush stroke. You don't have to raise your brush as you would with Opacity, which makes it perfect for progressively adding elements like color, light, and shadows!

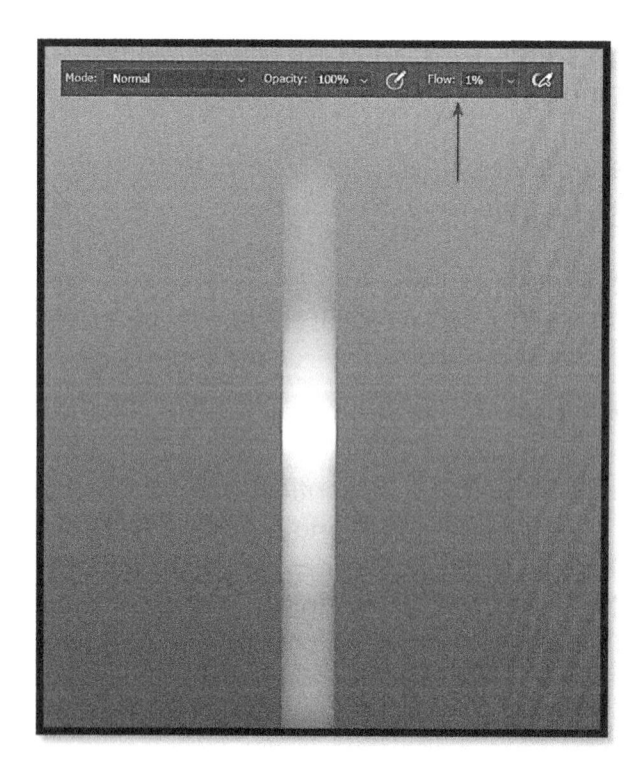

What Is the Brush Settings Panel?

A specific brush behavior or Brush Preset can be created, edited, saved, and loaded using the Brush Panel. Here, you can adjust some parameters, including the brush tip shape, scattering, opacity jitter, flow jitter, and controls specific to each variation. Select **Window > Brushes** to bring up the Brush Settings Panel. To activate the Brush Preset options, you must also choose the Brush Tool from the Tools toolbar. Let's make a Custom Brush now and give it a few different versions.

MAKE A WET BRUSH

When you first open Photoshop, a "**Welcome**" screen including multiple options for document creation will appear. One way to go about it is to make a "**Wet Brush**." First, open the "**Brushes**" tab to create a Wet Brush. The Window drop-down menu at the top of your screen is where you can find this panel. Click the icon that resembles a paintbrush with water drops in the Brushes section. The Wet Brush options will then be accessible.

Three options are available for Wet Brush:

- **Dry Brush**: Selecting this option will result in a dry brush devoid of any water droplets. This is the default option.
- **Wet Brush**: Selecting this option will result in a wet brush that contains water droplets.

You can modify the "Wetness" slider to regulate the quantity of water droplets.

- **Wet-on-Dry Brush**: Selecting this option will result in a wet-on-dry brush that contains water droplets. You can modify the "Wetness" slider to regulate the quantity of water droplets.

You can change the size and shape of your brush by clicking on the "**Size**" and "**Shape**" options in the Brushes panel after choosing your preferred Wet Brush option. By selecting the "**Color**" option in the Brushes panel, you can also change the color of your brush. The Brushes panel can be closed by clicking the "**OK**" button once you have completed modifying the brush settings. Now you can paint on your canvas with your Wet Brush!

How Do You Make a Wet Brush in Photoshop?

Using Photoshop, you can create a Wet Brush by navigating to the Brushes panel and choosing the icon that resembles a paintbrush with water drops. Dry Brush, Wet Brush, and Wet on Dry Brush are the three Wet Brush options. The "**Size**" and "**Shape**" options in the Brushes panel are where you can change the size and shape of your brush.

MIXING COLORS WITH THE MIXER BRUSH

The first thing you need to do is locate the Mixer Brush, which shouldn't be too difficult. Although it is likely concealed beneath the ordinary brush, it can be found on the toolbar on the left side of the screen, along with the other tools. **Click and hold** (or **right-click**) on the brush tool to open the menu of tools hidden behind the top one. Select the **Mixer Brush Tool** from the list.

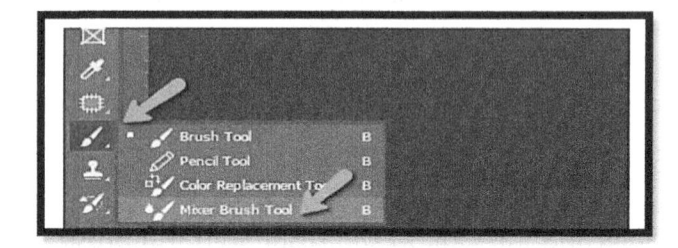

Step 1: Select a Color

Simply click the foreground color swatch that is located toward the bottom of the toolbar on the left side of the screen to change the color of your brush. Let's choose something dark so that we can more clearly see how the brush is behaving, and let's get started.

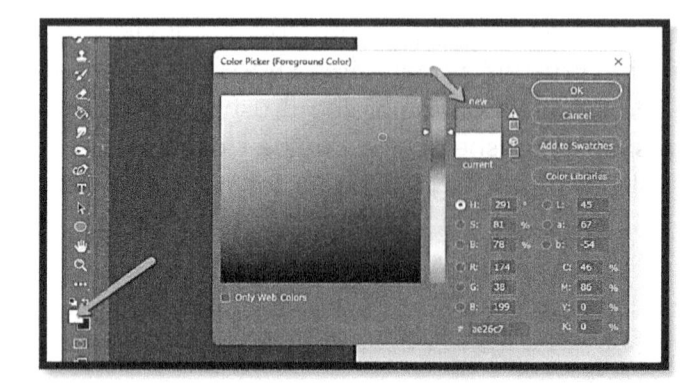

You can also determine the color of the paint by looking straight at the canvas. When you are attempting to blend several colors, this comes in handy. To load canvas paint, you must first select the color you wish to pick up by holding **Alt** and clicking or **Option** and clicking on it. You can also **Load and Clean** the brush using the buttons in the **Options** panel.

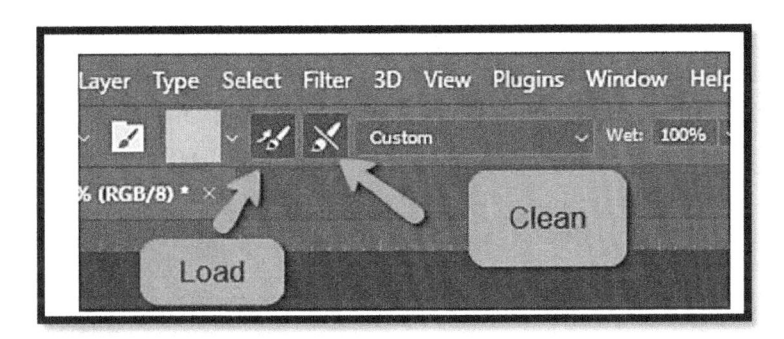

When you give the new brush a few strokes, you will see that it does not paint with the color as solidly as you are accustomed to seeing with the traditional brush. Since we haven't yet mixed any two colors, you might be wondering why we're doing this.

Well, actually we do.

Photoshop will treat any color you have on your canvas as if it were wet paint, regardless of what color it actually is. That encompasses the background color you've chosen for the page. Therefore, the color is rather muted in this area since there is a significant amount of white being blended in.

Simply by adjusting the settings for your brush, you can determine how this blending will take place.

Step 2: Choose Your Brush Settings

As is customary, the parameters for your brush can be changed in the **Options** bar. To select the brush tip, size, and degree of stiffness, you can do so by clicking the arrow next to the preview of the brush's tip.

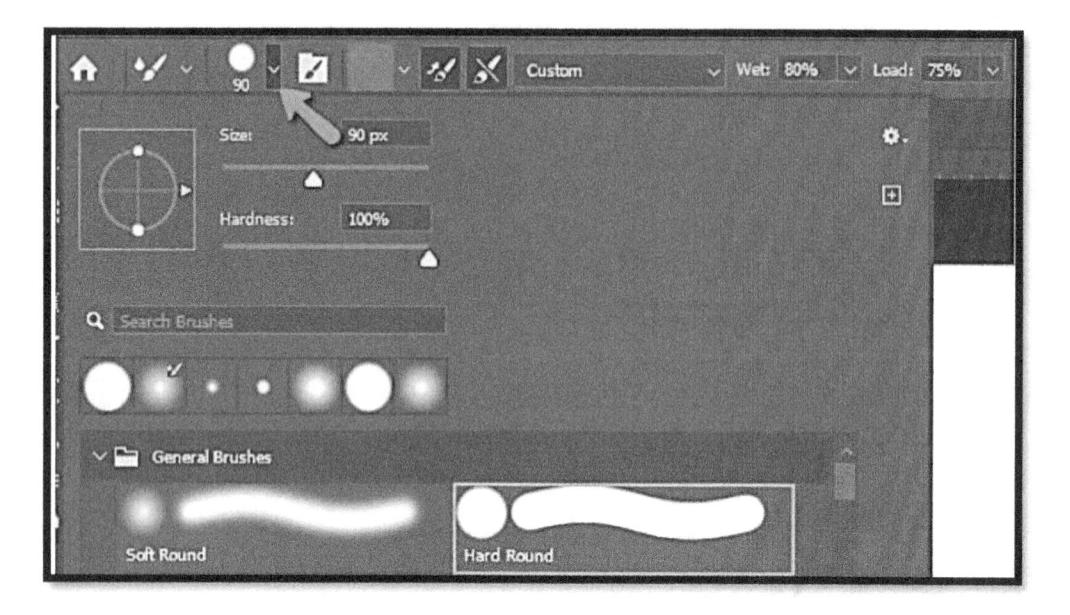

However, in addition to the standard Opacity and Flow options found on a regular brush, we have access to a few additional and unique settings. Let's look at each one in greater detail, shall we?

Wet

You have control over how "**wet**" the paint is on your canvas when you use Wet. Therefore, increasing the setting will lead the brush to pick up more color from the canvas, just as if the paint were still relatively wet. A low setting will give the impression that the paint on the canvas is already drying, resulting in a less seamless blending of the colors. You can see a comparison of how it looks when the Wet setting is set to 80 and when it is set to 5 below. Because there is less white "**paint**" being blended in, the color in the image on the right is not only darker but also more vibrant.

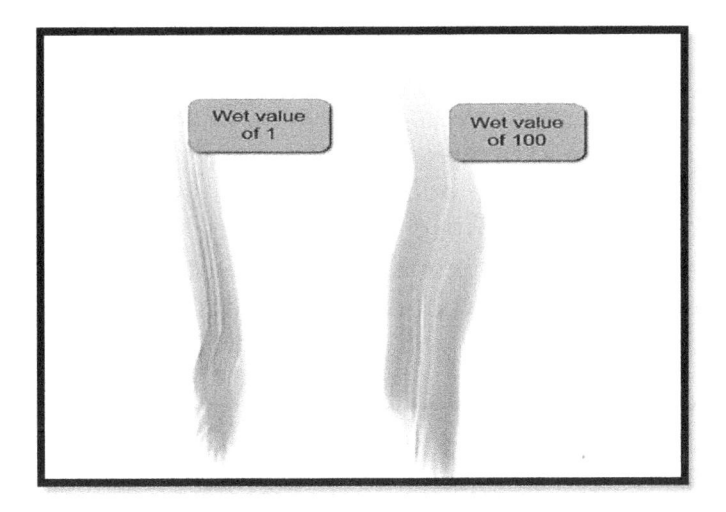

The Wet setting cannot be at 0 because this will prevent the brush from functioning correctly. If Wet is set to 0, the brush will behave similarly to the standard brush and simply paint a solid color onto the canvas.

Load

The value of the Load parameter determines how much paint you load onto your brush before beginning a stroke. If you were painting on a real canvas, this is the color you would select from your paint palette to use. A larger value causes more of the color you want to be picked up by the brush, while a lower value causes a smaller quantity to be picked up. Since the difference is rather small, it can be challenging to comprehend the significance of this value. Take a look at the difference between a Load value of 1 and a Load value of 100.

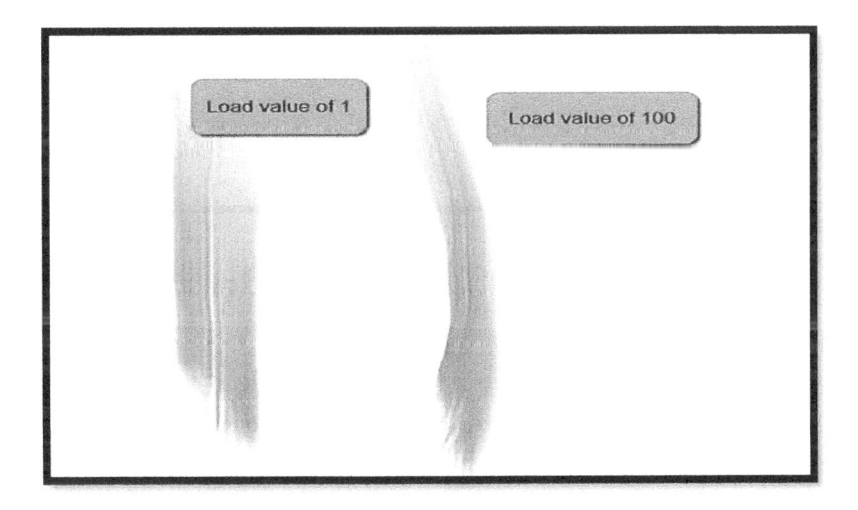

Mix

The paint is stored in a reservoir within the brush. When you load your brush, paint goes into this reservoir instead of directly onto the brush. By adjusting the Mix setting, you can control how much of the paint comes from the reservoir and how much comes directly from the canvas. Therefore, increasing the Mix value will result in a greater amount of your preferred color being applied to the canvas. A lower mix value, on the other hand, will pick up more paint off the canvas, which will be added to the mix.

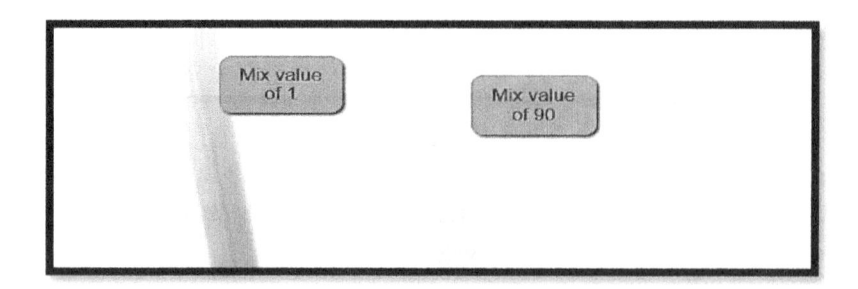

Flow

You can also control the flow, and this works the same way as it does with the standard brush. With a higher flow value, the paint will flow more easily and freely than with a lower one.

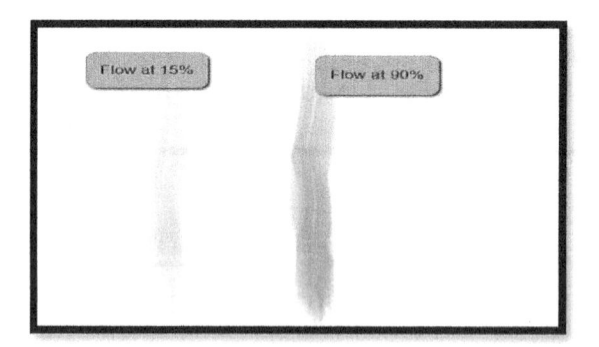

CREATE AND SAVE A CUSTOM BRUSH PRESET

Create a Brush Preset

Let's take a look at some of the different alterations that can be made to a brush preset by adjusting the jitters, counts, and pressure. When building a brush preset, the first thing you should do is select a brush tip from the library or, as is the case above, begin working with a custom brush tip. If you select a brush tip from the library, you can also start working with a custom brush tip.

Brush Tip Shape

The brush tip is the first component that can be altered to your liking.

1. The **Size** value indicates the actual number of pixels that make up the Brush Tip.
2. The checkboxes for the **Flip Axis** feature allow you to rotate the tip about its relevant axis, either horizontally or vertically.
3. Changing the **Angle** parameter will rotate the brush by the number of degrees you choose.
4. The **roundness** of the brush tip is measured in elliptical roundness, and a roundness of 100% corresponds to a perfect circle.
5. **Spacing** is the percentage of space between images when you draw a stroke on the canvas, using a mouse or a pen tablet. The larger the percentage, the bigger the distance.
6. One last thing: if the situation calls for it, you can also change the **Hardness** value of the tip. Hardness functions properly when used with the spherical brush tip that is provided by default; but, if you construct a brush tip from an image like we have, and then it will not function properly.

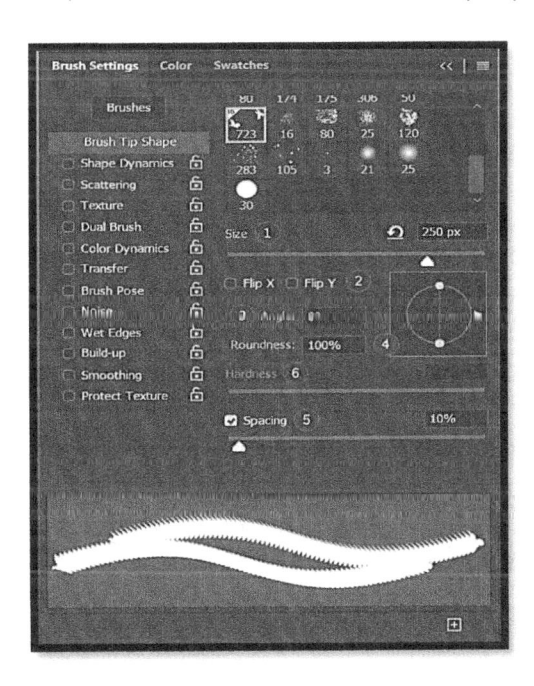

Shape Dynamics

The randomness of the **Size, Angle, Roundness, and Axis** values can be managed using some different options thanks to shape dynamics' availability. The greater the proportion, the less predictable the outcome will be.

Control

It will become apparent to you that many of the brush characteristics, such as Jittering and Scattering, can be adjusted by selecting one of the options from the Control dropdown.

You can choose from the following several Control options:

- **Off** indicates that there will be no control imposed at all.
- The brush stroke is gradually reduced in size from its starting diameter down to its minimum value by using the **Fade Control** feature.
- The values of the **pen pressure** are provided by an external device (such as a graphics tablet in this example), and the "Pen Pressure" setting adjusts the brush diameter based on those values.
- **Pen Tilt** and **Stylus Wheel** function in the same manner as Pen Pressure, but instead use the tilt and stylus wheel values that are stored in the hardware. These settings are not compatible with the usage of a mouse.

Scattering

The amount of scattering in a stroke will impact the quantity of brush marks as well as their placement. When the scattering % is higher, there is a greater degree of mark distribution.

1. Selecting the checkbox for **Both Axes** makes it possible to scatter along both the X and Y axes. If you deselect this option, the scattering will be done in a direction that is orthogonal to the stroke direction.
2. The **Count slider** allows you to specify the number of brush marks that are laid down at any given moment; a high number indicates that several brush marks will be laid down at once as opposed to simply one.
3. **Count Jitter** introduces an element of chance into the process of counting the marks on a stroke. There will be instances when it only places one, and other times when it will add more.

Color Dynamics

This setting determines how the paint's color shifts when it is moved over the canvas. The operation of it is not overly complicated. It just adds some arbitrary **color marks in a range that falls between the colors of the background and the foreground.**

- **The Jitter Percentage** determines the degree to which the colors are mixed at random.
- The difference between the Front Color Hue and the Foreground Color Hue can be adjusted with the use of the **Hue Jitter** control. The magnitude of the color difference will increase in direct proportion to the percentage.
- "**Saturation Jitter**" defines the proportion by which the saturation of a stroke fluctuates between the colors used for the foreground and the background. When the percentage is higher, there is a greater range of possible saturations.
- The **Brightness Jitter** feature is quite similar to the option that came before it, with the exception that it modifies the Brightness value. If the percentage is higher, then the difference in color intensity between the front and back colors is greater.
- **Purity** increases or decreases the overall saturation of the color.

Dual Brush

Let's try this one with a different brush tip, shall we? This one produces a blended mark by combining the effects of two different tips. Only the places where the primary brush's stroke and the secondary brush's stroke intersect are painted, and the second brush texture is applied within the primary brush stroke itself. To blend the primary tip with the second tip as well as all of the typical brush tip variations, you can select a Blending Mode.

Texture

Textured brushes have a pattern that is used to make brush strokes appear as if they were painted on a textured surface. Textured brushes are used in digital painting. To begin painting with texture, select a texture from the pop-up box, and then adjust the Pattern Scale to the desired percentage. You have access to a wide variety of pattern parameters that you can implement. If you paint a mark while the **Texture Each Tip** checkbox is selected, the program will apply a new instance of the texture to the mark each time it is painted. If this is left unchecked, the texture will continue to flow throughout the stroke in its entirety. The **Blending Mode** setting determines how the texture is combined with the color of the brush tip, while the Depth setting determines how much contrast the texture will have. Finally, some textures allow for the **Depth Jitter** to be activated by allowing for a controllable fluctuation between the Depth percentage and the Minimum Depth percentage. Although this control is rarely used, it is something that you can play about with.

More Dynamics

There are a few more dynamics on the list:

1. Adding **Noise** to a Brush Mark will add some noise to the brush mark's borders.
2. The effect created by **Wet Edges** gives the impression of a watercolor painting, with the stroke boundaries appearing darker than the center of the image.
3. Since **Build Up** is a simulation of conventional airbrushing, holding down the mouse button for a longer period results in a larger mark. There is a direct correlation between the Build Up option and the Airbrush option in the options bar.
4. When you're in a hurry to paint, you can benefit from **smoothing** because it makes the curves in your brush strokes more rounded. Excellent for using a mouse to create a drawing. You can also find this in the options bar located at the top of the screen.
5. The **Protect Texture** setting applies the same pattern and scale to all of the brush presets that include a texture, regardless of whether or not the settings for those brush presets are different. This is wonderful if you want to repeat the same pattern on some different brush tips.

How to Create a New Preset Brush

After making adjustments to the brush options, you can quickly save the brush by selecting the icon labeled **Create New Brush**, which is located in the bottom right-hand corner of the Brush Settings panel. Check that the box labeled **Include Tool Settings** is selected. After giving the brush a name, press the **OK** button. Your newly created brush will now show up in the Brush Settings Panel with all of its previous configurations preserved; however, if you reset the brushes library, your brush will no longer be available.

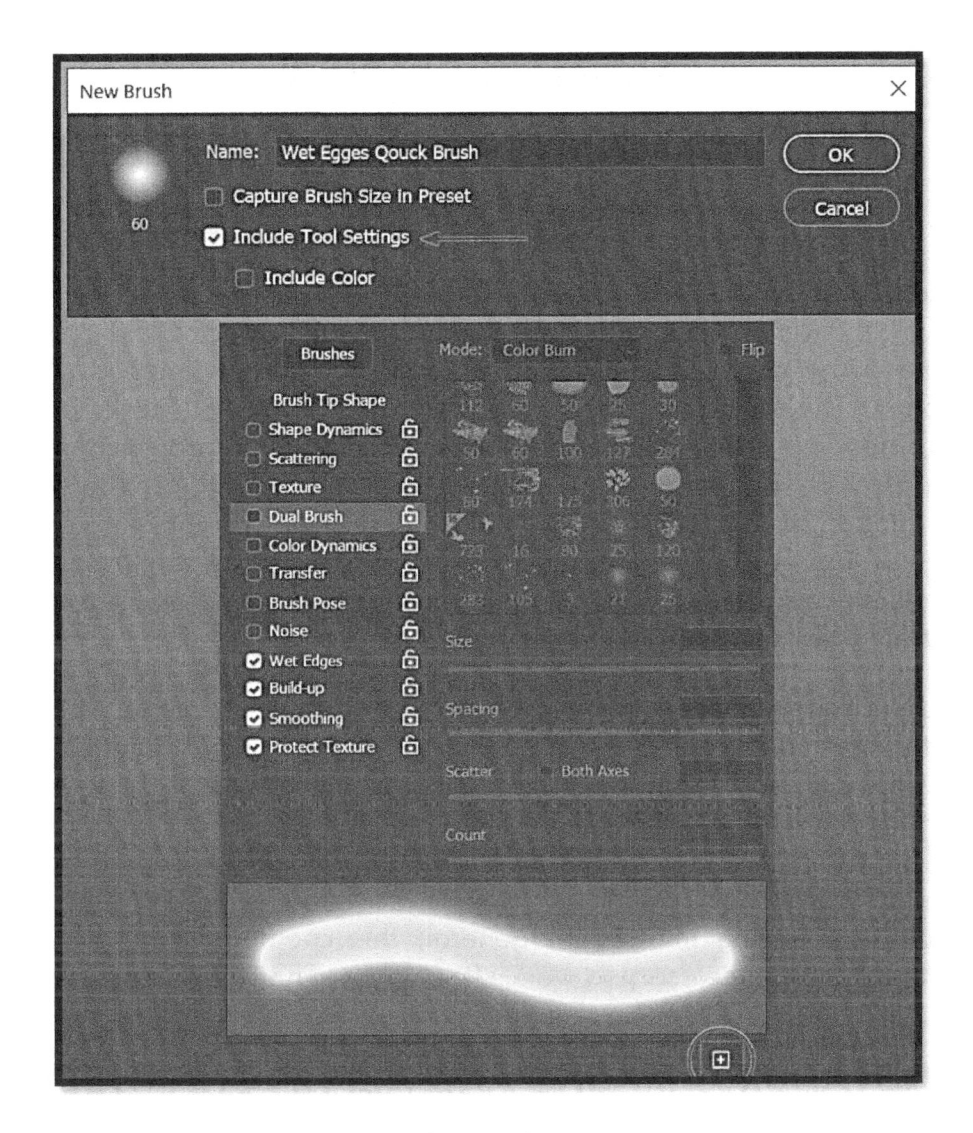

Save and Load Brushes in Photoshop

Click the "**Export Selected Brushes**" button in the Brush Preset Picker window. This will allow you to save your custom brushes as an ABR file, which is the format that Photoshop uses for its brushes. You can then give these brushes to a friend or keep them for yourself. To load a brush library that was previously stored, go to the Brush Preset Picker menu and click on the **Import Brushes** option. In addition to that, you can delete a single brush or an entire set of brushes by right-clicking the brush you want to delete and selecting "Delete Brushes." You can re-access the default brush group that was pre-installed in Photoshop by using the Append Default Brushes command.

CHAPTER ELEVEN
CREATING MASKS AND CHANNELS IN PHOTOSHOP

The process of developing masks and channels in Photoshop is the main topic of this chapter. It covers a wide variety of the fundamental principles of dealing with masks and alpha channels, which are essential for precise image editing and manipulation. The chapter starts by introducing the ideas of masks and alpha channels, underlining the importance of these concepts in the process of managing the transparency of an image and constructing complex selections. You will get an understanding of how to construct masks, improve their accuracy through further refining, and improve the appearance of mask edges through the application of global refinements. Within the realm of image manipulation, this section emphasizes the significance of accurate masking.

This chapter also provides an introduction to the idea of quick masks, which are an effective tool for making selections and refining image sections. The Puppet Warp feature, which can be used to creatively alter and manipulate images, is another subject that is discussed. In addition, the chapter offers instructions on how to create shadows by utilizing alpha channels and how to replace backgrounds by utilizing layer masks. This enables users to obtain more complex results when altering images and composing images. In general, this chapter teaches readers the fundamental abilities necessary to work effectively in Photoshop using masks and channels.

UNDERSTANDING MASKS AND ALPHA CHANNELS

A mask is a grayscale image in Photoshop that is used to determine the level of opacity or transparency of particular regions of a layer. Masks are a crucial tool for image editing and compositing because of how frequently they are used to hide or show sections of an image in a way that is not damaging.

The following is an explanation of the most important information regarding masks in Photoshop:

1. **Layer Masks:**
   - Layer masks control the visibility of the content on individual layers by being associated with those layers and controlling which parts of the content are shown.

- The contents of a layer are hidden when the layer mask has black sections, but white portions disclose the contents of the layer. Transparency can be altered to varied degrees depending on the shade of gray.

2. **Quick Masks:**
   - Quick Masks are temporary masks that are used for making precise selections or generating complex masks using brushes and other selection tools. Quick Masks can be created by clicking the "New" button in the "Mask" menu.

3. **Vector Masks:**
   - Vector masks are constructed using paths, and they are very useful for making clean, accurate selections with smooth curves.

4. **Clipping Masks:**
   - Clipping masks are used to restrict the visibility of a layer to the shape of another layer. These masks are frequently used for texturing and applying effects.

5. **Masking Techniques:**
   - To construct and edit masks in accordance with your specifications, you can make use of a wide variety of tools and procedures, including gradients, brushes, or the pen tool, amongst others.

Alpha Channels in Photoshop

On the other hand, a grayscale channel is known as an alpha channel, and it is responsible for storing information regarding the transparency of an image. Alpha channels are not limited to a single layer; rather, they can be used to specify transparency for the entire image as well as for many layers at the same time.

The following is a list of significant properties of alpha channels:

- **Creating Alpha Channels**: An alpha channel can be created by making a selection and then storing it with the "alpha channel" filename extension. When you wish to preserve complicated selections for later use, this is a helpful feature to have.
- **Editing Alpha Channels**: You can edit alpha channels by utilizing painting tools, gradients, or filters to adjust the information on the channel's transparency.
- **Loading Alpha Channels and Saving Them**: You can import alpha channels as selections, and then utilize those selections to create accurate masks or make a variety of modifications. In addition, alpha channels can be saved to a file and loaded into a separate project at a later time.

Key Differences between Masks and Alpha Channels

- **Layers Specificity**: Masks are only applicable to the individual layers they are placed on, whereas alpha channels can affect many layers or the entire image.
- **Functionality**: Masks are used to regulate which layer content is visible, while alpha channels are used to define how transparent an image is.
- **Color Information**: Masks are grayscale and manage transparency through the use of varying shades of gray. Alpha channels make use of grayscale as well, although they are specifically built to handle data relating to transparency.

Practical Uses

It is essential to have a solid understanding of the distinctions between masks and alpha channels to edit images in Photoshop effectively. When it comes to fine-tuning the visibility of certain layers, masks are the best tool for the job, while alpha channels are great for managing global transparency modifications and preserving complex selections.

CREATING A MASK

1. Open File
   - Startup "Photoshop." There is a menu bar that can be found at the very top of the screen. Locate the file, and then click on it. You need to decide which of the following to take now:
     - Click the Open... menu item, and then double-click on a project file to launch it from your local computer.
     - Click the New... button to initiate the creation of a new document, and then move on to the next step, which is to upload the image you want from your local computer.

2. Go to the Layers Panel and pick a layer to work with.

You will find a button labeled **Add layer mask** at the very bottom of the Layers panel; select this option. Next, a white layer mask thumbnail will appear on the layer that has been selected. This thumbnail will display everything that is contained in the layer that has been selected.

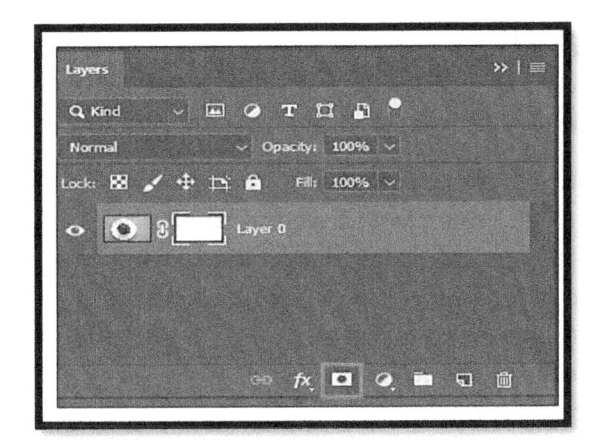

3. Select the Brush Tool

Because the entire task can be completed using the Brush Tool, navigate to the Toolbar and select the Brush tool from there. After that, head on over to the bar of options. To select the brush size and hardness, click on the **Brush Picker** button located in this area.

4. Make the foreground color black.

Make sure that the foreground color is set to black if you wish to hide a layer that uses the Photoshop mask. You have the option of doing it by hand, or you can press the D key. When you press the D key on your keyboard, the colors will revert to their standard settings, which are black and white respectively. When you press the X button, the colors will immediately change. You will achieve the desired effect of setting black as the foreground color in this manner. Simply paint over the image in the document window while the layer mask is selected and black will be added to the mask. The mask layer can be hidden by using the color black on the layer mask. Because of this, it is easy to view the layer right below it, as well as the checkerboard background, which is translucent.

5. Make the foreground color white.

Simply switching the foreground color to white will allow you to see through any layer that has the mask applied to it. You can change the color of the foreground to white by pressing the X key on your keyboard. This will also adjust the color of the background to the one you have currently selected.

To reveal the content that you had previously hidden behind a layer mask, simply paint over it with white at this point.

6. Apply Finishing Touches

While you are painting on a layer mask, this time you should go back and forth between black and white. When you use a soft brush to produce shadows, the region of the mask layer that you are working on will be partially masked.

REFINING A MASK

Follow these steps to easily modify and perfect any existing layer masks:

1. In the Layers panel, choose the layer that contains the mask you wish to edit.
2. In the Layers panel, select the **Mask thumbnail**.
3. Select an **editing or painting tool** from the available options. When the mask is activated, the foreground and background colors will both change to their respective default grayscale values.
4. **Carry out any one of the following:**
   - Painting the mask white will disclose the layer underneath while also removing part of the mask.
   - Painting the mask with gray will partially reveal the layer if you want to see it. The level seems less opaque when darker grays are used, and more transparent when lighter grays are used.
   - Painting the mask black allows you to add to the mask while simultaneously hiding the layer or group. The layers beneath are brought into view.
5. To edit the layer itself rather than the layer mask, instead, choose the layer by clicking its thumbnail in the Layers panel. **This step is optional**. A border is displayed around the layer thumbnail that is displayed.

Clicking the layer mask thumbnail in the Layers panel while holding down the Alt key (Windows) or the Option key (Mac) will select and display the mask channel, allowing you to paste a copied selection into a layer mask. Select **Edit > Paste**, followed by **Select > Deselect** in the menu bar. The selection is then grayscaled and added to the mask after it has been processed. To deselect the mask channel, click the thumbnail of the layer that is now selected in the Layers panel.

REFINING MASK EDGE WITH THE GLOBAL REFINEMENTS

Select and Mask is the name of the workspace in Photoshop that houses a collection of tools whose primary purpose is the creation and improvement of masks. When you're inside the **Select and Mask** window, you'll utilize the Select Subject tool to get a head start on the mask that will differentiate the model from the background. This will allow you to work more efficiently. After that, you will make adjustments to the mask using the various tools available in the Select And Mask palette, such as the Quick Selection tool.

1. In the Layers panel, ensure that both layers are visible, and then choose the Model layer.

The Select and Mask button becomes accessible in the options bar whenever any selection tool is selected to be in use. You can still use the Select > Select And Mask command even if the Select And Mask button is disabled in your editor.

2. **Go to the Select menu and select Select And Mask.**

The image is displayed when Select and Mask first launches. Masked sections are indicated by an "**onion skin**" overlay that is only partially transparent. Since you have not yet determined which parts of the image should be unmasked, the checkerboard pattern will continue to cover the entire picture for the time being. When you utilize Select and Mask for the first time, a little lesson may appear for you to peruse. You can choose to view it now, view it later, or close this window by clicking the corresponding button.

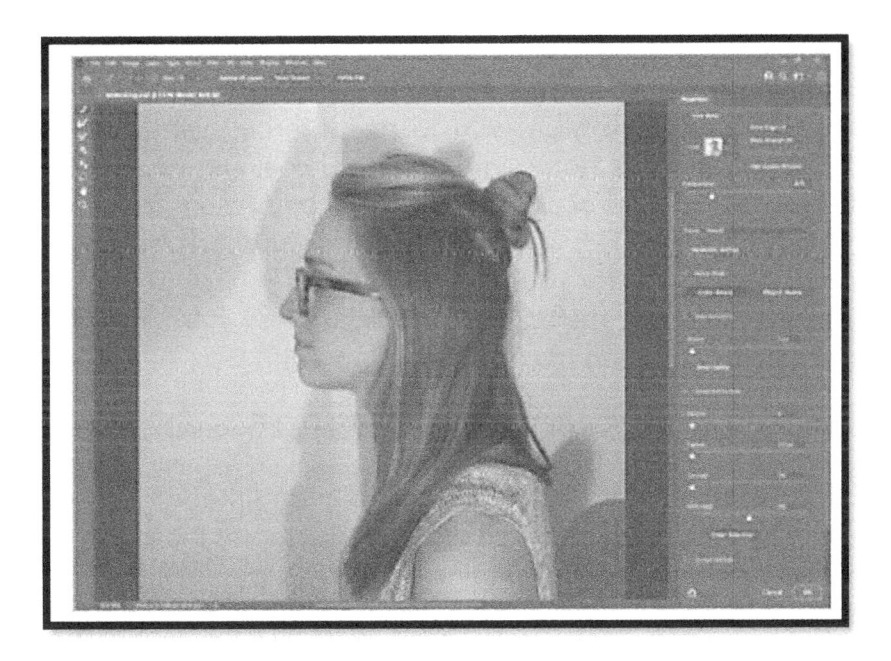

4. In the View Mode section of the Properties panel, click the View menu, and then select Overlay from the drop-down menu.

Instead of appearing as a checkerboard pattern made of onion skin, the masked area is now displayed as a transparent red color. It is reliable because nothing has been concealed as of yet. Instead of looking for the command in the menus, you can enter Select and Mask by clicking the Select and Mask button in the options bar when a selection tool is active on the document. This saves you time.

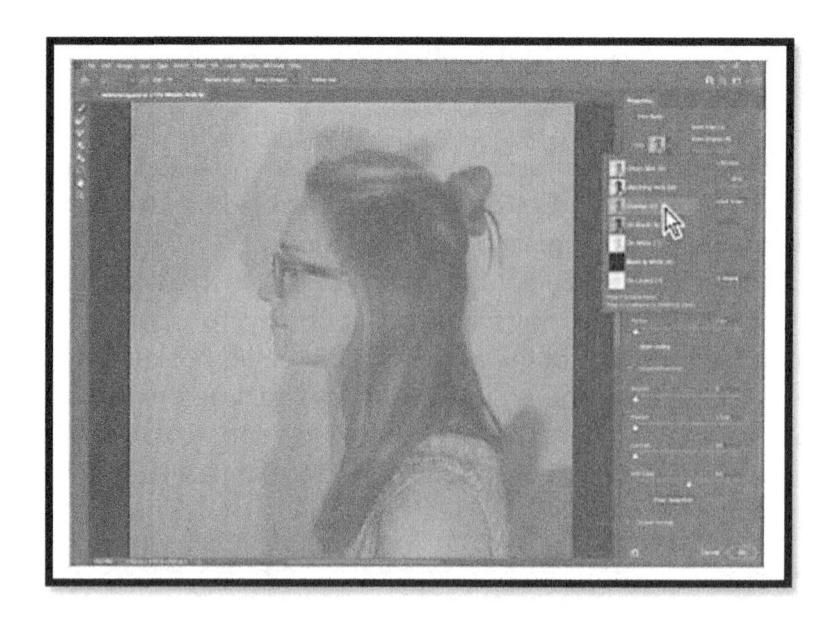

Simply tapping the F key will allow you to move through the View Modes in a whirlwind. When you view the game in a variety of settings, you are better able to identify faults in the selecting process that might not be so clear in other modes. You can see the mask more clearly over a variety of backgrounds by using the various View Modes, which are given for your convenience. In this scenario, the red overlay will make it easier to identify missed regions and edges where loose hair isn't fully covered. This is because the red overlay is transparent.

4. In the Options box, select the button that says Select Subject.

If the Select Subject button is not visible in the Select and Mask task space, check to see if the Quick Selection tool, which is located at the top of the toolbox, is selected. The Select Subject function is educated to recognize typical subjects of a photograph, such as people, animals, and objects, and then creates a selection for them using cutting-edge machine learning technology. This process takes place before the shot is ever taken. Although the selection might not be ideal, it is typically close enough for you to be able to improve it straightforwardly and expediently using additional selection methods. To utilize the **Select > Subject** command, the **Select and Mask** dialog box is not required to be open and active on the screen. Even if a selection tool is not active, you can still access it. Additionally, if you want to refine the selection, you can use **Select Subject** first, and then input **Select And Mask** after that.

> 5. In the View Mode section of the Properties panel, click the View menu, and then select Black & White from the list of options.

Using this View Mode will assist in making the mask edge more visible.

6. **If necessary, open the Refine Mode section in the Properties window, and then click the Color Aware button.**

If a message comes up, click the OK button. The edge of the mask shifts. Both of the refined modes take a somewhat different approach to interpreting potential subject edges. When working with straightforward backgrounds like the one used in this tutorial, Color Aware can perform well. **Object Aware** can perform better on more intricate backgrounds. You can toggle between the two results by selecting **Edit > Toggle Last State** whenever you wish to compare the two sets of findings.

7. Click the View menu in the View Mode section of the Properties panel, and choose Overlay to better compare the edge to the actual image.

It has been brought to your attention that the program Select Subject skipped over a few spots on the chest. Using the tool for quick selection, you can quickly add them to the selection.

8. **Verify that the Quick Selection tool is active in the editor. In the options bar, select the brush you want to use, and give it a size of 15 pixels.**

If increasing the magnification during the editing of a selection helps you identify regions that you may have overlooked, do so.

8. **To include the areas that were skipped in the selection, drag the Quick Selection tool across the sections that were left out (being sure not to drag it into the background).**

It has been brought to your attention that the Quick Selection tool automatically completes the selection by filling in the gaps as it finds the boundaries of the material. It is not a problem if you let go of the button on the mouse more than once when dragging.

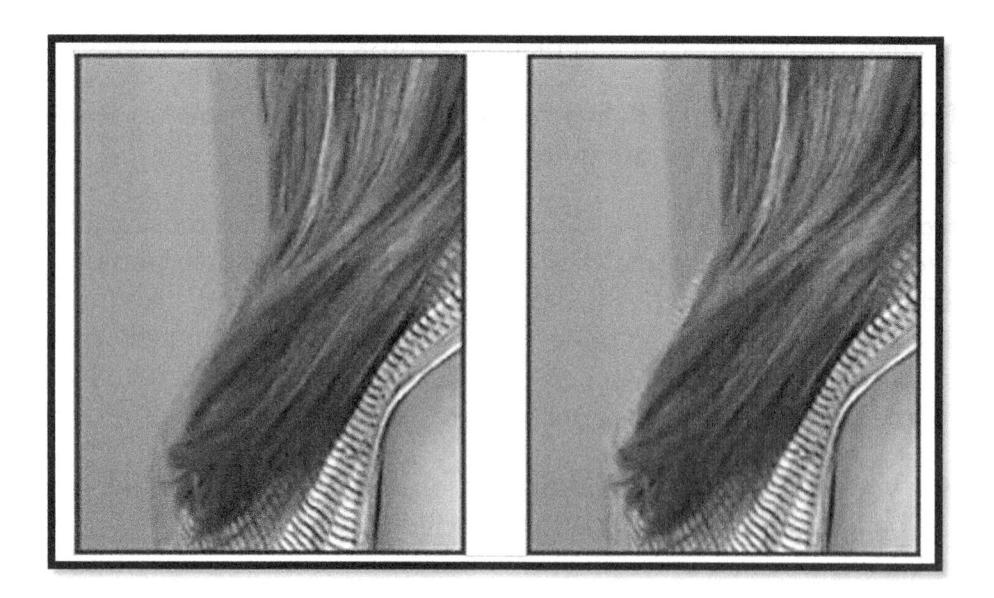

The direction in which you drag tells the Quick Selection tool which parts of the image do not belong to the mask and should be shown. Do not drag the Quick Selection tool beyond the edge of the model into the background. Doing so will teach the Quick Selection tool to include a portion of the background in the mask, which is something that you do not want to happen. If you made an error and added undesirable areas to the mask by accident, you can either select **Edit > Undo** or you can undo the edit by drawing over it using the Quick Selection tool while it is set to the **Subtract** mode. Simply clicking the "**Subtract from Selection**" icon located in the options bar will make the Quick Selection tool's "**Subtract Mode**" available for use.

You can alter the amount of light that passes through the onion skin by dragging the **Transparency slider**, which is located in the View Mode options. When you drag the Quick Selection tool over the model, the overlay is removed from the regions that you are marking to be revealed. This happens as you move the tool. At this point, you shouldn't stress about reaching absolute perfection.

9. Select on Layers from the View menu of the View Mode section after clicking the View menu once more.

This demonstrates how the current settings for Select and Mask appear over any layers that are located underneath this layer. You are getting a preview of how the current settings will mask the Model layer over the Episode Background layer in this instance.

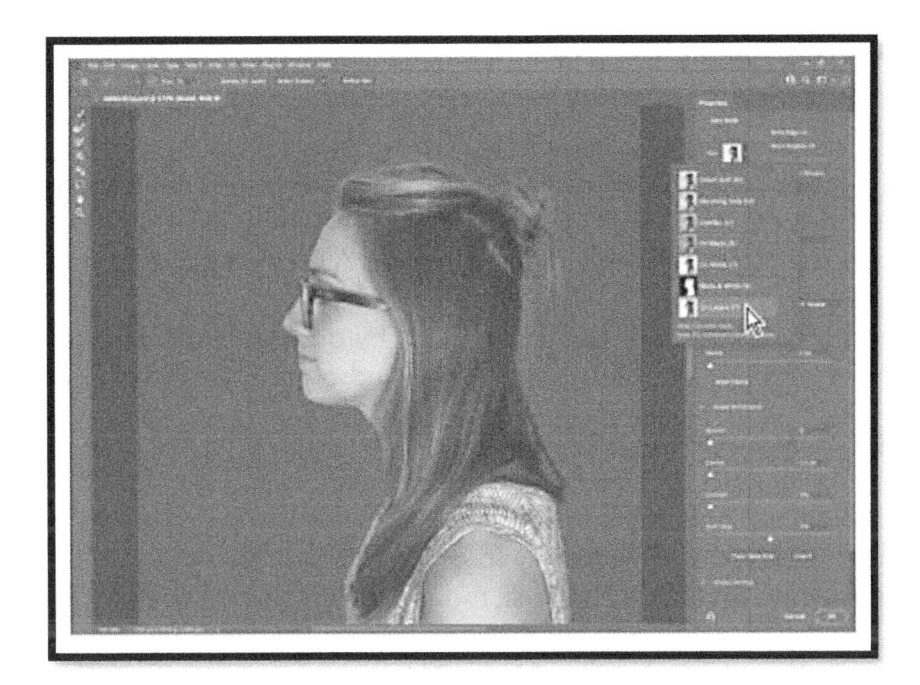

Perform a close examination of the model's borders using a high magnification, such as 400%. Although there is a possibility that some of the original bright background is visible between the model's edge and the background of the podcast, the Select Subject and Quick Selection tools should have, on the whole, been able to construct clean edges for the shirt and face.

GENERATING THE MASK OUTPUT

Clipping Masks and Vector Masks are the two types of output masks that can be generated in Photoshop. A quick guide on how to use each of them is as follows:

Clipping Masks

- You will need two layers to construct a clipping mask. The layer below the bottom determines which parts of the layer above it are visible.
- The content on the layer above it is visible anywhere the layer below it has actual content (pixels, shapes, or type).
- If there is any portion of the layer below that is transparent, then the portion of the layer above it that corresponds to that transparency will be obscured.
- You can make a clipping mask by going to the Layer menu and selecting the Create Clipping Mask option.

Vector Masks

- A vector mask is a path that is not reliant on the layer's resolution and is used to clip out the contents of the layer.
- Select **Layer > Vector Mask > Reveal All** from the menu bar to produce a vector mask that exposes the entirety of the layer.
- By selecting **Layer > Vector Mask > Hide All**, you can build a vector mask that conceals the entirety of the layer.
- You can modify the opacity of the mask by dragging the **Density** slider, and you can feather the edges of the mask by dragging the **Feathering** slider.

CREATING A QUICK MASK

Start with a selection, and then either add to it or take away from it to produce the mask. Using the Quick Mask mode, you can quickly generate and alter selections by using this method. In the Quick Mask mode, you can even construct the complete mask from scratch. The unprotected zones are denoted by a different color than the protected ones. When you exit the **Quick Mask** mode, the regions that were not previously protected become a selection.

Note:

While you are working in **Quick Mask** mode, the Channels panel will display a one-off temporary channel named **Quick Mask**. On the other hand, you do all of the editing to the mask in the image window.

- Select the portion of the image that you wish to modify using any of the available selection tools.
- To use the Quick Mask mode, select the "**Quick Mask**" button in the toolbox.

The area that is not part of the selection is hidden and safeguarded by a color overlay, which functions similarly to a rubylith. This mask does not protect certain parts of the image. In Quick Mask mode, the protected area is colored with a transparent red overlay that has a 50% opacity setting.

- To make changes to the mask, go to the toolbox and choose a painting tool. The swatches in the toolbox are converted to a black-and-white format automatically.
- To pick more of an image, paint with white. This will remove the color overlay from the parts of the image that you have painted white. To deselect a region, simply paint over it with black (the color overlay will hide any areas that have been painted with black). The use of gray or another color to paint generates

a semitransparent area, which can be beneficial for feathering or anti-aliased effects. (When you **exit Quick Mask** mode, semitransparent areas may not appear to be selected; however, you are selecting them.)
- To disable the fast mask and revert to the initial version of your image, navigate to the toolbox and select the **Standard Mode** button. A selection border will be seen surrounding the portion of the fast mask that is not covered.

When a feathered mask is transformed into a selection, the boundary line of the selection runs along the middle of the mask gradient, midway between the black pixels and the white pixels. The selection boundary denotes the transition between pixels that have been selected to a degree of less than 50% and those that have been selected to a degree of more than 50%.

- Make the adjustments to the image that you require. Only the area that is selected will be affected.
- To deselect the items, go to the Select menu and select Deselect.

Change Quick Mask options

1. To switch to the **Quick Mask** Mode, click its button located in the toolbox twice.
2. **Make your selection from the available display options below:**
   - **Masked regions**: This function turns black (opaque) the regions that are masked and white (transparent) the areas that are selected. While painting with black will increase the area that is masked, painting with white will increase the area that is selected. When this option is selected, the Quick Mask button in the toolbox changes to look like a gray circle with a white circle inside of it.
   - **Selected Areas**: Makes masked areas transparent by setting them to white, and makes selected areas opaque by setting them to black. While painting with white will expand the area that is masked, painting with black will expand the region that is selected. When this option is used, the Quick Mask button in the toolbox transforms into a circle with a gray center and a white background.

Note: If you want to switch between the Masked Areas and Selected Areas options for quick masks, you can do so by clicking the Quick Mask Mode button with either the Alt key (Windows) or the Option key (Mac OS).

3. Simply click the color box and make your selection from the drop-down menu to change the color of the mask.
4. To adjust the opacity, enter a number that falls between 0% and 100% in the box provided.

The color and opacity options solely affect how the mask appears; they have no bearing on how the underlying sections are protected. By adjusting these parameters, you might be able to make the mask stand out more clearly against the colors in the image.

MOULDING AN IMAGE USING THE PUPPET WARP

You can reshape and mold components within an image as if they were puppets on strings with the Puppet Warp tool in Photoshop. This is a powerful feature that allows you to reshape and mold elements within an image. The Puppet Warp tool is a useful tool to have in your arsenal of image modification tools because it allows you to shift the position of an object, modify the shape of a person's body, or create creative distortions.

You can use it to do any of these things.

1. **Opening Your Image:**
   - Start by opening your image in Adobe Photoshop. Ensure that you have a layer containing the object or subject you want to manipulate.
2. **Select the Puppet Warp Tool:**
   - Select the "**Puppet Warp**" tool from the toolbar. It looks like a pin icon with a triangle.
3. **Adding Control Points:**
   - Click on the image where you want to add control points. These points act as pins and will serve as anchor points for the areas you want to keep fixed. Place pins strategically to define the areas you don't want to distort.
4. **Defining the Mesh:**
   - After placing pins, Photoshop generates a mesh over the selected area. You can adjust the density of the mesh by altering the "Density" option in the top toolbar. A denser mesh allows for more precise control.
5. **Moving and Distorting:**
   - Click and drag any part of the mesh to warp the image. Photoshop will automatically adjust the surrounding pixels to create a distortion based on the pins' positions. You can also rotate or resize areas by clicking and dragging a pin.
6. **Adding More Pins:**

- As you make adjustments, you can add more pins if needed. For complex distortions, additional pins can help maintain control and achieve the desired result.

7. **Protecting Areas:**
    - You can choose to protect certain areas from being distorted by selecting them and then clicking the "Pin Depth" option in the toolbar. This allows you to maintain the depth of these areas while manipulating the rest of the image.

8. **Commit the Changes:**
    - Once you are satisfied with your adjustments, press Enter or click the checkmark in the toolbar to commit the changes. Photoshop will apply the distortion to your image.

9. **Refining the Result:**
    - After applying the Puppet Warp, you can further refine the result by using other tools and techniques, such as the Clone Stamp tool, Healing Brush tool, or additional adjustments and filters.

10. **Saving Your Work:**
    - Save your manipulated image by going to File > Save or File > Save As to keep the original image intact and save the distorted version as a new file.

Tips for Using Puppet Warp Effectively

- Start with a copy of your layer or image to keep the original intact.
- Practice and experimentation are key. It may take some trial and error to get the desired effect.
- Use the Puppet Warp tool for subtle adjustments or creative distortions, but be mindful not to overdo it.

CREATING A SHADOW WITH AN ALPHA CHANNEL

Channels allow you to access certain types of information, similar to how various layers in an image hold different sorts of data. Grayscale images are saved in the alpha channels when selections are made. Channels of color information are used to hold data regarding each color in an image; for instance, a red, green, and blue (RGB) image will always have red, green, blue, and composite channels. If you want to avoid getting channels and layers confused, just think of channels as containing an image's color and selection information, and think of layers as containing painting, shapes, text, and other content. This will help you avoid getting them confused. To make a shadow, you will first make a selection of the sections of the Model copy layer that are transparent, and then you will fill that selection with black on another layer. Because the selection will be modified to create the shadow, you will now save the selection in its current form as an alpha channel.

This will allow you to load the selection once more if it is required in the future.

1. Click the layer thumbnail icon for the Model Copy layer in the Layers panel using either the Ctrl (Windows) or Command (macOS) key on your keyboard. The area that was disguised has been selected.
2. Click the **Select** menu, and then click **Save Selection**. Make sure that the **New channel** is selected in the Save Selection dialog box before you save the selection. After that, give the channel the name Model Outline, and then click the OK button.

The Layers panel as well as the window that displays the document remains unchanged. On the other hand, the Channels panel now includes an additional channel with the name Model Outline. The option is still available for choosing.

Tip: Now that the initial selection outline of the model has been preserved as an alpha channel, you can reuse that selection at any time by choosing the **Select > Load Selection** command in Photoshop. You can even load that selection from another document.

3. At the very bottom of the Layers panel click the "**Create a New Layer**" button. Simply dragging the new layer below the Model Copy layer will place the shadow in the correct position, which is below the model's image. To rename the new layer, double-click on its name, and then select Shadow from the drop-down menu.

NOTE: There are a few different image file formats that give the user the option to save an alpha channel along with the image document. Photoshop will generate an alpha channel for the composite image if you select this option. This channel will contain all of the parts of the image that are not filled by an opaque pixel.

4. After making sure the Shadow layer is chosen, go to the Select menu and select **Select and Mask**. This action loads the selection that is currently being used into the **Select and Mask** task space.
5. In the Properties panel, under the View Mode heading, click the **View** menu, and then select **On Black** from the list of available options.
6. In the area titled "**Global Refinements**," adjust the Shift Edge slider so that it reads +36%.
7. In the section labeled "**Output Settings**," make sure that "**Selection**" is chosen in the menu labeled "**Output To**," and then click the "**OK**" button.
8. Select Fill under the Edit menu. Select "**Black**" from the "**Contents**" menu located in the Fill dialog box, and then clicks the "**OK**" button.

On the Shadow layer, the model's outline is shown as being filled in with a dark color. Because a person's shadow is not typically as dark as the person who casts it, the opacity of the layer must be decreased.

9. In the Layers panel, reduce the opacity of the layer to thirty percent.

The shadow can't be noticed because it is in the same position as the model. You are going to move it.

10. To clear the selection, go to the Select menu and then click Deselect.
11. Select **Edit > Transform > Rotate** from the menu. You can manually rotate the shadow, or you can put -15 degrees into the **rotate field** in the options bar. The shadow should then be moved to the left, or the value 545 should be entered into the X field in the options bar. To accept the transformation, either press **Enter or Return** on your keyboard, or click the "**Commit Transform**" button (commit_button.jpg) located in the options bar.
12. To view the Episode Background layer, choose the eye symbol for that layer in the layer stack, and then erase the Model layer, which is the one without the mask.
13. To save your work so far, go to the File menu and select Save.

PUTTING A NEW BACKGROUND FOR THE LAYER MASK

1. Open Your Image:
   - Start by opening your image in Adobe Photoshop. Make sure you have a subject or object you want to extract from the current background.
2. Prepare Your Background:
   - Before you start, have your new background ready. You can create one in Photoshop or use an existing image.
3. Duplicate the Background:
   - In the Layers panel, right-click on your image layer and select "Duplicate Layer." This ensures that you have a backup of your original image.
4. Add a Layer Mask:
   - With the duplicated layer selected, click the "Add Layer Mask" icon at the bottom of the Layers panel. This will add a white layer mask to the layer.
5. Select the Subject:
   - Use any selection tool you prefer (e.g., Magic Wand, Quick Selection, or Pen Tool) to select the subject or object in your image. Ensure that your selection is accurate.
6. Refine the Selection:

- After making the initial selection, you may need to refine it for better accuracy. You can use the Select and Mask tool (Select > Select and Mask) to fine-tune the edges.

7. **Apply the Selection to the Layer Mask:**
    - With the selection active, click on the layer mask in the Layers panel. This will apply your selection to the mask, revealing the subject and hiding the background.

8. **Adjust the Layer Mask:**
    - You can fine-tune the layer mask to improve the blend between the subject and the background. Use a soft brush and paint with black or white to hide or reveal parts of the subject as needed. This helps create a more seamless transition.

9. **Place the New Background:**
    - Drag and drop your new background image onto the Photoshop canvas. Make sure the new background layer is positioned below the subject layer in the Layers panel.

10. **Resize and Position the Subject:**
    - Use the Move tool (V) to adjust the position and size of the subject to fit the new background as desired.

11. **Final Touches:**
    - Make any necessary adjustments to the subject and the background to ensure they match in terms of lighting, color, and perspective.

12. **Save Your Work:**
    - Save the image with the new background using File > Save or File > Save As. You can save it in various formats, including JPEG, PNG, or PSD, depending on your needs.

Tips for a Professional Finish

- Pay attention to lighting and shadows to make the composite look natural.
- Match the color temperature and tone between the subject and the new background.
- Use filters, adjustments, and layer styles to further blend the subject with the background.

CHAPTER TWELVE
WORKING WITH SELECTION

The numerous methods and tools that can be utilized while working with selections in Photoshop are the primary emphasis of this chapter. It provides users with access to a wide variety of selection methods and tools, which enables them to make accurate and well-controlled selections for editing and design. It begins by providing an overview of the Marquee Tools, which can be used to create and modify selections of various shapes, such as elliptical and rectangular selections. In addition to that, it includes shortcut keys for rapidly shifting selections around. Readers will gain knowledge of the Lasso Tools, which can be used to make freehand selections, as well as the skills necessary to switch intelligently between the Lasso and Polygonal Lasso Tools. In addition to that, it explains how to use the Magnetic Lasso Tool to make more intricate selections, as well as how to rotate and scale those selections.

This chapter explores many types of selections, including color, edge, and content-based selections, and demonstrates how to make selections using the Magic Wand Tool and the Quick Selection Tool. In addition, it investigates the Object Selection Tool to satisfy more complex and exact selection requirements. In general, this chapter provides users with a full overview of the selection processes and tools available in Photoshop, empowering them to create precise and time-efficient selections for their artistic endeavors.

MARQUEE TOOLS SELECTION

Any Photoshop user should be familiar with the Marquee tool, and if you aren't already, now is the time to become familiar with this important function. If you don't already know how to use it, you should learn how to use it right away. You don't need to precisely outline the items you choose to select; **square, rectangular, or circular** shapes will do. Because the option appears to be "**marching ants**" while using this tool, the term "**marching ants**" is frequently used to refer to it. Using this function, you can alter the color as well as the saturation of individual objects without affecting the layer as a whole. Use the Marquee tool to make an object vanish completely from the image if you want to completely remove it from the picture.

What Does the Marquee Tool Do?

One of the various selection tools available to you in Photoshop is called the Marquee tool, and it just so happens to be the one with the simplest interface. Only the Marquee tool allows you to choose an entire portion of your document—or the entire document—with a single swift sweep of your mouse. The Lasso tools are ideal if you need accurate outlining, and the Magic Wand is appropriate if you have clearly defined color ranges. But that's not the only thing it can accomplish.

Common Uses for the Tool

In Photoshop, the Marquee tool can be utilized in a variety of ways, each of which makes your work just a little bit simpler.

You can quickly and simply do the following with the Marquee tool:

- Choose which objects should have their colors changed
- Remove specific objects from an image.
- Transfer objects to a new layer by cutting them.
- Create a new object to replace a portion of an existing image

You can feather a selection using the Marquee tool, or you can add to it using the addition or subtraction buttons on your keyboard. Both of these options are available to you. This can be a faster option than adding dots all around the selection. Imagine if you don't like the color of the model's outfit in your image; in that case, you can draw a rectangle around the model's dress, and then use the subtraction keys to remove her arms from the selection you've made. Because of this, altering the shade of the clothing to a different color does not necessitate a corresponding change in the coloring of her arms.

Fixed Ratio Selection

If you feel like you need a little bit more accuracy, you can utilize the **Fixed Size or Fixed Ratio settings** that are accessible from the **Options** bar. You can specify the precise height-to-width measurements for your selection when you use **Fixed Ratio**. You can select the precise height and width using the Fixed Size option. If you have a project that requires a certain size, you will find these parameters to be helpful. Using the Marquee tool, you can make speedy selections, alter the color tones of your selections, delete items, and feather your selections. This is one of the simplest tools that Photoshop has to offer, but it is also one of the tools that has the greatest potential applications.

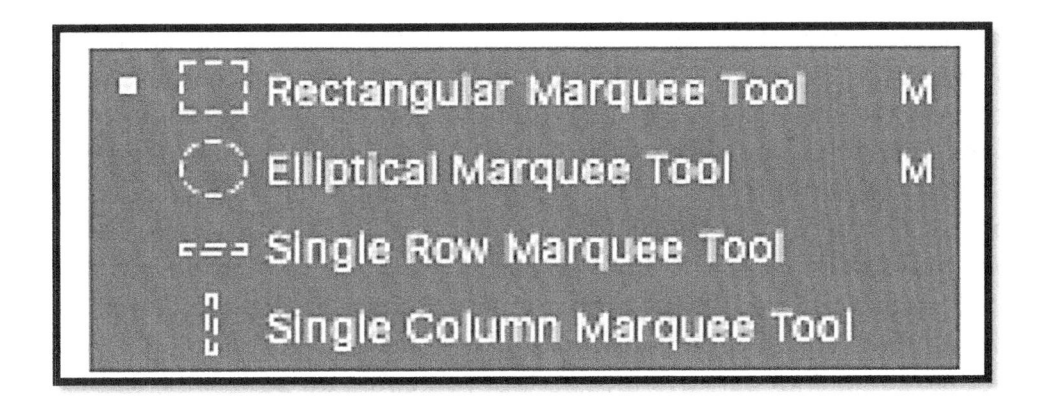

More specifically, let's talk about the Marquee Tools in Adobe Photoshop, such as the Rectangular Marquee, Elliptical Marquee, Single Row Marquee, and Single Column Marquee:

Rectangular Marquee tool

The Rectangular Marquee tool in Photoshop is a complex selection tool that allows users to produce rectangular selections on an image. Users can do this by clicking and dragging over the area of the image they want to choose. A photograph can be resized and cropped with the help of this utility. The tool can be used for a variety of tasks, such as cropping a photo, choosing a certain piece of an image, or isolating a certain sector of an image for additional editing. To use the Rectangular Marquee tool in Photoshop, you will first need to open the image that you want to edit. After that, click the "**File**" menu and select "**Open**."

Following that, select the **Rectangular Marquee tool** from the toolbar located at the very top of the screen. It is the tool represented by an icon in the form of a rectangle. Next, create a rectangle selection by clicking and dragging the cursor over the image to the desired location. Adjustments to the size of the selection can be made by dragging the selection's sides or corners in the appropriate direction. While dragging the selection, you can also maintain the aspect ratio by holding down the Shift key. This will allow you to maintain the selection's original dimensions. Because of this, you will be able to maintain the selection in the same proportions as before.

Once you have formed the selection, you will be able to do a range of editing operations on the region that you have chosen once you have established the selection. You have several options available to you when working with selections. For example, you can move the selection to a new location within the image, apply a wide range of effects or adjustments to the selection, or copy and paste the selection into a new layer or project. One of the most common uses of the Rectangular Marquee tool is the act of cropping an image. To accomplish this, open the picture in the editing software that you are using, create a selection around the part of the image that you wish to keep, and then go to the picture menu and select Crop. If you perform this action, the size of the picture will be decreased until it is comparable to that of the selection. In addition to its other use, the Rectangular Marquee tool can be used to cut out a specific area of a photograph so that it can be edited separately later. If, for example, you wanted to apply a certain effect or correction to the face of a person who was present in a group image, you would first need to isolate that person's face so that you could do so.

To accomplish this, you must first make a selection around the face by utilizing the Rectangular Marquee tool, and once you have finished doing so, you must duplicate the selection and then paste it onto a new layer. After that step, you can apply any effects or adjustments that you want to the new layer and the rest of the photo will not be affected by any effects or modifications. In addition to the standard Rectangular Marquee tool, users of Photoshop have access to a wide range of other selection tools, such as the Elliptical Marquee tool, the Single Row Marquee tool, and the Single Column Marquee tool. These tools allow users to choose areas of an image in a variety of different ways. The Tools menu is where you can locate all of these different tools. Because each of these tools has its own unique set of specialized traits and capabilities, users can select particular areas and shapes within an image with more ease and precision.

Elliptical Marquee tool

With the help of Adobe Photoshop's Elliptical Marquee tool, which is a sophisticated selection tool that is a feature of the program, you can generate a circular or elliptical selection of a region of a picture. This is one of the many benefits of using Adobe Photoshop. When it comes to the design of rounded shapes or the choosing of round objects like buttons or logos, this tool is really helpful and comes in very handy. When you first select the Elliptical Marquee tool, some options will appear in the top menu bar. These options give you the ability to change the size and shape of the selection you have made. You can accomplish this by dragging the corner handles or the center point of the selection. Both of these options are available to you.

The following is a rundown of useful tips and step-by-step directions on how to make effective use of the Elliptical Marquee tool in Photoshop:

1. **Creating a circular selection**: To create a selection in the shape of a circle that is round, hit and hold the Shift key while dragging out the selection with the Elliptical Marquee tool. This will allow you to produce an exactly circular selection. The selections are limited to those that have a circular shape that is perfectly circular as a result.
2. **Creating an elliptical selection**: To create an elliptical selection, you must first move the selection in an outward direction while using the Elliptical Marquee tool. This will result in an elliptical selection being produced. To modify the size of the ellipse, press and hold the Shift key and then drag any one of the selection handles to the left or right. Because of this, you will have the ability to alter the shape of the ellipse.
3. **Feathering the selection:** This includes diminishing the sharpness of the selection's boundaries to make it blend in more naturally with the background. To feather the selection, go to the Select menu, select the Feather option, and then select a value that is between one and one hundred pixels.
4. **Inverting the selection**: There can be times when you need to choose the background rather than the foreground. In these cases, you will need to invert the selection. Either navigate to the Select > Inverse menu option on the top menu bar of your computer or use the keyboard shortcut Ctrl + Shift + I (Windows) or Command + Shift + I (Mac). This will bring the desired result.
5. **Using the Marquee tool to create particular shapes**: There are several various kinds of Marquee tools available in Photoshop, and the Elliptical Marquee tool is only one of them. You can create selections that are either square or rectangular by using the Rectangular Marquee tool. On the other hand, you can select one row or column of pixels at a time by using the Single Row Marquee tool or the Single Column Marquee tool. Both of these tools belong to the Marquee selection category.
6. **Adding to or subtracting from the selection:** You can add to the selection by holding down the Shift key while making a new selection. This will allow you to add more items to the selection. You will be able to add more items to the selection as a result of this. You can minimize the size of the existing selection by making a new selection while simultaneously holding down the Alt key (on Windows) or the Option key (on Mac). This will allow you to generate a smaller selection.

7. **Duplicating the selection** After you have completed making a selection using the Elliptical Marquee tool, you can duplicate the selection onto a new layer by selecting Layer > New > Layer via Copy from the menu bar or by using the keyboard shortcut Ctrl + J (Windows) or Command + J (Mac).
8. **Moving the selection**: Once you have established a selection by using the Elliptical Marquee tool, you can move it across the canvas by using the Move tool or by hitting the arrow keys on your keyboard. This step is optional.
9. **Applying effects to the selection**: After you have created a selection with the Elliptical Marquee tool, you can then modify it using some other effects, such as blurring, color adjusting, and applying filters. The effect can be used by merely selecting it from the appropriate menu or dialog box to put it into action.
10. **Saving the selection**: After you have made a selection with the Elliptical Marquee tool, you have the option of saving it as a new selection so that you can use it again in the future. Choose **Select > Save Selection**, and before you save the selection, give it a name before doing so. After that, whenever you wish to load the selection, you can do so by going to Select > Load Selection and choosing the selection you want to load from the list that shows after clicking on the Select menu item.

You can produce circular or elliptical selections in your images by using Adobe Photoshop's Elliptical Marquee tool, which is a strong and helpful tool. To provide a summary, this tool allows you to create selections in your photographs that are either circular or elliptical. If you are familiar with the various methods and options that are available with this program and make full use of all of its features, you can rapidly construct accurate selections and add some effects to them to produce outstanding results in your images.

Single Row Marquee tool

The Single Row Marquee tool is one of the selection tools that are available for usage in Adobe Photoshop. You can use it to pick many rows at once. It allows you the opportunity to make a selection on a photo that is contained inside of a single row, either horizontally or vertically, giving you the flexibility to choose how you want to view the image. This tool is highly useful for selecting particular parts of an image that are only one pixel wide or for cropping a particular row of pixels in an image. Both of these tasks can be accomplished in an image. In addition to that, you can use this tool to choose particular portions of an image that have a height of exactly one pixel. To get started with the Single Row Marquee tool in Photoshop, you will first need to open the image that you want to edit. After that, you will select the area of the image that you want to modify. After that, locate the toolbar on the left side of the screen and select the Single Row Marquee tool. It is the tool that is denoted by the icon that consists of a solitary line running horizontally.

After that, click somewhere on the photo to indicate where you want to start the selection, either vertically or horizontally, and then drag the mouse across the image to produce a row selection that is one pixel wide. If you need to choose many rows or columns, you can easily repeat the process by creating a new selection for each row or column as required. This can be done by just repeating the previous step. This will provide you the ability to choose many rows or columns at the same time. Once you have formed the selection, you will be able to do a range of editing operations on the region that you have chosen once you have established the selection. You have several options available to you when working with selections. For example, you can move the selection to a new location within the image, apply a wide range of effects or adjustments to the selection, or copy and paste the selection into a new layer or project.

The Single Row Marquee tool is frequently utilized in the process of cropping a specific row of pixels located within an image. To accomplish this, first, make a selection around the row of pixels using the Single Row Marquee tool, and then navigate to the Image menu and select the Crop option from the drop-down menu. If you perform this action, the size of the picture will be decreased until it is comparable to that of the selection. The Single Row Marquee tool can also be used to choose particular areas of a photograph that have a width of exactly one pixel. This is one of its many uses. This is only one of many possible applications for it. It's possible, for example, that you'll need to choose a single pixel line of text to move it to a different part of the picture or apply a specific effect to it. To accomplish this, first, construct a selection that spans the row that is one pixel wide by using the Single Row Marquee tool and then copy and paste that selection onto a new layer after you've created the new layer. After that step, you can apply any effects or adjustments that you want to the new layer and the rest of the photo will not be affected by any effects or modifications.

Single Column Marquee tool

The Single Column Marquee tool in Adobe Photoshop is a selection tool that gives you the ability to produce accurate vertical selections of an image that are only one pixel wide. You can use this tool to choose certain areas of an image. This tool is highly useful for making thin strips inside of an image that has a preset width, as well as for selecting a particular column of pixels for editing. As soon as you select the Single Column Marquee tool for the first time, a set of options will appear in the top menu bar. These options allow you to change the dimensions and shape of the selection you have made. You can do this task by dragging the corner handles or by dragging the marquee's corners themselves.

The following is a rundown of some useful tips and advice about the application of Photoshop's Single Column Marquee tool:

1. **Creating a single-column selection**: To make a selection of a single column, just click on the picture's border at the location where you want the column to begin, and then drag the selection tool down until it reaches the bottom of the image. At this stage, the selection's breadth can be adjusted by dragging the selection handles to either the left or right side of the screen.
2. **Converting a rectangular selection to a single column selection**: If you already have a rectangular selection and you want to change it into a selection of a single column, all you need to do is select the Single Column Marquee tool and click on the edge of the rectangular selection where you want the column to begin. This will convert your rectangular selection into a selection of a single column. The selection of the rectangular area will then be altered. After that, to create a selection of a single column, you can construct that selection by dragging the selection tool down to the bottom of the picture.
3. **Feathering the selection**: This includes diminishing the sharpness of the selection's boundaries to make it blend in more naturally with the background. This is the third and last step in the selection process. To feather the selection, go to the Select menu and select the Feather option. Then, in the next window that appears, enter a number that is between 1 and 100 pixels.
4. **Inverting the selection**: There can be times when you need to choose the background rather than the foreground. In these cases, you will need to invert the selection. Either navigate to the **Select > Inverse** menu option on the top menu bar of your computer or use the keyboard shortcut **Ctrl + Shift + I (Windows) or Command + Shift + I (Mac)**. This will accomplish the desired result.
5. **Adding to or subtracting from the selection**: You can add to the selection by holding down the Shift key while making a new selection. This will allow you to add more items to the selection. You will be able to add more items to the selection as a result of this. You can minimize the size of the existing selection by making a new selection while simultaneously holding down the **Alt key (on Windows) or the Option key (on Mac)**. This will allow you to generate a smaller selection.

6. **Duplicating the selection**: After you have created a selection with the Single Column Marquee tool, you can duplicate it onto a new layer by selecting **Layer > New > Layer via Copy** from the menu bar or by using the keyboard shortcut **Ctrl + J (Windows) or Command + J (Mac)**. You can also use the keyboard shortcut **Ctrl + J (on Windows) or Command + J (on Mac)**.
7. **Moving the selection**: Once you have established a selection with the **Single Column Marquee** tool, you can move it across the canvas by using the Move tool or by hitting the arrow keys on your keyboard. Alternatively, you can use the Shift key on your keyboard. This step is completely optional.
8. **Applying effects to the selection**: Once you have made a selection using the Single Column Marquee tool, you can then apply a range of effects to it including blur, color correction, or filters. You can do this by clicking the Effects button in the top menu bar. Simply selecting the option from the appropriate menu or dialog box is all that is required to apply the effect.
9. **Saving the selection**: When you are finished making a selection with the Single Column Marquee tool, you have the option of saving it as a new selection that you can use in the future. If you do this, you will have the option to reuse the selection in the future. Choose **Select > Save Selection**, and before you save the selection, give it a name before doing so. After that, whenever you wish to load the selection, you can do so by going to **Select > Load Selection** and choosing the selection you want to load from the list that shows after clicking on the Select menu item.

You can make vertical selections in your images that are only one pixel wide when you use the **Single Column Marquee** tool in Adobe Photoshop. This tool is both precise and convenient, and it allows you to generate vertical selections in your photographs. If you are familiar with the various methods and options that are available with this program and make full use of all of its features, you can rapidly construct accurate selections and add some effects to them to produce outstanding results in your images.

Repositioning a selection marquee while creating it

When you're trying to choose between ellipses and rectangles at the same time, it can be challenging. Sometimes the selections won't be centered the way they should be, or the width-to-height ratio won't be the appropriate fit for what you want. Both of these things can be very frustrating. During this activity, you will learn techniques such as two crucial keyboard-mouse combinations that can make your work in Photoshop simpler, and you will also get the opportunity to practice using these techniques. These methods might be of significant assistance in some circumstances. During this exercise, you should make sure to follow the directions very carefully, and you should also make sure not to forget to keep the mouse button or any other specified keys pressed the entire time. If you accidentally let go of the mouse button at the wrong time, you will need to start the exercise all over again from the very first step. There is no need to worry about anything else.

We are currently working with a plate that contains a variety of shells.

1. After selecting the Zoom tool (🔍), click the plate of shells that is located at the bottom of the document window. Next, zoom in to a view that is at least 100% larger than the original (use a view that is 200% larger if the entire plate of shells can still be seen in the document window on your screen).
2. Select the Elliptical Marquee tool (⬭), which can be found hidden away under the Rectangular Marquee tool (▢).
3. After positioning the pointer above the photo, slide it in a diagonal path across the oval plate while holding down the left mouse button to create a selection. It is not an issue at all if the shape of the plate that you have chosen does not yet correspond to it in any way.

NOTE: You do not need to include every pixel on the plate of shells in your selection; nevertheless, the selection should be the form of the plate and should comfortably include the shells. If you accidentally let off the button on the mouse while you are drawing the selection, you will have to start the process all over again. The new alternative is selected instead of the older one in the overwhelming majority of cases, such as the one we are discussing right now.

4. You can continue to move the selection by pressing and holding the space bar while at the same time pushing and holding the left mouse button. You are no longer resizing the selection as you did previously; instead, you are now shifting it. Make necessary adjustments to the position of the selection so that it can be brought into better alignment with the plate.
5. After releasing the spacebar (but without removing your finger from the mouse button), continue to drag the selection around while striving to make its dimensions and shape conform as closely as possible to the oval plate of shells. If it is necessary to do so, press and hold the space bar once again, and then use your mouse to move the selection marquee into position around the plate of shells. This step is only necessary if it is necessary to do so.

TIP: Other drawing tools in Photoshop, such as the shape tools and the Pen tool, can also benefit from the method of sketching while holding down the spacebar to edit the drawing as it is being generated. This can be done to make changes to the drawing as it is being made.

6. After you have determined that the boundary of the selection is at the appropriate location, you can release your grip on the mouse button.
7. You can reduce the zoom level of the view by selecting **View > Fit On Screen** or by using the slider in the Navigator panel. This will allow you to see all of the components of the document window. Alternatively, you can see more of the objects by selecting **View > Zoom Out** from the menu bar.

MOVING A SELECTION WITH SHORTCUT KEYS

Using the shortcut keys on your keyboard, you can swiftly relocate a selected portion of an image while working in Adobe Photoshop. You can move objects within your image using this straightforward and user-friendly method.

This is the procedure to follow:

1. Make Your Selection:
   - To begin, open **Photoshop** and make a selection using one of the many selection tools available to you (for example, the Marquee, Lasso, or Magic Wand tool).
2. Use the Arrow Keys:

Once you have an active selection, you can move the region that is selected by using the arrow keys located on the top row of your keyboard.

The operation is as follows:
   - The **up arrow** moves the option one level higher.
   - The **down arrow** moves the selection to the bottom of the screen.
   - If you press and hold the **left arrow** key, the selection will move to the left.
   - To move the selection to the right, use the **right arrow** key.
3. Nudge the Selection:
   - Move the selection in the desired direction by pressing the arrow keys in that direction. Each time you hit one of the arrow keys, the selection moves forward by a very slight amount—typically just one pixel.
4. Hold Shift for Larger Movements:
   - To move the selection in larger increments, hold down the Shift key while hitting the arrow keys on your keyboard. This will allow you to move the selection more precisely. This will move the option further than it would have otherwise moved.
5. Deselect when you're Done:

- To clear the selection, either hit the **Ctrl and D keys** on your keyboard (or the Cmd and D keys on a Mac) or select **Select > Deselect** from the main menu.

Tips:
- To navigate in a diagonal direction, you can use the arrow keys in conjunction with the Shift key. If you hold down the Shift key and press the up and right arrow keys at the same time, for instance, the selection will be moved diagonally up and to the right.
- If you wish to move an entire layer rather than just a selection, you can use the Move tool (V) and then the arrow keys to move the layer in its entirety. This is possible since the Move tool can also move selections.

You can save time and improve the accuracy of your image edits in Photoshop by making use of these shortcut keys for moving selections around in the program. It is a useful method for relocating parts inside your design or making fine-tuned alterations to your selections, and it is a technique that has been around for quite some time.

LASSO TOOLS SELECTION

Because they enable users to make exact selections of irregular shapes and objects within an image, lasso tools are an essential part of the toolset of everyone who works with Photoshop. The basic Lasso Tool, Polygonal Lasso Tool, and Magnetic Lasso Tool are just a few of the options they provide to meet the requirements of customers with varying preferences.

The Standard Lasso Tool

The Lasso Tool is a core component of Adobe Photoshop that gives users the ability to manually choose and highlight certain regions inside an image using a lasso-like tool. It functions as a flexible tool for producing freehand selections and provides users the ability to capture irregular shapes, objects, or locations with a high degree of precision. The Lasso Tool is an essential component of the toolkit of digital artists, graphic designers, and photographers because it enables seamless isolation and manipulation of certain sections of an image. These skills are all essential to the creative process. The Lasso Tool allows users to create selections directly on the image canvas. It can be accessed from the toolbar or by hitting the 'L' key on the keyboard. It gives users the ability to accurately define the limits of the region that they desire to pick by tracing along the contours using a mouse or graphic tablet. This gives users more control over the selection process. When working with organic shapes, delicate features, or irregular shapes that cannot be effectively recorded by more automated selection approaches, this tool is very beneficial because of its ability to provide a solution.

Even while it provides users with a high level of manual control, the Lasso Tool can be difficult to use for persons who are looking to make exact selections, especially when working with shapes that are complex or detailed. When working with images that require a high level of detail and exactness, users frequently find that it is challenging to generate smooth and accurate selections. This is especially true when working with vector graphics. Nevertheless, despite its limitations, the Lasso Tool continues to be a useful resource for a variety of image editing tasks, such as isolating objects, producing cuts, or making detailed edits to particular areas within an image. It offers a hands-on approach to image alteration that allows for a more delicate and artistic touch in the editing process, making it a popular choice for both novices and seasoned Photoshop users alike.

- **Basic Selection**: Simply select the Lasso tool from the toolbar, click and hold down the mouse button at the beginning of the selection, and then draw a circle around the item while continuing to hold down the mouse button. This will complete the selection. After you have navigated back to where you started, you can end the selection process by letting off the button on your mouse.
- **Straight Edge Lasso**: While making a selection with the Lasso tool, hold down the Alt (Windows) or Option (Mac) key. This will allow you to use the Straight Edge Lasso. You can keep using the Lasso tool even as you carve out segments of straight lines using the method described above.
- **Magnetic Lasso**: This automated selection tool allows you to make selections around an object by automatically snagging to its edge, giving you the ability to create selections around the object. To use the Magnetic Lasso tool, first select it from the toolbar's Lasso tool button, then click and hold down the button to select it. Once you have clicked once on the edge of the object you wish to choose, the tool you are using will automatically begin to adhere to the edge of the item as you move it around the item.
- **Adding to a Selection**: To add to a selection that is already made, simply use the Lasso tool while holding down the Shift key on your keyboard. You will be able to add to the selection using this method without having to deselect the region that you have already chosen.
- **Subtracting from a Selection**: To remove objects from an existing selection using the Lasso tool, keep the Alt (Windows) or Option (Mac) key pressed down while doing so. If you follow these steps, you will be able to remove

sections from the selection without losing the ability to access the ones you chose in the past.
- **Feathering selections**: If you feather your selections, you can give them smoother edges, which will make it simpler to incorporate them into the background of the picture. Feathering your selections is a feature of Adobe Photoshop. From the Select menu, select the Feather option, and then enter the required amount of feathering to apply to a selection.
- **Intersecting Selections**: You can use the Lasso tool to make a circle around the location where two selections cross each other by holding down the Shift key while you draw the circle with the Lasso tool. Doing so will result in the creation of a selection that only include the areas where the parameters of the two selections intersects.
- **Copying and Pasting Selections** After making a selection with the Lasso tool, you can copy and paste the selection by selecting *Edit > Copy (Ctrl+C on a computer running Windows or Command+C on a Mac) and Edit > Paste (Ctrl+V on a computer running Mac)*.
- **Saving Selections**: You can store selections for later use by selecting the Save Selection option from the Select menu. You will be able to retrieve the selection at a later time even after Photoshop or the photo has been closed if you follow these steps.

Polygonal Lasso Tool

When it comes to selecting selections in Photoshop, one of the most useful tools is the Polygonal Lasso Tool since it considerably improves both the accuracy and the speed of the process. This tool gives users a practical approach to constructing selections with straight lines and acute angles, which enables detailed and accurate outlining of specified sections of an image. Users can create selections with this tool. When working with photos that require precise and complicated selections, as well as when trying to select objects that have defined edges, it is especially helpful to have this tool available. When working with the Polygonal Lasso Tool, it is vital to have a firm grasp of its functions and be familiar with how to create selections without causing any disruptions. Launch Photoshop and select the image you want to work on to get started. Pick the Polygonal Lasso Tool from the toolbar. This tool is typically found in the same area as the other lasso tools, such as the **regular Lasso Tool and the Magnetic Lasso Tool.**

Once the Polygonal Lasso Tool has been selected, you can begin making selections by clicking on various places along the boundaries of the object that you want to choose. Each click will result in the creation of a segment of a straight line, and each consecutive click will continue to build further segments of the line. It is essential to position the points correctly to guarantee that the decision will be correct. You can finish the selection by either clicking on the initial point or by double-clicking, which will cause the shape to finish automatically for you. When working with selections, it is not uncommon to run into circumstances in which you will need to fashion curved portions within the selection itself. Utilizing some discrete sections of straight lines that are relatively small in length is one method that is useful for accomplishing this goal. You can create the illusion of a curving line by strategically placing these short pieces, which will allow you to easily make more complex selections. This will also save you time.

In addition to that, the Polygonal Lasso Tool provides other functions that can make the choosing process more straightforward. On a Mac, pressing and holding down the "Alt" key (which corresponds to the "Option" key) allows you to exclude certain areas from the selection. When you need to modify the selection or eliminate undesired bits from the defined region, this feature is helpful because it allows you to do both. When picking fine features or several objects inside an image, you can achieve greater flexibility and precision by holding down the "Shift" key while making your selections. This allows you to add areas to the selection you have already made. In addition, while working with the Polygonal Lasso Tool, making use of the zoom function can significantly improve your ability to make correct selections. This is especially true when working with images that have fine details or elements that are relatively small. When you zoom in, you will be able to see the image at a more granular level, which will make it much simpler for you to accurately position the selection points along the margins of the object you want to choose.

After you have completed the selection, you can apply various editing operations, such as making modifications, making color corrections, or applying filters, to the selected area alone, without having those operations affect the remainder of the image. When dealing with intricate compositions or when you need to isolate specific pieces for additional editing or manipulation, this tool is especially useful.

Magnetic Lasso Tool.

When working with photographs that have items that have well-defined edges and high contrast, the Magnetic Lasso Tool in Photoshop is an additional useful function that streamlines the process of creating selections. This is especially true when dealing with images that contain well-defined text. This application simplifies the selection process by utilizing an algorithm that automatically recognizes and snaps to the borders of objects inside an image. As a result, users can produce precise selections promptly that are both rapid and effective. When utilizing the Magnetic Lasso Tool, it is necessary to have a solid understanding of its features and the best way to put those capabilities to use. Open the image you wish to work on in Photoshop, and then select the Magnetic Lasso Tool from the toolbar. This tool is often found in the same area as other lasso tools, such as the regular Lasso Tool and the Polygonal Lasso Tool.

Once the Magnetic Lasso Tool has been chosen, you can initiate the process of producing selections by clicking within a few pixels of the boundary of the object you wish to isolate. The tool will automatically detect the edges of the object as you move the cursor along its boundary, and it will then attach the selection line to the nearest edge points. This will result in the creation of a selection path that closely follows the contours of the object. It is necessary to modify the settings of the tool so that it can fulfill the specific needs of the image to achieve the best possible outcomes. The "**Width**" option controls the width of the area that the tool analyzes, which in turn influences the distance at which the selection line adheres to the boundaries of the object being selected. By modifying this setting, you will be able to tailor the sensitivity of the tool to better meet the qualities of the image as well as the complexity of the object's edges.

In addition, the "**Contrast**" setting is an essential component in improving the tool's capability of accurately detecting edges in a given image. You can fine-tune the selection process and make certain that the tool accurately captures the finer details of the object by modifying the contrast level. This allows you to choose how much contrast the tool should detect along the edges of the object. In addition, the **Magnetic Lasso Tool** gives users the option to either add to or take away from the selection while they are in the process of making the path. You can remove elements of the selection by depressing and holding down the "**Alt**" key (or the "**Option**" key on a Mac), which enables exact refinement of the area that has been selected. Holding down the "**Shift**" key, on the other hand, allows you to add regions to the selection. This gives you the ability to more precisely define the borders of the selection and incorporate extra components as required.

In addition, making use of the zoom function can considerably improve your ability to make exact selections using the Magnetic Lasso Tool. This is especially true when working with photos that contain delicate details or objects that are rather small. When you zoom in, you will be able to examine the boundaries of the object more closely, which will allow you to make tweaks and alterations to the selection path with a greater degree of precision and control. After the selection has been finished, you will have the ability to carry out some different editing actions, such as applying modifications, retouching particular parts, or removing the selected object so that it can be further manipulated or placed into a different background. Because of this feature, the Magnetic Lasso Tool is an extremely useful tool for undertaking jobs that need precise selections and extensive editing.

SWITCHING BETWEEN LASSO AND POLYGONAL LASSO TOOLS

When making selections in Photoshop, switching between the Lasso tool and the Polygonal Lasso tool can considerably improve your efficiency and precision, particularly when working with pictures that contain a combination of curved and straight edges. You must be aware of when and how to make a smooth transition between these two tools to maximize the efficiency of your workflow and get precise selections. To be able to make educated judgments about when to transition between different tools, it is essential to have a solid understanding of the unique capabilities offered by each one. Because it allows for freehand sketching of selections, the basic Lasso Tool is perfect for collecting irregular shapes and objects that have smooth, flowing edges. The Polygonal Lasso Tool, on the other hand, is most effective when used to choose objects that contain both straight lines and acute angles. This tool enables users to make exact selections that have delineated edges.

It is essential to evaluate the nature of the object you are trying to choose inside the image to make an informed decision regarding whether to use the Lasso tool or the Polygonal Lasso tool. Using the standard Lasso Tool would be more effective in capturing the organic curves and complex features of the object if the object has mostly curved or irregular edges. This is because the standard Lasso Tool has a smaller working area. On the other hand, if the object mostly consists of straight edges or has well-defined geometric shapes, you should use the Polygonal Lasso Tool to generate selections because this tool excels in outlining objects with definite lines and angles. This will allow you to produce selections with higher accuracy and speed than if you were to use the traditional Lasso Tool.

In addition, when working with complicated photos that have a mix of curved and straight edges, switching between the Lasso and Polygonal Lasso tools strategically can assist in simplifying the selection process and ensure that all of the vital aspects of the object are accurately captured. This is especially helpful when dealing with images that contain a combination of both curved and straight edges. In addition, you can further improve the efficiency of your workflow by making use of the keyboard shortcuts that are available for switching between various tools. You can substantially enhance your productivity by being familiar with the keyboard shortcuts, such as typing "L" to switch to the regular Lasso Tool and pressing "**Shift+L**" to cycle through the various lasso tools. This will allow for a more seamless transition between the two tools whenever it is necessary. In addition, utilizing the benefits of the Magnetic Lasso Tool for particular regions of the image that require exact edge detection can complement the usage of the conventional and Polygonal Lasso tools, allowing you to capture subtle features and refine selections with greater accuracy. This can be done by using the Magnetic Lasso Tool for certain regions of the image that require precise edge detection.

ROTATING AND SCALING A SELECTION

In Adobe Photoshop, rotating a selection is an easy technique that enables you to introduce unique perspectives or rearrange objects within your image. This feature gives you the flexibility to perform either of these things. You can easily adjust your choices, regardless of whether it is a geometrical shape or a more detailed freeform outline.

The following is an in-depth process that will teach you how to rotate a selection in Photoshop:

1. **Select the Appropriate Layer:** To begin, open your image in Photoshop and access the Layers panel. Click on the layer that contains the area or object you wish to rotate. Ensure that you select the correct layer if your project involves multiple layers.
2. **Create Your Selection**: Using one of the various selection tools, such as the Rectangular Marquee tool or the Lasso tool, specify the area that you want to rotate. Once you have done this, create your selection. As you make your selections, a moving dashed outline will highlight the location that you select, drawing attention to the fact that you have made a decision.
3. **Access the Transform Options**: After making your selection, head to the Edit menu and pick "Transform" > "Rotate." As an alternative, you can activate the Transform tool by using the keyboard shortcuts Ctrl+T (Windows) or Cmd+T (Mac).
4. **Activate the Bounding Box:** After activating the Bounding Box, you will see a box with handles appear around your selection. The box will have a border around it. These handles are necessary for the rotation procedure to be completed successfully. To change the angle, you can do so by clicking and dragging any of these handles. You are at liberty to rotate the selection in any one of the available directions.

5. **Precise Rotations**: as dragging the handle, if you want to limit the rotation to increments of 45 degrees, hold down the Shift key as you move the handle. This is helpful for correctly reaching specific angles that are being sought after.
6. **Relocate the Selection:** You can reposition the selection within the bounding box by clicking and dragging the selection itself while you are in the process of rotating the selection. This can be done while you are in the process of rotating the selection. This allows you to adjust its positioning to your liking.
7. **Apply the Rotation**: When you have the rotation angle that you want, you can apply the transformation by pressing the **Enter key (on Windows) or the Return key** (on Mac), respectively. Your selection will be adjusted accordingly when it has been spun.
8. You can get the same result by using the keyboard shortcut **Ctrl+D (Windows) or Cmd+D (Mac)** to deselect the selection. If you want to erase the outline of the selection, go to the **Select** menu and pick "**Deselect**." Another option is to go to the **Edit** menu and choose "**Remove Selected Items**."

You have completed the task of rotating a selection in Photoshop with flying colors! It is important to keep in mind that the act of rotating a selection can have a major impact on the composition of your image. To create the intended visual impression, it will be necessary to experiment with a variety of angles and placements. In addition, you must remember to save your work frequently as a recommended best practice so that you can simply revert to prior states if revisions are required in the future.

Selecting from a center point

When certain conditions are met, it is more straightforward to generate elliptical or rectangular selections by beginning the selection process at an object's center point and working outwards.

This approach will be utilized in the process of selecting the appropriate screw head to use for the shadow box corners.

1. You can magnify the photo by somewhere in the neighborhood of 300% by using the Zoom tool ( ). Make sure that the document window you're using can display the entire photo head.
2. Select the Elliptical Marquee tool ( ) from the **Tools** panel.
3. Position the cursor so that it is roughly in the middle of the image.

4. Once you've clicked, you can begin dragging. Then, while you are dragging the selection to the edge of the picture, make sure that you are holding down the Alt (Windows) or Option (MacOS) key.

The selection is currently positioned such that it is halfway between its starting point and its current location.

TIP: To choose a complete circle, keep the Shift key pressed while you drag the selection tool. While dragging the Rectangular Marquee tool, holding down the Shift key will allow you to select an exact square.

5. After the complete picture head has been selected, you should first let go of the mouse button, then press Alt or Option (and the Shift key if you used it), and finally release it.
6. If necessary, adjust the location of the selection boundary. If you accidentally let go of the Alt or Option key before releasing the mouse button, then you will need to select the screw once again.

Resizing and copying a selection

Ensure that the picture is selected before you start.

- Select **View > Fit on Screen** from the menu bar to make the entire image fit within the confines of the document window.
- Select the **Move tool** from the section labeled Tools on the interface.
- Move the cursor to the desired location inside the picture selection.

As you drag the selection, the pointer will transform into an arrow that looks like a pair of scissors (✂), indicating that the selection will be cut from its current location and moved to the new spot when you do so.

- To place the image in the shadow box, drag it into the lower-right corner.
- Under **Edit > Transform**, select the Scale option. A bounding box is displayed around the selection.

TIP: If the photo won't move or resize smoothly, appearing as if it has "**gotten stuck**," hold down the Control key to temporarily turn off snapping to the magenta Smart Guides when dragging. You can deactivate them permanently by deselecting the **View > Show > Smart Guides** command.

- When the picture has been reduced to around forty percent of its original size or is small enough to fit on the frame of the shadow box, slide one of the corner points so that it points inward.

When you change the size of the object, the selection marquee adjusts itself to match the new dimensions. Both will adjust their size proportionately automatically.

- To finalize the modification and get rid of the transformation bounding box, press either **Enter or Return** on your keyboard.

- After you have resized the picture, use the Move tool to relocate it so that it is placed in one of the corners of the frame for the shadow box.

Holding down the Shift key while dragging one of the corner handles of a transformation bounding box is what you need to do if you do not want the scale to maintain the same proportions as the original.

- To save your work, make sure the image is selected first, then go to the **File menu** and pick **Save**.

Moving and duplicating a selection simultaneously

If you need to replicate an object or region more than once within the same picture, you can save a ton of time and effort by moving and duplicating a selection at the same time in Adobe Photoshop. This is especially helpful when you need to move a selection more than once. It is necessary to make a copy of the selection to move it to a new location while utilizing this strategy. **Carry out the following to simultaneously move and replicate a selection in Photoshop:**

- Using one of the selection tools available in Photoshop, such as the Rectangular Marquee tool or the Lasso tool, make a selection around the item or region that you wish to reproduce and move.
- Once you have made your selection, copy it to the clipboard by selecting Copy from the Edit menu or by using the keyboard shortcut Ctrl+C on a computer running Windows or Cmd+C on a Mac. You can also use the shortcut directly.
- To paste the copied selection into a new layer, choose Paste from the Edit menu once more, or use the keyboard commands Ctrl+V or Cmd+V on a Mac or Windows computer, respectively. Alternatively, you can drag and drop the selection onto the new layer.

- While the new layer is selected, you can move the selection to its new location by using the transfer tool (the shortcut for which is the letter V). Simply clicking and dragging the selection will allow you to move it wherever on the canvas.
- Move the selection you want to replicate while maintaining pressure on the Alt (Windows) or Option (Mac) key. When you duplicate a selection, the Move tool pointer will display a plus sign next to it to indicate that you are doing so.
- First, let go of the button on the mouse, and then let go of the Alt or Option key. You will now have two copies of the selection present in your image that are similar to one another.

Repeat this process as many times as needed to create additional duplicates. That sums it up nicely. You have successfully moved and duplicated a selection in Photoshop at the same time. This method can help you save a ton of time when you need to duplicate an item or region within the same picture. All you have to do is follow the steps. Keep in mind that this method works best with selections that have a clear form and color, while more sophisticated selections may require additional adjustments after they have been made. Additionally, make sure to save your work frequently if you need to return to it and make modifications.

Copying selections

You can use the Move tool to copy selections as you drag them about within or between photographs, or you can use commands from the Edit menu to copy and move selections. Both of these options are available when using the Move tool. The Move tool takes up less memory than other tools because it does not make use of the clipboard. **Under the Edit menu in Photoshop, you'll find some different copy-and-paste options, including:**

- **Copy**: When you pick this action, the selected region of the active layer will be copied to the clipboard.
- **Copy Merged**: This operation creates a single copy from all of the visible layers in the region that you specify by merging them.
- **Paste**: When you select Paste, the contents of the clipboard will be placed in the center of the image. When you copy something from one image and paste it into another, a new layer is created.

In addition, Photoshop's Edit menu includes a subfolder under Paste Special, which contains specialized pasting commands that provide you with additional options when specific conditions are met:

- **Paste without Formatting**: If you select the option to **Paste without Formatting**, any font or size formatting that may have been added to the text when it was copied will be removed before the text is pasted. It assures that text copied from another application or document is formatted to match a text layer in Photoshop, even if the text was copied from somewhere else.
- **Paste in Place**: When you select this option, the content of the clipboard is placed in the same location as it was in the original photo, rather than in the middle of the document.
- **Paste Into**: When you select this option, the content of the clipboard will be moved into the region that is now selected within the same or a different picture. The area that lies outside of the source selection is converted into a layer mask, and the selection made from the source is then placed on a new layer.
- **Paste Outside**: This option is quite similar to the Paste Into option; however, instead of pasting information into the selection, Photoshop creates a layer mask for the area that is now selected and pastes the information outside of the selection.

When you paste content across two pages that have different pixel dimensions, it may appear as though the size of the content changes. This is done so that the original pixel dimensions of any content that is copied into a document that has different pixel dimensions are maintained. The picture quality may degrade if a pasted selection is enlarged, but it can be resized.

COLOR, EDGE, AND CONTENT-BASED SELECTIONS

You can make selections in Adobe Photoshop utilizing a variety of methods, such as those based on color, edges, or content, amongst others. According to several criteria, each method allows you to isolate particular regions or objects in your photographs. These methods of selection can be applied singly or in conjunction with one another to accomplish the aimed-for result.

Discussing them further down the page:

MAKING SELECTIONS WITH MAGIC WAND TOOL

The Magic Wand Tool in Photoshop is a selection tool that works by picking parts of an image that have colors that are similar to those selected. This tool is frequently represented in Photoshop's toolbar with an icon that looks like a magic wand. When you need to make selections based on color regions rather than precise shapes or paths, this is a great option to go with. The tool's primary purpose is to facilitate the manipulation of raster graphics, which include scanned images and photographic images. The **Tolerance setting** controls the range of tonal levels that the Magic Wand tool will select, beginning with the pixel that is now selected as the starting point. When you click on a color, a tolerance value of 32, which is the default, will select that color in addition to 32 shades lighter and 32 shades darker versions of that color. If the Magic Wand tool is not choosing the entire region that you want it to, you can try increasing the value of the Tolerance attribute to see if that helps.

It may be necessary to reduce the value of the Tolerance parameter if the tool selects an excessive number of objects.

1. Choose the **Zoom tool** from the Tools panel, and then zoom in until you can see the complete sand dollar in its entirety with all of its intricate details.
2. Choose the **Magic Wand** tool ( ), which can be found tucked away beneath the **Object Selection tool** ( ).
3. Make sure that the value of the Tolerance option is set to **32**. Note that this value affects which colors are available to be selected by the wand.
4. To use the Magic Wand tool, select the area outside of the sand dollar that has a red background.

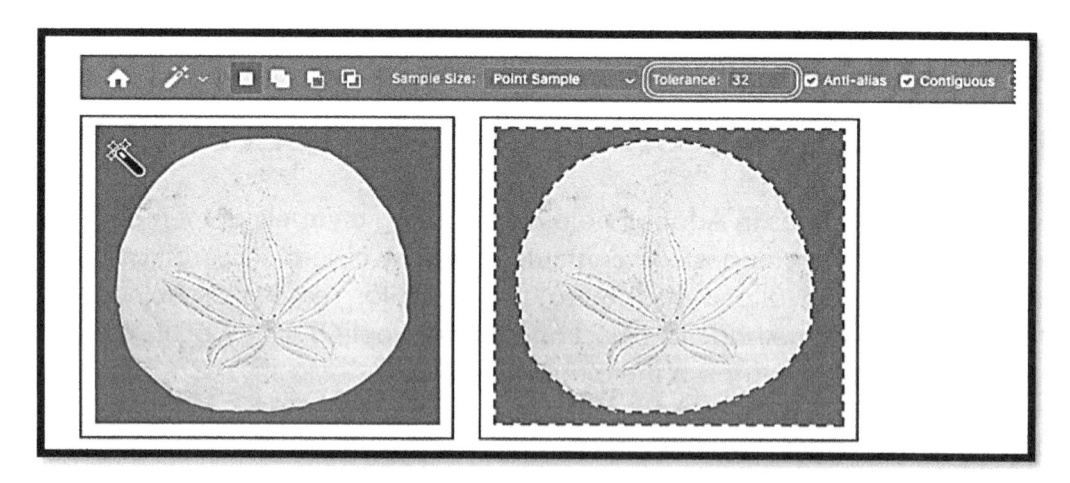

Because all of the colors in the background are within the 32 levels specified in the Tolerance option, the Magic Wand tool accurately picked the red background. This is because the clicked pixel is close enough to all of the colors in the background. This is because the setting for Tolerance allows for up to 32 different levels. However, the part of the snail that interests us is the shell, so let's start the process over again.

TIP: If a selection made using the Magic Wand tool takes up an excessive number of identical colors outside of the region you wish to choose, you may want to try enabling the **Contiguous** option that can be found in the settings bar. You can find this option in the upper-right corner of the settings bar.

5. Pick **Select > Deselect** menu item.
6. After positioning the **Magic Wand tool** such that it is over the sand dollar, you can then click on it.

It is important to pay great attention to the moving marquis that appears over the sand dollar and serves as a selection. If this was a perfect selection, the marquee that tells which objects have been chosen would very precisely follow the rim of the sand dollar. Be aware, however, that some of the more interior parts of the **Sand Dollar feature** selection marquees. This is because the colors of these places are more than 32 levels different from the color you clicked on, which is the value for the tolerance. The option that is now being used is useless because it does not contain all of the available interior color options.

When you want to pick a subject that is generally the same color and value as the background, against a decently solid background, you can frequently solve this problem by boosting the value of the Tolerance parameter. This works especially well when you want to pick a subject that is uniformly the same as the background in terms of color and value. However, the intricacy of the subject or background has a direct correlation with the possibility that a broad Tolerance number will also choose undesirable parts of the background. It is strongly suggested that you utilize a different selection tool, such as the Quick Selection tool, when confronted with a circumstance such as the one that you are currently experiencing. That will be your next step, but before you take it, let's remove the currently chosen items from the selection.

7. Choose **Select** then **Deselect**.

Using the Magic Wand tool, one can eliminate the background of an image from a picture, which is a common application of that tool. To accomplish this, you will initially need to use the Magic Wand tool to select the color of the background. The following step is to reverse the selection, which can be done by selecting the "**Inverse**" option from the **Select** menu. This will select the item, as opposed to picking the background. After that, you can change the background or effect by copying the selection and then pasting it into a new layer or document. After that, you can apply the new background or effect. The Magic Wand tool can be used in different ways, one of which is to change the color of a specific section within an image. To accomplish this, you will first need to use the Magic Wand tool to select the section of the image whose color you wish to modify. Once you have done this, you select Adjustments from the **Image** menu, and then pick **Hue/Saturation** from the list of options found under **Adjustments**. After that, you can edit the hue, saturation, and brightness of the color to change the color of the selected region.

MAKING SELECTIONS WITH THE QUICK SELECTION TOOL

In Photoshop's toolbar, the icon for the Quick Selection Tool looks like a brush that has a + sign superimposed over it. It is built to produce selections by intelligently recognizing and selecting areas in an image that share similar colors and textures. This is how it accomplishes its selection tasks. In contrast to the Magic Wand Tool, which requires you to zero in on a particular spot and adjust the tolerance level, the Quick Selection Tool requires you to simply paint over the regions that you wish to choose.

1. To quickly choose items, use the Quick Selection tool ( ), which can be found in the Tools panel. It is located in the same group as the Object Selection tool as well as the Magic Wand tool.
2. In the options menu, select the **Enhance Edge** option.

You should be able to make a selection of higher quality by selecting the **Enhance Edge** option. This will result in edges that are more accurate to the item being selected. If you are working on a machine that is particularly sluggish or very old, you can notice a slight delay whenever you utilize Enhance Edge.

3. You can move about the image by clicking and dragging within it, but you can't get outside of it.

If the Quick Selection tool includes parts of the image that do not belong to the subject, you can exclude those parts from the selection by clicking or dragging over them while holding down the **Alt (Windows) or Option (macOS) key**. This will remove the unwanted parts from the selection. This will delete the places that are not desirable from the selection. You can select the icon in the options bar that is titled "**Subtract from Selection**" by using this shortcut, which will take you there. The Quick Selection tool determines what type of content is most likely linked with the region where you clicked or dragged, recognizes the entire edge automatically, and then selects the complete sand dollar as a result of its investigation into what type of content is most likely associated with that region. Because it is so easy to use, the Quick Selection tool can single out the sand dollar for focus and attention right away. You have the option of manually completing the selection if the Quick Selection tool does not quickly finish it for you. To do this, click or drag over the areas that you wish to include in the selection, and then release the mouse button.

Moving a selected area

The ability to move a selected area is one of the most useful features that can be found in Adobe Photoshop when it comes to editing pictures. Because of the flexibility to move a selection, users can rearrange objects, make compositional tweaks, and create one-of-a-kind picture combinations. Some tools inside Photoshop, including the Move tool, the Arrow keys, and the Transform tools, can be utilized to relocate a location that has been selected. The Edit menu provides access to all of these different tools. To move a selected area using the Move tool, first choose the area you want to move using any of the selection tools that are available in Photoshop, such as the Lasso tool, the Magic Wand tool, or the Rectangular Marquee tool. Next, select the area you want to move using the Move tool. Finally, move the area using the Move tool. Next, using the Move tool, choose the region whose position you want to change. Finally, using the Move tool, move the area that has been selected. After you have made your pick, navigate to the toolbar and select the Move tool from the menu on the toolbar. It is the piece of equipment depicted by the image of an arrow that has four heads.

The next thing to do is to click and drag the section that has been selected so that it can be moved to the new location. In addition, you can advance the selection in increments of one step at a time by using the arrow keys that are accessible on your keyboard. When attempting to move the selection with the arrow keys, pressing the Shift key in conjunction with those keystrokes will cause the selection to move in larger steps. If you need to resize or rotate the picked region while you are transferring it, you can utilize the tools that are located in the Transform tab. You can access the tools in the Transform category by simply pressing the keyboard shortcut Ctrl+T (on Windows) or Command+T (on Mac). You also have the option of going to the Edit menu and selecting the Transform option from there. When you do this, the Transform controls will become active around the selected zone. This will allow you to resize and rotate the region once it has been selected. You can relocate the selected region whenever you are in the Transform mode by clicking and dragging within the Transform controls. This will cause the region to be relocated. You can also move the selection in increasingly smaller amounts by using the arrow keys on your keyboard while you are in the Transform mode. This option is available on most modern computers.

In addition to the Move tool and the other tools found in the Transform category, Photoshop offers a variety of other tools, such as the Content-Aware Move tool and the Puppet Warp tool, which can be used to move particular parts of an image. These tools can be found under the Move subcategory. The information-Aware Move tool is ideal for the retouching and editing of digital photographs because it enables users to move selected areas while automatically filling in the surrounding region with information that is analogous to the moved selection. The Puppet Warp tool is great for the development of one-of-a-kind; stylistic effects since it enables users to distort and warp selected areas in a variety of different ways. This makes the tool very versatile. When you move a certain area about in your image, it is essential to maintain the layer structure of your picture in mind. This is especially important to keep in mind if you are using layers. When you move a selection on a layer that has areas of transparency, the layer below it will be shown; but, when you move a selection on a layer that has a solid background color, all that will happen is that the selection will be moved on top of the background. This is the only thing that will occur when you move a selection on a layer that has a solid background color.

EXPLORING THE OBJECT SELECTION TOOL

The Object Selection Tool is a clever selection tool that makes it simpler to pick out and isolate objects in an image, regardless of their irregular shapes or complicated backgrounds. Using Adobe's Sensei AI technology, this tool can automatically identify and pick objects in an image.

To use the Object Selection Tool in Photoshop to choose an object, please follow these steps:

Step 1: Select the **Object Selection Tool**. The Photoshop Toolbar has the Object Selection Tool, which you can locate if you're not sure where it is.

Step 2: Choose your method for selecting an item.

- Using the Rectangle mode, you can draw a rectangle around the object.
- Using the lasso mode, you can draw a free-form lasso around the object.

For my example, I will be utilizing the rectangle mode.

Step 3: Encircle the object you want to pick with a rectangle. The dotted lines ought to round the object as indicated once you've drawn all around it.

In my image, the dotted lines only indicate the object I want to choose; but, in more complex images, it may also select other objects in your pictures. Selecting one of the following options and clicking it from left to right will deselect the other objects. New choice, Add to the list: Select **Subtract from selection** or **Intersect with selection** from the Object Selection Tool's options.

From the available options, choose the Lasso or Rectangle mode:

Once you've clicked Add to selection in the options box, draw a new rectangle or lasso around the space. Apply the same process to each missing region that you wish to have included in the selection. The Rectangle or Lasso modes can be used to make selections. However, where the two differ most is in the shape of the selections they generate. As the name suggests, you can use the Rectangle mode to create a rectangular selection around an object in a photograph. Conversely, you can create a free-form border around your image using the Lasso method. Both strategies work well for removing objects from photos, but if you're having trouble choosing one over the other, you might want to try another one. Everything is based on how intricate your image is. The more intricacy involved, the more time it takes to choose the most effective approach.

CHAPTER THIRTEEN
IMAGE RETOUCHING IN PHOTOSHOP

The skill of Photoshop image editing is examined in this chapter. It offers tips and methods for boosting and developing images. It starts by going over the fundamental strategy for image retouching and stresses how crucial it is to customize the retouching procedure to the particular goal of the image. A variety of retouching operations are covered, including cropping and straightening photographs to improve composition. It presents altering or removing image parts with ease using the Content-Aware Patch tool. This chapter covers the use of the Clone Stamp tool to repair image regions and flaws, and the Healing Brush tool to eliminate wrinkles and blemishes. Additionally, readers will discover how to enhance photographs by utilizing tools such as the **Sponge and Dodge tools** to modify color and brightness. The chapter describes how to obtain a polished and professional look in portrait photography by adjusting levels and fixing skin tones. In summary, this chapter provides readers with the skills and information required to use Photoshop effectively for image retouching, whether the purpose is to improve overall images or enhance portraits.

APPROACH FOR RETOUCHING

Retouching in Photoshop is a process of enhancing or improving the quality of a photo, often by fixing imperfections, adjusting colors, and overall making the image more visually appealing. It's a common practice in photography and graphic design.

Here's a step-by-step approach for retouching in Photoshop:

1. Organize Your Workflow:
   - Before starting, make sure your project is well-organized. Create a duplicate layer of your image, so you always have the original to reference.
2. Correct Exposure and Color:
   - Adjust the exposure, contrast, and color balance if needed. Use the Levels, Curves, and Color Balance adjustment layers for these corrections.
3. Blemish and Spot Removal:
   - Use the Healing Brush Tool or the Spot Healing Brush Tool to remove blemishes, acne, spots, or other imperfections. Create a new layer for non-destructive retouching.
4. Dodge and Burn:

- Create a new layer set to "Overlay" blending mode. Use the Dodge Tool to lighten and the Burn Tool to darken specific areas. This helps add depth and dimension to the image.

5. **Frequency Separation:**
   - Create a frequency separation setup by duplicating the background layer and splitting it into a high-frequency and a low-frequency layer. Use this technique to retouch skin texture while maintaining skin tones and colors.

6. **Skin Retouching:**
   - On the low-frequency layer, use the Clone Stamp or Healing Brush Tool to remove larger imperfections, wrinkles, and unwanted skin textures.
   - On the high-frequency layer, use a soft brush at a low opacity to even out the skin texture without removing important details.

7. **Enhance Eyes and Teeth:**
   - Brighten the whites of the eyes using the Dodge Tool. For teeth, use the same tool but on a new layer to gently brighten and whiten.

8. **Hair Retouching:**
   - For hair, use the Clone Stamp or Healing Brush Tool to remove stray hairs or frizz. Create a new layer for this to maintain flexibility.

9. **Adjust Lips and Lips Lines:**
   - Enhance the color and definition of lips using the Brush Tool. Remove any fine lines around the lips using the Healing Brush or Clone Stamp.

10. **Sharpening:**
    - Apply sharpening to the entire image using the Unsharp Mask or Smart Sharpen filter. Use a light hand to avoid oversharpening.

11. **Final Color and Tone Adjustments:**
    - Make any final adjustments to color balance, contrast, and saturation using adjustment layers. The **Color Balance and Curves** adjustment layers can be especially useful here.

12. **Save Your Work:**
    - Save your retouched image in a format suitable for your intended use. PSD format retains layers for further editing, while JPEG is often used for sharing the final image.

13. **Compare with the Original:**
    - Always compare the retouched image with the original to ensure you haven't overdone any aspect of retouching.

14. **Revisit if Necessary:**
    - If you notice anything that needs further attention or if you receive feedback, go back to the appropriate layer and make adjustments.

STRAIGHTENING AND CROPPING AN IMAGE

Cropping an image in Photoshop

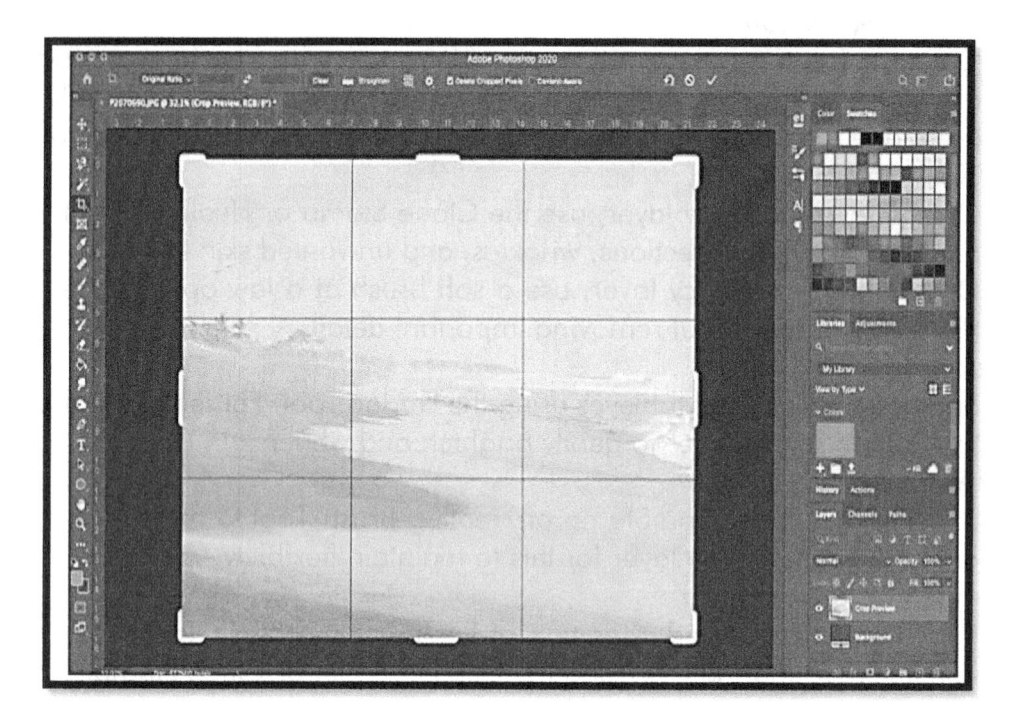

1. Select the crop tool

To pick the crop tool, either navigates to the toolbar on the left of the screen and click on the icon that looks like a square with overlapping corners, or press the **C** key on your keyboard. This is one of the keyboard shortcuts that Photoshop offers that makes sense. After the option has been chosen, a box will appear over the image, and white borders will appear at the photograph's corners and midpoints to illustrate the size and shape of the crop.

2. Choose an aspect ratio (Optional)

When you use the crop tool in Photoshop, the program will automatically utilize the aspect ratio that was originally used for the photo, or it will use the ratio that you chose the last time you used it. You'll need to modify the photo's aspect ratio if you want the shot to be in a particular shape, such as a square for Instagram or an 8 by 10 for printing. Examples of this include printing the photo as an 8 by 10 or sharing it as a square on Instagram.

Select the desired aspect ratio by using the menu that drops down from the top of the page (it will state "original ratio" by default). For instance, a ratio of 1:1 is square, whereas a ratio of 4:5 corresponds to the shape of an 8-by-10-inch print. If you do not want to be restricted to a specific aspect ratio, you can use a free-range crop tool by using the "**clear**" button that is located on the top toolbar.

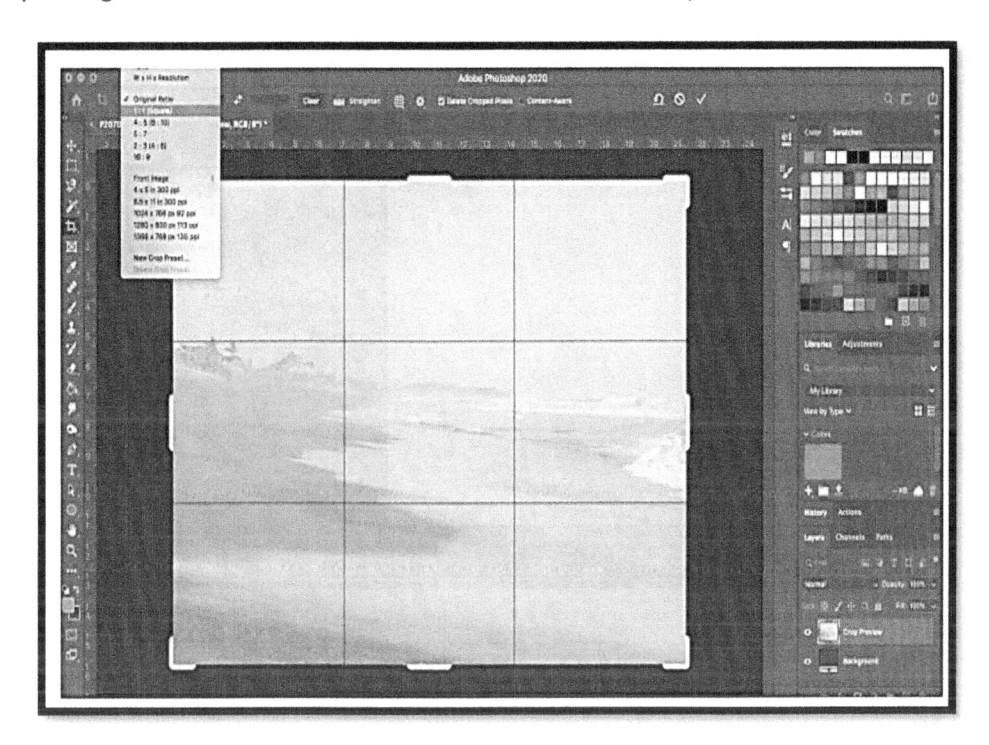

3. Resize

Take hold of the four corners of the crop box and drag them until the selection in the photo contains only the elements that you want to keep. You can also click and hold anywhere in the middle of the crop box to move it around the shot, altering the frame while preserving the original size of the photo.

4. Straighten (Optional)

While the crop box is still active, move the mouse pointer over one of the crop box's outside corners until the curving arrow with two heads appears. The image can then be reoriented by clicking and dragging the corners of the crop box until it is in the desired position. You also have the option of using the "**straighten**" tool, which can be found in the top menu. After that, make use of the tool to draw a line across a component of the image that ought to be straight, such as the horizon. After you have created the line, Photoshop will immediately begin to straighten the image for you. If your shot is already straight, you can skip this step. If it isn't, however, it is a simple and fast technique to correct a skewed horizon.

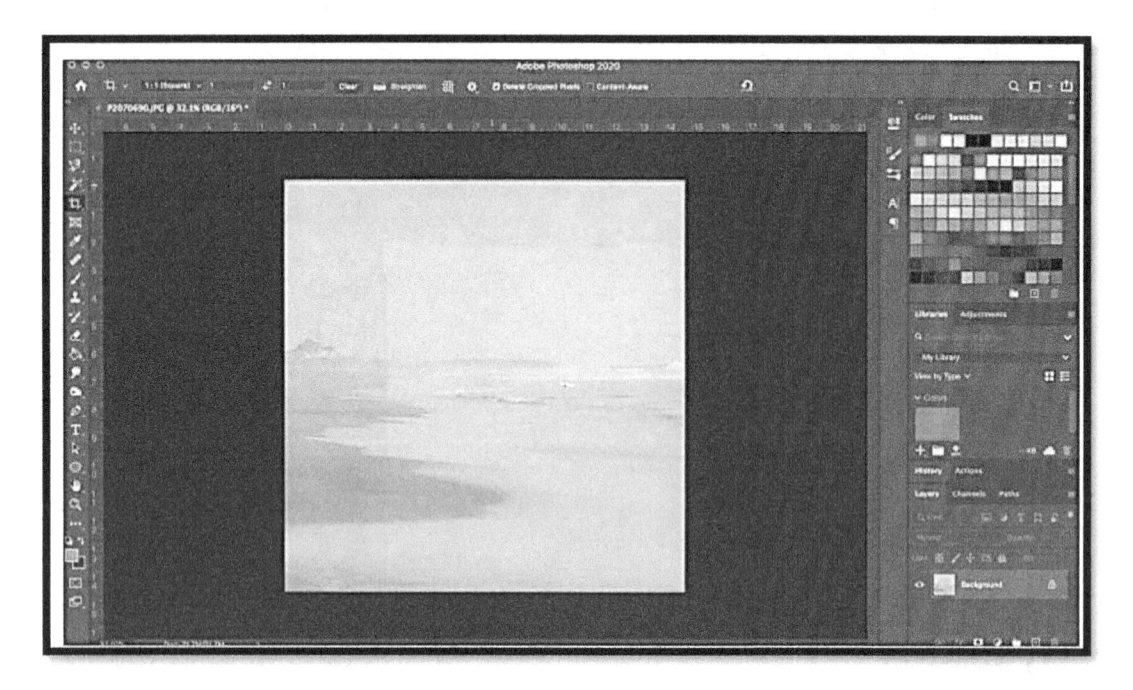

5. Lock in the crop

Simply hitting the enter key will complete the cropping process. However, before you proceed with this, you should make sure that the "**Delete Cropped Pixels**" option on the top toolbar is not selected. In that case, once you have completed the cropping process, you won't be able to undo it and make changes to it (except making it smaller). Because, in contrast to Lightroom, cropping in Photoshop is designed to be destructive by default, we recommend turning off the option to Delete Cropped Pixels unless you are certain that you won't need to make any adjustments to the image.

Straightening an image in Photoshop

The crop tool is the best and easiest technique to straighten a crooked photo simply because the photographer was not holding the camera level when the photo was taken. However, the process of adjusting lines that are slanted as a result of perspective is more complicated. This is something that frequently occurs when the shot is taken looking up at something or from a location that is slightly off-axis rather than straight on. It's also a problem frequently seen in pictures of buildings and other structures.

"You are in luck because Photoshop contains the tool you need to correct this."

1. Select the perspective crop tool

Instead of picking the standard crop tool from the toolbar, click and hold on the crop tool icon until the sub-menu appears. This will bring up more cropping options. To use the perspective crop tool, click on it. (The Shift-C key combination can also be used to cycle among the various crop tool options.)

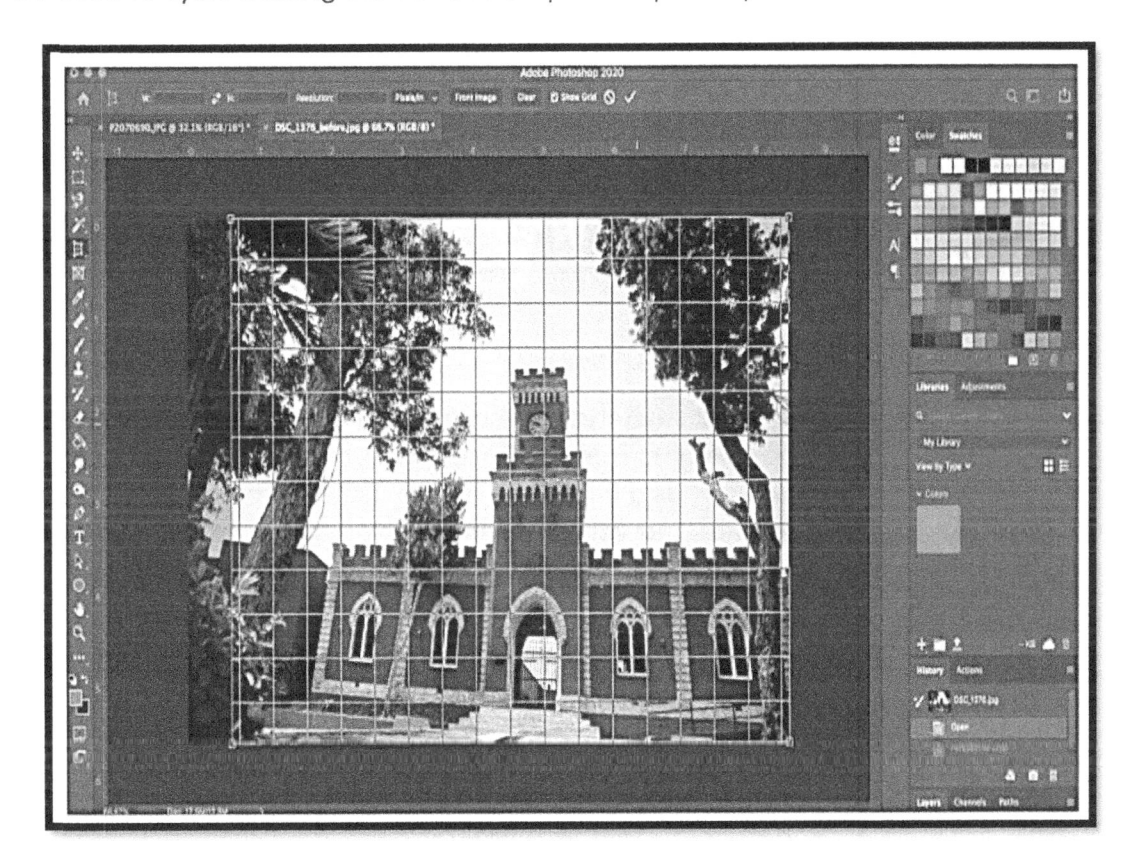

2. Select the cropped area

Create a rough box around the area of the photo that you want to retain in the final crop by drawing a box over it.

3. Adjust the edges

Next, slide the corners of the box such that they are parallel to the edges of objects in the image that should be straight. This will ensure that the edges of the box are straight. Make use of the gridlines as a guide. Be sure to use each of the four corners so that the lines in the horizontal and vertical directions will fit the grid.

4. Hit enter to finish

After you have checked the alignment of the lines and determined that it is satisfactory, press the enter key. If you would like the image to have a particular aspect ratio, you can continue altering it at this point by making use of the usual crop tool.

USING A CONTENT-AWARE PATCH

When it comes to removing unwanted elements from an image or filling in blank spaces, retouching it with Adobe Photoshop can be a time-consuming process. This is especially true when it comes to eradicating unwanted objects. The Content-Aware Patch tool is an exceptionally helpful function that provides you the power to quickly and undetectably extend or replace areas of an image. This capability is one of the many reasons why Photoshop is so popular. Below, for your convenience, are detailed the steps that must be taken to use the Content-Aware Patch tool that is included in Adobe Photoshop.

Step 1: Select the Area to Be Patched

To successfully apply a content-aware patch, the first thing you will need to do is determine which component of the system is broken and needs to be corrected. Using any of the various selection tools, you can form a selection around the item or region that you want to repair. This selection can then be repaired. During this example, the Lasso tool will be utilized to draw a boundary around the area that needs correction.

Step 2: Choose the Patch Tool

When you are finished making your pick, go back to the toolbar and select the Patch tool. The Patch tool is represented by an icon that looks like a patch or Band-Aid ( ). When you have the Patch tool selected, the options bar that is located at the very top of the screen will display some different choices for you to make. From this menu, you can change the size of the tool, as well as its hardness and transparency.

Step 3: Drag the Selection to a Similar Area

After picking the area that needs to be patched and then selecting the Patch tool, it is time to drag the selection to a region in the picture that is pretty similar to the one you just picked. This will complete the patching process. You need to find a zone that has a texture and color that is similar to the area that has to be patched, and you should look for this region. If you want to fix a cloud that's in the center of a blue sky, for example, you should look for a portion of the sky that has a color and texture that's comparable to the cloud's own. Only then can you fix the cloud.

Step 4: Apply the Patch

While the selection is still active, you can click and drag it to the position where you have decided it should be replaced by clicking and dragging it to that spot. As soon as you let go of the button on the mouse, Photoshop's content-aware technology will immediately begin to fix the area automatically. Depending on the complexity of the image as well as the size of the selection, this process could take as little as a few seconds or as much as a few minutes.

Step 5: Touch Up the Patch

After the patch has been stitched on, there can be some seams or defects in the area that were previously unaffected by these issues. Previously, these issues were not present. Use the Spot Healing Brush tool and set the brush size such that it is just slightly larger than the patch itself to make some little tweaks to the patch. After that, use the tool to mix the borders of the patch with the pixels that are around it. It is essential to keep in mind that the Patch tool and the Spot Healing Brush tool both make use of the same content-aware technology to function properly. This indicates that it will automatically sample and blend the pixels in the surrounding region to get a seamless result.

Step 6: Adjust the Patch Tool Settings

If the output from the initial process does not live up to your standards, you can adjust the settings of the Patch tool in the options bar to generate a result that is more in line with your requirements. You can modify the parameters for the tool's size, mixing, and color adaptation to achieve the result that is optimal for your image.

Step 7: Apply the Patch to Complex Areas

If you are trying to apply a content-aware patch to an area that is extremely intricate or textured, you could find that you need to use the Clone Stamp or Healing Brush tools instead of the Content-Aware Patch tool. With the use of these tools, you can manually choose the pixels from the source, and then use those pixels to apply them to the target area. To make use of these tools, first choose them from the toolbar. Next, select the pixels that will serve as the source by pressing the Alt key (on Windows) or the Option key (on Mac), depending on your operating system. After that, you need to apply the patch by painting over the area that needs fixing.

FIXING IMAGE AREAS WITH THE CLONE STAMP TOOL

One of the most important and versatile tools in Adobe Photoshop is called the Clone Stamp, and it can be found in the History palette. It allows you to copy pixels from one part of the image and paste them into another part of the image, which gives you the ability to fix broken or flawed parts of a picture. This tool is particularly useful for retrieving images from the distant past as well as touching up pictures that were captured in more recent times.

Step 1: Select the Clone Stamp tool

First, select the **Clone Stamp tool** from the menu.

Choose the **Clone Stamp tool** (🔨) from the Tools panel. In addition, you can select the tool by pressing the letter S on your keyboard.

Step 2: Choose the source area

To make changes to the source area, you need to click while maintaining a depressed position on the **Alt (Windows) or Option (Mac) key**. This will activate the cursor for the Clone Stamp tool, which, once it has been activated, will appear as a target icon in the tool's toolbar. Put the cursor in the area of the picture that you want to use as the foundation for the cloning process, and do so by clicking and dragging it. Simply making one click will select the location of the source.

Step 3: Choose the brush size and hardness

Using the Options bar that is located at the very top of the screen, you can adjust the brush's size as well as the amount of abrasiveness that it has. Adjusting the size of the brush so that it is just slightly larger than the area that needs to be cloned is something that needs to be done. By adjusting the level of brush stiffness, you can customize the amount to which the edge is rounded.

Step 4: Start cloning

When you are ready to start cloning, move the cursor to the area of the picture that needs to be fixed after first determining the size of the brush and then the amount of pressure it should have. After doing this, you can begin the cloning process. Click and drag the mouse over the portion of the image that is broken or defective to clone pixels from the source region into the target area.

Step 5: Adjust the brush settings

As you continue to clone, you might find that the settings for the brush need to be adjusted. For instance, if you want to clone extremely small or extremely large regions, you might need to adjust the brush size by either increasing or decreasing it. You can change the degree to which the edge is rounded by adjusting the degree to which the brush has a firm texture.

Step 6: Blend the cloned area

You can blend the newly cloned region with the pixels in the surrounding area by using either the Smudge tool or the Blur tool. These tools can help round off the corners of the copied region, making it appear more natural and integrated with the rest of the picture.

A few helpful hints while utilizing the Clone Stamp tool:

- **Use a light touch:** When cloning, avoid leaving noticeable repeated patterns in the image by using a light hand.
- **Clone small areas:** To avoid over-cloning or producing strange patterns in the image, clone small pieces at a time.
- **Use many sources:** When working with complex regions, it's best to clone from multiple sources to prevent the creation of a repeating pattern.
- **Refrain from cloning over crucial aspects:** Take care not to clone over the image's crucial details, such as mouths, eyes, or other prominent features.
- **Preview frequently:** You should zoom in and out of the image to frequently preview the results. This can be used to assess how well the duplicated region blends in with the surrounding pixels.

REMOVING BLEMISHES AND WRINKLES WITH HEALING BRUSH TOOLS

The Healing Brush tool in Photoshop is a typical retouching technique that is used to remove imperfections and wrinkles from photos to improve the subject's appearance and make the portraits look more professional.

You can use the Healing Brush tool in the following manner:

1. **Open Your Image:** Start by opening your image in Adobe Photoshop.
2. **Create a New Layer:** It's essential to work non-destructively. Create a new layer by clicking the "**New Layer**" icon in the Layers panel. This layer will be used for your retouching.
3. **Select the Healing Brush Tool:** In the Tools panel on the left, select the **Healing Brush** tool. You'll find it grouped with the Spot Healing Brush and Patch tool.
4. **Adjust the Brush Settings:** At the top of the screen, you can adjust the brush settings. You'll want to set the brush size to match the size of the blemish or wrinkle you're trying to remove. You can also choose "**Sample: All Layers**" to ensure that your changes are applied to the new layer.
5. **Alt/Option-Click:** To sample a source area, press and hold the Alt key (Option on Mac) and click on an area near the blemish or wrinkle that has

similar skin texture and color. This will be used to replace the **unwanted details**.
6. **Paint over Blemishes and Wrinkles**: Release the Alt/Option key and carefully paint over the blemish or wrinkle. The Healing Brush tool will automatically blend the sampled area with the surrounding skin.
7. **Repeat as Needed**: Continue to Alt/Option-click and paint over each blemish or wrinkle one at a time. It's essential to work slowly and carefully for a natural look.
8. **Zoom In**: To get more precise results, zoom in on your image as needed.
9. **Adjust the Layer Opacity**: After you've retouched all the blemishes and wrinkles, you can adjust the opacity of the retouching layer to control the overall effect. Reducing the layer opacity makes the retouching look more natural.
10. **Save Your Work**: When you're satisfied with the result, save your image.

Keep in mind that even if retouching can substantially improve a portrait, it is necessary to keep up a natural appearance. Because an unnatural and plastic appearance can be achieved by using the Healing Brush tool excessively, use it with moderation at all times. In addition, it is best practice to maintain the integrity of the original image by always working on a layer that is separate from the rest of the image.

Tips for Effective Use

The following are some ideas that can assist you in making more efficient use of the tool known as the Spot Healing Brush:

1. **Use a small brush size.** Using a small brush size is the best option if you want to improve the accuracy with which you determine the area of the photo that has to be touched up. When working on areas of the character that have minute details, such as the facial characteristics or the hair, it is extremely important to keep this in mind.
2. **Modify the brush's hardness**: The brush's hardness will affect the degree to which the pixels in the selected region are sharply blended with those in the surrounding area. For gentler blending, use a lower hardness setting.
3. **Sample from nearby pixels**: It is necessary to collect a color sample from adjacent pixels that are similar to the color of the surrounding area whenever you are modifying a region. This will contribute to the process of ensuring that the pixels in the modified region blend in precisely with those in the areas that surround it.

4. **Use multiple passes**: When working on larger or more complex areas, you may need to make multiple runs with the tool Spot Healing Brush to get the outcome you desire. Be very careful and take your time to ensure that the area that was changed looks completely natural and does not stick out from the rest of the picture in any way.

Advanced Techniques

In addition to the fundamental use of the Spot Healing Brush tool, you can build more complex retouching effects by employing a range of different ways that are not directly related to the tool. These methods are located in the extra panel where they can be accessed.

The following are some examples that illustrate this point:

1. **Eliminating larger objects**: You can use the Content-Aware Fill feature to remove larger objects from an image. This option is available in most image editing programs. Adobe Photoshop includes this functionality in its program. Because of this function, you can choose the item and replace it with a sampled region that is taken from the pixels that are neighboring, all while maintaining the texture and color of the area that surrounds the selected item. This feature is available on all devices.
2. **Fixing skin blemishes**: You can repair skin imperfections such as acne scars or other forms of scars by combining the Healing Brush tool, the Spot Healing Brush tool, and the Clone Stamp tool. These tools can be used in conjunction with one another. To get started, you will need to get rid of the flaw by utilizing a tool called the Spot Healing Brush. After that, you can give it a more genuine appearance by using the Healing Brush or the Clone Stamp tool to blend the edited region with the texture and color of the skin around it. This will give it a more natural look.
3. **Editing hair:** To retouch the hair, use the Spot Healing Brush tool in conjunction with the Clone Stamp tool. This will allow you to make any necessary adjustments. To get rid of any stray hairs or blemishes, you should launch the Spot Healing Brush tool as your first step. The following step is to make use of the tool known as the Clone Stamp to copy and paste individual strands of hair from surrounding spots to either fill in any gaps or produce a more consistent appearance.

SPONGE AND DODGE TOOLS

The Dodge, Burn, and Sponge tools are wonderful techniques to change the focus point of a shot that did not turn out as you had imagined it would. They are modeled after traditional darkroom processes that were applied to photographs to correct underexposed or overexposed areas. To put it another way, the Sponge tool can either saturate or desaturate the color in an area, whilst the Burn tool can darken the color and the Dodge tool can lighten it.

There are a few things you should be aware of before you reach for these controls, and they are as follows:

- The editing techniques of Dodge, Burn, and Sponge are considered to be harmful. That indicates the modifications are performed straight to the image itself. Because of this, avoiding making changes to the layer that serves as the background is recommended. Making multiple layers and dealing with those allows you to throw out errors if you push things too far.
- You "paint" with these tools because they are brushes. You can adjust the size of the brush by hitting the [key to make it larger and the [key to make it smaller.
- Dodging or burning an area is accomplished by painting over it. When you paint over a region that has previously been dodged or burned, the effect will be reapplied to the pixels that are being painted.
- The number 0 is the command for the keyboard shortcut that will provide you access to these tools.

Working with the Dodge, Burn, and Sponge Tools

In the Layers panel, choose the layer that serves as the background, and then create a duplicate of that layer. You should avoid working on the original because of the destructive potential of the equipment at your disposal.

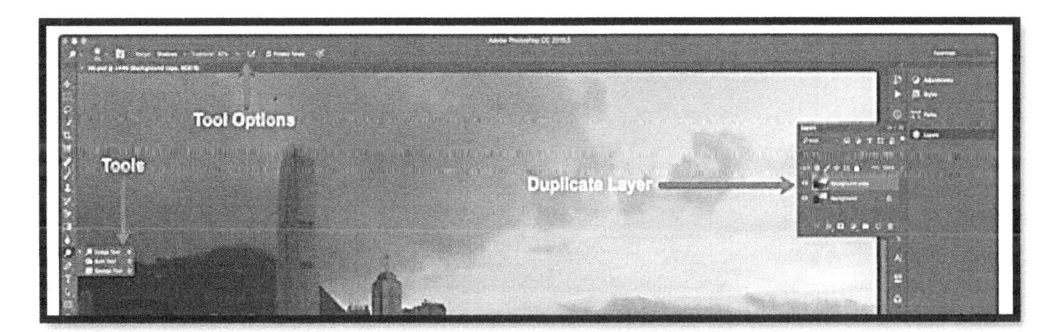

After that, navigate to the menu bar and select the Dodge tool. If you need to use the Burn tool or the Sponge tool, choose the little arrow in the tool icon's lower-right corner, and then choose the relevant tool from the drop-down menu that appears. Choose the Dodge tool if you need to bring more light into a specific region. Select the Burn tool if you want to make an area significantly darker. Choose the Sponge Tool if you need to decrease or enhance the amount of color in a specific region.

In the menu bar, you'll find that each choice has its own individual set of options. A summary of each item is as follows:

- **Dodge and Burn Tool Options**: The Shadows, the Midtones, and the Highlights are the three different Ranges. Your choices will only affect the aspects of the problem that are relevant to the categories you select. The intensity of the effect can be adjusted using the Exposure slider, which has values ranging from 1% to 100%. The default value is 50 percent. Only the midtones are affected, and they are darkened or lightened to a maximum of 50% of their original value if the midtones are set to 50%.
- **Sponge Tool Options**: There are two different modes to choose from: desaturate and saturation. Desaturate decreases the amount of color intensity, whereas Saturate increases the amount of color intensity in the area that is being painted. The flow is not quite the same. The figure, which can be anything from 1% to 100%, indicates the rate at which the effect is put into play.

The Dodge tool, for instance, is the greatest option for brightening the tower in this image.

Using Adobe Photoshop's Dodge and Burn Tools

When you are painting, you should approach the subject as though it were a coloring book, and you should make sure to keep within the lines. When it comes to the tower, put a mask on it in a layer that is a duplicate and call it Dodge. Because you are using a mask, the brush cannot influence any places that are outside of the lines of the Tower.

Focus your camera on the Tower, then switch to the Dodge tool. I enlarged the size of the Brush, chose Midtones as the starting point, and decreased the Exposure to 65%. From that vantage point, I painted over the tower and added some additional detail. The open and airy space at the very top of the tower was one of my favorites.

After decreasing the exposure to 10% and painting over it once more, I was able to make it stand out more. After that, I changed the Range to Shadows, zoomed in on the foundation of the Tower, and shrunk the size of the brush. In addition to that, I decreased the Exposure to approximately 15% and painted over the shadowy region that was at the base of the Tower.

Applying the Sponge Tool in Adobe Photoshop

There is a hint of color between the clouds on the right side of the image. This is caused by the setting sun. I decided to make it a little bit more obvious, so I duplicated the Background Layer, gave the copy the name Sponge, and then chose the Sponge tool from the toolbox.

Take special note of the sequence in which the layers are stacked. As a result of the masked tower, the Sponge layer is located beneath the Dodge layer. This explains why I didn't duplicate the Dodge Layer earlier in the process. After that, I selected the **saturate mode**, increased the **Flow setting** to **100 percent**, and then began painting. It is important to keep in mind that as you continue to paint over an area, the colors in that region will get more intense. When you are pleased with the result, you can release your grip on the mouse. The art of Photoshop is all about being subtle. It is not necessary to make significant alterations to make some aspects of a photograph "**pop**." When trying to prevent "**overproducing**" an image, it is important to take your time to analyze it, formulate a plan, and go cautiously.

ADJUSTING LEVELS

You need to have a fundamental understanding of image tones in relation to photo editing before you can progress to the next step of learning how to modify the Levels in Photoshop. When we talk about the tones of an image, we are ignoring the color. Instead, they focus on the amount of light or darkness present in particular places (or pixels). Photoshop makes use of a numerical representation technique to convey this sense of brightness. In Photoshop, the values of the image's tones can range from 0 up to 255 at any given time. If the value of an image tone is 0, the resulting tone is black; if the value is 255, the resulting tone is white. Gray tones are those that have values that are in between black and white. When the value is higher, the gray seems lighter, and vice versa when the value is lower. The percentage of white that is contained in the tone is an alternate method that is utilized by certain picture editors such as Affinity Photos. When the tone of an image reaches 0%, the resulting picture is black because there is no white present. However, a value of 100% represents a completely white color. To reiterate, grey is the result of any value between 0% and 100%.

In the illustration that follows, you can compare the two different systems.

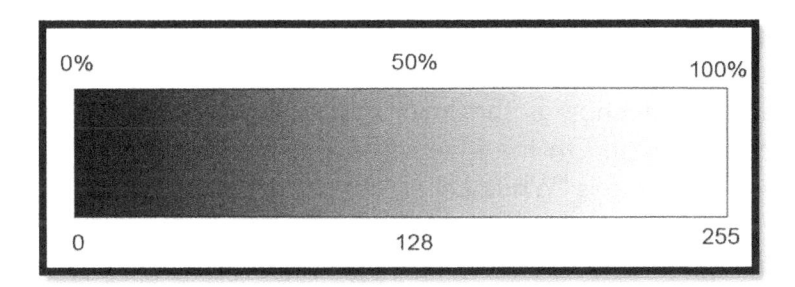

The Photoshop Levels Dialog

Now that you have an understanding of image tones, let's look at how you can use this knowledge to make adjustments in Photoshop using the Levels panel. The following snapshot of Photoshop's Properties box demonstrates the level adjustments that can be made in the program.

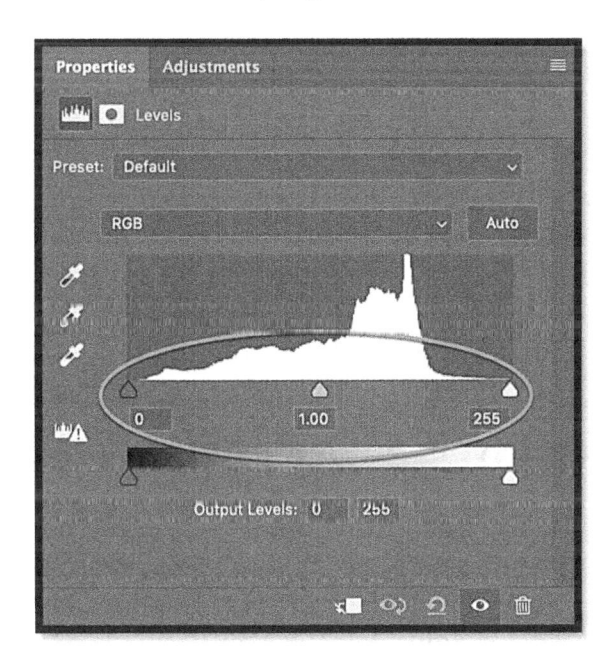

A histogram that displays the image's tones can be found in the Levels dialog box in Photoshop. The histogram displays the distribution of tones across the entire image, beginning with black on the left and progressing up to white on the right. You can see a box containing numbers right below the histogram, as well as three-pointers immediately below the histogram itself. These are the Photoshop Input Levels, which we can use to make adjustments to the various tonal values in the image.

Reading the Photoshop Levels

The Black Level in Photoshop is the level that is located on the left and has the number 0 directly below it. On the inverse end of the scale, the White Level has a value of 255, and its name is **"White Level."** The Photoshop Midtone Level is located in the center of the image and has a value of 1 directly below it. This uses a slightly different numbering system and represents the brightness of a midtone gray. If you go to the left side of the histogram in the Levels panel, you'll see that it goes all the way to the left but stops short. This is because it doesn't go all the way to the left. The Black Level and the beginning of the histogram are separated by a space in this diagram. This informs us that the image does not now contain a black tone; rather, the tone that is the darkest is a dark gray. If you look to the right side of the histogram, you will see that the same thing holds there as well. The histogram does not reach up to the White Level where it would meet it. This indicates that there are currently no white tones present in the image that you are looking at. In its place, we have a very light gray.

How to Adjust the Levels in Photoshop

The image will not have sufficient contrast because it does not contain any black or white, simply varying shades of grey. It is supposed to have a flat appearance. This may, of course, be ideal for some photographs; for instance, a photograph of a foggy area would have a low contrast. However, if you determine that the contrast has to be adjusted, you can use Photoshop's levels adjustment to make the necessary changes.

Step 1 – Add a New Levels Adjustment Layer

In Photoshop, adding a Levels Adjustment Layer is the first step you need to take before adjusting the levels of an image. You can accomplish this in Photoshop by going to the **"Layer"** menu and selecting **"New Adjustment Layer"** followed by **"Levels..."** Because the **Levels adjustment** is non-destructive, we apply it to a new layer rather than directly to the image itself so that we can take advantage of its benefits.

Step 2 – Adjust the Black Input Level

You can now see the Levels dialog after the Levels Layer was applied to the image. We'll now adjust the Black and White Input Levels. To begin, slide the **Black level** toward the center of the screen by dragging it to the right. You will see that the image becomes noticeably darker when you make adjustments to the Black Level. You want it to have a slight overlap with the left side of the histogram, but you don't want it to cut into it. Clipping is the term that describes what happens to a histogram when it is clipped into. This results in the dark image tones becoming completely black, which can be detrimental to the shadow detail in the image.

Step 3 – Adjust the White Input Level

You must now perform Step 2 once more, but this time use the White Level. To move the white level to the left, use the mouse to click and drag it until it is almost even with the right side of the histogram. You will see that the image gets brighter as you continue to do this, and the contrast will also get higher. Once more, highlight clipping is caused when you cut into the histogram, so try to avoid doing that.

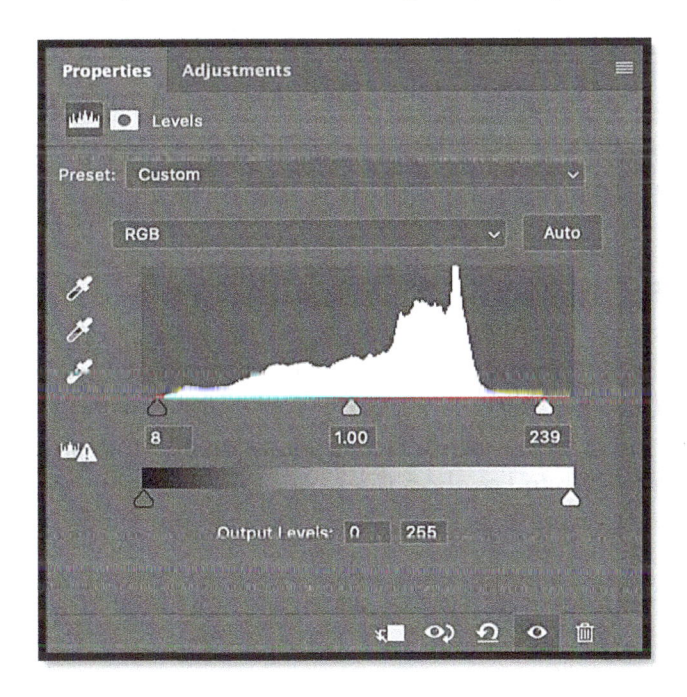

If you examine the screenshot in great detail, you will notice that the dark level has a value of 8 located below it.

Reading the Input Level Numbers

This tells us a few things:

- o Before, the value of the image tone that was the darkest had been set to 8, rather than 0 (which represents black).
- o Because of the adjustment to the Black Level, all of the tones in the image that previously had a value of 8 now have a value of 0.
- o Because adjusting the Black Level caused all of the other tones in the image to go darker, the figures for each of them became lower when you measured them.

When we take a look at the White Input Level, we notice something very similar:

1. The White Level is now at a value of 239 as of 1. This tells us that the previous image tone that was the lightest was 239, which is also known as light gray.
2. We remapped the lightest image tone so that it now has a value of 255, which is white, by sliding the White Level slider to the left.
3. After that, Photoshop will redistribute the other tones in the image over the tonal range, which will result in the image becoming a little bit brighter.

Before, the image had a tonal range of 8 to 239 available to it. The new tonal range in Photoshop is 0 to 255, and it can be achieved by adjusting the Input Levels. This provides contrast to the image, preventing it from seeming as though it is lacking in depth.

Adjusting the Photoshop Output Levels

If you look at the Levels dialog, you will find a second strip with sliders down the bottom of the dialog. This strip is located in the middle of the Levels dialog. In the same way that we have been altering the Input Levels, this strip also has a Black Level on the left and a White Level on the right. You will then see the words "**Output Levels**" followed by two numbers below this.

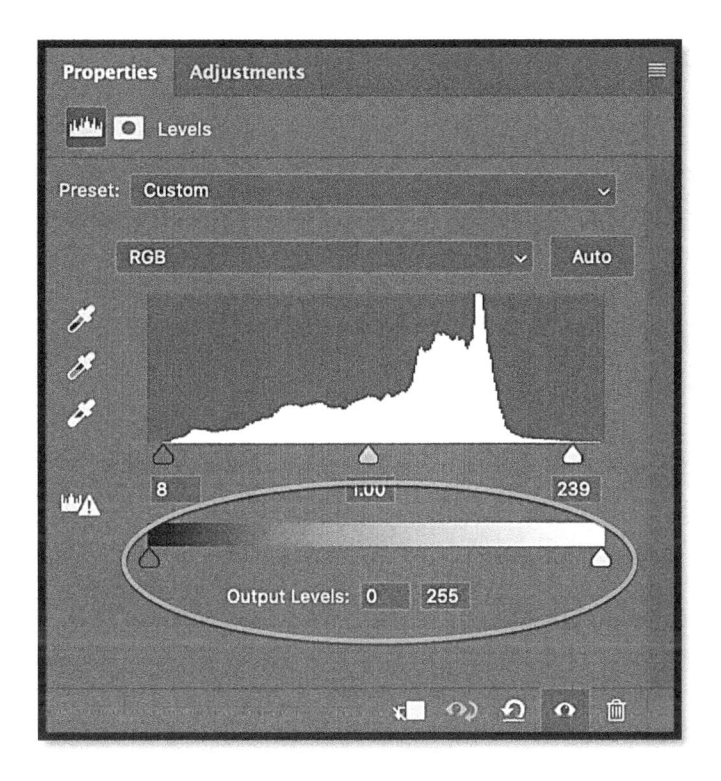

You can control the tones by adjusting the Black and White Output levels, but the process works in the opposite direction of how it does with the Input Levels. If we want the dark tones to be even darker, we can use the Input Levels, but if we want them to be brighter, we can use the Output Levels. If you check to the left, where it says "**Black Output Level**," you'll see that its default setting is 0. This is the significance of the first of the number boxes. If you adjust the slider for the Black Output Level to the right, you'll see that this figure rises. As you continue to do this, you'll also notice that the image is getting brighter.

What's going on here is that the Black Output Level determines how much darker the image's darkest tone can get. This is how it works. If you have it set to 0, it indicates that black can be the tone that is the darkest. If you move it to the right to the number 30, for example, Photoshop will only allow dark grey to be the darkest possible tone for the image. The White Output Level accomplishes the same goal, with the exception that it places a cap on how brilliant the image's whitestone can seem. If you shift the slider to the left from its default position of 255, which corresponds to white, the strongest possible tone will be gray.

What's happening in the Photoshop Levels Adjustment

The actual process that is taking place is that the Black and White Input Levels are using the Black and White Output Levels as a mapping tool for the dark and light image tones. When we changed the settings for the input levels, it just so happened that the output levels were 0 and 255. When you're just starting with the Level adjustment in Photoshop, this can be a little difficult to understand. However, you should not give up because the results will justify your efforts.

The Photoshop Midtone Level

Both the Input and Output levels have been discussed up to this point. Adjusting the levels in Photoshop is something you should be familiar with if you've been following along with the image editing tutorials. However, there is one level that we haven't discussed yet, and that's the Midtone Input Level. The Midtone Input Level is responsible for regulating how tones are distributed across the image. If you drag the Midtone level to the right, more of the image's tones will be displayed to the left of the Level. This results in a darker overall appearance of the image. When the Midtone Level is moved to the left, a greater percentage of the image's tones are displayed to the right of the level. This results in a brighter appearance of the image. There is nothing else to the Midtone Level that can make it any more sophisticated than this. You can use it to brighten or darken the image, but you should do so only after you have established the levels for the input and output.

CORRECTING SKIN TONES

Step 1 – Open the Image to Select Skin Tones

To modify the skin tone of an image in Photoshop, you will first need to either open the image or choose the layer from the layers menu.

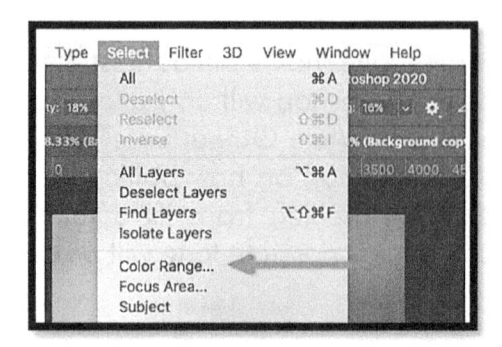

Open the color range window by going to the Select menu in the top-right corner of the screen, selecting Color Range, and then selecting the photographs whose skin tones require editing. You can use Color Range to select just the skin tones in the image you've chosen. You will be able to concentrate on refining the skin tones because the remainder of the image will not be affected by your changes. Open the drop-down menu that is located next to Select in the Color Range window, and then select the Skin Tone option. You'll find it much simpler to alter with the skin tone option because it automatically detects skin color.

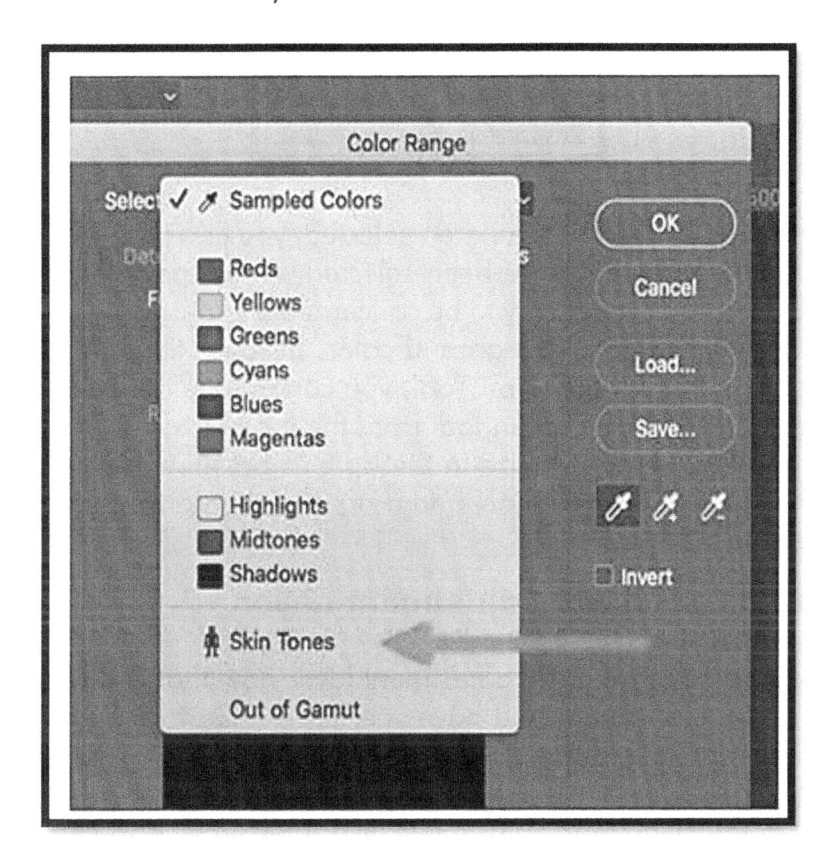

Step 2 – Select the Target Area

Because you probably won't want to change the entire image, having software like Adobe Photoshop that can magically detect faces and choose skin tones can be helpful. Move the pointer up and down the Fuzziness slider to make adjustments to the range of the currently selected area. You can raise or reduce the quantity of the image that is picked simply by sliding the pointer to the right or left side of the image.

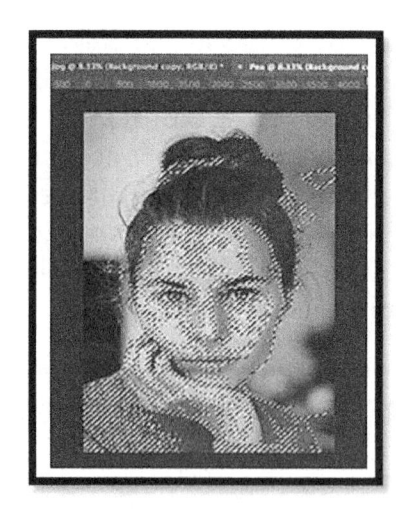

Once you have the desired skin tone area selected, you can proceed by clicking the OK button. The locations that have been selected will be indicated on your image by marching ants. It is not necessary to be concerned if undesirable areas have been selected, such as hair color or foreground color, because they are comparable to skin tones. Using the Quick Selection Tool, you can quickly deselect these if you so choose. Choose the Quick Selection tool from the toolbar, or hit the "W" button on your keyboard. Check the brush size in the options box, then hold the Alt key (on Windows) or the Option key (on Mac) and drag over the portions of the image that you do not want to be deselected.

Step 3 – Create a Curves Adjustment Layer

It is time to build a selective color adjustment layer now that you have highlighted the region that requires editing and have selected it. Go to the **Adjustment Panel** and then choose the **Curves** icon; doing so will open the Curves Panel. In the panel that displays the layers, a new Adjustment Layer for Curves will be made. This allows you to return to the skin color adjustment at a later time. You can target a very specific skin tone by using the RGB tab to make your selection. Choose Red from the color palette drop-down menu if you wish to adjust the amount of red tones in the skin tone. Alternatively, if you need to alter the tints of blue or green, you can select the Blue or Green option. To adjust the tones, you need to click on the line, and then drag the curve. You can drag and curve anywhere along the line, including the middle of the line as well as the edges. Keep an eye on the image until you find the precise skin color that you want. You now have the final image with the ideal skin color after completing the entire process.

CHAPTER FOURTEEN
WORKING WITH LAYERS

This chapter digs into the fundamentals of working with layers in Photoshop and covers a variety of topics. The use of layers, an essential component of the program, enables exact control over and arrangement of the various components that make up a composition. The Layers panel, which is the key hub for managing layers in Photoshop, is the focus of the first section of this guide, which explains how to navigate it. This includes converting layers from one kind to another as well as converting layers between different types. You will learn how to add new layers, copy existing layers, rename existing layers, as well as show and hide layers. The addition of layer styles, the modification of stacking order, and the adjustment of layer opacity are also covered in this section.

This chapter discusses many methods for altering the appearance of a layer's final product, including ways for rotating and resizing layers, duplicating those layers, and employing different blending modes. Important subjects covered in this chapter include dealing with gradients, layer styles, and adjustment layers, as well as applying filters, inserting text with special effects, and working with layer styles. In addition to that, it discusses the process of adding borders to photographs as well as merging, flattening, and saving files. In addition, the chapter offers advice on designing patterns that can be used to build borders for photos, which is something that can help add embellishments to pictures. The reader will emerge from this chapter with an in-depth understanding of how to deal with layers in Photoshop, which will enable them to construct intricate and aesthetically pleasing compositions with a high level of precision and originality.

ADOBE PHOTOSHOP LAYERS

Every Photoshop file consists of at least one content layer. Once a new layer is added to an image, the picture appears to have a translucent quality until further elements such as text or artwork are added to it. The method of working with layers is analogous to the technique of arranging pieces of a drawing on translucent sheets of film, similar to those that can be seen through an overhead projector: It is possible to make changes to, reorganize, or delete individual sheets without affecting the functionality of any other sheets that have been modified. It is possible to see the entirety of the composition once the sheets have been laminated. It is common practice to add a background layer in Photoshop files that are intended for printing. This is also common practice for digital camera shots and scanned photographs.

Likely, Photoshop files created specifically for mobile devices and websites won't include a background layer in their structure. For example, photos intended for websites might need to have certain portions that are transparent so that they won't hide the page's background or other elements.

There is not the slightest shred of doubt that the utilization of layers in Adobe Photoshop is without a doubt the single most important aspect of this program. There is nothing worth doing in Photoshop that can be done without layers, or at the very least, there shouldn't be anything that can be done without layers. They are believed to be of such value that Photoshop gives them their very own Layers panel in addition to their very own Layer category in the Menu Bar that runs along the top of the screen. This is because Photoshop considers layers to be of such significant importance. You can create new layers, remove existing layers, name and rename existing layers, group layers, move layers, mask layers, blend layers together, add effects to levels, alter the opacity of layers, and much more! Your layout might benefit from the addition of some text, doesn't it? It will show as its separate entry on the Type layer. Instead of utilizing raster shapes, why not try using vector shapes? They will be displayed on separate Shape layers each in their own right. The most crucial component of Photoshop is the Layers panel. It's a good thing that once you have your bearings beneath you, layers are so easy to use and understand since that's when you'll appreciate having them. At the very least, the fact that they are so straightforward is a benefit in disguise.

NAVIGATING AROUND THE LAYERS PANEL

You can view the layers that are contained within our document by selecting the Layers panel from the menu. On the other hand, the Layers panel has a lot more capability than it initially appears to have. It serves as the command and control center for the layers. When we need to perform any actions in Photoshop that involve interacting with layers, we go to the Layers panel to do so. Anything that has to be done in Photoshop will be carried out in that program. The Layers panel is where we go to add new layers, remove existing layers, rename layers, move layers around, turn layers on and off in the project, apply layer masks and layer effects, and a variety of other tasks. This panel has an almost infinite number of applications that might be used for various purposes. Additionally, any changes can be made from within the Layers panel.

When the software is first opened, the Layers panel can be found in the bottom right corner of the screen. You can access the Layers panel (as well as any of Photoshop's other panels) by going to the Window menu in the Menu Bar that runs along the top of the screen and selecting Layers. This will allow you to access the Layers panel even if it is not currently displayed on your screen. You will now have access to all of Photoshop's panels as a result of doing this.

If there is a checkmark to the left of the name of a panel, this indicates that the panel is now visible on the screen at some location:

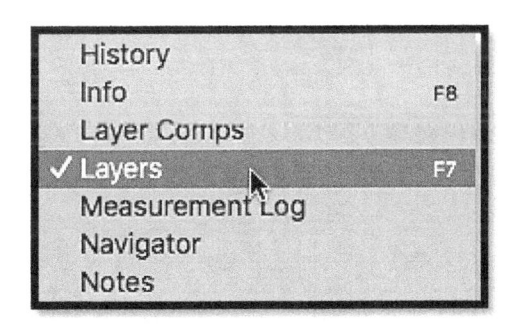

History
Info   F8
Layer Comps
✓ Layers   F7
Measurement Log
Navigator
Notes

Because Photoshop contains a large number of panels, it can be challenging to display all of them on the screen while still maintaining a sufficient amount of working space. As a result of this, Adobe concluded that the best way to conserve screen real estate would be to group certain panels and call such groups panel groups. To go to a different panel inside a group, you need just click on the tab that corresponds to the panel. The tab of the panel that is presently open in the group is highlighted. This occurs when the group is opened. You shouldn't let the fact that the Layers panel is crammed in between these two other panels throw you off; still, you need to pay attention to what you're doing to avoid making any mistakes. While we concentrate on the Layers panel, we may safely ignore the Channels and Paths panels because they are not connected to the Layers panel in any way, shape, or form. The only similarity between the Channels and Paths panels and the Layers panel is that both are utilized frequently in Photoshop.

The Layer Row

When we open a new picture in Photoshop, the computer automatically generates a new document that is tailored to that particular image and places the image on a layer. In Photoshop, the Layers panel, which is a representation of the layers in the project, provides each layer in the document with its row. This row serves as a label for the layer. In relation to the layer, we are given a new piece of information about each row. Because my project only contains one layer at the moment, the Layers panel is only displaying one row of information in its grid. This is because there is only one layer to display. On the other hand, as we continue to add more layers, we will eventually build more rows.

The Layer Name

When a new photo is made in Photoshop, it will automatically be saved under a layer that is labeled Background. Because of the function that it serves in our paper, this part should be referred to by its proper name, the background. For our convenience, the name of each layer has been included in the row that corresponds to it. When working with Photoshop, one of the different types of layers that you can add to your document is called the **Background layer**.

The Preview Thumbnail

To the left of the layer's name is a small image that serves as a thumbnail preview. Since it gives a sneak peek at the content of the layer in question, this thumbnail image is referred to as the layer's preview thumbnail. This is because it displays a preview of the content. In my case, the preview thumbnail reveals that my image is situated on the Background layer of the layer stack. This information is provided by the layer stack itself.

Adding a New Layer

If you want to add a new layer to a document, you can do it by selecting the Layers panel and then clicking the "**New Layer**" icon that can be found at the bottom of the panel: There is now a new layer that has been created that can be found in the Layers panel directly above the Background layer. Photoshop will automatically give names to any new layers that are produced in the program. In this particular scenario, it referred to the layer as "**Layer 1.**" If you take a look at the preview thumbnail for the new layer, you will see that it has a checkerboard pattern. You can see in the software that Photoshop uses a checkerboard pattern to represent transparency. This pattern is visible in the program. Because the preview thumbnail does not display anything outside its default contents, you can deduce that the newly created layer does not include any content at this time. This indicates that the new layer is now vacant for use.

Moving Layers

Simply dragging a layer in the Layers panel will allow us to move it either above or below another layer in the stack. This is one of the many useful features of Adobe Photoshop. Layer 2 is currently positioned above Layer 1, but I can shift it so that it is below Layer 1 by clicking on Layer 2, holding down the left mouse button, and dragging the layer downward until a highlight bar appears between Layer 1 and the Background layer. This will change the position of Layer 2 from above to below Layer 1. Because of this, Layer 2 will migrate from its present location above Layer 1 to its new location below Layer 1. You are free to let go of the button on your mouse once the highlight bar appears.

In Photoshop, the layer is moved to its new position in the following manner:

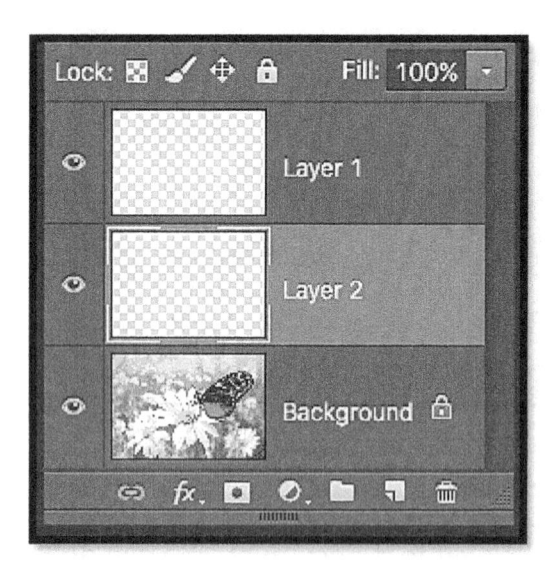

Only the Background layer in the Layers panel cannot be altered; all other layers can be rearranged freely. In addition, we are unable to move any additional levels underneath the Background layer. This is a limitation of the software. Every other layer can be changed to whichever location is required, even if it means moving it over or below previous levels.

The Active Layer

If a layer is highlighted, this signifies that it is the layer that is now being used in the editing process. Any modification that we make to the document itself will result in corresponding alterations being made to the contents of the layer that is currently active. Nevertheless, we can manually change which layer is the active layer by simply clicking on the layer that we want to use as our new active layer. When we add a new layer to a project in Photoshop, the program will immediately set the newly added layer as the active layer.

Deleting a Layer

To get rid of a layer, click on it, and then, while keeping pressure on the left mouse button, drag it until it drops onto the trash can symbol at the bottom of the Layers panel. This is how you get rid of layers. You can release your grip on the button on the mouse once you have reached the appropriate height above the icon.

Copying a Layer

We can learn not only how to add a new blank layer to a project but also how to generate a clone of an existing layer by making use of the Layers panel in Adobe Photoshop. To make a copy of a layer, first choose the layer you want to copy by clicking on it, and then while holding down the left mouse button, drag the selected layer onto the icon labeled New Layer. When you are in the position where you can see the icon for the New Layer, you can release the button on your mouse. On top of the original layer, you will see a copy of the layer that has been duplicated.

Renaming a Layer

Either double-click on the layer in the Layers Panel (click on Window, then choose Layers) or select the layer on the Canvas, then go to "**Layer**" in the main menu, then select "**Rename Layer**" to rename the layer in Photoshop.

Rename a layer in Photoshop by making use of the Layers Panel

Double-clicking on the layer's name in the "**Layers**" panel is the simplest, quickest, and most common way to rename it. This method is also the most common. It should get highlighted and chosen once you double-click on it. The following thing you need to do is use the "**Backspace**" button on your keyboard to get rid of the current name. After you have removed the previous name, you will need to write in the new name for the layer that you want to use, and then either press **Enter** (on Windows) or Return (on a MAC).

Rename a layer in Photoshop by using "Layer" in the main menu

Utilizing the option that can be found in the main menu is the second method for renaming the Layer. If you wish to alter the name of only one layer, you can do it by selecting the layer on the Canvas, going to the main menu, clicking on "**Layer**," and then selecting "**Rename Layer.**" Rename it and after you finish, press **Enter** (Windows) or **Return** (MAC). If you want to rename a group, select it, and in the same way rename it, but this time, choose the **"Rename Group"** option.

The Layer Search Bar

Using the Search Bar, we can quickly navigate through a document's various layers. Because of this, we can recognize a certain layer, examine only a specific category of layers, or see only the layers that meet a given set of requirements. To utilize the Search Bar, select a filter type from the menu that appears to the left of the bar. Because the filter type is set to Kind by default, when we use it, we will be instructing Photoshop to show only a particular layer category. This is because the Kind setting is the default for the filter type. You will see some alternatives to the right of the box indicating the type of filter that you have chosen, and the specifics of these options will change depending on the type of filter that you have chosen. When you select the Kind option, a row of icons will show up in front of you. Each icon in this row represents a different category of layer. From left to right, this graphic demonstrates pixel layers, adjustment layers, type layers, form layers, and smart objects. The order of these layers is left to right. When you select one of these icons, the layers in your project will be filtered so that you can view only the layers that are associated with a particular category. This will allow you to work more efficiently. You can view two or more distinct kinds of layers at the same time by clicking on multiple icons within the layer window. A simple double-click on an icon will deselect it and remove it from the search entirely.

In the document that we are currently working on, for instance, there is currently one adjustment layer as well as two-pixel layers present. If we were only interested in viewing the pixel layers, we could select the icon that is labeled "**pixel layers**" from the menu. Because of this, our adjustment layer would be hidden from view in the Layers panel, revealing only the two-pixel layers that are listed below:

However, it is essential to bear in mind that filtering layers in the Layers panel will not turn off the other layers that are present in the document. This is something that must be kept in mind at all times. The fact that they are hidden is the sole thing that renders them invisible in the Layers panel itself.

Even if the Hue/Saturation adjustment layer is not now being shown in the Layers panel, the effects of the layer can still be observed when we look at our photo in the manner shown below:

SHOW/HIDE LAYER

Simply clicking on the small eye icon that is located to the left of the layer's thumbnail within the Layers panel will cause that layer to be hidden from view. To view it once more, click the spot where the Eye icon was previously displayed. If you want to see only one specific layer (and conceal all the others), hit and hold the Option (PC: Alt) key, and then click on the Eye icon that corresponds to the layer you want to see. Only the layer that you're currently looking at will be visible in the future, with the other layers being hidden away. Option-clicking on the Eye icon again will bring them all back.

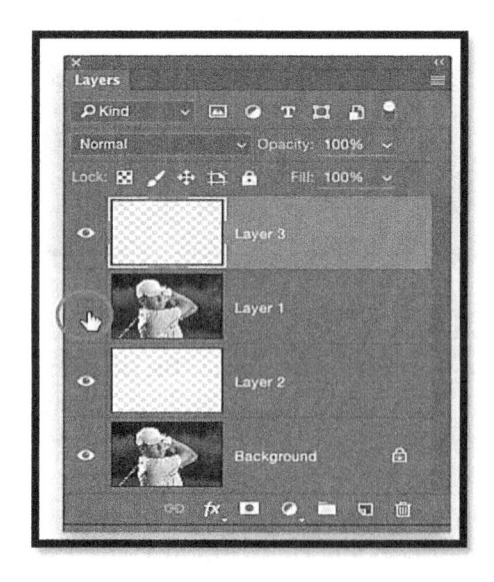

Locking Layers

The Layers panel also gives us a selection of options that we can use to lock particular aspects of a layer. We may utilize these options to prevent accidental changes. For example, if part of a layer is transparent, we can lock those transparent pixels so that we can only change the content of the layer itself and not the transparent sections. This prevents accidental changes to the transparent areas. Because of this, we will not inadvertently be able to change the appearance of the transparent areas. We also have the option of locking all of the pixels, regardless of whether or not they are translucent. This will prevent us from making any changes to the layer that is currently active. We also have the option of locking the location of the layer, which stops us from accidentally moving it within the document itself and gives us more control over how it looks.

You can also select from four distinct locks, each of which is marked by a small icon, and they are located directly below the Blend Mode option in the menu. **Lock Position, Lock Image Pixels, Lock Transparent Pixels,** and **Lock locking** all of the pixels on the layer, even the ones that are transparent will lock the position and all of the pixels on the layer. From left to right, these are all the possibilities that are open to us as we move through the various selections. Simply click the symbol of the lock option you want to use to activate it. By selecting the same lock option a second time, the lock can be unlocked. It is essential to bear in mind that before any of the lock options may become available to you; you will first need to select a real pixel layer, such as our Blur layer. This is a prerequisite that cannot be overlooked.

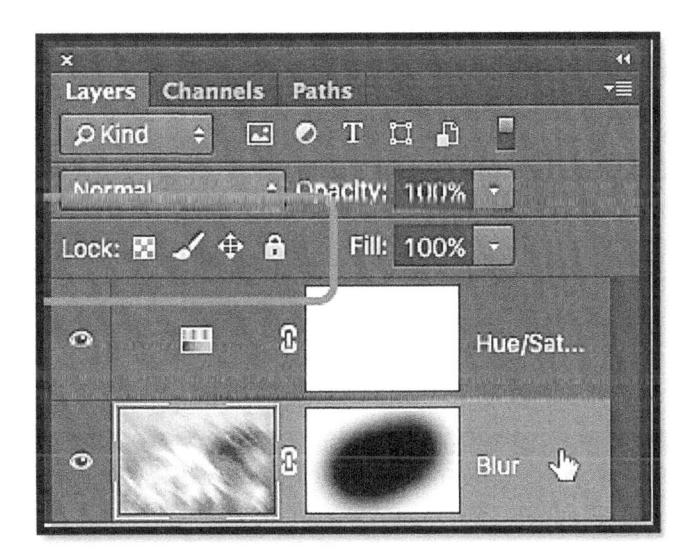

You will notice a little lock symbol appears on the far right of the locked layer, which is locked by default if any of these choices are chosen, and you can pick any or all of these options.

ADDING LAYER STYLE TO A LAYER

Additionally, at the bottom of the Layers panel is the icon for the Layer Styles. The "fx" mark in the icon should be interpreted as Layer Effects because Layer Styles are occasionally referred to as such. Layer styles give us simple ways to apply many different kinds of effects to layers, including glows, strokes, and shadows, among many others. A menu with a variety of effects will show up when you use your mouse to pick the Layer Styles icon.

Let's examine some of the most popular layer styles in more detail, along with some tips for using them.

1. **Drop Shadow**: This layer style gives the layer underneath it a shadow. This effect is great for adding dimension and depth to your work. You can alter the shadow's color, size, opacity, angle, and distance.
2. **Bevel & Emboss**: Using this layer style, your layer appears three-dimensional. By choosing from a range of bevel and emboss styles, such as Inner Bevel, Outer Bevel, and Pillow Emboss, you can change the effect's size, depth, and angle.
3. **Inner Glow**: Your layer has a faint sheen thanks to the Inner Glow layer style. This effect is great for creating an appearance of something glowing or backlit. You can adjust the glow's hue, blending mode, opacity, and size.

4. **Outer Glow**: This layer style adds a subtle sheen to the edges of your layer. This effect is useful for creating aura or halo effects. You can adjust the glow's hue, blending mode, opacity, and size.
5. **Stroke**: A border surrounds your layer when you use the Stroke layer style. The size, color, and opacity of the stroke can all be altered, as can its placement inside the layer.

LAYERS STACKING ORDER

Complex composites of several layers deep can be made. With Photoshop, you can work with several layers as a single object by grouping them into a stack and moving them around quickly. Lock a layer to prevent inadvertent modifications to your work.

Change the order of layers and layer groups

You can do any of the following to alter the arrangement of layers and layer groups:

- In the Layers panel, drag the layer or group up or down. When a highlighted line appears where you wish to position the chosen layer or group, release the mouse button.
- Drag a layer to the group folder to add it to a group. The layer is positioned at the bottom of the group if it is closed.
- After selecting a group or layer, select **Layer > Arrange**, then pick a command from the menu. The command affects the group's stacking order if the item you have chosen is part of it. The command affects the Layers panel's stacking order if the selected item is not part of a group.
- Select **Layer > Arrange > Reverse** to change the order of the selected layers. If you do not have at least two layers chosen, some options appear darkened.

The background layer is always at the bottom of the stacking sequence by definition. Consequently, the selected object is positioned immediately above the background layer when using the Send to back command.

ADJUSTING THE OPACITY OF A LAYER

1. **Open Your Image**: Start by opening the image or document you want to work on in Photoshop.
2. **Select the Layer**: In the Layers panel, locate the layer that you want to adjust the opacity for. Click on the layer to select it.
3. **Adjusting Opacity with the Opacity Slider**:
    - **Method 1**: Directly on the Layers Panel

- In the Layers panel, you will see an "Opacity" slider at the top of the selected layer.
- Click and drag the slider left to decrease opacity (making the layer more transparent) or right to increase opacity (making the layer more opaque).
- Release the mouse button when you reach the desired opacity level.
- **Method 2**: Through the Layer Blending Options
    - Right-click on the layer in the Layers panel.
    - From the context menu, select "Blending Options."
    - In the Layer Style dialog that appears, locate the "Opacity" slider under the "General Blending" section.
    - Adjust the slider as needed to change the opacity of the layer.
4. **Using the Opacity Field**:
    - Alternatively, you can manually enter the desired opacity percentage in the field next to the opacity slider.
5. **Preview and Confirm**:
    - As you adjust the opacity, you will see real-time changes in your document. This allows you to preview the effect.
    - When you are satisfied with the opacity level, you can either click outside the opacity slider or press Enter/Return to confirm your changes.
6. **Save Your Work**: Once you are happy with the opacity adjustment, don't forget to save your image or document to preserve the changes.

Adjusting layer opacity is particularly useful for various tasks, such as:

- **Creating Fades and Transitions**: You can improve the visual attractiveness of your designs by creating seamless transitions between various elements by decreasing the opacity of a layer.
- **Text Overlays**: To make sure that the text doesn't entirely hide the underlying image when you place text over it, you might need to decrease the opacity. This is typical of typography and design.
- **Adding Depth**: You can give your artwork more depth and dimension by varying the opacity of the highlights, shadows, and other effects.
- **Adding Watermarks**: Reducing the opacity of the watermark layer guarantees that it remains visible while not detracting from the main content if you wish to add one to your photographs.
- **Blending photos**: Modifying the opacity of a layer facilitates the smooth blending of elements when compositing or blending numerous photos.

Recall that adjusting a layer's opacity is a non-destructive editing method, which means that the original image or layer is not permanently changed. As you work creatively, you can always go back and change the opacity as necessary.

ROTATING AND RESIZING LAYERS

To alter the appearance of objects, text, and other visual elements in your design, you can modify the size and rotation of layers in Adobe Photoshop. This lets you resize, reposition, and orient the information to better fit your arrangement.

You can resize a layer by using the Free Transform tool, which also allows you to skew, distort, and scale its content. As follows:

1. Select the layer you wish to resize from the Layers panel.
2. Press Ctrl+T on a PC or Command+T on a Mac to launch the Free Transform tool, or select Edit > Free Transform.
3. You can click and drag any of the bounding box's corner handles to resize the layer accordingly.
4. To skew or distort the layer, hold down the Ctrl key (or the Command key on a Mac) and drag any of the corner handles.
5. Hit **Enter (or Return)** to save the modification.

A separate set of handles is available for the Free Transform tool, which can also be used to rotate a layer. As follows:

1. Select the layer you wish to rotate from the Layers panel.
2. Press Ctrl+T on a PC or Command+T on a Mac to launch the **Free Transform** tool, or select **Edit > Free Transform**.
3. Hover your cursor over the area outside the bounding box until you see a double-headed, curved arrow.
4. Use the mouse to click and drag the layer to rotate it.
5. Hit **Enter (or Return)** to save the modification.

As an alternative, you can use the rotate tool to accurately rotate a layer. As follows:

1. Select the layer you wish to rotate from the Layers panel.
2. Select **Edit > Transform > Rotate** (or hit Ctrl+Shift+R on a PC or Command+Shift+R on a Mac) to launch the Rotate tool.
3. Click and drag the mouse outside the enclosing box to rotate the layer.
4. Hit **Enter (or Return)** to modify.

Using the menu options under Edit > transform, you can also access more transformation tools such as warp, scale, skew, distortion, and perspective. Because each of these tools allows you to modify a layer's content in a variety of ways, you have more control over the aesthetic elements of your design. Remember that when extending and rotating layers, excessive stretching or extreme angle rotation can cause them to become pixelated or distorted. Wherever you can use high-resolution photographs, and try to keep your edits within reasonable bounds to avoid this. Furthermore, you can use the Align and Distribute options under the Layer menu to align multiple layers or distribute them evenly throughout your canvas. By doing this, you can create compositions that are more precise and harmonious.

BLEND MODES

Blending Modes are mathematical equations that blend layers based on their hue, saturation, brightness, or any combination of these three characteristics. Blending Modes are used in Adobe Photoshop. Without having to create layer masks, you can target certain portions of your image and apply overlays, textures, or target modifications by using Blending Modes. Blending Modes are a fantastic tool for creating effects in a way that is not damaging. The pixels themselves are unaffected by the blend you apply; only the visual output is altered. The Blending Mode can be altered at any time, or it can be removed entirely.

You must have at least two layers for the Blend Modes to function properly. The layer that comes before the Blend layer is called the Base layer. The layer that comes after it is called the Blend layer. The Blending Mode controls the type of blending operation that is carried out on the Blend layer. Photoshop performs a blend operation on each pixel of the Blend layer against its matching pixel in the Base layer to blend the pixels while dealing with Blending Modes. To explain it another way, the blend is applied to a single pixel at a time to obtain the desired outcome.

Blending mode descriptions

- Choose from the **Mode pop-up** menu in the options bar.

Note:

- In the pop-up menu for the Blend Mode, you can see how different selections look on your image by scrolling over them in the menu. On the canvas, Photoshop presents a real-time preview of the various blend modes.

- The only blending modes that are accessible for 32-bit pictures are Normal, Dissolve, Darken, Multiply, Lighten, Linear Dodge (Add), Difference, Hue, Saturation, Color, Luminosity, Lighter Color, and Darker Color.

Normal mode

Edits or paints each pixel to change its color to the desired effect. This is the mode that is chosen by default. (When you are working with a bitmapped or indexed-color image, the Normal mode will be referred to as the Threshold mode.)

Dissolve

Edits or paints each pixel so that they all have the same color as the final result. However, the color that is produced is a result of randomly replacing the pixels with either the base color or the blend color, and this color is determined by the opacity of each pixel.

Behind

Edits or paints solely on the portion of a layer that is translucent when using the Behind mode. This mode can only be used in layers that do not have the **Lock Transparency** option enabled. It functions similarly to painting on the reverse side of sections that are transparent on a sheet of acetate.

Clear

Clear makes each pixel transparent after being edited or painted by the user. This mode can be used with the Fill command, the Stroke command, the Paint Bucket tool, the Brush tool, the Pencil tool, and the Shape tools when the fill region checkbox is chosen. To use this mode, you need to be in a layer that does not have the Lock Transparency option set.

Darken

Examines the color information included in each channel, then chooses as the result color either the base or blend color, based on which of the two is darker. Pixels that are darker than the blend color will not change, while pixels that are lighter than the blend color will be replaced.

Multiply

Multiply performs an analysis of the color information contained in each channel before multiplying the blend color by the base color. The end color is invariably a shade darker than the starting color. Any color, when multiplied with black, will give the color black. White does not affect the hue of any color when multiplied with other colors. When painting with a color other than black or white, each subsequent stroke you make with a painting tool will result in a color that is a darker shade than the previous one. The effect is comparable to sketching the image with some different marking pens at the same time.

Color Burn

This examines the color information contained in each channel, and then darkens the base color so that it more accurately reflects the blend color by increasing the contrast between the two colors. There is no discernible difference after blending with white.

Linear Burn

This is a technique that examines the color information in each channel, and then reduces the brightness of the base color to make it darker so that it reflects the blend color. There is no discernible difference after blending with white.

Lighten

Examines the color information included in each channel, then chooses as the result color either the base or blend color, based on which of the two is lighter. Pixels that are lighter than the blend color are not affected by the change, whereas pixels that are darker than the blend color are replaced.

Screen

This examines the color information from each channel and multiplies it by the inverse of the colors used for the blend and the base. The end color is invariably one shade lighter than the starting color. The color will not be affected when black is used as a screen. When screened with white, the result is white. The appearance is comparable to that achieved by superimposing some photographic slides on top of one another.

Color Dodge

Performs an analysis of the color information contained in each channel and, based on the results, either increases the brightness of the base color or decreases the contrast between the two colors. There is no discernible difference after blending with black.

Linear Dodge (Add)

This takes into account the color information contained in each channel and then boosts the brightness of the base color so that it more accurately reflects the color of the blend. There is no discernible difference after blending with black.

Overlay

Depending on the color used as the base, it either multiplies or screens the colors. Patterns or colors are superimposed on top of the pixels that are already there, but the highlights and shadows of the underlying color are kept intact. The base color is not changed; rather, it is combined with the blend color to achieve the desired degree of lightness or darkness in the finished product.

Soft Light

Changes the hue by either darkening or lightening it, depending on the color of the blend. The effect is comparable to shining a spotlight that is somewhat dispersed on the image. When the blend color, also known as the light source, is darker than 50% gray, the image is darkened so that it appears to have been dodged. If the blend color is darker than 50% gray, the image will appear to have been burned in since it will get darker. When you paint with pure black or white, the resulting area will be noticeably darker or lighter, but it will not be black or white in its purest form.

Hard Light

Depending on the hue of the blend, hard light either multiplies the colors or screens them out. The result is something like throwing a bright spotlight on the picture. When the blend color, also known as the light source, is darker than 50% gray, the image is darkened so that it appears to have been screened. The addition of highlights to an image is facilitated by using this tool. When the blend color is darker than 50% gray, the image is darkened as if it were doubled. This has the same effect as if the blend color were black. The addition of shadows to an image is facilitated by using this tool. When you paint with pure black or white, the resulting color is also pure black or white.

Vivid Light

Depending on the color that is being blended, Vivid Light will either "**burn**" or "**dodge**" the colors by raising or diminishing the contrast. If the blend color (light source) is lighter than 50% gray, then the contrast in the image will be decreased, which will result in the image appearing lighter. If the blend color is darker than 50% gray, then the contrast of the image will be increased to make the image darker.

Linear Light

Depending on the color of the mix, Linear Light either "**burns**" or "**dodges**" the colors by diminishing or boosting the brightness of the colors. The brightness of the image is increased to lighten it if the blend color, also known as the light source, is lighter than fifty percent gray. If the blend color is darker than 50% gray, then the brightness of the image will be decreased to make the image darker.

Pin Light

Replaces the colors in a blend, based on the hue of the mix. Pixels darker than the blend color are replaced, but pixels lighter than the blend color do not change if the blend color (light source) is lighter than 50% gray. Pixels lighter than the blend color are replaced whereas pixels darker than the blend color do not change when the blend color is darker than 50% gray. When modifying an image with this, several special effects can be applied.

Hard Mix

The RGB values of the base color are modified by the addition of the values from the blend color's red, green, and blue channels. If the final sum for a channel is larger than 255, then that channel is assigned the value 255; if the final sum is less than 255, then that channel is assigned the value 0. As a consequence of this, the values of the red, green, and blue channels of every blended pixel are either 0 or 255. This modifies each pixel such that it is white, black, or one of the three major additive colors (red, green, or blue). Note that when you use the Hard Mix filter on a CMYK image, all of the pixels are converted to one of the three fundamental subtractive hues (cyan, yellow, or magenta), white, or black. 100 is the highest possible value for the color.

Difference

Examine the color information contained in each channel and then either remove the blend color from the base color or remove the base color from the blend color, depending on which of the two colors has a higher brightness value. When blending with white, the basic color values are inverted, while blending with black does not affect the color.

Exclusion

The Exclusion mode produces an effect that is analogous to that of the Difference mode but has lower contrast. When you mix a base color with white, the values of the base color are inverted. There is no discernible difference after blending with black.

Subtract

Takes into consideration the color information included in each channel, and then subtracts the base color from the blend color. Any resulting negative values in 8-bit and 16-bit pictures are trimmed to zero before being saved.

Divide

Examine the color information contained in each channel, and then calculate the ratio of the base color to the blend color.

Hue

Produces a result color that has the luminance and saturation of the base color as well as the hue of the blend color. Hue can be used in conjunction with Saturation and Luminosity.

Saturation

The luminance and hue of the base color are used to create the result color, while the saturation of the blend color is used to create the result color. When using this mode to paint on a gray area, there is no change to the region as a result of the painting.

Color

Produces a new color with the brightness of the base color combined with the hue and saturation of the blend color in the result color. This is handy for coloring monochrome photos as well as tinting color images because it maintains the gray levels that were there in the original image.

Luminosity

Produces a new color that takes on the hue and saturation of the base color while taking on the brightness of the blend color as its output. This mode produces an effect that is opposed to that of the Color mode.

Lighter Color

Displays the color that has a greater value based on a comparison of the sum of all the channel values for the blend and the base color. Lighter Color does not produce a third color, which can result from the Lighten blend, because it chooses the highest channel values from both the base color and the blend color to create the result color. This prevents the creation of the third color that can occur from the Lighten mix.

Darker Color

Displays the color that has a lower value after comparing the blends and the base color's sum of all channel values for each of the colors. Because it selects the channel values with the lowest absolute value from both the base color and the blend color to create the result color, the Darker Color adjustment does not result in the production of a third color like the Darken blend can.

APPLYING A FILTER TO CREATE A DESIGN

Step 1: Open Your Image or Start with a New Canvas

- Either open an image that is already saved on your computer or create a new canvas by selecting "**File**" > "**New**" and entering the dimensions and resolution that you want for your creation.

Step 2: Create or Import Your Design Elements

- Include the design components that you intend to use in your work. This can incorporate text, shapes, photos, or any other graphic components you like. In Photoshop, you have the option of either creating these items from scratch or importing them from external sources.

Step 3: Select the Layer to Apply the Filter

- In the Layers panel, choose the layer that includes the design element that you want to apply the filter to. This will ensure that the filter is applied correctly. Be sure that you are working on the appropriate layer if you are manipulating numerous components at once.

Step 4: Apply the Filter

- While keeping the layer selected, navigate to the "Filter" option located in the main menu. You will see a dropdown menu that provides access to a variety of filter categories, some of which are **Artistic, Blur, Distort, and Stylize**, among others.
- Determine which of the available filter categories best fits the concept of your design. You could, for instance, select "Artistic" to apply a filter such as "Oil Paint" or "Cutout," or you could select "Stylize" to apply filters such as "Glowing Edges" or "Wind." The impact that you are going for will determine the filter you end up going with specifically.
- Once you have chosen a category for the filter, you will be shown the available filter options. You can customize the impact by adjusting these options to suit your preferences. The available options could change based on whatever filter you choose.
- When you are finished modifying the settings, click "OK" to apply the filter to the layer that is now selected.

Step 5: Review and Modify

- After applying the filter, you should examine the output carefully for a while. You can undo the filter by selecting "**Edit**" > "**Step Backward**" from the menu bar on a Mac or by using the Ctrl+Z or Command+Z keys on Windows.

Step 6: Combine Filters and Effects (Optional)

- You can make designs that are intricate and one-of-a-kind by applying various filters and effects to the same or separate layers in your project. Try out a variety of various combinations until you find the one that best suits you.

CREATING TEXT AND ADDING SPECIAL EFFECT

The application of special effects to text is a fantastic method for drawing attention to the text in question. The usage of Photoshop is currently one of the most popular methods for adding special effects to text, although there are many more methods available. In Photoshop, opening a new document and creating a new project are the first steps in applying special effects to text. Then, in the toolbar that is located at the very top of the screen, select the "T" icon. This will open the Type tool for you to use. You can manually type out the text to which you want to apply special effects by using the tool labeled "**Type**."

PRO TIP: Adding special effects to text in Photoshop can be fun, but it's important to be careful. If you're not careful, you could end up with text that is hard to read or doesn't look quite right.

When you have finished typing out your text, you can move on to the next step, which is to apply special effects. To accomplish this, select the "**FX**" symbol located in the layer panel and click on it. This will bring up a list of different special effects that you can use on the text layer that you're working on. Drop shadows, glows, and bevels are three of the most well-liked special effects now in use. Try out a variety of different effects up until you locate one that you particularly enjoy.

When you are satisfied with the effect that you have applied, you can exit the layer panel by clicking the "OK" button. After that, you can choose to either save your document or view it in your web browser to observe how it appears on a real website. Bringing attention to text is simple and effective when you use special effects in creative ways. You can modify the appearance of your text with a wide range of unique effects by using Photoshop. Simply type out your text, clicks on the "**FX**" icon located in the layer panel, and then play with the numerous effects available until you find one that you like.

APPLYING A GRADIENT TO A LAYER

Step 1: Create a new layer

In Photoshop, begin by making a new layer by clicking the "Create a new layer" button at the bottom of the Layers panel. Moreover, you can hit "**Command + Shift + N**" on a Mac or "**Ctrl + Shift + N**" on a PC.

Step 2: Select the Gradient tool

Next, select the Gradient tool from the toolbar on the left-hand side of the screen ( ).

Step 3: Choose a gradient type

From the options bar at the top of the screen, choose the type of gradient you wish to use. Photoshop offers a variety of gradient types, such as **linear, radial, angle, reflected, and diamond**. Select the option that most closely matches your design.

Step 4: Select the colors for your gradient

Click on the color swatches in the options bar to select your gradient colors. You can create your custom colors or select from a selection of pre-set colors by clicking on the color swatch and using the Color Picker.

Step 5: Apply the gradient

After choosing your colors and the Gradient tool, click and drag the tool over the layer to apply the gradient. You can adjust the gradient's length, angle, and placement by dragging the tool in different directions or by using the settings in the options bar.

Step 6: Adjust the gradient using layer styles

If you want to further refine the gradient, you can use layer styles to add effects like glows, strokes, and shadows. To apply a layer style, double-click the layer in the Layers panel and select "**Layer Style**" from the menu. From there, you can adjust the style's characteristics and select the style you wish to use.

Step 7: Save your work

Once your gradient is to your satisfaction, save your work by selecting **File > Save** or File > Save As.

Photoshop Gradient Application Tips

- **Experiment with different gradient types**: Photoshop offers a wide range of gradient types, so don't be afraid to try out different styles and angles to find the one that best fits your design.

- **Use multiple gradients**: You can make gradients that are more sophisticated by combining different gradient layers and layer styles. Using a radial gradient on one layer and a linear gradient on another, for example, can produce a more dynamic appearance.
- **Modify the opacity**: If the opacity of your gradient is too strong, you can use the Opacity slider in the Layers panel to lessen it. By doing this, you'll be able to convey a more subtle message.
- **Use layer masks**: If you just want to apply a gradient to a portion of a layer, you can use a layer mask to mask out the areas you don't want to include in the gradient. After adding a layer mask to your layer, just use the Brush tool to paint over the areas you wish to mask out.
- **Create custom gradients**: If you can't find the perfect gradient among Photoshop's preset selections, create your own by clicking on the gradient color swatches in the options bar and choosing "**New Gradient**" from the menu. After that, a new gradient can be made using the Gradient Editor.

About Adjustment Layers

A set of incredibly useful editing tools called Adjustment Layers can be discovered within the layers domain. With the help of these tools, you can easily modify your photos. To use most of Photoshop's features and achieve the same result, there are several ways to go about things. You can make changes, save the document as a Photoshop document (PSD), and then years later, undo or amend those edits when working with adjustment layers in Photoshop, in addition to other types of layers. Your original image is kept whole because no pixels are added, subtracted, or changed in any other way. Alright, let's start with the basics of using Photoshop's Adjustment Layers.

Accessing Photoshop Adjustment Layers

Accessing the Photoshop Adjustment Layers can be done in one of two methods.

1. To begin, pick **Layer > New Adjustment Layer** from the Layers menu. From the several options that appear, choose an adjustment type (described below).
2. Click the half-white, half-black circle at the bottom of the Layers Panel to open it, and then select the adjustment type you wish to work with from the drop-down box that appears.

Adjustment Layer Types

1. Brightness and Contrast

Two settings let you easily adjust the brightness and contrast of the image. These are called brightness and contrast. Each pixel in your image will have its overall lightness (or blackness) altered by adjustments to the brightness. You can enhance a photograph's highlights and tonal values by dragging the Brightness slider to the right.

To decrease a picture's tonal values and increase the shadows' depth at the same time, move the Brightness slider to the left. Conversely, the contrast option alters the difference in brightness between the different parts of your image. Every pixel will get lighter as the brightness is raised. Conversely, the light regions will get lighter and the dark portions will get darker if the contrast is increased.

2. Levels

You can change your picture's tone range and color balance with the levels tool. It achieves this by adjusting the shadow, midtone, and highlight intensities of the picture, in that order. Levels Presets can be instantly applied to additional photos after being saved.

It should be noted that no new layer will be created if you access the levels tool from the Image menu (**Image->Adjustments->Levels**). Rather, the alterations will be applied directly—and potentially disastrously—to the layer holding your picture. Therefore, choosing it from the Adjustment Layers menu is the best approach to obtaining this incredibly useful tool.

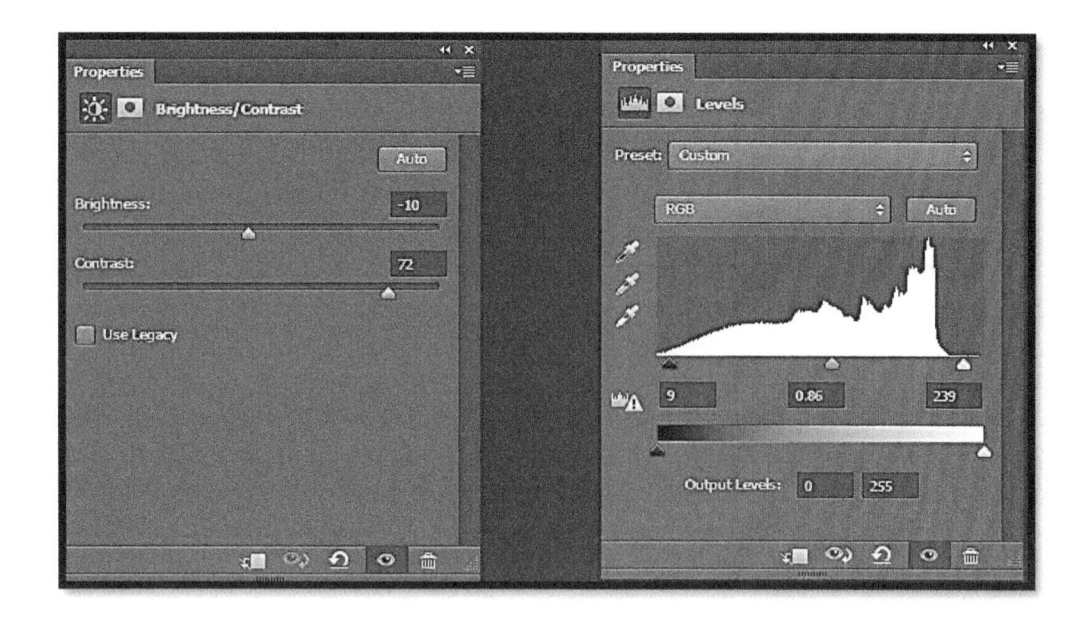

3. Curves

The Curves adjustment allows you to select the percentage of the tonal range that you would like to modify, as opposed to the Levels adjustment, which allows you to adjust all of the tones in your image proportionately. The highlights are displayed in the upper-right area of the Levels graph, while the shadows are displayed in the lower-left corner. If your image's contrast is off, you can adjust its tone by applying one of these adjustments (levels or curves) (too high or too low). The Levels Adjustment feature is particularly useful if you need to make a general tone adjustment to your recording. If you would like to make more targeted changes, you should utilize the Curves tool. This includes making adjustments to a small portion of the image's tonal range or just changing the image's lighter or darker tones.

4. Exposure

The goal of properly exposing a photograph is to capture the optimal brightness, which will allow you to see details in the subject's highlights and shadows. Three sliders are available for modifying the exposure, offset, and gamma of the picture in Photoshop's Adjustment Layers Exposure Adjustment panel. To make adjustments to the image, move the Exposure slider to alter the highlights, the Offset slider to alter the mid-tones, and the Gamma slider to focus solely on the dark tones of the image.

5. Vibrance

Using the Vibrance Adjustment Layer, you can make the colors in your photo look better. Increasing an image's vibrance has the lovely effect of highlighting areas with lesser saturation levels while leaving the colors that are currently at their peak unaltered.

6. Hue/Saturation

You can adjust the overall color hue of your image as well as the saturation level of the color with the help of hue and saturation. Maintaining "**Master**" selected in the dropdown menu will allow you to change the overall picture's tone (color); this is the default setting. Alternatively, you can click on the individual color whose hue you want to change after choosing it. You can choose from the following colors: magenta, cyan, blue, yellow, green, and red. In addition to editing the visible hue and saturation of your image's colors, this Photoshop Adjustment Layer allows you to alter the brightness of your image overall as well as the hue and saturation of individual colors. It's crucial to remember that adjusting the overall saturation of an image will impact its tonal range.

7. Color Balance

In addition to being a helpful tool for color modifications, the Color Balance Adjustment layer can be used to alter the overall color composition of an image. Whether you want to change an image's highlights, midtones, or shadows is the first thing you need to decide when adjusting the image's tonal range.

Before making any color alterations to your image, make sure to choose the **"Preserve Luminosity"** checkbox if you want the luminosity values to stay the same, regardless of how bright or dark they are. To increase or decrease the intensity of a color, move the slider closer to the desired color and farther away from the desired color.

8. Black and White

As its name implies, the black-and-white adjustment layer allows you to rapidly convert your photos to a grayscale format or alter the color of the image entirely. There are several techniques to process images; one of them is using black and white. The Photoshop Adjustment Layer for Black and White is among the most helpful. It helps enhance the quality of your black-and-white conversion by allowing you to brighten or darken specific color ranges. For instance, simply moving that slider will increase the blues' saturation when your color image is converted to black and white. You can change the brightness or darkness of individual colors to change the amount of contrast you see.

Important: While most of these adjustments can be accessed under the Image menu (Image > Adjustments), their usefulness in that particular context differs greatly. The primary difference is that when they are applied directly to the image, it is transformed, as opposed to when they are applied using Adjustment Layers. You can turn the adjustment on or off by selecting and deselecting the "eye" icon in the layers panel once it has been completed under Adjustment Layers. This will determine if the tweak is effective or not.

ADDING A BORDER TO THE IMAGE

Creating a solid border

Sometimes the best option is to go with a plain border. A solid border can make a big difference to an image. You can choose to use a color that highlights specific elements of your photo or stick with the classic white.

Step 1: Open your image in Photoshop.

Before you apply a border to your photo, make sure that any necessary Photoshop adjustments have been made. If there is no need to make changes to the document, move on to step three.

Step 2: Flatten the Edited Image

If you made any changes to your image, the resulting file will contain multiple layers, which you must first flatten or combine. Locate and click on the Layers Panel in the lower right corner of the screen. From the list of options, select "**Flatten Image**" when the drop-down selection appears.

Step 3: Unlock the Layer of Your Image

To apply a border, you might need to unlock the layer of your image. If needed, you can use the Layers Panel to achieve this. Navigating to the **Layers Panel** (bottom right corner of the screen) will allow you to find your picture. It is necessary to display a small padlock next to the picture. Click the padlock to release it. You can change the name of the layer that holds your photo when you first select it; it will initially be called **Layer 0**.

Step 4: Adjust Your Image Canvas Size to Accommodate a Border

Now is the time to make some room for the border. Select Canvas Size from the drop-down menu by navigating to the **Image tab** located at the top of the toolbar.

Step 5: Fill Out the Dialog Box Properly

It should display a "**Canvas Size**" dialog box. There are a few necessary actions to take at this point, but selecting "Relative" should be your initial step.

Step 6: Choose Your Border Dimensions

The width of your border is the next setting to be made in the **Canvas Size** dialog box. You can adjust this by sliding the sliders. The ideal fit is between one and two inches, but you can play about with the size of your image canvas. Generally speaking, one or two inches is ideal.

Step 7: Select a Color for the Border

The color that will be used for your border must be decided upon next. At the very bottom of the Canvas Size dialog box, next to a drop-down menu with a variety of color possibilities are the words "**Canvas extension color**." Just click on the color you wish to choose.

Step 8: Press OK.

Select OK from the menu that appears in the dialog box's top right corner to accept the changes and view your border. Once you press "**OK**," don't forget to save your photo.

Creating a Grunge Border

Step 1: Choose an Image of a Skyline

Whether the picture was shot outdoors or in a city is irrelevant. After starting Photoshop, open the file.

Step 2: Prep Your Image to Create the Grunge Border

Yes, the foundation for the grunge border you make is the picture of the skyline. Clicking on Image will take you to the main menu, where you can choose Adjustments and then Threshold. Setting the threshold to an extremely high value will result in a black-and-white image.

Step 3: Open a New Blank Canvas

Control/Command + A can be used to pick the image, and then **Control + C** can be used to copy it. To paste the image onto a fresh, empty canvas, copy it and then hit Ctrl or Command + V.

Step 4: Transform the Skyline Image

From the menu at the top of the screen, select **Edit**. Move the entire black-and-white image to the center of one of the edges by selecting **Free Transform** from the menu. Right now, you are just using one edge of your Grunge Border.

Step 5: Duplicate the Skyline Image into More Layers

So that you can create the remaining border sides, you must duplicate the layer. By navigating to the Layer panel and using the duplicate layer option, you can create three more sides.

Step 6: Build Your Border

After selecting each layer separately, use the "**Transform**" option to rotate and resize it so that it fits one of the image's sides. Continue doing this until the border is rectangular.

Step 7: Blend the Layers

You will need to alter each side of the rectangle such that it no longer looks uniform to create a true grunge border. Select **Blending Options and Layer Style** from the menus that show up in the Layer panel. Try creating slightly different sides for each layer until you achieve the desired outcome.

MERGING LAYERS

As more layers are added to an image, the file size of the image may see a substantial expansion. When multiple layers of an image are merged into one, the total size of the image's file might be reduced. You shouldn't merge layers until you have finished all of the necessary modifications to get the picture you want from the separate layers you have been working with individually. You have the option to combine only the layers that are connected, only the layers that are now visible, only a layer with the layer below it, or only the layers that you have chosen to merge. You also have the option of combining the contents of all visible levels into a single layer while maintaining the integrity of the other visible layers in the process. However, this will not result in a reduction in the overall size of the file. You can flatten an image once all of the processing on it has been performed and you are satisfied with the results. Flattening an image involves combining all of the visible layers, erasing any layers that are hidden from view, and filling any transparent areas with white.

- Launch the Layers panel and make sure that each of the layers you intend to combine has a checkmark next to it before you proceed with the merge. Check to see that the eye symbol has not been blocked out.

Do one of the following:

- To merge selected layers, pick more than one layer while holding down the Control key (or the Command key on Mac OS) and clicking each layer individually. This will allow you to merge the selected layers. This will enable you to blend the layers that you have chosen. When you right-click, the context menu will give you the option to Merge Layers.

- To merge a layer with the one below it, pick the layer that is on top of the pair, and then choose Merge Down from either the Layer menu or the Layers panel flyout menu. This will join the two layers. This will merge the one on top with the one below it in the layer stack.
- To merge all visible layers, you must first hide any layers that you do not wish to combine, and then select Merge Visible from either the Layer menu or the flyout menu of the Layers panel. This will join all of the layers that are currently visible.
- First, choose one of the linked layers, then navigate to the Layers panel's flyout menu or the Layers menu itself, and choose the option to Merge Linked from any of those menus. This will aggregate all of the visible layers that are related.

Merge layers into another layer

When combining layers, use this procedure when you want to keep the original quality of each one even after they have been combined. **The completed product consists of the individual layers in their original forms as well as a newly combined layer.**

- Ensure that the eye icon is visible and not crossed out for the layers that you do want to merge by clicking the eye icon that is situated next to the layers that you do not want to merge and ensuring that the icon is crossed out for the layers that you do want to merge. Ensure that the icon is visible and not crossed out for the layers that you do want to merge by clicking the eye icon that is positioned next to the layers that you do not want to merge.
- Select a layer to serve as the final destination for the merging of all visible layers, and then click **OK**. In the Layers panel, you have the option of either creating a new layer to merge into or selecting an existing layer to merge into. You can also choose not to merge into any layers at all.
- Select "**Merge Visible**" from the Layers menu or the **More** menu on the Layers panel while simultaneously holding down the **Alt key** (or the Option key on Mac OS). This will result in all of the visible layers being combined into a single layer. In Photoshop, whenever you choose a layer, a copy of all of the layers that are now visible get merged into that layer.

Convert the Background layer into a regular layer

One of the layers that can be found at the very bottom of a photograph is referred to as the Background layer. It is common practice to look for the principal picture data of a photograph within the Background layer of the associated photograph;

however, this is not always the case. The Background layer is covered by subsequent layers that are built upon it. Since this helps to prevent unintentional alterations to the picture, the Background layer is always locked. Before you can change the layer's opacity, stacking order, or blending mode, you need to first convert it into a regular layer. This is a prerequisite for making any other adjustments to the layer.

Take action in one of the following ways:

- In the Layers panel, double-click the **Background layer** to activate it.
- Select **Layer > New > Layer from Background** from the drop-down menu.
- Select the **Background layer**, and then from the **flyout** menu in the Layers panel, select the Duplicate Layer option. This will preserve the original Background layer while also creating a duplicate of it as a new layer.

FLATTENING AND SAVING FILES

You can lower the size of the file by either flattening the layers in your image or merging them once you have completed modifying each of the image's layers. When you flatten an image, all of the individual layers are merged into a single background layer. After you have flattened the layers, you will no longer be able to make any changes to them in any way. As a result of this, you should hold off on flattening a picture until you are very confident that you are satisfied with all of the design choices you have made. It is recommended that you make a copy of the file with its layers preserved rather than flattening the original Photoshop document (PSD) that you are working with. If you find that you need to modify a layer in the future, you will have the ability to do so using this method.

Take note of the two numbers that appear in the status bar at the very bottom of the document window. These numbers reflect the size of the file you are working with. You will gain a better understanding of what is meant by flattening after reading this. The first value indicates how large the resulting file would be if the image were to be flattened. The second number indicates how big the original file was before it was flattened. Choose any tool other than the **Type tool (type.jpg)** if you want to make sure that you are not operating in the mode that allows you to edit text as you work. After that, pick File > Save (if it is an option) to ensure that all of your changes have been successfully incorporated into the file. If this option is not available, select **File > Close** instead.

- From the menu, select **Image** and then select **Duplicate**.

- Before selecting the "**OK**" button, make sure that you have given the duplicated image the name "**04Flat.psd**" in the dialog box that is titled "Duplicate Image."
- It is recommended that you keep the 04Flat.psd file open while you close the other file.
- Using the menu that is found in the Layers panel, choose the **Flatten Image** option.

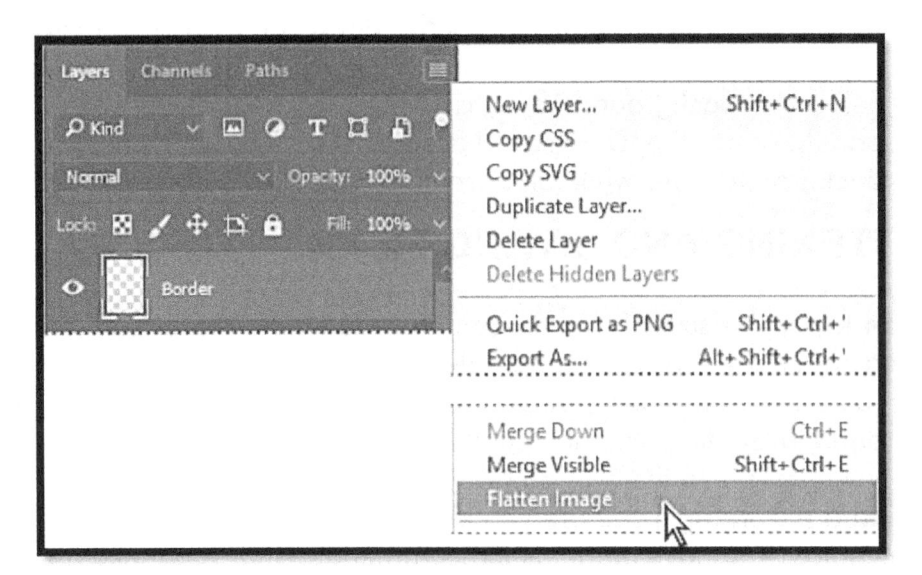

- To save your work, go to the "**File**" menu, then click "**Save**." Even though you choose Save rather than Save As, the Save As dialog box will continue to appear since this document has not yet been saved to the storage location you specified. Even when you choose to save, the situation remains the same.
- Ensure that the folder is selected as the destination, and then click the Save button to validate your decision to utilize the default settings and save the flattened file.

You have saved two separate versions of the file: one copy that has been reduced to a single layer and has been flattened and the other copy is the original file, which includes all of the layers in their unmodified form. You can hide the layers in the file that you do not want to flatten by clicking the eye icons in the Layers panel, and then you can select **Merge Visible** from the option in the Layers panel to flatten only the layers that you want to flatten. Because of this, you will be able to flatten only a portion of the layers contained in the file.

CREATING A PATTERN TO MAKE A BORDER

With the help of Photoshop's many features, which all collaborate to make this possible, you can build patterns in a way that is both quick and effective. In this section, you will develop a template for a new border that will be applied to the artwork that you have created and will surround it.

- Start up a file. Choose **Layer** > **Flatten Image** from the menu to flatten the image.
- Choose **Layer** > **New Fill Layer** > **Solid Color** (or whatever name you choose to give it), and then select the layer. Click the OK button, then use the color picker to select white for the Pattern Background, and finally, click the OK button once more.
- Navigate to "**File**" > "**Place Linked**," and following that "**Choose a folder**," "**Select a file**," before clicking "Click **Place**." After that, click "**OK**" from the "**Open as Smart Object**" dialog box, and once the graphic has been included in the document, press "Return" or "Enter" on your keyboard. Even though these are vector graphics that were generated with Adobe Illustrator, you will be able to create a pattern by merely utilizing the layers in Photoshop.

Select **View** > **Pattern Preview** from the main menu once you have zoomed out to a magnification of at least 30 percent but no more than that. If a warning message appears, you should dismiss it by clicking the **OK** option. Pattern Preview creates a simulation of what the document would look like if it were tiled as a pattern by repeating the content outside of the canvas. This creates a simulation of what the document would look like if it were tiled as a pattern. To include yet another element in the design, use the Ellipse tool to draw a dot in the right color, and then proceed to the next step.

You can refine your pattern by relocating, rotating, or scaling the picture and dot layers until you reach the desired appearance in the pattern preview. You can do this by clicking on the pattern and selecting the "**Edit Pattern**" option. You are free to add any number of additional layers that you see fit to the pattern. You can apply the modification by selecting **Edit** > **Define Pattern** from the menu bar, naming the pattern, and then clicking the OK button at the bottom of the window. By going to **View** > **Pattern Preview** and concealing the layers that comprise your design, you can deselect the pattern preview. Before continuing, you should make sure that the Pattern Background layer is the only one chosen. After that, go to **Layer** > **New Fill Layer** > **Pattern**, give the new layer the name Border, and then click the **OK** button. When you open the Pattern Fill dialog box, a pop-up menu with thumbnail samples of patterns will display. From this menu, you can select your brand-new pattern to use for the fill. After bringing the Scale down to the level you want, make any required alterations to the Angle, and then click the OK button when you're finished. You can unlock the Background layer by clicking the lock icon that is located on that layer. After that, you can click and drag the Background layer to the top of the stack to replace the Border layer. Choose **Edit > Free Transform**, and after that, reduce the size of the transformation so that the new boundary is visible. The Patterns panel has been updated to include your newly created pattern, and you can refresh the photo layer at any moment by double-clicking it in the Layers panel. You can make modifications to the design even after it has been added thanks to this feature.

CHAPTER FIFTEEN
IMAGE TRANSFORMATION

The approaches for transforming images in Photoshop are the primary subject of this chapter. It covers a wide variety of tools and techniques that can be used to improve and manipulate photos. The process begins with eliminating red-eye, a problem frequently seen in flash photography. It explains how to efficiently fix this problem. You will learn how to remove undesired objects from photos by using the Content-Aware Fill tool and how to relocate pieces by using the Content-Aware Move tool, both of which will allow for smooth adjustments after you have mastered them. The correction of camera distortion is yet another significant topic that is treated in this chapter. It discusses how to correct perspective and distortion problems in photographs, which might arise when using certain lenses or angles to take the picture.

This chapter describes the process of making panoramic images using the **Photomerge** function, which enables the stitching together of many shots to form a single, wide-angle view. These images can be seen in a variety of orientations, including portrait, landscape, and even overhead. There is also a discussion on brightening and correcting images, including ways to boost image exposure and overall quality. You will also gain an understanding of the Liquify filter and the various ways in which it can be utilized to adjust various aspects of an image, such as rearranging objects or retouching portraits. This chapter will teach you how to use the Liquify filter as a Smart Filter, which will enable you to make edits that are not damaging. It provides users with helpful tools and strategies for modifying and refining photographs in Photoshop, ranging from fundamental image repairs to more advanced forms of image modification.

RED EYE REMOVAL

The following steps will show you how to get rid of red eyes in Photoshop:

- **Step 1:** Select the **Red Eye Removal** tool.
- **Step 2:** Adjust the **Pupil Size** and Darken Amount settings as desired.
- **Step 3:** Click and drag to create a rectangular marquee around each eye.

You've just fixed the red eyes in Photoshop. Congratulations! This is without a doubt the quickest way to complete the task, but it's not usually the most effective way. You may need to take a more hands-on approach to fixing the red-eye shine in your photograph, depending on how much of it there is and where it's located.

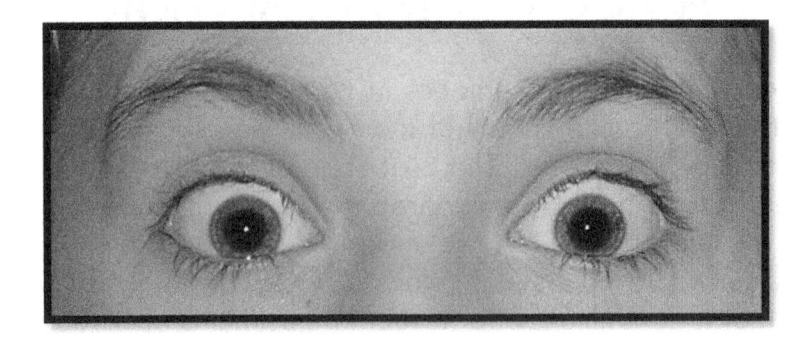

The Detailed Guide to Photoshop Red Eye Removal

Before you begin, you need to pay careful attention to the specular highlights in the eyes, which are also referred to as "**catchlights**." You can improve the realism of your edit and make it look more natural by keeping these highlight reflections the same or recreating them after you have finished working on the rest of it.

Step 1: Select the Glow

In the initial step of this process, you will need to build a selection around every pixel that shines in the pupil of your subject. This can be accomplished in a variety of ways; therefore, if you have a preferred approach that you would want to adopt, you are free to do so. If you are unsure about which tool to use, I would suggest beginning with the Object Selection Tool because it is the most basic tool. You can access it by using the toolbox (it's nested with the Magic Wand and Quick Selection tools), or you can hit the keyboard shortcut **Shift + W** to cycle through the nested tools until you reach the Object Selection Tool. The Object Selection Tool is located in the same folder as the Magic Wand Tool and the Quick Selection Tool.

After activating the Object Selection Tool, construct a rectangle marquee around the red glow emanating from the first eye by clicking and dragging to outline the area. While you should make an effort to maintain the selection area as close to the margins of the light as is practically practicable, you should also make sure that the glow is completely covered. After a little pause for thought, Photoshop will immediately begin the process of creating a selection for you. Because the red-eye glow is such a strikingly different color from the rest of your image, Photoshop should have no issue automatically picking the necessary pixels; having said that, the specifics of this process may change slightly depending on the subject matter of your photograph.

If the Object Selection Tool does a good job selecting objects for the first eye, it is reasonable to believe that it will similarly do a good job selecting objects for the second eye.

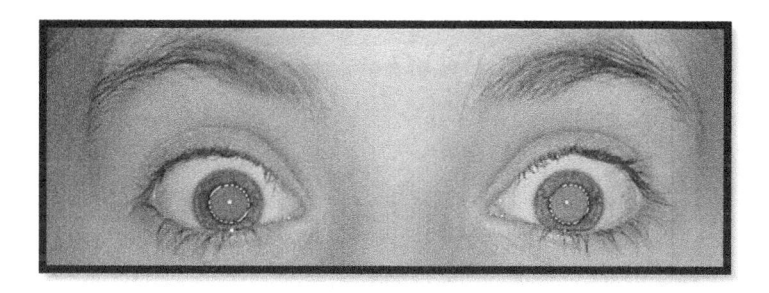

Keep the Shift key depressed to add to the selection you already have, and then click and drag over the red-eye light in the second eye to select it along with the first.

Step 2: Add a Curves Adjustment Layer

It is time to add a Curves adjustment layer now that you have finished selecting every last bit of the red-eye glow that you want to get rid of. When you add an adjustment layer to a document in Photoshop while you have an active selection, Photoshop will generate a layer mask by making use of your selection automatically.

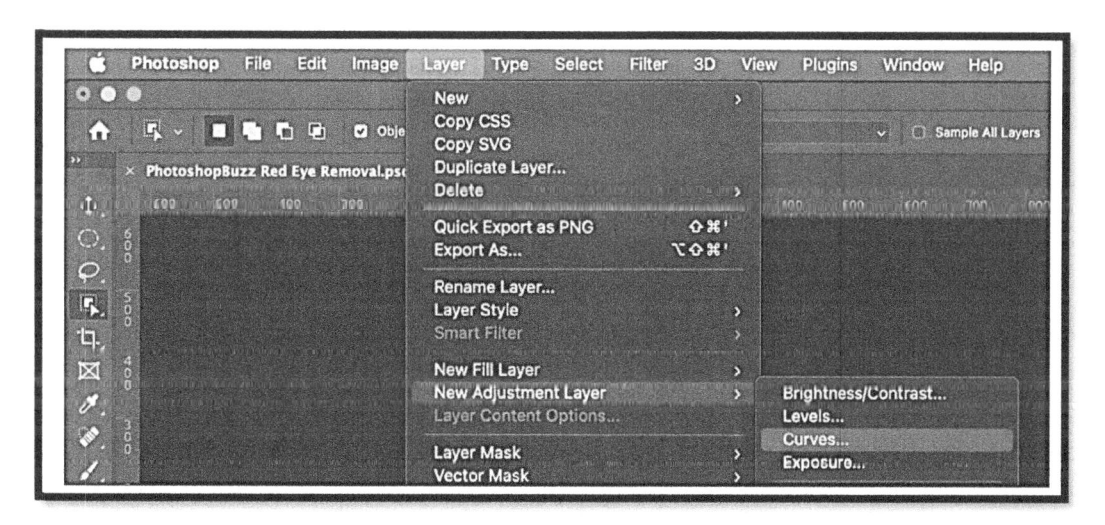

By accessing the Layer menu, navigating to the **New Adjustment Layer** submenu, and choosing the Curves button, you can add a Curves adjustment layer to your document. If you have the Adjustments panel open, you can also add one through there if it's already open. Find the **Properties** panel, which should now reflect the settings for your Curves adjustment layer. To adjust the black point, locate the black point slider at the bottom of the dialog box (it is highlighted with a red arrow below), click it, and then drag it over to the right side of the histogram.

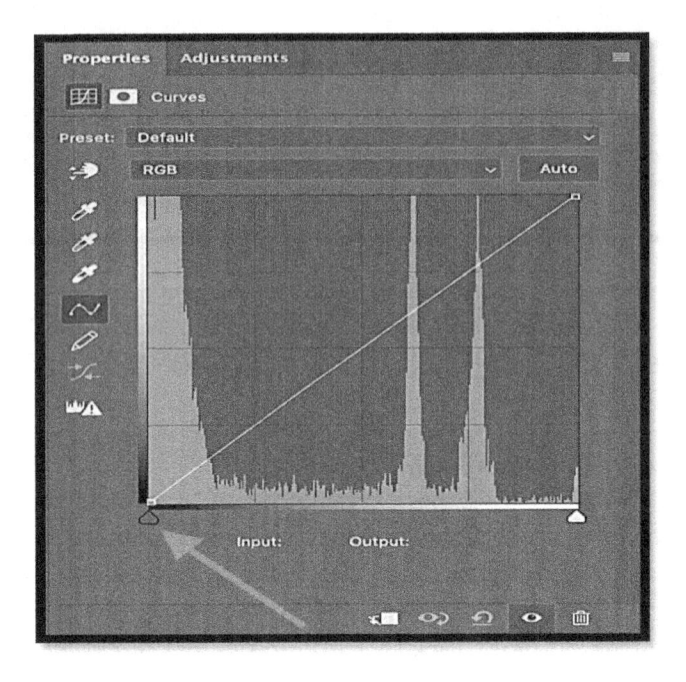

As you move the slider, pay careful attention to your image so you can judge when to stop. Don't drag the slider too much, either, as you want to preserve the highlights in the eyes if at all possible to make them look natural.

Step 3: Add a Hue/Saturation Adjustment Layer (Optional)

You can add a Hue/Saturation adjustment layer if you're not quite happy with how the colors are adjusted or if you want to change the hue of the catchlight that's seen in the eye. Using the keyboard shortcut **Command + Shift + R (or Ctrl + Shift + R on a PC)** will launch the **Reselect** command and restore the selection you made in Step 1. As in Step 2, this will also automate the process of creating a layer mask. Click **Hue/Saturation** after bringing up the Layer menu and choosing the **New Adjustment Layer** option. After adding the layer, navigate to the Properties panel and make any necessary adjustments.

To achieve a neutral catchlight, I usually find it helps to drastically reduce the Saturation slider; if you would prefer, you can also use the Hue slider to vary the reflection's color.

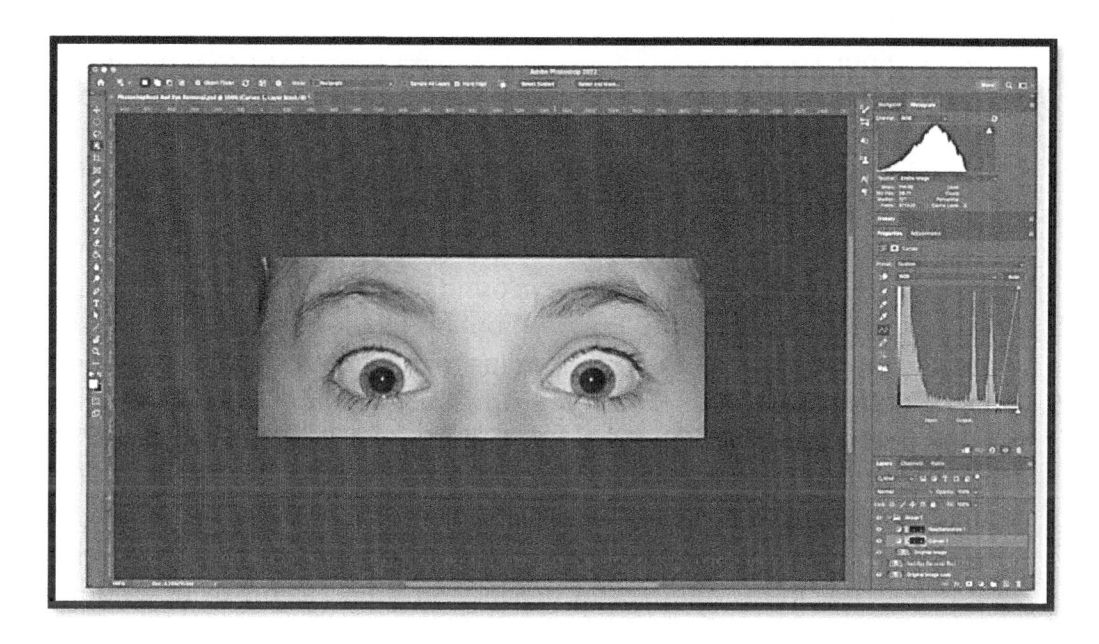

REMOVING OBJECTS WITH CONTENT-AWARE FILL

With Adobe Photoshop, you have a great tool called Content-Aware Fill that lets you remove objects from photographs and fill in the background in an elegant way.

Using Content-Aware Fill in Photoshop to eliminate objects can be done as follows:

1. **Open Your Image:** Start by opening the image you want to edit in Photoshop.
2. **Select the Object:** Use one of the selection tools, such as the Lasso Tool, Pen Tool, or Quick Selection Tool, to select the object or area you want to remove.
3. **Access Content-Aware Fill.** There are multiple ways to access the Content-Aware Fill feature:
    - Go to "**Edit**" > "**Content-Aware Fill**."
    - Right-click your selection, and from the context menu, choose "**Fill**." In the Fill dialog, set the "**Contents**" option to "**Content-Aware**."
    - Use the keyboard shortcut: **Shift + F5** (Fn + Shift + F5 on some keyboards).
4. **Adjust the Content-Aware Fill Settings:** The Content-Aware Fill dialog box will appear. Here, you can make several adjustments to get the best results:

- **Sampling Area:** Use the **"Sampling Area"** brush to specify the areas from which Photoshop should sample to generate the fill content. This helps ensure that the filled area matches the surrounding background.
- **Output To:** Choose **"New Layer"** to create a new layer with the filled content or select "Current Layer" to replace the selected area directly on the current layer.
- **Color Adaptation:** Adjust this setting to make the filled area match the color and lighting of the surrounding background more closely.
- **Rotation Adaptation:** Use this setting to adjust how the fill content is rotated to better match the surrounding area.

5. **Preview the Result:** Click the **"Preview"** button to see how the Content-Aware Fill will look. You can make further adjustments to the settings if needed.
6. **Apply Content-Aware Fill:** Once you are satisfied with the preview, click the "**OK**" button to apply the Content-Aware Fill. If you choose "**New Layer**" in the "**Output To**" settings, the filled content will be placed on a new layer, allowing you to further refine or adjust it as needed.
7. **Fine-tune the Result (if necessary):** You may need to fine-tune the result by using tools like the Clone Stamp or Healing Brush to make any additional adjustments or clean up any remaining imperfections.
8. **Save Your Work:** Save your edited image.

That is how you can utilize Photoshop's Content-Aware Fill to get rid of objects. Remember that the intricacy of the image and the settings you select will determine how effective this tool is, so you might need to make some manual tweaks to get the best results.

RELOCATION WITH THE CONTENT-AWARE TOOL

You can choose an object in an image and move it to a different location in Photoshop using the **Content-Aware Move Tool**. As a "**Content-Aware**" tool, it uses nearby matching pixels to magically fill in the missing pixels in the place where you moved the object. Let's examine the Content-Aware Move Tool's operation.

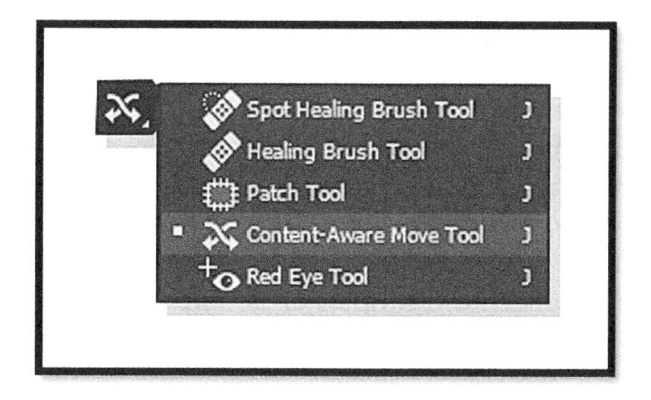

Draw a selection

First, from the left toolbar, choose the Content-Aware Move Tool. By default, it is located under the **Spot Healing Brush** Tool. The Content-Aware Move Tool is visible when you right-click and hold on to it. Make a selection around the object you wish to rotate, resize, or change position while the tool is selected.

Reposition, Resize, or Rotate

To move the object to a new location, drag the selection there. You will see both the original object in its original place and the one you previously picked in its new location as you are repositioning. By dragging on the handle points, you can simultaneously rotate or resize the selection. When you are satisfied with the new position, press Enter or the Check symbol above. The region you had initially chosen will thereafter appear to have miraculously filled in to match its surroundings! Your next photo shoot's creative output can be enhanced with the aid of this tool. With this easy technique, you can play around with different compositions and produce intriguing versions of your image.

CORRECTING LENS/CAMERA DISTORTION

A flaw called vignetting occurs when light leaks over the edge of the lens, darkening the corners of the picture. When a lens focuses on various hues of light in different planes, it causes chromatic aberration, which manifests as a color fringe around the borders of objects. Different faults can be seen in some lenses at specific focal lengths, f stops, and focus distances. You can choose the exact combination of settings that were used to create the image by using the Lens Correction filter.

Correct lens distortion and adjust perspective

Common lens imperfections including chromatic aberration, vignetting, and barrel and pincushion distortion are corrected with the Lens Correction filter. Only RGB or grayscale images with 8 or 16 bits per channel can be processed with this filter. The filter can also be used to correct perspective issues in images caused by horizontal or vertical camera tilt, as well as to rotate images. Compared to using the Transform command, these modifications are simpler and more precise when made using the filter's picture grid.

Automatically correct image perspective and lens flaws

The built-in Auto-Correction feature corrects distortion fast and precisely by using lens characteristics. Photoshop needs matching lens profiles on your system and Exif metadata identifying the camera and lens that took the picture to perform automated correction correctly.

1. Choose **Filter > Lens Correction**.
2. Set the following options:

Correction

- Decide which issues you wish to resolve. If the image is unnecessarily stretched or contracted beyond its original dimensions, choose Auto Scale Image.
- The Edge menu describes how to deal with blank spaces that come from perspective, rotation, or pincushion adjustments. You can expand the image's edge pixels or fill in any vacant spaces with color or transparency.

Search Criteria

- Filters the Lens Profiles list. Image sensor size-based profiles are shown first by default. Click the pop-up menu and pick **Prefer RAW** Profiles to see a list of RAW profiles first.

Lens Profiles

- Choose the appropriate profile. Photoshop only shows profiles that are compatible with the camera and lens that were used to take the original picture. (The camera model does not need to be an exact match.) In addition, Photoshop chooses a compatible sub-profile for the chosen lens based on the focal length, f-stop, and focus distance automatically. Right-click the lens profile that is now selected and chooses a different sub-profile to alter the automated selection.

If no lens profile matches, click Search Online to obtain other profiles made by the Photoshop community. Click the pop-up menu and select Save Online Profile Locally to store online profiles for later use.

Manually correct image perspective and lens flaws

You can apply manual correction alone or use it to refine automatic lens correction.

1. Choose **Filter > Lens Correction**.
2. In the upper-right corner of the dialog box, click the Custom tab.
3. (**Optional**) From the Settings menu, select a pre-made list of settings. Lens Default makes use of the camera, lens, focal length, f-stop, and focus distance settings that you have already saved to create the image. The parameters from your previous lens correction are used in Previous Conversion. Your saved groups of custom options appear at the bottom of the menu.
4. You can adjust your image by selecting any of the following settings.
   - **Remove Distortion**: This fixes pincushion (a form of optical distortion in which straight lines along the edge of a screen or a lens bulge towards the center) or lens barrel distortion. To straighten lines that bend toward or away from the image's center, move the slider in either direction. To fix this, you can also use the Remove Distortion tool. To adjust for barrel distortion, drag toward the image's center; to adjust for pincushion distortion, drag toward the image's edge. The Edge option on the Auto Correction tab can be adjusted to make up for any resulting blank image edges.
   - **Adjust Fringe settings**: Make adjustments to one color channel's size in relation to another to account for fringing.
   - **Vignette Amount**: Adjusts how much an image's edges are lightened or darkened. Fixes photos with darkening corners brought on by misaligned or defective lens shading.
   - **Vignette Midpoint**: Indicates the area's width that the Amount slider affects. To effect a larger portion of the image, enter a lower value. To limit the impact on the image's borders, enter a larger value.
   - **Vertical Perspective**: Adjusts perspective in images that result from up or down-tilting the camera. Creates parallel vertical lines in an image.
   - **Horizontal Perspective**: Makes horizontal lines parallel by adjusting the viewpoint of the image.

- o **Angle**: Rotates the picture to make corrections after perspective correction or to account for camera tilt. To fix this, you can also use the Straighten tool. To make a line in the image vertical or horizontal, drag it along.
- o **Scale**: Modifies the height or width of the image. The pixel dimensions of the image remain unchanged. The primary purpose is to eliminate regions of the image that are blank due to perspective, rotation, or pincushion adjustments. Cropping the image and interpolating up to the original pixel size are the effective outcomes of scaling up.

Adjust the Lens Correction preview and grid

To determine how much adjustment is required, adjust the grid lines and preview magnification.

- Use the Zoom tool or the zoom settings located in the lower-left corner of the preview image to adjust the magnification of the image.
- Use the **Hand tool** and drag the image preview to reposition it within the preview window.
- Select **Show Grid** from the dialog box's bottom to utilize the grid. Use the Size and Color controls to modify the grid's color and spacing, respectively. With the Move Grid tool, you can adjust the grid so that it aligns with your image.

Save settings and set camera and lens defaults

You have the option of saving the settings made in the Lens Correction dialog box so that you can use them with other pictures taken with the same camera, lens, and focal length combination. For distortion, chromatic aberration, and vignetting, Photoshop will save both the Auto-Correction settings as well as any Custom settings you may have used. The parameters for perspective correction are not retained because there is a high likelihood that they will be different for each image.

There are two ways that settings can be saved and used again:

- You'll need to save and load the settings manually. After making your selections in the corresponding dialog box, select **"Save Settings"** from the "Settings" menu. Choose the saved settings from the menu labeled **"Settings"** to apply them. (If you save your settings somewhere other than the default folder, you won't be able to find them in the menu; to retrieve them, use the **Load Settings** command.)

- Specify a default lens to use. You can preserve the current settings as a lens default if the image you're working with has **EXIF metadata** for the camera, lens, focal length, and f-stop. To make the changes permanent, select the **Set Lens Default** option from the drop-down menu. The **Lens Default** option will become available in the Settings menu once you have corrected an image to the point that it matches the camera, lens, focal length, and f stop. If your image does not have any EXIF metadata, you will not be able to use this option.

Reduce image noise and JPEG artifacts

Noise in an image manifests itself as haphazard, unnecessary pixels that aren't included in the image's detail. Underexposure, shooting in a dark environment with a slow shutter speed, and photography with a high ISO setting on a digital camera can all contribute to the appearance of noise in an image. Consumer cameras with lower resolution tend to have higher levels of image noise than higher-resolution cameras. Images that have been scanned could have noise in them because of the scanning sensor. The grain pattern of the film will frequently be visible in the scanned image. Image noise can manifest itself in two distinct ways: as luminance (grayscale) noise, which is responsible for giving an image a grainy or patchy appearance, or as color noise, which is typically seen in the form of colored artifacts in the image.

It's possible that one channel of the image, perhaps the blue channel, has higher luminance noise than the others. In **Advanced** mode, you can independently modify the noise for each channel. Examine each channel of your image independently before opening the filter to determine whether or not the noise is concentrated in one of the channels. When you modify just one channel instead of making a global adjustment to all of the channels, you keep more of the image's details.

1. Select "**Reduce Noise**" from the **Filter** menu under "**Noise**."
2. Increase the magnification on the preview image so that you can have a better look at the image noise.
3. **Choose your options:**
  - **Strength**: This setting determines how much of a reduction in luminance noise is applied to all of the image channels.
  - **Preserve Details**: This allows you to keep image details such as hair and texture objects, as well as image edges. The largest amount of visual detail is maintained at a value of 100, while the amount of luminance noise is

reduced the least. Adjust the settings for Strength and Preserve Details to achieve the desired level of noise reduction.
- **Reduce Color Noise:** This gets rid of pixels with unpredictable color combinations. A greater value decreases the amount of color noise.
- **Sharpen Details:** This brings out the finer details of the image. The image's sharpness will suffer if the noise is removed. To bring back the image's original sharpness, either utilizes the sharpening control that's located in the dialog box or one of the additional sharpening filters that are available in Photoshop later.
- **Remove JPEG Artifacts:** This gets rid of blocky image artifacts and halos that appear as a result of an image being saved with a poor JPEG quality preset.

4. If the luminance noise is more noticeable in one or two color channels, select the color channel from the Channel menu after clicking the advanced button. Reduce the amount of noise coming from that channel by adjusting the Strength and Preserve Details settings.

CREATING PANORAMA WITH PHOTO MERGE

1. Go to the **File** menu and select **Automate > Photomerge**.
2. In the Photomerge dialog box, add the photos that you want to utilize in the merged picture.

It is not necessary to include any pictures that completely obscure the top (called the zenith) or the bottom (called the nadir) of the scene. These photographs will be added at a later time.

3. Select **Spherical** for the Layout.

Note: If you took the picture using a fisheye lens, make sure that the Auto Layout and Geometric Distortion Correction are both selected. If Photoshop is unable to detect your lens automatically, you can use the free Adobe Lens Profile Creator, which can be downloaded from the Adobe website.

4. Choose either the "**Vignette Removal**" or "**Geometric Distortion**" option for the Lens Correction (this step is optional).
5. Choose Content Aware (this step is optional). Fill in the Areas That Are Transparent to prevent transparent pixels from appearing around the panoramic image's edges.
6. Press the **OK** button.

7. Select "**Spherical Panorama**" from the "**New Shape from Layer**" menu under "3D."
8. If you want to, you can manually add the top and bottom photographs into the sphere. This step is optional. You might also use the paint tool to cover up any transparent pixels that are still present in the 3D spherical panorama layer.

BRIGHTENING A PHOTOGRAPH

The method of brightening a photograph in Photoshop or any other image editing program is a frequent one and can be completed with little effort. You have the option of adjusting the brightness and contrast of the entire image, or you can choose to brighten only certain parts of the picture. This is the procedure to follow:

Method 1: Adjusting Overall Brightness and Contrast

1. **Open Your Image:** Start by opening the image you want to brighten in Photoshop.
2. **Create a Duplicate Layer:** It is recommended that you make a copy of your image's layer before making any changes to it. This is known as the duplicate layer. You can make modifications to the duplicate layer while the original layer remains untouched in this fashion. When you right-click on the background layer in the Layers panel, you can select "**Duplicate Layer**" from the context menu to duplicate the layer.
3. **Brightness and Contrast Adjustments**: First, select the duplicate layer, and then navigate to "Image" > "Adjustments" > "Brightness/Contrast." A modal dialog box will show up.
4. **Modify the Brightness**: Do this by moving the "Brightness" slider to the right to make the image more visible. You can also make adjustments to the "Contrast" slider to achieve the desired level of contrast in the image.
5. **Preview and Apply**: You can see the changes taking place in real time by activating the "Preview" option, and you can continue to make adjustments until you are satisfied. To put the changes into effect, click the "**OK**" button.

Method 2: Brightening Selective Areas

1. **Open Your Image:** Open your image in Photoshop.
2. **Create a New Layer:** Create a new layer by clicking on the "**New Layer**" icon in the Layers panel.
3. **Use Brush Tool:** Select the **Brush Tool (B)** and set the foreground color to white. Adjust the brush size and hardness as needed. Paint over the areas of the image that you want to brighten.

4. **Blend Mode:** Change the blend mode of the new layer to "**Screen**." This blend mode brightens the areas you painted while preserving the image's color.
5. **Adjust Opacity:** You can further control the intensity of the brightening effect by adjusting the opacity of the new layer. Reduce the opacity if the effect is too strong.
6. **Fine-Tune:** You can continue to fine-tune the effect by painting on the layer mask or adjusting layer opacity until you achieve the desired result.
7. **Save Your Work:** Save your edited image when you're satisfied with the brightness adjustments.

You have the option of brightening the entire image in these ways, or you can choose to selectively brighten certain parts. Pick the approach that caters best to your requirements as well as the picture that you are currently working on. When making alterations to the brightness of an image, it is important to constantly keep in mind the original lighting and intended visual style of the image.

ADJUSTING IMAGE WITH LIQUIFY

There are hundreds of different settings, filters, and other tools available in Adobe Photoshop for manipulating images. In Photoshop, the Liquify tool is a filter that can be applied to a region of a picture to modify it. Some of the options that can be used with this filter include Forward Warp, Twirl, Pucker, and Bloat.

Depending on which parameter you select to liquify an image, these settings affect the image in a variety of different ways. Even though most of the changes you make won't be quite as extreme, the Liquify tool can make some modest adjustments to your images so that they are more subtly refined. If you want to make crazy and abstract images, using the Liquify filter can be a lot of fun. If you want to rectify little things in your photographs, however, it can be an excellent tool. We are aware that Liquify can bend a portion of a photograph; however, this very effective and user-friendly application is capable of many more than simple transformations. The Liquify filter is a multi-functional filter that includes a variety of useful functions.

Forward Warp Tool

When you move your mouse, the Forward Warp Tool pushes pixels forward in the image. As is the case with the majority of the equipment, the magnitude of the brush's bristles can influence the amount of material that is advanced. You will see a Properties panel on the right side of the screen whenever you choose any of the tools, including this one. From this panel, you can make changes to the brush, the mask, and other options. The Forward Warp Tool is often the tool in the Liquify arsenal that receives the most use. With this tool, you can modify and edit virtually every aspect of your photographs.

Reconstruct Tool

The Reconstruct Tool allows you to undo any distortions that you may have introduced into your image. To utilize it, all you have to do is choose and drag.

Smooth Tool

The Smooth Tool performs exactly what it says it will do, which is to smooth out any wobbles in your image by making the curves less angular and more natural. This comes in handy if any of the image's edges become twisted when you are altering it. This device is ideal for smoothing out creases and wrinkles in fabric, particularly garments. It is therefore not an issue for the Smooth Tool even if you did not iron the shirt before the shot was taken.

Twirl Clockwise Tool

If you hold down the Alt key while using the Twirl Clockwise Tool, your photographs will be distorted in a counterclockwise direction instead of a clockwise one. You can give the sea or the clouds some movement with the help of this tool.

Pucker Tool

The Pucker Tool brings pixels closer to the brush's center from the edge of the brush area. This can be useful in reducing the size of certain face characteristics, such as eyes, dimples, and other facial features.

Bloat Tool

The Pucker Tool moves pixels toward the center of the brush area, while the Bloat Tool moves pixels away from the center of the brush area. This can come in helpful for helping to perk up a flat haircut, adding some extra curves to a physique, or even making clouds look more billowy.

Push Left Tool

Pixels can be moved to the right or left depending on whether the Alt key is held down while using the **Push Left** Tool. Although it is not a very frequently used tool, it can help make modest modifications to assist in correcting a slightly slanted image. This technique can help you nudge your subject into alignment if you didn't do a very good job of aligning it in the first place.

Freeze Mask Tool

When working with the Liquify filter, the Freeze Mask Tool is used to isolate a portion of the image that should remain unchanged regardless of the other adjustments that are made to the filter. This is a useful feature that will help you maintain control and accuracy over your edits.

Thaw Mask Tool

The mask that you've set on your shot can be removed with the Thaw Mask Tool. You can precisely control your modifications by combining Freeze and Thaw.

Face Tool

The Face Tool's primary function is to allow for the modification of facial features. When you initially choose this tool in Photoshop, the program will look for a face in the image. The software will alert you if it does not recognize a face. The steps to becoming a virtual plastic surgeon are as follows. Do you want to improve your appearance by getting rid of that double chin, straightening your teeth, or giving yourself a pouty smile? This is the tool that can make even the most imperfect face look perfect.

Hand Tool

The Hand Tool in Photoshop behaves the same way as the Hand Tool in all of the other versions of Photoshop. It can be used to reposition or otherwise alter your image.

Zoom Tool

You can zoom in on your image with the Zoom Tool, as well as zoom out of it. This is used for making little adjustments, such as those that require you to zoom in first, and then zoom out to see the final effects of your work. To zoom out, press and hold the Alt key on your keyboard.

1. Launch Photoshop and select an image from your hard drive to alter.
2. Navigate to the Filter menu and select Liquify, or use the shortcut Shift+Ctrl+X.

When you click on the Liquify tool, a new window will pop up. You are now in a position where you can select any of the tools that were discussed earlier.

Liquify Tool Properties

Once you've entered the Liquify interface, all of the tool's individual properties can be found on the right side of the screen. There are a great many parameters that you can alter to achieve the exact look you want, from changing the Brush Density to tinkering with the settings for the Mask area. The available parameters are broken down into categories below. Changes can be made to the Brush Tool Options, including the Size of the Brush, the Density of the Brush, the Pressure of the Brush, and the Rate.

Here is an explanation of what each setting does.

- **Size**: Alters the brush size in the same manner as it does on the primary Photoshop page. When using a larger brush, the resulting alterations are more nuanced.
- **Density**: This determines how the edges are feathered out as you use it and can be controlled by the user.
- **Pressure**: The alterations will be more dramatic when the pressure is higher and more intense. When making tiny adjustments, you should often apply less pressure.
- **Rate**: This controls the speed at which the brush moves, which varies depending on whether you move the brush or keep it still.
- **Stylus Pressure**: This is only accessible if you have a stylus in your possession. If you have a stylus and choose this box, the settings for the Brush Tool will be applied to the stylus rather than the brush tool.
- **Pin Edges**: This prevents you from pulling too much of an image's edge while you are using any of the other tools to distort an image. This comes in handy

for lowering the degree of background distortion, which manifests itself as a checkered pattern that is transparently gray and white.

When you use the Liquify tool, you also have a few other options at your disposal, which give you even more control over how and when the tool is applied to your image.

- **Face-Awareness Liquify** gives you the ability to make more precise adjustments to a more specific region of the face because it has separate controls for each facial feature. There are separate controls for the eyes, lips, nose, and overall shape of the face. Each of them can be customized in a variety of ways, including its width, height, and tilt.
- **Load Mesh Options** gives you the ability to store the Liquify distortions you've created so that you can use them in another picture.
- **Mask Options** provides you with the settings necessary to mask specific areas of your photograph.
- **View Options** provides you with extra viewing settings, such as the ability to reveal the mesh and enable the guide, so that you can see the mesh as you are making adjustments.
- **Brush Reconstruct Options** gives you the ability to customize the extent to which you want to revert the alterations made to your image.

APPLYING LIQUIFY FILTER AS A SMART FILTER

The Liquify filter is considered to be a smart filter because it not only supports Smart Objects but also Smart Object video layers. Meshes are now immediately stored in your document whenever you apply the Liquify filter to a Smart Object. When the Liquify filter is reapplied, meshes that have been applied to Smart Objects get compressed and are editable again. It is important to keep in mind that the file size will rise due to the embedded meshes, even the compressed ones.

To use the Liquify filter as a smart filter, please do the following:

1. In the Layers panel, select a layer that contains a smart object.
2. Select "**Liquify**" from the filter menu.

CHAPTER SIXTEEN
GROUPS IN PHOTOSHOP

This chapter will teach you the essential skill of building groups in Photoshop, which will create the groundwork for the rest of the book. In addition to that, it explores the fascinating field of layer effects. You will learn the skills necessary to apply a broad variety of effects to your grouped layers after completing this lesson. Adjustments to color, lighting, and contrast, as well as the use of filters and layer styles, are examples of the kinds of effects that could fall under this category. In this lesson, you will discover how to hide groups in Photoshop. You can temporarily conceal the contents of a group so that you can concentrate on other areas of your project when you hide the group. When you need to clear out clutter in your workstation or zero in on particular aspects of the design, this is a strategy that can be helpful. This chapter will discuss the appropriate procedure to use when removing a group from your project if it is determined that the group is no longer required. By removing a group from your workspace, you can ensure that it will remain uncluttered and well-organized. In addition to that, it demonstrates how powerful Photoshop's ability to duplicate groups can be.

You will get an understanding of how to produce identical clones of your groups, which can help you save time while working on activities that are repetitive or when creating variations of a design. Your workflow will be more efficient after you have a better understanding of this process. When this happens, it can be required to divide a group into its components or layers. This chapter will walk you through the process of ungrouping layers in Photoshop, which will allow you to recover individual control over each layer that is contained within a group. It is crucial to have this level of freedom to make exact tweaks and edits to your designs. As the chapter comes to a close, you are going to delve into the fascinating world of text grouping in Photoshop. By virtue of possessing this ability, you will be able to manage and manipulate text layers collectively, hence simplifying the process of editing and formatting text inside your projects.

What is a Photoshop Group

In Photoshop, photos, words, and other objects can all be organized in their layers. This indicates that even a large project can contain a multitude of layers. This can lead to the layers panel becoming cluttered very quickly. Using Photoshop's Group feature to organize your layers and prevent the Layers panel from growing too large is quite helpful. Because of the scale of the project, many of the layers will likely share the same layer styles and tools. It is possible to group numerous layers that share the same styles and tools, and once this has been done, the shared style can be added to the group. Adjustment layers and Fill layers can be added above the group, and once they are there, the properties of those layers will be inherited by all of the items in the group. The wonderful thing about a group is that if you drag and drop layers into the group, those layers will immediately take on the qualities of the group. This is one of the many benefits of using groups. This indicates that any impact that is being applied to the group will affect any new layers that are added to the group.

HOW TO CREATE A GROUP IN PHOTOSHOP

The formation of a group can take place in a few different ways. When you want to create a group, first pick the layers that you want to include in the group. Next, in the layers panel, go to the top menu and click Layers then Group layers, or press **Ctrl + G**. This will bring up a dialog box where you can name the group and add members to it.

You can also group layers by going to the layers panel, selecting the layers you wish to group, then going to the top right of the layers panel and clicking the menu button. This is another option. When the menu appears, select "**New group from layers**" from the list of options. The **New Group** from the layers window will appear, and you can give the group a name before clicking the **OK** button to finalize. The naming box for the new group will open when you touch the menu button on the layers style panel and select New Group from the drop-down menu that appears. After giving the new layer a name, you will need to confirm by pressing **OK**. The layers, on the other hand, will not be automatically added to the group. You will have to drag the layers and drop them on the new group.

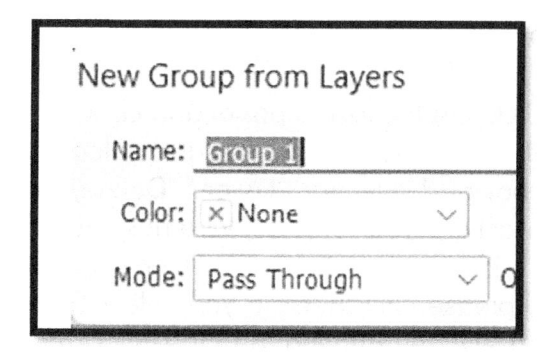

ADDING EFFECTS TO THE GROUP IN PHOTOSHOP

Having the ability to create groups in Photoshop is one of the program's many benefits. You can apply effects to several layers at once by first grouping all of the layers together and then applying the effect to the group that contains all of the layers. When there are multiple layers inside a project, it can be challenging to apply effects to all of the layers. You may want to apply the same effect to some different layers, but doing so individually would be a challenging and time-consuming process. A group can have layers added to it, and then that group can have an effect added to it. The effect created by the group will be consistent across all of the layers in the group. Simply move the adjustment layer to the top of the layers panel, above the group, if you want to apply the adjustment to all of the layers that are contained within the group. To add effects to the group, right-click on the group in the layers panel, then select "**Blending mode**" from the context menu that appears. The option window for the different sorts of layers will emerge. The layer styles that you prefer can be selected by you.

HIDING A GROUP IN PHOTOSHOP

There will be times when you are working on a substantial project that consists of a great deal of layers. Even if you have them arranged in groups and the layers panel is in order, the canvas will still have all of the things even after you have ordered them. In this situation, you can choose to conceal the groups so that you can work more efficiently without the other items being visible. When you are prepared to deal with the hidden items, you can choose to enable their visibility again. You can hide the group by clicking the eye icon that is located next to the thumbnail of the group. If you are working with a large number of layers, this is a speedy method for hiding numerous layers at once.

DELETING A GROUP IN PHOTOSHOP

To remove the group, pick it in the layers panel and click the **Delete** button. You can delete the group by either right-clicking on it and selecting "**Delete group**," or by going to the top menu bar and selecting "**Layer," "Delete," and "Group**." You will be presented with a menu asking you to select whether you want to delete the group alone, the group along with its content, or cancel the operation altogether. To select the desired alternative, please click here. If you select **Group only**, the folder that contains the group layers will be removed, and the layers will no longer be grouped. If you select **Group** and the content, the group as well as the layers included inside it will be removed. If you select **Cancel**, the options box will shut, but the group will not be affected in any way.

DUPLICATING THE GROUP IN PHOTOSHOP

A group and the content it contains can both be duplicated. Go to the layers panel, right-click on the group, and select the "**Duplicate group**" option from the context menu. A popup will pop up asking you to give the duplicated group a name; if you want to keep the default name, just press **OK** when the window appears. The group can also be duplicated by selecting it with the mouse and dragging it onto the icon that says "**Create a new layer**" which is located at the bottom of the Layers panel.

UNGROUPING LAYERS IN PHOTOSHOP

Ungrouping the layers in a group is possible if the group is no longer required. Right-clicking on the group in the layers panel and selecting "**Ungroup layers**" from the context menu gives you the option to ungroup the layers. You can also ungroup the layers by selecting the group, then going to the top menu bar, clicking **Layer**, and then clicking **Ungroup layer**, or by pressing **Shift + Ctrl + G**. Both of these methods will provide the same result. The group folder will be removed, and the layers in the layers panel will remain ungrouped after it has been done.

GROUP TEXTS IN PHOTOSHOP

To group the text layers, open the layers panel, hold down the Control key, and then click on each of the text layers that you want to include in the group. After you have selected all of them, go to the top menu bar and choose Layer, then click **Group Layer**, or press the **Ctrl** and **G** keys on your keyboard.

FREQUENTLY ASKED QUESTIONS ON PHOTOSHOP 2024

What are the system requirements for Photoshop 2024?

For your computer to operate Photoshop 2024 to its full potential, it must fulfill all of the necessary system requirements. A multicore Intel CPU that supports 64-bit architecture, a minimum of 8 gigabytes of random access memory (but 16 gigabytes is suggested for better operation), and an Internet connection are required for product activation and access to online services.

Does Adobe Photoshop 2024 support plugins created by third-party developers?

Indeed, Photoshop 2024 is compatible with plugins made by third-party developers. However, it is essential to keep in mind that the most recent version of Photoshop may not be fully compatible with all of the available plugins. It is recommended to check with the plugin vendor for specific details to be certain that compatibility will be maintained.

How will I be able to become familiar with the new features that have been added to Photoshop 2024?

Adobe provides customers with a variety of materials to assist them in becoming familiar with the new features that are included in Photoshop 2024. These tools provide you with access to community forums, user guides, and tutorials, all of which allow you to seek support and direction from other users as well as professionals.

Is it possible to install Photoshop 2024 on more than one computer?

There is no limit to the number of computers on which you can install Photoshop 2024. On the other hand, the number of devices that you can activate is subject to a cap. To be more specific, activation is restricted to a maximum of two machines for each individual who is affiliated with the membership. It is also essential to remember that you are not permitted to run the software on both of these devices at the same time.

Is Generative Fill a paid add-on?

There is no additional charge for using the Generate Fill feature. Adobe has come out with a new feature called Generative credits, which function similarly to a data plan. Subscribers who pay a fee are given quick processing credits; nevertheless, even if these credits are used, you can continue to generate without paying any further fees. However, if there is a significant volume of requests being processed by the servers, the processing speed may decrease.

What happens if you run out of credits?

It should not be a regular occurrence for the majority of users to lose all of their credits. You can keep using the Generative Fill option even if you go over your credit limit. This is because it is not tied to your credit limit. In these kinds of situations, you can have slower processing rates, or there might even be a daily limit put on the amount of data you can upload.

Is the resolution still limited to 1024 x 1024?

Yes, 1024 by 1024 pixels will continue to be the maximum resolution for any content that is generated. This means that the longest dimension of any material generated by the Generative Fill feature will never exceed 1024 pixels in length.

Where is High Resolution?

Adobe has stated that future capabilities may include the option for Higher Resolution in Generative Fill; however, this may come with the requirement of additional Generative Credits or may incur an additional fee.

Are there going to be any adjustments made to the prices?

Yes, Adobe has confirmed that it will be increasing the cost of its Creative Cloud membership service beginning on November 1st, 2023. This decision was made public in an announcement made by the company.

What is the difference between Photoshop 2024 and previous versions?

The new features included in Photoshop 2024 represent a significant improvement over its predecessors. These include better performance, more creative tools, and a more intuitive user interface, all of which combine to make it an even more powerful and user-friendly tool for digital artists and designers.

What is the Generative Fill feature in Photoshop 2024?

The unique function known as Generative Fill can be found in Photoshop 2024. This feature makes use of artificial intelligence to generate realistic patterns and textures. It is a wonderful tool for artists and designers who wish to quickly and easily develop complicated and one-of-a-kind creations and those people can benefit from using it.

How can I update to Photoshop 2024?

If you are currently a subscriber to Creative Cloud, updating to Photoshop 2024 is a simple process for you to go through. To obtain the most recent version of Photoshop, you need to launch the Creative Cloud desktop program, go to the "**Apps**" tab, locate Photoshop in the list of installed apps, and then click on the "**Update**" button.

What should I do if I am having problems with Adobe Photoshop 2024?

If you run across any problems when using Photoshop 2024, Adobe suggests looking for advice on how to fix them on their help website or in the community forums that they maintain. You also have the option of contacting Adobe Customer Support to receive more assistance with any technical issues that you may be experiencing.

Does Photoshop 2024 offer any new brushes or filters?

Yes, Photoshop 2024 comes with a wide range of brand-new brushes and filters to choose from. These extra tools broaden the scope of what can be created creatively and give users the ability to incorporate a greater variety of effects into their digital artwork.

Can I use Photoshop 2024 on a tablet?

Yes, Photoshop 2024 is compatible with the many tablets that are now available. Adobe recommends utilizing a tablet that satisfies their particular system requirements to guarantee a fluid and effective performance for the user. This will result in the greatest possible user experience.

What are the new features in Photoshop 2024?

Adobe Photoshop 2024 includes a plethora of fascinating new feature additions. One of the most notable of them is the Generative Fill tool, which is driven by artificial intelligence and enables the development of realistic textures and patterns, hence expanding the capabilities of design. In addition, customers may anticipate increased performance, which will result in a more streamlined and expedient workflow, as well as an upgraded user interface that will make the creative process easier to navigate. In addition, this version includes additional creative tools and brushes, increasing the number of options available to digital artists so that they can incorporate a greater variety of effects into their work.

Is there a free trial for Photoshop 2024?

Yes, Adobe normally provides a free trial version of its newly released product, which includes Photoshop 2024 when it does so. The trial edition of Adobe software is readily available on the company's main website, where it may also be downloaded. Before committing to a purchase, you will have the opportunity during this trial time to investigate and assess the features offered by the software.

Can I use my existing Adobe ID to use Photoshop 2024?

There is no question about it; you can continue to make use of Photoshop 2024 with the same Adobe ID you've always had. If you are already a subscriber to Creative Cloud, updating to the most recent version can be done without any problems through the Creative Cloud desktop app. This makes it straightforward for existing Adobe users to upgrade to the most recent version of the software.

What are the benefits of subscribing to Adobe Creative Cloud?

A subscription to Adobe Creative Cloud comes with a lot of different perks and benefits. You will always have access to the most recent tools and features thanks to the fact that it grants access to the most recent versions of all Adobe products, including Photoshop 2024. In addition, Creative Cloud provides you with useful extras like **cloud storage**, the option to construct portfolio websites, and access to premium typefaces, and social media tools, all of which can further improve the efficiency of your creative production.

How can I learn more about using Photoshop 2024?

Adobe provides customers with access to a wide variety of tools to aid in their education regarding how to get the most out of Photoshop 2024. These resources include an abundance of online lessons that cover a variety of facets of the software, extensive user guides that provide in-depth reference information, and active community forums in which you can seek help, ask questions, and share insights with other users. This ensures that you have access to the information and support you require to master Photoshop 2024 and bring out the full creative potential that you possess.

CONCLUSION

This Adobe Photoshop 2024 guide is intended to be a complete resource that can be used by both beginners and experienced users of Photoshop. It covers a broad variety of important subjects, tools, and methods across its many chapters, to assist users in realizing the full potential of the sophisticated picture editing program that they are using. The essentials of Photoshop, such as the program's interface and the core tools, are covered first in this guide's introduction to the program, which lays a strong basis for further exploration. Following that, it gets into more complex features and capabilities, such as working with layers, selections, and color modes, in addition to fine art painting, picture retouching, and image modification. One of the guide's strengths is its emphasis on practical application. Each chapter not only explains the concepts but also provides step-by-step instructions and real-world examples, allowing users to follow along and apply what they've learned to their projects.

In addition, the guide takes into account the ever-changing nature of Adobe Photoshop by including upgrades and new features that are specific to the 2024 edition. This ensures that users are familiar with all of the most recent tools and methods. This Adobe Photoshop 2024 guide is a great resource that can help you increase your abilities, accomplish your creative vision, and unlock new possibilities in the realm of digital imaging. Whether you're a photographer, graphic designer, digital artist, or just someone interested in image editing, this guide is for you. It can help you improve your skills, realize your creative vision, and open new possibilities. Users will be able to take their Photoshop skills to the next level and produce breathtaking graphics with confidence and accuracy thanks to the tools provided by this extension.

INDEX

"

"hidden" tool options, 25

3

32-bit Exposure, 41
3D Material Drop Tool, 35
3D Material Eyedropper, 31
3D rendering, 1
3D Text, 142

4

4 GB of storage space, 3

A

A 1080p monitor, 5
A dialog box, 23
A flaw called vignetting occurs, 335
A vector drawing, 120
About Adjustment Layers, 316
About path components, 122
Access all your work, 74
access the Interface category, 71
Access the Transform Options, 252
Accessibility Features, 97
Accessibility of Context Menus, 42
Accessing Photoshop Adjustment Layers, 316
Accessing Preferences, 104
accommodate a wide range of tasks, 22
accurate modifications, 24
ACR interface, 188
Activate the Bounding Box, 252
active community forums, 355
active screen stands, 47
actual dimensions, 114
Actual Pixels, 113, 114
ACTUAL PIXELS, 114
actual vector graphic, 120

Add a Curves Adjustment Layer, 331
Add a Layer Mask, 233
Add a New Levels Adjustment Layer, 284
Add a Threshold layer, 118
Add Anchor Point, 32
Add Anchor Point Tool, 32
Add Layer Mask, 163, 233
Add to Selection, 164
ADDED FEATURES TO CONTEXTUAL TASKBAR, 14
ADDED FEATURES TO CONTEXTUAL TASKBAR TO AID WITH MASKING AND CROPPING PROCESSES, 14
ADDING A BORDER TO THE IMAGE, 320
Adding an object, 15
Adding Depth, 304
ADDING EFFECTS TO THE GROUP IN PHOTOSHOP, 349
ADDING LAYER STYLE TO A LAYER, 302
Adding More Pins, 230
Adding to a Selection, 247
Adding to or subtracting, 239, 242
Adding to or subtracting from the selection, 239, 242
Adding Watermarks, 304
adjust 32-bit HDR images, 41
adjust for barrel distortion, 337
Adjust Fringe settings, 337
Adjust Lips and Lips Lines, 267
Adjust the Black Input Level, 285
Adjust the brush settings, 275
Adjust the edges, 272
Adjust the gradient using layer styles, 315
Adjust the Layer Mask, 234
Adjust the White Input Level, 285
adjust tone curves, 185
ADJUSTING CANVA SIZE, 84
adjusting graphics, 29
ADJUSTING IMAGE TONAL USING THE BASIC PANEL, 182
ADJUSTING IMAGE WITH LIQUIFY, 342
ADJUSTING LEVELS, 282
ADJUSTING THE OPACITY OF A LAYER, 303
Adjusting the Photoshop Output Levels, 286
adjustment layer, 43, 115, 116, 169, 290, 299, 320, 331, 332, 349
Adjustment layer, 118, 319

Adjustment Layer Types, 317
adjustments, 9, 36, 61, 66, 74, 75, 87, 105, 137, 164, 172, 178, 181, 182, 183, 185, 186, 188, 190, 198, 201, 216, 222, 229, 231, 234, 237, 238, 241, 244, 256, 267, 270, 278, 283, 284, 285, 289, 317, 318, 320, 325, 329, 332, 333, 334, 336, 337, 338, 341, 342, 344, 345, 346, 352
Adjustments, 22, 43, 47, 48, 49, 50, 52, 55, 56, 61, 155, 158, 169, 183, 237, 260, 267, 317, 320, 322, 332, 341, 347
Adjustments panel, 48, 49
Adobe Camera Raw, 172, 178, 181, 182, 189, 190
Adobe Creative Cloud, 15, 19, 20, 74, 117, 354
Adobe Drive, 40
Adobe Engineers, 64
Adobe Express Premium, 11
Adobe Illustrator or InDesign, 70
Adobe membership plan, 11
Adobe Photoshop, 1, 2, 3, 4, 5, 6, 8, 15, 18, 19, 24, 26, 28, 29, 33, 36, 41, 62, 65, 73, 75, 76, 90, 91, 95, 96, 97, 105, 112, 123, 141, 143, 159, 171, 175, 179, 181, 197, 230, 233, 237, 238, 240, 241, 243, 245, 246, 248, 252, 255, 257, 261, 272, 274, 276, 278, 280, 281, 289, 292, 296, 297, 305, 306, 333, 342, 351, 353, 354, 355
Adobe Photoshop 2024 guide, 355
ADOBE PHOTOSHOP LAYERS, 291
Adobe Portrait, 182
Adobe provides customers, 351, 355
Adobe Stock's images, 10
Adobe Stock's large collection, 10
Advanced Selection Tools, 164
Advanced Techniques, 278
Aero utilizing cloud documents., 74
Align Layers, 163
Alpha Channels and Transparency, 98
Alpha Channels in Photoshop, 219
alpha transparency, 93
alter the brush's color., 204
alter the color scheme of Photoshop, 73
Altering the direction lines, 138
altering the parameters for Clarity, 192
Am I going to be forced to save my documents to the cloud in Photoshop?, 74
an ageless cornerstone of innovation, 1
An example path, 121
An Internet connection is needed to activate the software, 3

anchor points, 27, 31, 32, 117, 120, 121, 122, 124, 129, 131, 134, 136, 137, 138, 140, 145, 230
Angle, 145, 213, 214, 328, 338
antivirus software, 6, 8
anti-virus software, 6
Application Bar, 21
Application Menu options, 154
application of choice for creating vector, 117
Applications folder, 8
Apply a Shadow, 144
Apply Finishing Touches, 221
Apply Image, 159
Apply sharpening, 267
Apply Sharpening, 186
Apply the Filter, 313
Apply the gradient, 315
Apply the Patch, 273, 274
Apply the Rotation, 253
Apply the Selection to the Layer Mask, 234
APPLYING A FILTER TO CREATE A DESIGN, 312
APPLYING A GRADIENT TO A LAYER, 314
Applying Edits, 178, 181
Applying effects to the selection, 240, 243
APPLYING LIQUIFY FILTER AS A SMART FILTER, 346
APPROACH FOR RETOUCHING, 266
appropriate background layer color, 146
appropriate choices and commands, 22
appropriate runtime libraries, 8
architectural design, 31
Archival and Long-Term Preservation, 97
Archival and Preservation, 96
Arizona's Grand Canyon, 16
Artboard Tool (V, 27
artificial intelligence, 10, 12, 13, 27, 353, 354
artistic blur effects, 35
artistic expression, 15
ask questions, 355
assurance for commercial initiatives, 10
asymmetrical proportions, 93
attractive graphics, 1
Auto Button, 181
Auto Recovery Feature, 41
Auto Tone, 159, 183
Auto-Connect Loops, 13
Automate, 161, 340
Automatically correct image perspective and lens flaws, 336

B

Background Eraser, 35
background layer, 115, 146, 234, 267, 291, 303, 325, 341
Background layer, 37, 226, 233, 294, 295, 296, 324, 325, 327
Background layer and the pixel layers, 37
Baseline and Progressive, 92
Basic Panel, 177, 179
Basic Selection, 164, 247
Basic Selection Tools, 164
Batch Processing, 90, 94
Behind, 205, 307
Behind Mode paints, 205
Behind, Clear, Normal, and Dissolve, 205
beneficial for picture compositing, 145
Best Applications, 92
Bevel & Emboss, 302
Big Sur, 4
Bit exposure, 39
Bitmap and vector graphics, 119
Bitmap and vector graphics strengths, 119
Bitmap and vector graphics strengths and weaknesses, 119
bitmap graphic, 119, 120
bitmap image, 112, 113, 114
Bitmap Image Exercise, 113
BITMAP IMAGES, 112
Bitmap mode, 194, 196
Bitmap pictures, 112
Black and White, 285, 287, 288, 320
Blemish and Spot Removal, 266
Blend Mode, 144, 301, 306, 342
BLEND MODES, 306
Blend the cloned area, 275
Blend the Layers, 323
blending color transitions., 35
Blending mode descriptions, 306
Blending Modes, 142, 162, 205, 306
Blending photos, 304
Bloat Tool, 344
Blur Tool, 35, 167
boosting contrast, 35
boundless creative power, 2
boundless creative power of Adobe Photoshop in 2024!, 2
breathtaking graphics, 355
BRIGHTENING A PHOTOGRAPH, 341
Brightening Selective Areas, 341
Brightness, 155, 156, 184, 215, 317, 341
broad variety of, 347, 355
broad variety of important subjects, 355
Brush Hardness, 168
Brush Modes, 205
Brush Preset Picker Contextual Menu, 205
Brush Reconstruct Options, 346
Brush Size, 168
Brush Tip, 203, 213
Brush Tool (B, 34, 167
Brush Tool Flow, 169
brush tool's size and shape, 38
build a corner point, 128, 139
build a document, 19
Build Your Border, 323
building complicated composite pictures, 14
Burn Tool, 36, 267, 280

C

Calculations, 159
Camera Calibration Panel, 178
Camera Raw, 172, 175, 176, 177, 178, 179, 181, 182, 183, 184, 185, 186, 187, 188
Camera RAW, 173, 174
Camera Raw is sharpening, 188
Can I use my existing Adobe ID to use Photoshop 2024?, 354
Can I use Photoshop 2024 on a tablet?, 353
Canon's.CR2, 172
Canvas Size, 86, 87, 88, 158, 321
capabilities of the program, 20
capable of exceeding, 9
Caps Lock, 152
Change Photoshop Ruler to Inches, 104
Change Quick Mask options, 229
Change the Document Color Profile, 200
Change the order of layers and layer groups, 303
change the viewpoint, 28
Changing the Order of Panels in a Group, 48
changing the print resolution, 83
Changing the print size changes the resolution, 81
Changing the print size, not the image size, 79
Changing the resolution changes the print size, 81

channel support, 94
Channels and Paths, 47, 57, 294
Character Panel, 141
Check Microsoft Visual C++ Installation, 7
checkmark, 55, 56, 231, 293, 323
Choose a gradient type, 315
Choose an aspect ratio (Optional), 268
Choose an Image of a Skyline, 322
choose the Eye Dropper Tool, 43
Choose the source area, 275
Choose Your Brush Settings, 210
Choose Your Starting Point and Create Path, 130
Choosing a Workspace, 202
CHOOSING A WORKSPACE, 202
CHOOSING A WORKSPACE AND SELECTING BRUSH, 202
CHOOSING A WORKSPACE AND SELECTING BRUSH SETTINGS, 202
choosing asymmetrical shapes., 27
CHOOSING FILE FORMATS, 91
Choosing Inches, 105
choosing Performance, 66
Choosing the Essentials Workspace, 44
Choosing the Right Format, 90
choosing the Undo option, 62
circular or elliptical selections, 27, 240
Clarity, 180, 192
Clarity Slider, 180
Clear, 102, 170, 205, 307
Clear shortcuts from a command or tool, 170
Click on the Finder Icon, 18
clicking and dragging, 27, 123, 128, 169, 230, 237, 252, 253, 256, 261, 262, 269, 273, 275, 330
clipping mask, 143, 144, 145, 227
Clipping Masks, 142, 219, 227
Clone small areas, 276
Clone Stamp Tool, 35, 167
Close and Go to Bridge, 161
Close File, 160
Close Tab Group, 54
Closing A Panel or Group from the Tab, 54
Closing a Single Panel, 53
cloud document, 74, 75
Cloud document, 74
Cloud documents, 73, 74
Cloud Documents, 19, 20
cloud file services, 40
cloud storage, 354

CMYK, 29, 96, 194, 195, 197, 199, 200, 201, 310
Collapse/Expand Layer Group, 163
Collapsing and Expanding Panel, 52
collapsing and extending panels, 53
Color Accuracy, 174
Color Adaptation, 334
Color and grayscale photos, 91
COLOR AND SWATCH SHORTCUTS, 168
Color Balance, 158, 169, 266, 267, 319
Color Burn, 308
Color channels in the original image, 197
Color Depth Flexibility, 95
Color Detail, 188
Color Dodge, 205, 309
Color Dynamics, 215
color information, 29, 31, 91, 92, 174, 195, 231, 307, 308, 309, 311
Color Information, 220
Color mode, 195, 196, 197, 312
Color Picker, 168, 169, 196, 204, 315
Color Range, 119, 165, 169, 289
Color Replacement, 25, 35
Color Sampler Tool, 31
Color Space, 91
Color Theme, 71
COLOR, EDGE, AND CONTENT-BASED SELECTIONS, 257
Combine Filters and Effects (Optional), 313
Command key, 65, 135, 136, 151, 155, 305, 323
Commit the Changes, 231
Common FAQs about Changing Photoshop Ruler to Inches, 105
common functions, 160
Common Use Cases, 98
Common Uses for the Tool, 236
Compact File Size, 97
comparable in terms of performance, 4
comparable vector graphic, 119
Compare with the Original, 267
Compared to JPEGs, 173
Compatibility, 94, 95, 189
complete tasks, 22
complex compositing, 1
complications, 6
Compressed RAW, 172
compressing an image, 93
Compression Artifacts, 93
Compression Settings, 92

359

compression technique, 91, 93
computer keyboard, 151
computer keyboards, 151
computer running Windows, 4, 248, 255
computer's central processing unit, 4
CONCLUSION, 355
confidence and accuracy, 355
confirmation message, 8
connecting slices, 29
Cons, 107
considerable number of commands, 155
consistent appearance, 278
contacting Adobe Customer Support, 353
contemporary applications, 152
Content Credentials, 12
content production options, 11
Content-Aware Fill, 157, 278, 329, 333, 334
Content-Aware Move Tool, 34, 334, 335
content-aware technology, 34, 273, 274
context menu, 24, 41, 42, 119, 143, 144, 304, 323, 333, 341, 349, 350
Context options, 42
Contextual Menus, 22
contextual taskbar, 9, 15, 17
Continuing paths, 128
Contrast, 155, 156, 159, 180, 182, 183, 187, 250, 317, 341
Control, 22, 38, 62, 63, 64, 65, 84, 135, 136, 151, 152, 155, 156, 173, 204, 214, 230, 254, 322, 323, 350
Control-click on macOS, 22
Convert Point, 32, 138, 139, 140, 168
Convert Point Tool, 32, 168
Convert your selection into a path., 119
Converting a rectangular selection to a single column selection, 242
Converting from a corner point to a smooth point, 138
Converting from a smooth point to a corner point, 139
CONVERTING RGB IMAGE, 199
Copying a Layer, 297
Copying and Pasting Selections, 248
Copying selections, 256
Correct Exposure and Color, 266
correct image perspective, 336, 337
Correct lens distortion and adjust perspective, 336
CORRECTING LENS/CAMERA DISTORTION, 335
CORRECTING SATURATION IN CAMERA RAW, 192

CORRECTING SKIN TONES, 288
CORRECTING THE WHITE BALANCE IN THE CAMERA RAW, 189
Correction, 335, 336, 337, 338, 340
Count Jitter, 214
Count Tool, 30
CPU, 3, 4, 5, 351
Create a Brush Preset, 212
Create a Clipping Mask, 144
create a curve, 125
Create a Curves Adjustment Layer, 290
Create a new Fill layer or Adjustment, 119
Create a new layer, 266, 267, 276, 314, 341, 350
Create a new object, 236
Create a New Swatch, 169
Create a solid color layer., 119
CREATE AND SAVE A CUSTOM BRUSH PRESET, 212
Create as a path, 121
Create custom gradients, 316
Create Layer Group, 162
Create New, 19, 118, 216
Create or Import Your Design Elements, 313
Create the anchor point, 128
Create Your Selection, 252
Creating a circular selection, 239
CREATING A CLIPPING MASK AND APPLYING A SHADOW, 143
Creating a Grunge Border, 322
CREATING A MASK, 220
CREATING A PATTERN TO MAKE A BORDER, 327
CREATING A POINT TYPE, 142
CREATING A QUICK MASK, 228
CREATING A SHADOW WITH AN ALPHA CHANNEL, 231
CREATING A SHAPE USING THE PEN TOOL, 123
Creating a single-column selection, 242
Creating a solid border, 320
Creating Alpha Channels, 219
Creating amazing visual storytelling, 1
Creating an elliptical selection, 239
Creating and Selecting Layers, 162
Creating Fades and Transitions, 304
CREATING MASKS AND CHANNELS IN PHOTOSHOP, 218
CREATING PANORAMA WITH PHOTO MERGE, 340
CREATING TEXT AND ADDING SPECIAL EFFECT, 314
CREATING TYPE ON A PATH, 145
creating vector art, 117

CREATING YOUR KEYBOARD SHORTCUTS, 152
Creative Cloud, 11, 19, 74, 99, 352, 353, 354
Creative Cloud desktop, 353, 354
creative expression, 1, 12
creative goals and expectations, 9
creative journey, 11
creative landscape, 2
creative software, 4, 12
creative tools, 19, 24, 352, 354
creative vision, 355
creative zone, 15
credentials, 12
Crop and Slice Tools, 24, 28
CROP AND SLICE TOOLS GROUP, 28
Crop Tool, 28, 37, 167
Cropping an image in Photoshop, 268
current enhancements, 19
current situation, 41
Current Tool, 39, 41
Curvature Pen Tool, 32
Curved line segments, 122
Custom Brush, 207
Custom Shape Tool, 32
Customizable Interface, 37
Customization, 22
customization choices, 141
Customizing Clipping Path, 131
Customizing the Toolbar, 26
Cut to New Layer, 157
cutting-edge tools, 11
Cycle through Tools, 168

D

Darken, 205, 307, 312, 329
Darker Color, 307, 312
deactivate **Windows Defender**, 6
defensible judgments, 31
Defining the Mesh, 230
degree of inventiveness, 10
Delete a set of shortcuts, 170
Delete Anchor Point Tool, 32
Delete Brush, 205
Delete Cropped Pixels, 270
Delete Swatch, 169
Delete the Photoshop Preferences File, 73
DELETING A GROUP IN PHOTOSHOP, 350

Deleting a Layer, 297
Deleting your path, 125
demonstration of Adobe's dedication, 11
Density, 228, 230, 345
Depending on your selections, 30
Desaturate, 158, 280
desaturate the color in an area, 279
Deselect when you're Done, 245
designing a path, 127
Destination Space, 200
Detail Panel, 178
develop compelling visual tales, 1
development of content, 11, 13
Device Preview panel, 58, 60
DICOM, 173, 197
DICOM format, 173
Difference, 108, 307, 311
DIFFERENCE BETWEEN RESIZING AND RESAMPLING, 84
Different color modes, 194
DIFFERENT MOTIVES FOR SAVING FILES, 99
DIFFERENT MOTIVES FOR SAVING FILES DIFFERENTLY, 99
different perks and benefits, 354
Different Projects Call for Different Units, 110
Digital Art, 99
digital artist, 1, 163, 355
digital artists use PSD files, 99
digital arts, 1, 117
Digital Imaging, 197
Digital Imaging and Communications, 197
Digital Imaging and Communications in Medicine, 197
Digital Negative, 188
Digital photographs and paints, 117
Dimensions, 77, 78, 84, 321
Direct Selection tool, 134, 135, 136, 137, 138, 140
Direct Selection Tool, 32, 145, 168
Direct Selection tool., 135
DirectX 12 support and 2 GB of memory, 3
Disable Home Screen, 20
Disable/Enable Layer Mask, 163
Dissolve, 205, 307
Distance, 145
distinct command, 63
Divide, 311
DNG format, 188

Do cloud documents in Photoshop have anything to do with Lightroom photos?, 75
DO I NEED CAMERA RAW IMAGES, 173
Document Dimensions, 39, 40
Document profile, 39
Document Profile, 40
Document Size, 40, 84, 106
Document Window, 22, 23
Dodge and Burn, 266, 280
Dodge Tool, 36, 267
Does image resolution affect file size?, 82
Does Photoshop 2024 offer any new brushes or filters?, 353
Don't fill in the prompt box., 17
Don't fill out the prompt box., 17
Dots Per Inch (abbreviated as DPI), 106
Double-click on "Adobe Photoshop, 19
Download the Software, 6
DOWNLOADING, 3
downsampling, 79
downward direction, 126
Drag the Selection to a Similar Area, 273
dragging and dropping tools, 26
Draw a selection, 335
Draw Loops for Removal, 13
draw triangles, 32
DRAWING & TYPE TOOLS, 31
DRAWING & TYPE TOOLS GROUP, 31
Drawing and Type Tools, 25
DRAWING CURVED LINES, 125
DRAWING STRAIGHT LINES, 124
Drop Shadow, 144, 302
Dropbox, 40
Dual Brush, 215
Duotone mode, 196
Duplicate Image, 159, 326
Duplicate the Background, 233
Duplicate the Skyline Image into More Layers, 322
DUPLICATING THE GROUP IN PHOTOSHOP, 350
Duplicating the selection, 240, 243
Dynamic Range, 174

E

Easy Corrections, 13
edit PICT files, 120
EDIT SHORTCUTS, 156

Edit Warp Text Live, 148
Editable Text and Vector Graphics, 98
edited photo, 17
Editing Alpha Channels, 219
Editing and Conversion, 97
Editing hair, 278
Editing Paths in Photoshop, 133
editing program, 97, 341, 355
Editing Transparency, 94
EDITING WITH CAMERA RAW EDITOR, 172
Edit-Undo, 62
Edit-Undo (Control/Command + Z), 62
Efficiency, 39, 41, 94
eliminate extraneous items, 35
Eliminating larger objects, 278
Ellipse Tool, 32
Elliptical Marquee tool, 238, 239
Elliptical Marquee Tool, 27, 167
Embark on an exciting learning journey, 10
embracing the most cutting-edge technology, 1
embracing the most cutting-edge technology and fashions, 1
empowered in equal measure, 11
Enhanced Generative, 14
Enhanced Generative AI Workflows, 14
enlarge a tab, 53
enormous potential, 11
equations that make up vector images, 117
Erase Unsuitable Background, 133
Eraser Tool, 35, 167
ERASING EDITING STEPS, 65
ERASING EDITING STEPS WITH THE HISTORY BOX, 65
ESSENTIAL REQUIREMENTS, 76
ESSENTIAL REQUIREMENTS FOR IMAGE EDITING, 76
essential to edit images, 76
Essentials area, 43, 44, 45
Essentials desk, 43
establishing personalized workplaces, 22
establishing web-specific features, 29
ethical sourcing and transparency, 12
ever-changing nature, 355
ever-changing nature of Adobe Photoshop, 355
ever-changing world of digital design, 1
Everyday Photography, 174
exact modifications, 33
examine PDF in more depth, 96
examples of raster graphics, 117
exciting new phase, 11

exciting new phase of your creative journey, 11
Exclusion, 311
Expanding a photo, 16
Expanding and Collapsing Secondary Panels, 59
expedient workflow, 354
experienced designer, 11
experienced users of Photoshop, 355
Experiment with different gradient types, 315
Experimenting with the direction lines, 126
exploiting material, 12
explore the New Features area, 19
explore the New Features area of Photoshop, 19
EXPLORING CONTEXT MENUS, 41
EXPLORING THE OBJECT SELECTION TOOL, 262
EXPLORING THE TOOLBAR, 24
Export Clipboard, 70
Export Options, 94, 142
Export Selected Brushes, 217
Exporting for Web, 90
EXPORTING KEYBOARD SHORTCUTS, 170
EXPORTING KEYBOARD SHORTCUTS IN ADOBE PHOTOSHOP, 170
Exposure Slider, 179
extensive user guides, 355
Extract the Software, 6
Extras, 166
Eyedropper Tool, 29, 31, 42, 167, 168, 169

F

Face Tool, 344
Face-Awareness Liquify, 346
FAMILIARIZING WITH THE PHOTOSHOP WORKSPACE, 21
fascinating world of Photoshop in 2024, 1
Feathering selections, 248
Feathering the selection, 239, 242
field of generative artificial, 12
Figure out an image's width and height., 39
FILE COMPRESSION, 90
File Info, 161
FILE SHORTCUTS, 159
File straight, 74
Fill Light, 184
Fill Out the Dialog Box Properly, 321
Filter Effects, 142
Final Touches, 234

Find "Adobe Photoshop, 19
Finding and choosing the necessary tools, 24
Finding the total number of pixels, 78
fine art painting, 202, 355
FINE ART PAINTING, 202
FINE ART PAINTING WITH THE MIXER BRUSH, 202
Fine-Tune, 342
FINE-TUNE CURVES, 184
Fine-tune the Result, 334
fine-tuning masks, 14
Fixed Layout, 96
Fixed Ratio Selection, 236
Fixed Ratio settings, 236
Fixed Size, 236
FIXING IMAGE AREAS, 274
FIXING IMAGE AREAS WITH THE CLONE STAMP TOOL, 274
Fixing skin blemishes, 278
Flatten All Layers, 199
Flatten Image to flatten, 199
Flatten the Edited Image, 321
FLATTENING AND SAVING FILES, 325
flawless installation, 6
Flow, 203, 206, 210, 212, 282
Foreground and Background Colors, 168
Foreground Color, 204, 215
Foreground/Background Color, 169
Formatting options, 37
Forward Warp Tool, 343
Frame Tool, 29
Free Transform, 142, 157, 305, 322, 328
Freeform Pen Tool, 31
Freeze Mask Tool, 344
Frequency Separation, 267
FREQUENTLY ASKED QUESTIONS ON PHOTOSHOP 2024, 351
Fresco, 74
fresh working environment, 18
FROM START TO FINISH, 192
full potential of Photoshop 2024, 1
Full Screen with Menus, 167
Functionality, 220
Future-Proofing, 174

G

game-changing addition, 11

363

game-changing features, 9
General preferences, 70
Generate Image Assets, 161
GENERATING THE MASK OUTPUT, 227
Generative AI model, 12
generative AI technologies, 9
Generative AI technology, 12
generative AI with relative ease, 14
generative credits, 11
Generative Credits, 11, 352
Generative credits in Photoshop, 11
GENERATIVE EXPAND, 9
GENERATIVE EXPAND ACCESSIBLE, 9
GENERATIVE EXPAND ACCESSIBLE IN PHOTOSHOP FOR COMMERCIAL USE, 9
Generative Fill, 9, 10, 12, 14, 15, 16, 17, 352, 353, 354
GENERATIVE FILL, 9
Generative Fill and Generative Expand, 9, 10, 12, 14
Generative Fill feature, 352, 353
Generative Fill tool, 354
Generative layer, 9
geometric polygons, 117
GET ACQUAINTED WITH THE HOME SCREEN, 19
GETTING ACQUAINTED WITH CAMERA RAW EDITOR WINDOW, 177
GETTING ACQUAINTED WITH COLOR MODE, 194
GETTING FAMILIAR WITH THE BASIC PANEL, 179
GETTING STARTED WITH ADOBE PHOTOSHOP SYSTEM, 18
GETTING STARTED WITH DRAWING ON PHOTOSHOP, 112
GETTING STARTED WITH TYPE, 141
GETTING USED TO PHOTOSHOP PANELS, 43
Go to the "Applications" Folder, 18
Google Drive, 40
go-to platform, 1
GPU, 3, 5
Gradient Map, 169
Gradient Tool, 35, 167
graphic design, 1, 38, 117, 199, 266
Graphic Design, 98
graphic designer, 1, 107, 108, 355
graphic designers, 95, 97, 98, 121, 176, 246
graphics card built, 5
graphics processing unit, 5
grayscale channel, 219

grayscale image in Photoshop, 218
Grayscale mode, 194, 196
greater frequencies, 4
greatest possible user experience, 353
Green mountain range with a calm lake, 16
GROUP TEXTS IN PHOTOSHOP, 350
GROUPS IN PHOTOSHOP, 347

H

Hair Retouching, 267
Hand Tool, 33, 166, 167, 344
Hard Light, 309
Hard Mix, 310
hard-edged strokes, 34
hardness, 68, 168, 204, 221, 273, 275, 277, 341
Hardness, 213
HDD, 3, 5
HDDs, 5
Healing Brush, 25, 34, 63, 168, 231, 266, 267, 274, 276, 277, 278, 334, 335
Healing Brush Tool, 34, 266, 267, 276
Healing Brush tools, 25, 63, 274
hexadecimal, 29
hexadecimal values, 29
hexagons, 32
Hidden tools, 38
Hidden Tools, 25
HIDING A GROUP IN PHOTOSHOP, 349
high cost per gigabyte of SSDs, 6
high-end graphics card, 5
higher numeric values, 108
Higher resolution vs. file size, 83
highest expectations prevalent, 10
Highlights, 180, 183, 185, 280
Highlights Slider, 180
High-Resolution photographs, 98
hint of color, 281
Histogram and Toolbar, 178
History Brush, 35, 66, 67, 68
History Brush Tool, 35
History panel, 58, 59, 65
Hit enter to finish, 272
Hit the **Generate** button, 17
Hold Shift for Larger Movements, 245
horizontal and vertical orientation., 143
Horizontal Distortion, 147

horizontal or vertical camera tilt, 336
horizontal or vertical ruler, 101
Horizontal Perspective, 337
Horizontal Type, 32, 141, 143
Horizontal Type Tool, 32, 141, 143
Horizontal Write Mask, 32
Horizontal Write Mask Tool, 32
How can I update to Photoshop 2024?, 353
How do I change my Photoshop ruler from pixels to inches?, 106
How Do You Make a Wet Brush in Photoshop?, 208
How Does Changing the Ruler Unit Affect Your Final Design Output?, 109
How does image resolution work?, 80
How does path work?, 120
How is Paths Utilized?, 121
How to Access the Photoshop Preferences, 69
How to Add a Guide Lines in Photoshop, 101
How to Adjust the Levels in Photoshop, 284
How to Change an Existing Canvas Size in Photoshop, 86
How to Change the Canvas Size on Export from Photoshop, 87
How to Change Unit / Increment of Your Rulers, 101
How to Change Your Grid Layout, 104
How to Create a Grid in Photoshop, 103
HOW TO CREATE A GROUP IN PHOTOSHOP, 348
How to Create a New Preset Brush, 216
How to Delete a Guide in Photoshop, 102
How to Display Rulers in Photoshop, 100
How to Lock Your Guides in Photoshop, 102
How to Make JPEGs and TIFFs Always, 176
How to Reset Photoshop Preferences, 73
HOW TO RESET TO THE DEFAULT SHORTCUT, 171
HOW TO RESET TO THE DEFAULT SHORTCUT IN ADOBE PHOTOSHOP, 171
How to turn a raster image into a vector image in Photoshop., 118
How to Turn Off the Photoshop Home Screen., 20
HOW TO UNDERSTAND THE TOOL PROPERTIES, 38
HOW TO UNDERSTAND THE TOOL PROPERTIES IN THE OPTIONS BAR, 38
How will I be able to become familiar with the new features that have been added to Photoshop 2024?, 351
HSL/Grayscale Panel, 178
Hue, 169, 215, 260, 299, 307, 311, 319, 332, 333
Hue/Saturation, 169, 260, 299, 319, 332

I

ICC Profiles, 198
identical actions, 63
identify the appropriate tool for your assignment, 24
Image Artifacts, 93
Image Editing, 98
Image Mode, 159
image modification, 1, 230, 329, 355
Image Preview, 177
Image production, 94
image resampling, 84
Image resizing, 84
IMAGE RETOUCHING IN PHOTOSHOP, 266
Image Rotation, 159
IMAGE SHORTCUTS, 158
Image Size, 77, 78, 82, 84, 90, 158
IMAGE TRANSFORMATION, 329
IMAGE/MODE/BITMAP, 117
Images in grayscale mode, 196
import alpha channels, 219
Import the image you want to vectorize into Photoshop., 118
Import your preferred image., 15
important system components, 4
imported CMYK pictures, 195
importing your image, 17
IMPORTING/EXPORTING KEYBOARD SHORTCUTS, 170
improve your images, 1
improve your skills, 355
increase consumer confidence, 12
InDesign, 114
Index mode, 194
Inner Glow, 302
innovative new feature, 12
INS, 152
Insert, 152
INSTALLING ADOBE PHOTOSHOP 2024, 6
installing the software, 8
instructions for adjusting saturation, 172
Intel or AMD processor, 3
intelligence algorithms, 13
Interactive Elements, 97
Interface Preferences, 71
Interlacing, 94
International Color Consortium, 198

365

International Committee, 191
International Committee of White Balance, 191
international keyboards, 152
international posters and banners, 108
Internet connection, 3, 351
Intersect with Selection, 164
Intersecting Selections, 248
intricate image compositions, 94, 98
INTRODUCTION, 1
Inverse Selection, 165
Inverting the selection, 239, 242
investigation of Photoshop's possibilities, 1
Is it possible to install Photoshop 2024 on more than one computer?, 351
Is the resolution still limited to 1024 x 1024?, 352
Is there a free trial for Photoshop 2024?, 354

J

JOINT PHOTOGRAPHER EXPERTS GROUP, 91
JPEG, 23, 74, 76, 83, 90, 91, 92, 93, 112, 145, 172, 173, 174, 175, 176, 189, 190, 234, 267, 339, 340

K

Key Differences between Masks and Alpha Channels, 220
Key Points about the Properties Panel, 37
keyboard shortcut, 17, 25, 26, 36, 62, 63, 99, 100, 144, 145, 152, 155, 156, 157, 168, 170, 239, 240, 242, 243, 253, 255, 262, 279, 330, 332, 333
keyboard shortcuts, 22, 26, 63, 151, 152, 156, 157, 158, 159, 160, 161, 170, 171, 177, 251, 252, 268
Keyboard Shortcuts, 22, 42, 64, 152, 153, 157, 170, 171

L

Large Document Format, 173, 196, 197
large selection of brushes and settings, 34
Lasso Selection tools, 24
Lasso Selections, 164
Lasso tool, 17, 129, 164, 167, 247, 248, 251, 252, 255, 261, 273
Lasso Tool, 27, 167, 235, 246, 247, 248, 249, 250, 251, 252, 333

LASSO TOOLS SELECTION, 246
launch the Creative Cloud desktop program, 353
Launch your Photoshop app., 15
Launching Adobe Photoshop, 18
LAUNCHING PHOTOSHOP, 18
Layer Alignment, 163
Layer Comps, 91, 98
Layer Filtering, 37
Layer Groups, 162
Layer Linking, 163
Layer Locks, 162
Layer Masking, 163
Layer Masks, 218
Layer menu shortcuts, 161
LAYER SHORTCUTS, 161
Layer Styles, 141, 163, 302
Layer Support, 98
Layer Visibility, 162
LAYER/FLATTEN IMAGE command, 116
Layers and transparency, 95
Layers panels, 46, 47
Layers Specificity, 220
LAYERS STACKING ORDER, 303
Layer-Specific Controls, 37
learning journey, 10
Learning on the Go, 14
Legacy Undo Mode, 64
Legacy Undo Shortcuts, 63, 64
legal dialog window, 16
lens bulge towards, 337
Lens Profiles, 336
leveraging various services and tools, 15
Lighten, 205, 307, 308, 312
Lighter Color, 307, 312
lightning-fast SSD, 6
Lightroom Classic, 75
Lightroom collection., 75
Lightroom-compatible file, 75
Lightroom-compatible file type, 75
Line Tool, 32
Linear Burn, 308
Linear Dodge (Add), 307, 309
Linear Light, 310
List of modifier keys, 151
Load Mesh Options, 346
Load Swatches, 169
Loading Alpha Channels and Saving Them, 219
loading of online pages, 28

Lock in the crop, 270
Lock Layers, 162
Locking Layers, 301
Long blond and wavy hair with red ribbon, 16
Look through the Preset Profiles, 181
looking at the Color, 46
Lossless compressed RAW, 172
Lossless Compression, 93
Lossless Editing Workflow, 95
lossy compression, 90, 91, 173, 190
lower latencies, 4
Lower resolution vs. file size, 83
Luminance, 187
Luminance Detail, 187
Luminosity, 307, 311, 312, 320

M

Mac running, 4
MacBook, 40
Magic Wand Selection, 164
Magic Wand tool, 25, 118, 164, 167, 245, 258, 259, 260, 261
Magic Wand Tool, 27, 167, 235, 257, 260, 330
Magnetic Lasso, 27, 129, 164, 167, 235, 246, 247, 248, 249, 250, 252
main measurement tools, 29
Maintaining a discriminating mindset, 7
MAJOR GROUPING OF PHOTOSHOP TEXT, 141
MAKE A WET BRUSH, 207
Make More Refinements to Your Edits, 182
Make the foreground color black, 221
Make the foreground color white, 221
Make Your Selection, 245
makes counting objects, 30
Making a corner point with direction lines, 139
Making a corner point with only one direction line, 139
Making a corner point without direction lines, 139
MAKING IT RIGHT WITH UNDO AND REDO COMMANDS, 62
making modifications, 178, 184, 249
MAKING SELECTIONS WITH THE QUICK SELECTION TOOL, 260
Making the transition, 127
manage your cloud documents, 19
Marquee selection category., 239

Marquee Selection Tool, 167
Marquee Selection tools, 24
Marquee Selections, 164
Marquee tool, 164, 235, 236, 237, 238, 239, 240, 241, 242, 243, 244, 253
MARQUEE TOOLS SELECTION, 235
Mask Options, 346
Masking, 14, 186, 188, 219
masking and cropping, 9
MASKING AND CROPPING, 14
masking tasks, 14
master Photoshop 2024, 355
Match Color, 159
mathematical equations, 117, 306
Measurement Scales, 40
measurement tool, 29
Measurement Tools, 24
measuring angles and distances, 24
MEASURING TOOLS GROUP, 29
memory slots, 4
memory storage components, 4
Menu Bar, 21, 55, 69, 73, 77, 166, 292, 293
menu shortcuts in Photoshop, 156, 161, 163, 165
Merge layers into another layer, 324
MERGING LAYERS, 323
Metadata, 93
Microsoft OneDrive, 40
middle of the working area, 22
midtone gray., 284
Midtone level, 288
millions of colors, 194
MINIMUM AND RECOMMENDED SYSTEM, 3
Mixer Brush Tool, 35, 208
Mixer Brush tool sets, 25
MIXING COLORS WITH THE MIXER BRUSH, 208
Mobility, 74
Modes Supported by Your Hardware, 109
modifier keys, 151, 152
Modify Selection, 165
modify specific handles, 32
Modify the Shadow Settings, 144
Modify the shadow's transparency, 145
Modify Your Warp Text, 147
Modifying path segments, 136
modifying slice features, 29
Monitor calibration, 198
Monitor Profiling, 198
monthly credits, 11

More Dynamics, 216
most recent version, 4, 6, 12, 63, 351, 353, 354
motherboard, 4
MOULDING AN IMAGE, 230
MOULDING AN IMAGE USING THE PUPPET WARP, 230
Move and Selection Tools, 24
Move Tool (V, 27, 167
Moving a selected area, 261
MOVING A SELECTION WITH SHORTCUT KEYS, 245
Moving and Distorting, 230
Moving and duplicating a selection simultaneously, 255
Moving curved segments, 136
Moving Layers, 296
Moving options bar, 38
Moving Panel, 60
Moving Panels between Groups, 49
Moving straight segments, 136
moving the cropping handles, 28
Moving the selection, 240, 243
Multichannel mode, 197
multiple layers, 252, 279, 306, 321, 323, 349
Multiple Monitors, 167
multiple times, 64
Multiply, 144, 205, 307, 308

N

navigate to the "**Applications**, 18
Navigate to the **Preferences** menu, 20
Navigate to the **Preferences** menu, then **General.**, 20
NAVIGATING AROUND THE LAYERS PANEL, 292
Navigation and Panning, 166
Navigation Tools, 25, 33
NAVIGATION TOOLS, 33
NAVIGATION TOOLS GROUP, 33
New Brush Group, 205
New Brush Preset, 205
New Features, 19, 20
New File, 160
New Fill Layer, 327
New Gradient, 316
NEW INTERACTIONS IN REMOVE TOOL, 13
New Layer, 115, 162, 232, 276, 295, 297, 334, 341
new tools, 13, 14

new universe of possibilities, 9
Nikon's.NEF, 172
Normal mode, 307
Normal Mode, 205
Notable artifacts, 93
Notes Tool, 30
noticeable increase in performance, 5
Nudge the Selection, 245
Num Lock, 152

O

Object Selection Tool, 27, 235, 262, 263, 264, 330, 331
older version of Photoshop, 107
On macOS, 18, 151
On Windows, 18
online lessons, 355
on-the-spot guidance, 14
opacity, 68, 98, 162, 163, 168, 206, 207, 218, 228, 230, 233, 267, 277, 291, 292, 302, 303, 304, 305, 307, 316, 325, 342
Opacity, 145, 162, 163, 168, 203, 206, 210, 277, 303, 304, 316, 342
Open a New Blank Canvas, 322
Open Adobe Photoshop, 8, 176
Open an image., 202
Open as Smart Object, 160, 327
Open File, 160, 220
Open images in Photoshop Camera Raw from Photoshop or Bridge, 175
open new possibilities, 355
Open **Photoshop**, 36, 146
Open Recent Files, 160
Open the Image to Select Skin Tones, 288
Open the Profile Panel, 181
Open vs. Active Panels, 56
Open your image, 118, 320, 341
Open Your Image, 181, 233, 276, 303, 312, 333, 341
Open Your Images, 144
Open your photo., 17
Opened red wine bottle next to an empty wine glass, 16
Opening files, 23
OPENING IMAGES IN THE CAMERA RAW EDITOR, 175
Opening Panels from the Window Menu, 55
Opening Your Image, 230

operating system, 4, 18, 70, 96, 274
Operating system, 4
Operating System, 3
optimal solution, 5
Optimization in Photoshop, 93
Option key on macOS, 33
Organize Your Edited Files, 189
Organize Your Workflow, 266
organizing your workplace, 26
original design, 199
original photo's surrounds, 16
Outer Glow, 303
Overlay, 205, 223, 225, 267, 309

P

Page Setup, 161
Paint Bucket Tool, 35
painting, 13, 21, 25, 34, 35, 66, 76, 99, 120, 167, 202, 203, 211, 215, 216, 219, 221, 222, 228, 229, 231, 274, 279, 280, 281, 282, 307, 308, 311, 342
Panel and Dialog Box Context Menus, 42
Panel Groups, 47, 50, 52, 60
Panels and Panel Groups, 22
Panel's Snapshots, 66
Paragraph and Character Styles, 141
Paragraph Panel, 141
Paragraph Text, 143
paragraph text layer, 143
Parametric Curve, 184, 185
Paste in Place, 257
Paste Into, 257
Paste Outside, 257
Paste without Formatting, 257
Patch Tool, 34, 273, 274
Path Selection Tool, 32
Pattern Preview, 327
Pattern Stamp Tool, 35
PDF, 76, 96, 97, 194, 196, 197, 201
PDF (PORTABLE DOCUMENT FORMAT), 96
Pen Tool, 31, 112, 123, 129, 130, 138, 145, 167, 168, 233, 333
Pencil Tool, 34
performance, 4, 5, 6, 9, 67, 69, 70, 352, 353, 354
performance benefits, 4
Performing edits, 138
personalize Photoshop's user interface, 69, 71

personalize the toolbar, 26
personalize your strokes, 34
Perspective Crop Tool, 28
photographer, 1, 11, 40, 173, 270, 355
Photomerge function, 329
PHOTOSHOP (PSD), 97
Photoshop 2024 draws, 1
PHOTOSHOP 2024 STRIKING FEATURES, 9
Photoshop format, 172
Photoshop from pixels, 104, 109
Photoshop Gradient Application, 315
Photoshop Gradient Application Tips, 315
Photoshop Midtone Level, 284, 288
Photoshop path-creation process, 129
Photoshop program, 74
Photoshop PSD files, 98
Photoshop RGB Color, 194
Photoshop running, 24
Photoshop system requirements by component, 3
Photoshop techniques, 202
Photoshop tools, 33, 38, 151
Photoshop works with raster images, 117
Photoshop's areas, 44
Photoshop's Edit menu, 256
Photoshop's large collection, 22
Photoshop's large collection of keyboard shortcuts, 22
Photoshop's layer-based editing system, 94
Photoshop's new Search Bar., 44
Photoshop's Preferences, 58
Photoshop's Sticky Panels, 56
Photoshop's workspace, 22
Pick a Profile, 182
Pick Reset Essentials, 45
pick the **Make Work Path** option, 119
picture compositing and design tasks, 145
picture editing, 1, 10, 38, 141, 172
piece of software, 1, 105
Pin Edges, 345
Pin Light, 310
pincushion distortion, 336, 337
Pink convertible sports car with the roof off, 16
pixel dimensions, 77, 81, 257, 338
pixelation, 112, 117
Place Embedded, 160
Place the New Background, 234
Play Around With Various Warp Effects, 148
plethora of fascinating new feature, 354

369

Plugins and Filters, 94
PNG, 12, 23, 74, 76, 90, 91, 93, 94, 95, 112, 145, 197, 234
Point text, 143
Polygon Tool, 32
Pop-Up Sliders, 42
PORTABLE DOCUMENT FORMAT, 96
PORTABLE NETWORK GRAPHICS, 93
power and accuracy of Photoshop, 9
powerful central processing unit, 4
powerful processor, 5
Practical Uses, 220
Precautions, 201
precise adjustments, 10, 346
precise measurements, 31
precise region, 13
Precise Rotations, 253
Preferences, 6, 20, 69, 70, 73, 100, 101, 104, 105, 106, 157, 176
pre-made frames or shapes, 29
premium price, 5
Prep Your Image to Create the Grunge Border, 322
Prepare Your Background, 233
Prepare Your Computer, 6
Preserve Details, 339, 340
preserving layout settings, 22
Preset Sync, 9, 15
PRESET SYNC DISCONTINUED, 15
PRESET SYNC DISCONTINUED WITH THE RELEASE OF PHOTOSHOP 25.0, 15
Preset Sync for the management, 15
Preset Sync in Photoshop 25.0, 9
Presets and Snapshots, 178
press the extra Alt key, 152
Press the **Generate Fill** button, 16
pressing **Control or Command Z**, 63
Pressure, 214, 345
prevalent misperception, 82
prevent "overproducing" an image, 282
Preview and Confirm, 304
Preview frequently, 276
Preview Profiles, 182
Preview Toggle, 181
previous step, 43, 241
primary advantages, 10
primary purpose, 30, 222, 258, 338
Print Design, 99

Print Screen, 152
print size changes, 81
Printer Calibration, 198
Printer profiling, 198
Print-Ready Format, 97
prioritize purchasing a computer, 4
produce artistic effects or gentle, 35
produces pixel-perfect, 34
producing appealing visuals, 1
producing artwork, 34
Professional Printing, 96
professional-grade, 10
progressing up to an immersion, 1
Progressive VS Baseline, 92
Properties, 10, 36, 37, 43, 46, 47, 48, 49, 50, 60, 61, 141, 223, 224, 225, 232, 283, 332, 343, 345
Protecting Areas, 231
PrtScn, 152
PSD, 23, 40, 74, 75, 76, 97, 98, 99, 115, 116, 172, 188, 234, 267, 316, 325
PSD files, 98, 99
Pucker Tool, 343, 344
Push Left Tool, 344
pushing the Color panel, 47
PUTTING A NEW BACKGROUND FOR THE LAYER MASK, 233
PV2010, 184
PV2010 and PV2003, 184
PV2012, 183
Pyramids in the desert, 16

Q

Quality, 74, 90, 92, 94, 95, 201
Quick Actions, 37
Quick Masks, 219
Quick Selection Tool, 25, 27, 235, 260, 290, 330, 333
Quit Photoshop, 73

R

RAM, 3, 4, 5, 6, 40, 41, 70, 82
RAM system needs, 5
Raster images, 117
Rasterize Text, 142
rasterize the twisted text, 149
rasters or vectors, 117

370

RAW + JPEG mode, 190
RAW files, 172, 173, 174
Reading the Input Level Numbers, 286
Reading the Photoshop Levels, 284
realm of digital imaging, 355
real-world examples, 355
recent version of Photoshop, 4, 12, 63, 351, 353
Reconstruct Tool, 343
Rectangle Tool, 32
Rectangular Marquee, 17, 27, 118, 164, 167, 237, 238, 239, 244, 252, 254, 255, 261
Rectangular Marquee tool, 17, 118, 237, 238, 239, 244, 252, 254, 255, 261
Rectangular Marquee Tool, 27, 167
RED EYE REMOVAL, 329
Red Eye Tool, 34
redistributable packages, 8
Reduce Color Noise, 340
Reduce image noise, 339
Refine the Selection, 233
REFINING A MASK, 222
REFINING MASK EDGE WITH THE GLOBAL REFINEMENTS, 222
Refining the Result, 231
Refrain from cloning over crucial aspects, 276
regular Lasso Tool, 248, 250
regular layer, 324, 325
Relaunch Photoshop, 73
Reliability, 74
Relocate the Selection, 253
RELOCATION WITH THE CONTENT-AWARE TOOL, 334
removal procedure, 13
Remove Background and **Select Subject**, 37
Remove Distortion, 337
Remove specific objects from an image, 236
Removing an object, 17
REMOVING BLEMISHES AND WRINKLES, 276
REMOVING BLEMISHES AND WRINKLES WITH HEALING BRUSH TOOLS, 276
REMOVING OBJECTS WITH CONTENT-AWARE FILL, 333
Rename a layer in Photoshop by making use of the Layers Panel, 297
Rename a layer in Photoshop by using "Layer" in the main menu, 298
Rename Brush., 205
Renaming a Layer, 297
Reopening and joining path components, 140

Reposition a Guide by Clicking and Dragging, 102
Repositioning a selection marquee while creating it, 243
Resetting options, 38
Resetting the Essentials Workspace, 44
Reshaping curved segments, 137
Resize, 234, 269, 335
Resize and Position the Subject, 234
Resizing and copying a selection, 254
resizing images, 84, 158, 159
Resizing Images, 90
RESOLUTION field, 114
Resolution Matters, 109
Restarting Photoshop, 20
retouching, 1, 21, 34, 115, 157, 251, 262, 266, 267, 272, 276, 277, 278, 329, 355
RETOUCHING & PAINTING TOOLS GROUP, 34
Retouching and Corrections, 174
Retouching and Painting Tools, 25
Revert to Saved, 160
Review and Modify, 313
Revisit if Necessary, 267
RGB Color mode, 194
RGB mode, 194, 195, 197
Rotate Brush, 168
Rotate Canvas, 158
Rotate View Tool, 33, 166
ROTATING AND RESIZING LAYERS, 305
ROTATING AND SCALING A SELECTION, 252
Rotation Adaptation, 334
roundness, 213
ruler systems, 110
Ruler Tool, 30
Rulers, Grids, and Guides, 166

S

Sample from nearby pixels, 277
Saturation, 169, 180, 185, 192, 193, 215, 307, 311, 332, 333
Saturation Slider, 180
Save a Backup of Your Work, 199
SAVE A COPY, 99
Save and Load Brushes in Photoshop, 217
Save File, 160
Save for Web, 90, 93, 160
Save Progress, 41

Save settings and set camera and lens defaults, 338
Save the edited photo to your local storage., 17
Save the image to your desktop., 17
Save the Vector Image as an SVG file, 119
Save your Image, 182
Save Your Path, 132
Save your photo., 16
Save your work, 315
Save Your Work, 234, 267, 277, 304, 334, 342
Saving as a Different Format, 90
SAVING CAMERA RAW EDITS, 188
SAVING CAMERA RAW EDITS AS NEW FILES, 188
SAVING IMAGE TO DUPLICATE THE IMAGE FILE, 99
SAVING THE IMAGE AS THE ORIGINAL, 99
Saving the selection, 240, 243
SAVING YOUR IMAGE AS PHOTOSHOP, 201
Saving Your Work, 231
Scattering, 214
schmancy structure, 186
Scratch Size, 39
Scratch Sizes, 40
Screen, 3, 19, 20, 77, 165, 166, 167, 245, 254, 308, 342
Screen Mode, 166, 167
Screen Resolution, 3
Scripts, 161
Scroll Lock, 152
Seamless Integration, 14
Search Criteria, 336
second anchor point, 126
secondary column, 58, 59, 60
Security Features, 96
select "Layer via Cut", 133
select a Blending Mode, 205, 215
Select a Color, 208, 321
Select All and Deselect, 165
Select and Mask, 164, 202, 222, 223, 224, 226, 232, 234
Select and Mask window, 222
Select Menu Commands, 165
SELECT SHORTCUTS, 164
Select Subject, 164, 222, 224, 225, 227
Select the Appropriate Layer, 252
Select the Area to Be Patched, 273
Select the colors for your gradient, 315
Select the crop tool, 268
Select the cropped area, 271
Select the Gradient tool, 315

Select the Language, 7
Select the Layer to Apply the Filter, 313
Select the OK button, 105
Select the part of the image you want to vectorize, 118
Select the perspective crop tool, 271
Select the Picture You Want to Use, 129
Select the Puppet Warp Tool, 230
Select the Subject, 233
Select the Target Area, 289
Select Tonal Areas with the Color Range, 119
Select Tonal Areas with the Color Range Command., 119
SELECTING A TOOL FROM THE TOOLBAR, 36
SELECTING AN ADOBE RAW PROFILE, 181
Selecting from a center point, 253
selecting particular parts, 240
Selecting paths, 133
Selecting Units & Rulers, 105
Selection Modification, 164
SELECTION TOOLS GROUP, 26
Selective Color, 169
separate layer, 9
separate panel, 47
SETTING PHOTOSHOP PREFERENCES, 69
Setting standards, 12
Setting standards for responsibility, 12
Setting standards for responsibility and transparency, 12
several devices, 15, 74
Shadows, 180, 183, 185, 280, 281
Shadows Slider, 180
Shape Dynamics, 214
Shape Tools, 37
Sharpen Details, 340
Sharpen Tool, 35, 167
Sharpening, 267
SHARPENING IMAGE WITH THE DETAIL PANEL, 185
SHOW/HIDE LAYER, 300
Show/Hide Rulers, 166
Shrinking and stretching, 137
shut panels, 53
significant modifications, 9
Single Column Marquee tool, 238, 239, 242
Single Column Marquee Tool, 27
Single Row Marquee tool, 238, 239, 240, 241
Single Row Marquee Tool, 27

Sitting brown and white corgi with its tongue out, 16
SKETCHING A PATH FROM A PHOTO, 129
Skin Retouching, 267
Slice Select Tool, 29
Slice Tool, 28, 29
Slices of HTML, 28
Smaller File Sizes, 174
Smart Objects, 98, 346
smooth anchor points, 32
Smooth Tool, 343
Smudge Tool, 35, 167
Snap Objects onto Guides or Grids, 103
Snap To, 103, 166
Soft Light, 309
Soft Proofing, 198
solid background color, 262
solid-state drive, 5, 6
solid-state drives, 5, 6
Some handy shortcuts, 135
Some International Keyboards, 152
Some other information, 39
Sony's.ARW, 172
Spacing, 213
specific components, 3
specific tool., 25
speed of Adobe Photoshop, 5
SPONGE AND DODGE TOOLS, 279
Sponge Tool, 36, 280, 281
Spot Healing Brush tool, 274, 278
Spot Healing Brush Tool, 34, 266, 335
SSD, 5, 6
SSDs, 5, 6
standard component, 11
standard hard disk drives, 5
start a new document, 19, 84, 123
Start cloning, 275
Start Installation, 8
Start Menu, 8
Start the Setup File, 7
Start with a New Canvas, 312
Status Bar, 22, 39
step by step instructions, 355
sticks of RAM leaves, 5
Storage, 5, 95
straight and curved lines, 127
Straight Edge Lasso, 247
Straight line segments, 122

Straighten (Optional), 269
Straightening an image in Photoshop, 270
STRAIGHTENING AND CROPPING AN IMAGE, 268
straightforward access, 14
straightforward method, 62
straightforward process, 18, 62
Streamlined Masking Workflows, 14
Subsampling, 92
Subtract, 164, 226, 261, 264, 311
Subtract from Selection, 164, 226, 261
Subtracting from a Selection, 247
Sunset at the beach, 16
supplementary software, 7
Support for a Wide Range of Color Depths, 93
Swatches panel, 47, 49, 53, 56
Swatches Panel, 169
Swatches panels, 49, 50, 56
switch to sketching a curve, 128
Switching between curves and lines, 127
SWITCHING BETWEEN LASSO AND POLYGONAL LASSO TOOLS, 251
Switching Between Panels in a Group, 47
SYSTEM REQUIREMENTS, 3
SYSTEM REQUIREMENTS, DOWNLOADING AND INSTALLING PHOTOSHOP 2024, 3

T

TAGGED IMAGE FILE FORMAT, 95
Tall buildings full of windows, 16
Technique, 137, 138
Temperature and Tint, 180, 189, 190, 191, 192
Temperature Slider, 181
Text & Typography, 95
Text and Image Integration, 96
Text Effects, 141
Text Export, 142
Text Filters, 142
Text Masking, 142
Text on Path, 142
Text Overlays, 304
Text Presets, 142
Text tools, 25
Text Tools, 141
Text Transformation, 142
Text Warp Defined, 146
Text Warped and Distorted, 150

Textual Information, 94
Texture, 215, 216
Textured brushes, 215
Thaw Mask Tool, 344
the "**Customize Toolbar**" dialog box, 26
the "**Edit**" menu, 26, 149
The "**Edit**" menu in Photoshop, 156
the "**Pick up Path**" cursor, 128
The "**Source Space**" area, 200
the "**Update**" button., 353
the "**Window**" menu, 36
The action starts, 10
The Active Layer, 297
The actual components, 122
the **Adjustment Panel**, 290
the **Adjustments panel** tab, 48
the Adobe Photoshop symbol, 18
the Basic panel, 172, 177, 179, 181, 182, 184, 192
The Basics, 203
The Black Level in Photoshop, 284
the **Brush**, 25, 34, 41, 43, 167, 168, 169, 202, 203, 205, 207, 213, 216, 217, 221, 267, 276, 281, 307, 316, 341, 345
The Brush Preset Picker menu, 205
the Clone Stamp, 63, 167, 231, 266, 267, 274, 275, 276, 278, 334
the CMYK mode, 195
the **Color or Swatches panels**, 43
the **Color panel**, 46, 47, 50, 51, 52, 56
the Color Panel, 47
The Color panel, 52
the **Color panel's** tab, 47
The context options in Photoshop, 41
The Contextual Task Bar, 14, 15
the Control key in addition, 155
The **Count slider**, 214
the **Count Tool**, 30
the current version, 63
The Default "Essentials" Workspace, 43
the Design Editor, 142, 143
The Detailed Guide to Photoshop Red Eye Removal, 330
the dialog window, 69
The Difference between Pixels and Inches, 108
The Direct Selection tool, 134
The **Dissolve Mode**, 205
The Document Window, 22

the Edit menu, 62, 63, 64, 65, 66, 170, 232, 252, 253, 255, 256, 262
the **Edit Menu**, 63
The editing techniques of Dodge, 279
the **Essentials workspace**, 43, 45
The fields labeled Width, 78
the File menu, 23, 99, 176, 233, 255, 340
The Freeform Pen tool, 129
the full potential of the sophisticated picture, 355
The General Preferences, 70
the general steps to launch Photoshop, 18
the **Group menu** option, 49
the History Panel, 65, 66
The Home Screen, 19
The icon view mode, 59
the **IMAGE menu**, 114, 115
the **Image Size** dialog box, 78, 82, 84
The Image Size dialog box, 77
the IMAGE SIZE option, 114
The image's pixel count, 81
the **Import Brushes** option, 217
The Jitter Percentage, 215
The Layer Name, 294
The Layer Row, 294
The Layer Search Bar, 298
the **Layers panel**, 36, 37, 42, 43, 57, 118, 119, 145, 163, 220, 222, 223, 232, 233, 234, 252, 276, 279, 292, 293, 294, 295, 296, 297, 299, 300, 302, 303, 304, 305, 313, 314, 315, 316, 323, 324, 325, 326, 328, 341, 346, 347, 350
The Layers panel, 46, 47, 57, 232, 291, 293, 301
The Learn area offers access, 19
the **left mouse button** down, 48
the Liquify filter, 329, 342, 344, 346
the Liquify tool, 342, 345, 346
The Main Panel Column, 46
the menu bar, 16, 36, 65, 73, 102, 103, 147, 166, 201, 222, 228, 240, 243, 245, 254, 280, 313, 327
the Menu Command, 155
the **mouse button**, 48, 50, 51, 101, 123, 129, 140, 203, 216, 244, 245, 247, 254, 261, 303, 304
the navigation bar, 21, 181
the **New Adjustment Layer** submenu, 332
the numerous panels, 22
The Options Bar, 21, 38
The Options Menu, 21
The paint application speed, 206
The Panel Area, 45

374

the panel's symbol, 59
the Patch Tool, 34
The Path Component Selection tool, 134
The path to vectors., 117
the *Paths* **tab**, 125
the pen tool, 121, 219
The Photoshop Levels Dialog, 283
the **Photoshop panels**, 45, 46, 55
the Photoshop toolbar, 24, 25, 145
The Pixel Grid, 76
The Preferences Dialog Box, 69
the Preferences panel, 69, 70, 73
The **Preferences** panel, 69
The Preset Picker panel, 205
The **Preset Sync** feature, 15
The **Preset Sync** feature of Adobe Photoshop, 15
The Preview Thumbnail, 295
The price of solid-state drives, 5
the **primary panel** column., 58
the **Properties panel**, 10, 43, 48, 49, 50, 60, 61, 223, 224, 225, 232, 332
The Properties Panel, 37
The Recent section, 19
the Remove tool, 13
the **Resample Image** option, 84
the **Resample** option, 79, 81, 83
The **Resample** option, 79
The resolution of a bitmap image, 119
The RGB model, 195
the Rubber Band option, 124
the same menu button, 54
the second anchor point, 126
The Secondary Panel Column, 58
the shapes tool, 121
the Sharpen Tool, 35
the simpler UI, 72
The Split Toning panel, 178
the standard Lasso Tool, 251
the **Step backward** command, 63
the **Swatches panel**, 47, 52, 56, 169
the Taskspaces., 154
The text pointer, 145
The TIFF integration, 96
the Tools palette, 129, 134
The Transitions Involved, 109
The unique function, 353
The value of the Load parameter, 211
The vast majority of users, 5

The Width, Height, and Resolution connection, 78
THE WORD PIXEL, 76
The workplace, 22
Threadripper, 4
three-panel columns, 45
THRESHOLD, 116
TIFF, 74, 75, 76, 95, 96, 113, 117, 173, 175, 176, 188, 189, 196, 197
TIFF (TAGGED IMAGE FILE FORMAT), 95
TIFF file, 113, 117, 175, 176
TIFF files, 74, 95, 96
Timeline (for Animation), 166
Timing, 39, 41
Tint Slider, 181
Tips for a Professional Finish, 234
Tips for Effective Use, 277
Tips for Using Puppet Warp Effectively, 231
Toggle Last State, 63, 225
Toggle text orientation, 143
Tone Curve Panel, 177
Tool Selection, 26
TOOL SHORTCUTS, 167
Toolbar Layout, 24
Toolbar Organization, 42
Tools Panel, 21
Tools toolbar, 204, 207
Tool-Specific Context Menus, 41
Tool-specific settings, 38
Touch Up the Patch, 274
traditional hard disk, 5
traditional Lasso Tool., 251
Transfer objects, 236
Transform Selection, 157
Transform the Skyline Image, 322
transformative capabilities, 11
Transparency, 93, 94, 95, 219, 226, 307
Transparency and Layers, 95
Transparency Masks, 94
Triangle Tool, 32
Turn the Clipping Path into Dotted Lines, 132
Twirl Clockwise Tool, 343
Two-dimensional digital images, 117
Type Layers, 37
Type Tool, 143, 145
Typefaces & Font Size, 109
Types of anchor points, 122
Types of line segments, 122
typical path in Photoshop, 121

U

Uncheck Advertising, 7
Uncompressed RAW, 172
uncover the limitless possibilities, 2
UNDERSTANDING CALIBRATION, 197
UNDERSTANDING CALIBRATION AND PROFILING, 197
UNDERSTANDING MASKS AND ALPHA CHANNELS, 218
UNDERSTANDING VARIOUS RAW FILE FORMATS, 172
Undo and Redo, 63, 156
UNGROUPING LAYERS IN PHOTOSHOP, 350
unique tasks and projects, 14
Universal Compatibility, 96
unlock new possibilities, 355
Unlock the Layer of Your Image, 321
Unsharp Mask, 186, 267
Unsharp Mask dialog box, 186
UPDATED SHORTCUTS COMMAND, 151
updating to Photoshop 2024, 353
upgrade to Windows 10, 4
upper right part of the Photoshop screen, 44
upsampling, 79
Use a light touch, 276
Use a small brush size, 277
Use Brush Tool, 341
Use layer masks, 316
Use multiple gradients, 316
Use multiple passes, 278
Use the Arrow Keys, 245
Users of Photoshop, 12
USING A CONTENT-AWARE PATCH, 272
Using Compression Software, 90
using Photoshop 2024, 353, 355
using Photoshop tools, 38
using the Detail panel, 172
Using the Inch Measurement System in Photoshop, 107
Using the Lightroom top menu, 75
USING THE PRESETS, 190
Using the Remove tool, 13
Using the RGB paradigm, 194
USING THE STATUS BAR, 39
USING THE TEMPERATURE & TINT SLIDERS, 190
USING THE WHITE BALANCE TOOL, 191
utilize the "Warp Text" option, 145
utilize the Patch Tool, 34
utilizing tools, 63, 266

V

Variations, 17, 159
variety of editing tasks, 21
variety of formats, 112
variety of tools and actions, 14
VARIOUS RAW FILE, 172
VECTOR GRAPHICS, 117
Vector Image, 119
Vector Masks, 219, 227, 228
vector-based tools and capabilities, 120
Vectors are an excellent format, 117
Versatile Usage, 95
VERSION 25.0, 6
Vertical Distortion, 147
Vertical Perspective, 337
Vertical Type Mask Tool, 32
Vertical Type Tool, 32, 141, 143
Vibrance, 180, 192, 319
Vibrance and Saturation, 180
Vibrance Slider, 180
View a list of current shortcuts, 170
View menu shortcuts, 165
View Options, 346
VIEW SHORTCUTS, 165
Vignette Amount, 337
Vignette Midpoint, 337
visibility of the Adjustments panel, 48
Vivid Light, 310
voyage of exploration and mastery, 1

W

Wait for Installation to Complete, 8
Warp and Distort Text in Photoshop?, 146
Warp Transform, 142
Warp Your Text, 147
Warped Text, 142, 149
WARPING TEXT, 146
Web design, 99
well-defined geometric shapes, 251
Wet reflective pathway, 16
Wet-on-Dry Brush, 207
What am I doing wrong? I've tried switching the unit of measurement on my ruler to inches, but it hasn't worked out so far., 107

What are the benefits of subscribing to Adobe Creative Cloud?, 354
What are the new features in Photoshop 2024?, 354
What are the system requirements for Photoshop 2024?, 351
What Does the Marquee Tool Do?, 235
What happens if you run out of credits?, 352
What is a Photoshop Group, 347
What is DPI and how does it relate to changing rulers into inches?, 106
What is image size?, 77
What is the difference between cloud documents, 74
What is the difference between Photoshop 2024 and previous versions?, 352
What is the Generative Fill feature in Photoshop 2024?, 353
WHAT KNOWLEDGE DO YOU HAVE OF PATHS?, 120
What should I do if I am having problems with Adobe Photoshop 2024?, 353
What's happening in the Photoshop Levels Adjustment, 288
When to use raster images., 117
When to use vector images., 117
Where is High Resolution?, 352
WHICH COLOR MODE SHOULD I CHOOSE?, 194
Whites and Blacks, 180
Why go from raster to vector?, 118
Why would I need to change my ruler unit from pixels to inches?, 106
Window Document, 22
Window menu, 55, 56, 57, 65, 293
Window menu in Photoshop, 55
Windows, 3, 4, 6, 8, 18, 21, 38, 54, 62, 63, 64, 69, 73, 99, 100, 113, 135, 136, 138, 144, 151, 152, 155, 156, 157, 158, 159, 160, 161, 162, 163, 164, 165, 166, 175, 176, 202, 204, 222, 229, 232, 239, 240, 242, 243, 247, 252, 253, 254, 255, 256, 261, 262, 274, 275, 290, 298, 313
Windows 10 (64-bit) version 1809 or later, 3
Windows 7, 4

Windows drop-down menu, 38
Windows or macOS, 4, 18
WMF, 120
WMF files, 120
working in Photoshop, 53, 118
Working more efficiently through familiar units, 110
working on refining selections, 14
Working Space, 198
WORKING WITH BRUSHES, 203
WORKING WITH BRUSHES AND WETNESS OPTIONS, 203
WORKING WITH CLOUD DOCUMENTS, 73
WORKING WITH IMAGE RESOLUTION, 78
WORKING WITH IMAGE RESOLUTION AND DIMENSION, 78
WORKING WITH LAYERS, 291
Working With Photoshop's Panels, 45
WORKING WITH SELECTION, 234
Working With the Dodge, Burn, and Sponge Tools, 279
WORKING WITH THE RULERS AND GUIDES, 100
WORKING WITH THE TOOL PROPERTIES, 36
Workspace Layout, 22
Wrap Text, 147

Y

Your Design Process, 110
Your Edits as a DNG (Digital Negative) File, 188

Z

Zoom and Navigation Tools, 22
Zoom Factor, 39
Zoom Tool, 33, 168, 345
Zooming back out to view the image, 77
Zooming In and Out, 165

Made in the USA
Monee, IL
19 November 2023